Nothing but
History

Nothing but History

Reconstruction and Extremity
after Metaphysics

David D. Roberts

UNIVERSITY OF CALIFORNIA PRESS
Berkeley   Los Angeles   London

University of California Press
Berkeley and Los Angeles, California

University of California Press
London, England

Copyright © 1995 by The Regents of the University of California

Library of Congress Cataloging-in-Publication Data

Roberts, David D., 1943–
    Nothing but history : reconstruction and extremity after
metaphysics / David D. Roberts.
        p. cm.
    Includes bibliographical references and index.
    ISBN 0-520-20080-2 (alk. paper)
    1. History—Philosophy. I. Title.
D16.8.R62 1995
901—dc20   94-43786
                                                      CIP

Printed in the United States of America

1 2 3 4 5 6 7 8 9

For Robert Freeman

Contents

Preface   xi

1 Postmetaphysical History   1

A Difficult Adjustment   1
Dissolving and Inflating the Historical   3
Expansion and Polarization in Empirical Historiography   10
A Historical Approach to the Changing Culture of History   15

2 Tentative Steps into History: From Vico to Dilthey   22

The Question of Modern Historical Consciousness   22
Individuality and Completeness in Vico and Hegel   23
Historicism and Historiography after Hegel   30
Dilthey and the Unfinished Revolution   34

3 The Reduction to History   40

New Confrontations with Time and History   40
This Particular World   50
History, Language, and Individual Experience   52

4 Nietzsche: The Innocence of Becoming   58

The Trouble with History   58
Emptiness and Connectedness   62
Reshaping the Past   66
Affirming the Particular Totality   70
Nietzsche's Triple Legacy   78

5 Croce: History as Thought and Action   81

Croce's Uncertain Legacy   81
A Postmetaphysical Historicism   85
Knowing the World as History   90
Experiencing Action as History   97
Commitment and Collaboration, Humility and Faith   102
Croce's Limits   107

6 Heidegger: Historicism, Disengagement, Holiness   111

Heidegger and the Reduction to History   111
Being and Time and After   117
Being and History, Our History and Nihilism   119
The Scope for an Active Response   125
Out the Other Side of Historicism   135
Attuning Ourselves to the Sending   143

7 Gadamerian Hermeneutics: Belonging to a Growing Tradition   153

Interlude: Pathways in a New Terrain   153
Heidegger, Gadamer, and Croce   158
Belonging to History   160
Confinement and Openness   165
Concealment and the Fusion of Horizons   172
The Authority of Tradition   175

8 Deconstruction: The Uses and Limits of Perversity   180

Deconstruction and the Cultural Displacement   180
Foucault and the End of Man   183
Derrida and the Dissolution of Metaphysics   192
The Premium on Disruption   202
Plausible Extremity   207
Overreaction and Preclusion   215

9 Pragmatism, Historicism, Aestheticism   226

Rorty's Neopragmatism   226
From Foundations to History   229
From Philosophy to Textualism   235
Irony, Redescription, Autonomy   237
Suffocation, Weightlessness, and the Prophets of Extremity   241
Reconnection and Truth   247

10 Past, Process, and Contest in Contemporary Historiography   252

Historiographical Openness   252
Processes to the Present   254

Contents

The Uncanny Past   268
Scott versus Himmelfarb   280
Groups, Processes, and Axes of Contest   283
Polarization and Revitalization   289

11 Responding to the World as Historical   291

Postmetaphysical Moderation   291
Care, Learning, and Truth   297
The Process of Interaction   301
Between Rational Critique and Disruptive Play   306
Openness and Risk in Historiography   312
The Extremes and the Middle Ground   316

Index   319

Preface

Nothing but history? Hyperbole, to be sure, and I ask the reader's indulgence. But I seek to show that a kind of reduction to history has been one cultural tendency in light of the eclipse of "metaphysics"—the term I use for foundationalist or essentialist philosophy and all the cultural weight it has carried. A new, post-Hegelian sense of the world as historical has been central to our recent experience, despite occasional suggestions that "history" ends along with traditional philosophy or modernity. My aim in this book is to understand this reduction to history, first by asking how it has played out in our own intellectual history over the past century or so, then by seeking to assess the cultural possibilities it affords us. At issue are not only the uses of historical understanding but also some fundamental aspects of personal experience.

My study is primarily an exercise in intellectual history, but it also has critical and even prescriptive dimensions. I emphasize, however, that in referring to "nothing but history" my aim is not to foster some sort of historiographical imperialism, affording professional historians new domain over the stuff of science, or art, or religion. We still seek the suprahistorical in many forms: novelists explore the universal human condition; natural scientists seek to discover the structure of an independently existing physical world; philosophers and theorists strive to establish truths that are not merely historically specific; in our more or less religious moments, we all wonder about the source or purpose of it all. Recent humanistic discussion suggests only that history stands in tension with these adjacent cultural domains. But by following the historical strand, clarifying what "history" has come to encompass, we can better explore the tensions along the areas of intersection.

In its prescriptive dimension, my study seeks to show, first, what is necessary for a new culture of history to settle out as one autonomous component, in tension with others, in a postmetaphysical culture. But that historical component is itself tension-ridden, and I also seek to show what is required for a "moderate," reconstructive strand to emerge, playing off the extreme responses that also merit a place, but not an exclusive place, within a postmetaphysical culture of history. In any case, I venture into this somewhat prescriptive mode not to claim the last word but simply to contribute what I can to the ongoing conversation, the evolving cultural mix. I believe the argument of the book itself will make clear the spirit in which it is offered.

In bringing this study to completion, I have had the benefit of help and support from many quarters, and my acknowledgment here can only begin to express my gratitude. My way of comparing Benedetto Croce with his German contemporaries in an earlier study elicited some penetrating comments from Martin Jay that helped me see what I needed to do next. In the initial phases of this project, during the mid-1980s, I learned a great deal from the interdisciplinary study group fostered by the Humanities Department of the University of Rochester's Eastman School of Music. My particular thanks to my former colleagues Jonathan Baldo, Douglas Dempster, Thomas Donnan, Ruth Gross, Aimée Israel-Pelletier, and John McGowan. My Rochester connections also brought me together periodically with Hans Kellner, whose friendship I valued, just as I did the intellectual challenge he offered. I also take this occasion to remember the late Ann Clark Fehn, whose contributions to interdisciplinary discussion at the University of Rochester enriched us all.

Since moving to the University of Georgia in 1988, I have especially appreciated the encouragement of Lester Stephens, the interested but skeptical eye of Kirk Willis, who remains curiously partial to the British philosophical tradition, and the efforts of Bernard Dauenhauer, who did so much to foster humanistic discussion as founding director of the university's Humanities Center. I have also profited from the chance to discuss recent intellectual history with my doctoral student Mark Clark. In addition, I thank the University of Georgia Research Foundation for the Senior Faculty Research Grant that enabled me to devote much of my effort to this project during 1989–1990.

Speaking engagements in Italy during 1992 and 1994 gave me a chance to discuss my work in progress with several Italian colleagues. I am especially grateful to Mario Corsi, who helped me keep my recasting of Benedetto Croce in bounds. (For reasons that will become clear, I did not wish to play out of bounds.) I have also valued the comments of Domenico Settembrini and Vittorio Stella in response to my effort to place Croce in wider context.

In preparing the final manuscript for the University of California Press, I had the benefit of astute readings by Allan Megill and a second, anonymous reader. My revisions will not fully have satisfied either of them, but the book is surely stronger thanks to their objections, questions, and suggestions. For helping me through the several hurdles, I am grateful to the three sponsoring editors at California who have had a hand in this project, Alain Hénon, Eileen McWilliam, and Edward Dimendberg. It has also been a pleasure to work with Michelle Bonnice and Sheila Berg in bringing the manuscript into print.

The continuing support and tolerant good humor of my family have been essential to me as I labored on this book. So thanks again to Ellen, Trina, and Anthony for their patience—but also for their growing interest in my work. As they have become a formidable and engaging audience, I have fleetingly felt that having three children in college at the same time isn't so bad after all. And thanks to Beth, as always, for her unfailing, if occasionally bemused, support. As she knows, only her bemusement enables me to place my work in such perfect perspective.

The book is dedicated to Robert Freeman, Director of the University of Rochester's Eastman School of Music, where I had the privilege of teaching as a member of the Humanities Department from 1978 to 1988. Without his friendship, encouragement, and support at that pivotal stage of my career, this book would not have been possible.

Postmetaphysical History

A Difficult Adjustment

Over the past century or so, cultural changes centering on the erosion of foundationalist metaphysics have called forth an ever more explicit effort to specify the contours of a postmetaphysical culture. That effort has encompassed earlier thinkers like Friedrich Nietzsche, Benedetto Croce, and Martin Heidegger, and it has brought hermeneutics, deconstruction, and neopragmatism to center stage in recent decades. All the strands in our culture, from philosophy and science to literature and politics, have been at issue in this discussion, but the place of "history" has been central—and especially elusive. Sometimes explicitly, often only implicitly, thinkers prominent in this cultural reassessment have thought anew about what is historical and about the role of historical inquiry and understanding. Taking for granted the waning of metaphysics, this study examines its implications for the place of history, as one competing cultural strand.

As Richard Rorty has emphasized, the foundationalist assumptions of our tradition have been gradually eroding for the last one hundred fifty years, as philosophers have chipped away at such notions as "self-validating truth," "transcendental argument," and "principle of the ultimate foundation of all possible knowledge."[1] After Nietzsche, Heidegger, John Dewey, Ludwig Wittgenstein, W. V. Quine, and Donald Davidson, there are few foundationalists to be found on either side of the notorious divide between Continental and Anglo-American philosophy. And because our whole philosophical tradition has been

1. Richard Rorty, *Essays on Heidegger and Others* (Cambridge: Cambridge University Press, 1991), 109–110.

fundamentally metaphysical, what is apparently unraveling is not simply a delimited philosophical genre but also epistemology and any possibility of privileged methods or decision procedures affording access to certain, suprahistorical truth. But what is left, and how do we make our way in the world that remains to us?

This change in the intellectual landscape has had implications for history in both its customary senses—as *res gestae,* the past, the stuff that historical inquiry seeks to apprehend, and as *historia rerum gestarum,* the past as related or conveyed, the historical account. At issue, in fact, have been broad questions about the human relationship to a world that sometimes seems fundamentally historical in a new, radically post-Hegelian sense. But whereas some of the answers seem to portend an expanded cultural role for history, others seem to undermine even the role—modest by some measures, grandiose by others—that history came to play by the late nineteenth century. Indeed, assaults on "history" have been central to a number of the cultural responses to the eclipse of metaphysics, and history itself is sometimes assumed to be ending along with foundationalist philosophy.

Even the terminology surrounding history has become ever more complex and uncertain as the wider intellectual framework has changed. The term "historicism" has remained central to humanistic discussion, even taking on yet another lease on life by the latter 1980s as "the new historicism" became a catchphrase in literary studies, then spilled over to influence historiography. What historicism might entail proves crucial to any effort to assess the status of history after metaphysics, yet even within the same intellectual camp, some refer to it approvingly, others disparagingly.[2] Those seeking to place our situation in historical perspective often refer to an earlier "crisis of historicism," yet they do not seem to understand the crisis in the same way, or even to date it at the same time.

Among thinkers responding to the waning of metaphysics, the now-familiar sequence of Nietzsche, Heidegger, Michel Foucault, and Jacques Derrida has been especially influential. Their efforts, taken together, constitute a culture of extremity, as Allan Megill showed in his influential *Prophets of Extremity,* published in 1985. Although some found the extremes nihilistic in implication, many embraced them as liberating from the authoritarianism of our metaphysical tradition. Also prominent, by the 1980s, was a more general aestheticism that similarly contested metaphysically grounded approaches, though its relationship with the extremes was complex. This aestheticism affected readings of Nietzsche and Heidegger, gave a certain spin to deconstruction, and led to a particular recasting of the hermeneutic and pragmatist strands within our tradi-

---

2. For a good assessment of the term and its recent uses, see Georg G. Iggers, "Historicism: The History and Meaning of the Term," *Journal of the History of Ideas* 56, no.1 (January 1995): 129–152.

tion.[3] The understanding of postmetaphysical possibilities that resulted from the combination of extremity and aestheticism seemed to have unfavorable implications for history.

However, some who welcomed the postmetaphysical turn sought an alternative response, though their efforts were disparate and their alternative hard to characterize. In one sense, it was to be "moderate"—no longer metaphysical, and thus not "authoritarian," yet eschewing the extremes at the same time. But though moderate in this sense, such an alternative might prove more radical than the extremes, which, despite their apocalyptic quality, seemed to some to undermine the scope for any politically significant radicalism. At the same time, those seeking this moderate alternative were leery of aestheticist tendencies and clung to the scope for truth. Rather than accent personal edification, they played up the human role in the ongoing reconstruction of the world in history. And the approach they envisioned seemed to entail an enhanced cultural role for empirical historiography.

The outcome of the waning of metaphysics has so far been a kind of field of forces, including an array of extreme responses, not all of them compatible, a generically aestheticist tendency, and a quest for a moderate, constructive alternative. In my view, there is value, or at least plausibility, to a great many of these impulses, including extremes that some find merely nihilistic. But the sources of these diverse responses, their implications and the connections among them, have not been well understood. Moreover, uncertainty regarding the baggage that "history" must carry has produced confusion and excess. As a result, our understanding of postmetaphysical cultural possibilities has been prejudicial and limiting.

Dissolving and Inflating the Historical

The status of history was already in question before the waning of metaphysics forced the more insistent reconsideration of cultural priorities that has marked the period since about 1960. Indeed, it has long been a commonplace that the break into twentieth-century culture was bound up with a retreat from the premium on historical approaches that marked "the great age of history" in the nineteenth century.[4] Somehow the sphere of public, objective history, which

3. "Aestheticism" is central to Allan Megill's account in *Prophets of Extremity: Nietzsche, Heidegger, Foucault, Derrida* (Berkeley, Los Angeles, and London: University of California Press, 1985). See also Alexander Nehamas's aestheticist reading of Nietzsche in *Nietzsche: Life as Literature* (Cambridge: Harvard University Press, 1985); and Richard Rorty's discussion of the category in *Contingency, Irony, and Solidarity* (Cambridge: Cambridge University Press, 1989), 119n.

4. Introducing the pioneering modernism of Vienna, Carl Schorske refers to "our century's a-historical culture" almost in passing. See Carl E. Schorske, *Fin-de-Siècle Vienna: Politics and Culture* (New York: Random House, Vintage, 1981), xviii.

had seemed deeply meaningful, grew blurry, and the focus shifted to subjective temporal experience or, at most, to one's own personal history. The advent of Freudian psychoanalysis has frequently been cited as the most significant example.[5] In addition, the modernist use of simultaneity and collage seemed to challenge the notion of linear time and thus to undermine the confidence in linear narrative that was apparently essential to any historical approach.[6]

At the same time, the cataclysmic events of the twentieth century seem to have constituted such a rupture that history, with its connotations of continuity, coherence, and intelligibility, must surely diminish as a cultural component. In his widely admired *The Great War and Modern Memory*, Paul Fussell notes that World War I "was perhaps the last to be conceived as taking place within a seamless, purposeful 'history' involving a coherent stream of time running from past through present to future."[7] Especially insofar as "history" necessarily carries this particular baggage, it seems to have been undermined by the events of history itself in the twentieth century. Some insist that only literature, even if still in narrative form, can get at the real, lived reality of what is commonly taken as a historical experience or event, such as the First World War.[8]

Indeed, changes in the cultural situation seemed to thrust a new kind of leadership on the literary culture, even responsibility for what once seemed part of the historians' domain. The distinguished critic Harold Bloom noted this tendency with a certain grim resignation in the early 1970s, when he pondered the special difficulties we have come to encounter in conceiving the relationship between our present experience and our tradition or history:

> The teacher of literature now in America, far more than the teacher of history or philosophy or religion, is condemned to teach the presentness of the past, because history, philosophy and religion have withdrawn as agents from the Scene of Instruction, leaving the bewildered teacher of literature alone at the altar, terrifiedly wondering whether he is to be sacrifice or priest. If he evades his burden by attempting to teach only the supposed presence of the present, he will find himself teaching only some simplistic, partial reduction that wholly

5. Stephen Kern, *The Culture of Time and Space, 1880–1918* (Cambridge: Harvard University Press, 1983), p. 63; Schorske, *Fin-de-Siècle Vienna*, chap. 4.

6. See, for example, Eugene Lunn's lucid discussion of this direction, especially as represented by Brecht and resisted by Lukács, in *Marxism and Modernism: An Historical Study of Lukács, Brecht, Benjamin, and Adorno* (Berkeley, Los Angeles, and London: University of California Press, 1982), 48–55, 121–124. See also Gianni Vattimo, *La fine della modernità* (Milan: Garzanti, 1985), 18, for a comparable argument about the impact of the modern media, especially television, in dehistoricizing our experience through simultaneity.

7. Paul Fussell, *The Great War and Modern Memory* (London: Oxford University Press, 1975), 21.

8. Modris Eksteins, in *Rites of Spring: The Great War and the Birth of the Modern Age* (Boston: Houghton Mifflin, 1989), 290–291, 296, argues explicitly that literary writers proved better able than historians to get at the reality of World War I. The war itself had undermined the historical imagination, so that history could not make sense of the experience.

obliterates the present in the name of one or another historicizing formula, or past injustice, or dead faith, whether secular or not. Yet how is he to teach a tradition now grown so wealthy and so heavy that to accommodate it demands more strength than any single consciousness can provide, short of the parodistic Kabbalism of a Pynchon?[9]

Only one chunk of the cultural terrain is at issue in this passage, and for Bloom responsibility for it falls to the literary culture by default, not as the booty of confident imperialist conquest. But the notion that literature must assume responsibility for a historical world grown too overwhelming for the competence of historians was central to the overall rethinking of cultural priorities.

If history was still to contribute to the wider culture, it seemed to need major recasting in light of the twentieth-century experience. Writing in 1966, Hayden White argued that "the historian serves no one well by constructing a specious continuity between the present world and that which preceded it. On the contrary, we require a history that will educate us to discontinuity more than ever before; for discontinuity, disruption, and chaos is our lot."[10] But as even categories ancillary to historiography, such as continuity, chronology, and narrative, became suspect, the notion that "history" is ending, along with God, metaphysics, and the true world, became widespread in humanistic discussion.

Poststructuralists like Foucault and Derrida were widely assumed to have shown "that there really is no such thing as 'history.' "[11] All we can do is think instead in terms of sheer becoming, or mere flux, or slippage, or the play of differences. Throughout his *Radical Hermeneutics*, John D. Caputo falls back on the notion of "flux," which he takes to be a kind of neutral, premetaphysical category capable of withstanding even the postmodernist critical onslaught.[12] It comes to seem that in shaping the formless ooze into "recorded history," we are simply seeking an antidote to "the primitive terror" we feel in the face of the real nothingness of the flux.[13]

Tainted with metaphysical prejudices, historical-mindedness came to seem but another Western pretense, even a form of domination by the winners, who

9. Harold Bloom, *A Map of Misreading* (Oxford: Oxford University Press, 1975), 39.

10. Hayden V. White, "The Burden of History," reprinted in his *Tropics of Discourse: Essays in Cultural Criticism* (Baltimore: Johns Hopkins University Press, 1978), 50.

11. David Hoy, "Jacques Derrida," in *The Return of Grand Theory in the Human Sciences,* ed. Quentin Skinner (Cambridge: Cambridge University Press, 1985), 48–49, referring to the stance of Foucault, Derrida, and "other modern Nietzscheans." See also pp. 59–60, and, in the same volume, Mark Philp, "Michel Foucault," 78–79, for further indications that any premium on continuity or tradition has come to seem conservative, limiting, even authoritarian.

12. John D. Caputo, *Radical Hermeneutics: Repetition, Deconstruction, and the Hermeneutic Project* (Bloomington: Indiana University Press, 1987); see, for example, pp. 97–98.

13. See T. S. Eliot, "The Dry Salvages," in *Four Quartets* (San Diego: Harcourt Brace Jovanovich, 1971; orig. pub. 1943), 39, lines 96–103. See also Hans Kellner's way of making the point in his "Beautifying the Nightmare: The Aesthetics of Postmodern History," *Strategies* 4–5 (1991): 292–293.

enforce remembrance of the course of the actual and forgetting of all the rest. History is always written by the victors, and victory conflates with domination and exclusion.[14] From this perspective, any premium on historical thinking is inherently conservative, since it justifies the present power configuration by affording privilege to the course of the actual and thus the status quo.

However, another body of evidence suggests that what ends with the erosion of metaphysics is not history writ large but simply a certain approach to history—and a certain way of understanding our own place within our particular history. Our idea of history had indeed come to carry a good deal of metaphysical baggage, but to jettison that baggage may force us to take history seriously in ways inconceivable before.[15]

Recent antihistorical thinking often simply assumes that *any* notion of history must carry such baggage. There is a tendency to conflate the coherence and continuity that do seem necessary, if we are to speak of "history" at all, with the progressivism and even teleology that may not be. Indeed, postmetaphysical discussions of history persistently slip in G. W. F. Hegel at key junctures, as if a cultural emphasis on history necessarily entails Hegelian assumptions.[16]

The metaphysical tradition rested on the belief that, on some level, things are a certain way that we might discover, that there are stable, suprahistorical foundations or essences, origins or purposes, "firsts" or "ends." In one form or another, metaphysics seemed to specify a kind of container for all the variable and contingent stuff of history. For Rorty, in fact, traditional philosophy was fundamentally "an attempt to escape from history—an attempt to find nonhistorical conditions of any possible historical development."[17] But if so, then something like history might seem what remains as, with the end of metaphysics, we recognize that any such suprahistorical realm is inaccessible, even inconceivable.

14. See especially Walter Benjamin, "Theses on the Philosophy of History," in *Illuminations*, ed. Hannah Arendt, trans. Harry Zohn (New York: Schocken, 1969), 253–264. See also Václav Havel, *Disturbing the Peace: A Conversation with Karel Hvížďala*, trans. Paul Wilson (New York: Random House, Vintage, 1991), 166–167, for a more recent example of this tendency.

15. What it means "to take history seriously" is crucial. See David Couzens Hoy's way of framing the issue in "Taking History Seriously: Foucault, Gadamer, Habermas," *Union Seminary Quarterly Review* 34, no. 2 (Winter 1979): 85–95.

16. For Michel Foucault, "our age . . . is attempting to flee Hegel." See "The Discourse on Language" (1970), published with *The Archaeology of Knowledge*, trans. A. M. Sheridan Smith (New York: Harper and Row, Colophon, 1976), 235. See also Megill, *Prophets of Extremity*, 186–187, on Foucault's enduring preoccupation with Hegel; and Vattimo, *La fine della modernità*, 10–17, on the effort to escape Hegel in Nietzsche and Heidegger. In questioning the Hegelian legacy, Jacques Derrida, like Vattimo, worried plausibly about the notion of *Aufhebung*, or "overcoming," but a sense that the ghost of Hegel lurked everywhere may have led these thinkers to load certain categories with unnecessary baggage. See especially Jacques Derrida, *Of Grammatology*, trans. Gayatri Chakravorty Spivak (Baltimore: Johns Hopkins University Press, 1976), 25.

17. Richard Rorty, *Philosophy and the Mirror of Nature* (Princeton: Princeton University Press, 1979), 9.

In one sense, the modern subjectivism that began with René Descartes was a new, more radical attempt at a suprahistorical metaphysics in the face of Renaissance skepticism. With the Cartesian recasting of Western philosophy, subjectivity or consciousness became the bedrock, that which could not be doubted. Taking form as the self or ego, subjectivity was a priori and somehow transcendent, capable of seeing the world whole, even mastering it.

In some of our accounts, to be sure, we accent the sense in which modern subjectivism was itself postmetaphysical. As the old metaphysics no longer seemed to hold, a new kind of humanism emerged, accenting the scope for human beings to make their own world on earth. Thus the Enlightenment project and the several political strands that followed from it; thus, eventually, the idea of progress and the particular relationship to history that it entailed. In this sense, the departure from antihistorical metaphysics involved embracing history as meaningful—as the arena for making the world, thereby creating or revealing ourselves. But even insofar as modern subjectivism entailed this premium on action in history, the ahistorical core of that tradition remained in place. The metaphysical tradition led us still to posit a universal rational standard, a congruence between mind and reality, and a direction, even a telos, to history itself.

What happens when "modernity," combining still-metaphysical assumptions with one brand of historical consciousness, loses its aura? Most basically, the subjective ego or consciousness no longer seems a priori and transcendent but is "thrown" into some particular context. And this means not only that individual subjectivity is always historically specific but also that my selfhood emerges only through the larger historical happening into which I am thrown. My self-understanding begins in a past I did not create and is projected into a future I cannot control.[18] But it is equally crucial that with the waning of metaphysics, we cannot conceive this history as an overarching process of human self-realization, of "becoming what we are." Because there is no a priori human essence, there is no scope for fulfilling ourselves by overcoming some fragmentation or alienation.

So the subject is neither transcendent nor in process of self-realization but is rather bound up with some specific situation that is historical in a non-Hegelian sense. It would seem, then, that a post-Hegelian form of historical inquiry might replace subjectivity or consciousness as the key to self-understanding.

From within the modern framework, "modern" was an honorific term expressing our sense of ourselves as the privileged culmination of a benign historical process. The West was superior, and Western modernity was the culmination of human development, because scientific reason afforded a

18. Georgia Warnke makes the point nicely in specifying the central Heideggerian insight influencing Hans-Georg Gadamer. See her *Gadamer: Hermeneutics, Tradition and Reason* (Stanford: Stanford University Press, 1987), 40.

privileged access to the truth of things—and thus an increasing technological mastery of the world. But on this level, too, we come to seem more significantly bound up with history as our modern world comes to seem merely a contingent historical resultant, "modern" in no more than a neutral chronological sense and certainly not metaphysically privileged. As modernity loses its aura, we become postmodern, relating to our earlier pretensions in a newly self-conscious way, perhaps through parody or nostalgia.[19] But the res gestae, the stuff history deals with, still may be sufficiently coherent to make possible historical inquiry, and such inquiry may have deeper cultural import precisely insofar as history is *not* progressive, with an a priori frame.

For over a century, those assaulting the metaphysical tradition have found themselves face-to-face with something like history—but not the history that nineteenth-century advocates of a historical approach had in mind. Even as he deplored the implications of the hypertrophy of one kind of historical consciousness, Nietzsche reduced reality to perpetual becoming and emphasized the contingent constructedness of the worlds we fashion for ourselves. By the first decade of the century, Croce was submerging philosophy within history as he sought to posit an absolute historicism. Heidegger thought through first the centrality of historicity to human living, then the particularity of our world as a purely historical resultant. By midcentury, Wittgenstein had reacted against his earlier attempt to provide a suprahistorical map of language and was suggesting that, on every level, we may alter or devise the rules as we go along, subject to the historically specific form of life in which we find ourselves. A bit later, Thomas Kuhn modestly proposed "a role for history" even in the self-understanding of the natural sciences, thereby initiating one of the most fruitful discussions of the century. By the 1980s, Robert C. Solomon was offering a strikingly contemporary Hegel whose "closing" telos proves the empty yet liberating awareness that the world is perpetually incomplete; Michael Ryan was suggesting that "history" is another name for the undecidability that Derrida allots us; and Richard Rorty, underscoring the historical contingency of what once seemed the inevitable philosophical problems, was proposing that history affords the only therapy when we find ourselves intellectually befuddled. More recently still, Brook Thomas concluded that, with the end of all we have encompassed under the term "metaphysics," ours is "a historically contingent world" in which "there are only historical ways of knowing."[20]

19. Jean-François Lyotard's *The Postmodern Condition: A Report on Knowledge*, trans. Geoff Bennington and Brian Massumi (Minneapolis: University of Minnesota Press, 1984; orig. French ed. 1979) focused attention on these possibilities within the postmodern discussion.

20. Robert C. Solomon, *In the Spirit of Hegel* (New York: Oxford University Press, 1983), 14–16, 636–637; Ludwig Wittgenstein, *Philosophical Investigations*, trans. G. E. M. Anscombe, 3d ed. (New York: Macmillan, n.d.), no. 83 (p. 39e); Michael Ryan, *Marxism and Deconstruction: A Critical Articulation* (Baltimore: Johns Hopkins University Press, 1982), 21; Brook Thomas, *The New Historicism and Other Old-Fashioned Topics* (Princeton: Princeton University Press, 1991), 215–216. I discuss Rorty in chap. 10.

Examples could be multiplied, and, though disparate, they have a significant family resemblance. For a hundred years, some have suggested that as we cease to believe in foundations, essences, or "metanarratives," we are left with a world that is particular and provisional, endlessly differing, forever incomplete; ever more of reality seems but a contingent historical resultant. A kind of "inflation of history" or "reduction to history" seems to have been at work. With the dissolution of metaphysics, history could no longer be understood simply as the mundane testing ground specified in our religious tradition, or as the revelation or dramatization of truths, principles, or values already there, or as the path to a goal given beforehand. Rather, history was left standing alone, naked, for the first time—as all there is.

But whether what is left can usefully be termed "history" obviously depends on the baggage the term must carry. Perhaps, to avoid metaphysical heresies, we must settle for empty becoming, or, with Caputo, mere flux. However, it is possible that we must understand the world more fully as "historical" than ever before, but "historical" in a new, "weak" way in the absence of metaphysical buttressing.[21] Even if we find ourselves doing so, however, it is not obvious how the human relationship to such a world is to be conceived. Nor is it clear how we might respond to a purely historical world. A simple dichotomy between pro- and antihistory does not seem sufficient to sort out the cultural directions that have opened in response to this inflation of history.

At this point, it is enough simply to grasp the overall line of questioning that these preliminaries suggest. If our conventional ways of understanding history prove to rest on outmoded metaphysical assumptions, are we left with sheer becoming, mere flux, or the play of differences, or can we make new sense of history, both as a conception of what "there is" and as a mode of inquiry and understanding? If our world seems to reduce to nothing but history, what is the range of plausible responses? Does the mix of extremity and aestheticism rest on a fair reading of the possibilities, or has there been something prejudicial about the way the alternatives have been sorted out? What is the scope for a moderate, constructive orientation toward history within a postmetaphysical culture, and how would any such orientation relate to the extremes?

21. The notion of "weakness" in recent humanistic discussion is associated especially with the Italian Gianni Vattimo, whose thinking derives from his innovative and illuminating synthesis of Nietzsche and Heidegger. For a good brief introduction, see his "Dialettica, differenza, pensiero debole," in *Il pensiero debole,* ed. Gianni Vattimo and Pier Aldo Rovatti (Milan: Feltrinelli, 1983), 12–28. In English, see Gianni Vattimo, *The End of Modernity: Nihilism and Hermeneutics in Postmodern Culture,* trans. Jon R. Snyder (Baltimore: Johns Hopkins University Press, 1988; orig. Italian ed. 1985). Although I am indebted to Vattimo's work, I depart from his position in accenting the divergence between Nietzsche and Heidegger within the postmetaphysical space, as well as the scope for a constructive alternative between the extremes they were the first to establish. Thus my use of the term "weak" is not precisely congruent with Vattimo's.

Expansion and Polarization in
Empirical Historiography

Although the growing theoretical ferment, with its apparent extravagance and apocalyptic aura, put off many practicing historians, changes in the wider intellectual framework clearly had implications for the cultural place of empirical historiography. And by the late 1980s, interest in theoretical matters was growing remarkably within the historical profession. But because departures that some found exciting and liberating seemed, to others, to compromise historiography's cultural role, the most obvious result was polarization between an assertive "new," or postmodern, history and a defensive "old," or modern, history.

The points at issue followed first from the most striking feature of historical writing in recent decades—the expansion of the range of questions asked by practicing historians. That expansion was associated initially with the new social history, which focused on neglected groups and ordinary people. But as the expansion proceeded to encompass adolescence and retirement, sexuality and gender roles, it became clear that the wider inflation of history was at work. It had become possible—and necessary—to ask an expanding range of historical questions as ever more of what shapes the lives of all of us came to seem contingent, constructed, merely historical. At the same time, historical questions, often radical and particularly fruitful, were increasingly raised from outside the historical profession, most notably by philosophers. The efforts of those like Alasdair MacIntyre, Charles Taylor, and Richard Rorty suggested that with the waning of metaphysics, even what had seemed the stuff of philosophy required a kind of historical questioning.[22]

To some, postmodernism portended a further expansion by freeing the historian from "modern" limitations on ways of approaching and representing history. Departure from the pretense of a single master narrative entailed a welcome pluralism, an opening to the stories of long-excluded others. There was much interest in the "microhistories" of those like Carlo Ginzburg and Emmanuel Le Roy Ladurie, which turned from what had seemed the master process, culminating in the present, to focus on the marginal or anecdotal. These histories afforded access to mentalities and worlds of experience somehow hidden before. This direction converged in some respects with the "new historicism" that Stephen Greenblatt and others were developing from within literary studies.

But though this expansion suggested a broader cultural role for historical

---

22. See, for example, Charles Taylor, *Sources of the Self: The Making of Modern Identity* (Cambridge: Harvard University Press, 1989). Although his aims were decidedly antihistoricist, the work of Alasdair MacIntyre similarly appeals to historical argument and stresses the import of the contingent historical level. See especially his *After Virtue: A Study in Moral Theory* (Notre Dame: University of Notre Dame Press, 1981).

understanding, it also raised troubling questions about criteria of significance and hierarchies of importance. Some worried that if, as this expansion suggested, history can be about anything at all, historical writing was in danger of lapsing into triviality. It became ever more difficult for the wider public to know what was important, and some worried that the historians were losing their audience, becoming culturally marginal.[23] Yet demands for a clear hierarchy of importance or a unified "master narrative" seemed to others to be inherently authoritarian—attempts to justify some actual state of affairs and preclude alternatives. So even as historiography radically expanded, there were calls for still greater pluralism and openness.

There was polarization especially because the effort to expand the focus led some to embrace epistemological innovations from the wider discussion. With the erosion of metaphysics, historians could no longer be conceived as disinterested inquirers representing the past as it actually happened. Thus they could play a more active, creative role, asking new kinds of questions based on their own present concerns. Joan Wallach Scott found in the French poststructuralists Foucault and Derrida the keys to the "new epistemology" that she found necessary for a more significant feminist history. For Scott, it was time to come to terms not only with the historian's present involvement but also with the contested, broadly political nature of the process through which some subjects come to be studied at the expense of others.[24]

Changes in the accents of the theory or philosophy of history pointed in the same direction. During the 1950s and 1960s, the analytical philosophy of history, assessing the truth value of historical claims against the model of the natural sciences, dominated historiographical discussion. That enterprise could be reassuring, as it showed how causation and explanation function in historiography, or disturbing, insofar as it showed why history was inherently incapable of measuring up to the model of the real sciences. But beginning with Hayden White's pathbreaking *Metahistory* in 1973, a new current concerned with textuality, language, rhetoric, and narrative gradually established its predominance, shifting the basis of comparison for historiography from science to art.

White drew on literary theorists from Northrop Frye to Roland Barthes, and his work brought together theoretically minded historians, philosophers of history, and literary intellectuals in an interdisciplinary discussion with wide resonance. Although their accents differed, these narrativists deepened consideration of the historian's active role by examining the process through which the "archive," the stuff of the past, gets constructed, through language, into a recognizably historical account. Historical texts are emplotted in

23. On the concern about splintering and loss of focus, see the lucid discussion by the social historian Olivier Zunz in his introduction to *Reliving the Past: The Worlds of Social History*, ed. Olivier Zunz (Chapel Hill: University of North Carolina Press, 1985), esp. pp. 4–6.

24. Joan Wallach Scott, *Gender and the Politics of History* (New York: Columbia University Press, 1988), 1–11, esp. p. 4.

narratives just like fictional texts. To write a history is to construct one kind of story, not to represent the past as it actually happened.

In confronting historians with the constructedness of their own histories, narrativists like White and Hans Kellner claimed to be freeing historiography to play a more fruitful cultural role. Following Barthes, especially, they tended to find the notions of "truth" and "reality," long central to the self-understanding of historians, to be not merely irrelevant but to constitute an authoritarian obstacle to the more open, pluralistic kind of historiography they envisioned. Kellner noted, almost casually, that " 'Truth' and 'Reality' are, of course, the primary authoritarian weapons of our time."[25]

With their tendency to portray historical writing as one kind of fiction, these narrativists fostered a kind of aestheticism, which meshed interestingly with the neopragmatist accents of Richard Rorty and the political emphases of historians like Scott. By undercutting the authoritarian ideal of a single true account, this direction seemed to invite a more creative and pluralistic historiography, welcoming many stories, including the stories of those others long excluded from the mainstream master narrative. As the old imperatives of detachment and objectivity became suspect, innovators like White and Scott seemed to invite historians to become presentist and political with a good conscience.[26]

To his book on language and historical representation, Kellner added a deliberately provocative subtitle—*Getting the Story Crooked*—that mocked the ideal of "getting the story straight" that had long seemed essential to the historians' self-understanding. And he noted that the new scrutiny of the historians' discourse, a scrutiny formerly reserved for novels, "must generate a certain anxiety in a profession whose identity is based upon precisely the distinction between its own prose and that of the writer of fiction."[27]

Such anxiety there was, and it fueled some concerted attempts at resistance by more conventional historians. Because White's emphasis on rhetorical categories in *Metahistory* seemed to come at the expense of any concern for truth, the historians among his critics found his strategy incongruent with his stated aim to free history to play a more central cultural role.[28] If history writing

---

25. Hans Kellner, *Language and Historical Representation: Getting the Story Crooked* (Madison: University of Wisconsin Press, 1989), 301; see also p. 24. For the Barthes argument so central to Kellner and other narrativists, see especially Roland Barthes, "Historical Discourse," trans. Peter Wexler, in *Introduction to Structuralism,* ed. Michael Lane (New York: Basic Books, 1970), 145–155, esp. p. 154.

26. Peter Novick notes "the casual, matter-of-fact fashion" in which new historians like Scott "signaled their abandonment of traditional objectivist axioms." See *That Noble Dream: The "Objectivity Question" and the American Historical Profession* (Cambridge: Cambridge University Press, 1988), 598.

27. Kellner, *Language and Historical Representation*, 292.

28. For example, Arnaldo Momigliano, "The Rhetoric of History and the History of Rhetoric: On Hayden White's Tropes," in *Comparative Criticism: A Yearbook*, vol. 3, ed. E. S. Shaffer (Cambridge: Cambridge University Press, 1981), 259–268. See also Robert F. Berkhofer, Jr., "The Challenge of Poetics to (Normal) Historical Practice," *Poetics Today* 9, no. 2 (1988): 449.

merely provides a story that *seems* true because of certain rhetorical conventions, why should anybody pay attention to it, especially when the novelists generally manage to construct more engaging stories? Reflecting the concerns of many mainstream historians, Gordon S. Wood worried, and Oscar Handlin insisted, that historical writing must rest on precisely the old-fashioned "positivism," with its ideal of a stable, objective truth, that was falling into disrepute in the wider humanistic culture.[29]

In the same way, traditionalists worried that the accent on presentism and political commitment invited histories that simply confirm the starting point of the inquirer. Even as historical understanding seems to become more central, doubts about the scope for genuinely learning from historical accounts may lead us to listen only to what we want to hear. Charging those like Scott with violating the past for present political purposes, Gertrude Himmelfarb invoked the long-standing historiographical imperative, insisting that when we look into the past, it is *their* history we should be seeking—and seeking to *re*construct.[30]

By the end of the 1980s, there was much interest in Peter Novick's *That Noble Dream*, which made it clear that concerns about involvement, relativism, and truth have come up periodically in the American historical profession, especially as historiography sought self-understanding in a culture dominated by the image of the natural sciences. Novick brought the discussion up to date in a somewhat resigned spirit, for he worried that the founding ideals of the discipline were at last dissolving for good, with very little chance of recovery. It was widely viewed as symptomatic when Simon Schama, a distinguished Harvard historian known for, among other attributes, his abilities as a storyteller, overtly blended what seemed fact with what seemed fiction in *Dead Certainties*, published in 1991. Schama's book not only blurred the genres but, as he himself put it, "deliberately dislocated the conventions by which histories establish coherence and persuasiveness."[31]

In a sharply critical review, Gordon Wood traced Schama's effort to the fashionable postmodernist and deconstructionist theories of the day. And for Wood, those theories threatened to undermine the fragile, historically specific conventions essential to the integrity of historiography, because once such blurring of history and fiction is allowed, we can never be sure which is which in any account, and we come to doubt the truthfulness of the whole.[32] Wood's effort to resist these tendencies reflected the stubborn insistence of the

29. Oscar Handlin, *Truth in History* (Cambridge: Harvard University Press, 1979), 405; see also pp. 100–101, 118, 157, 377. Gordon S. Wood, contribution to "Writing History: An Exchange," *New York Review of Books*, 16 December 1982, 59.

30. Gertrude Himmelfarb, "Some Reflections on the New History," *American Historical Review* 94, no. 3 (June 1989): 665–670; Gertrude Himmelfarb, *The New History and the Old* (Cambridge: Harvard University Press, 1987), 15–24.

31. Simon Schama, *Dead Certainties (Unwarranted Speculations)* (New York: Random House, Vintage, 1992), 321.

32. Gordon S. Wood, "Novel History," *New York Review of Books*, 27 June 1991, 12, 15.

traditionalists that, though historians, too, tell stories, historical inquiry can get at truth, or reality, in a way that literature does not and that the distinction remains culturally central.

There was dispute not only between innovators and traditionalists; the innovators themselves fell out over some of the central points at issue. White found something facile about the "new historicist" reaction against formalism or structuralism, while proponents of postmodernism found quite different implications for historiography.[33] And Dominick LaCapra, who was central in mediating Derrida, Gadamer, and others to intellectual historians, sharply criticized Carlo Ginzburg's widely admired microhistory, *The Cheese and the Worms,* and, especially, the arguments used by proponents of the microhistorical approach. With unconcealed bitterness, LaCapra noted that though these historians claim to resist hegemonies and to open up historiography, their way of affording privilege to oral, popular culture

> functions to reinforce hegemonic relations in professional historiography. If a certain level of culture represents primordial reality, then it is a very short step to the assumption that those who study it are the 'real' historians, those who focus on the most important things. . . . [A] number of historians have taken this step. The result is a bizarre and vicious paradox whereby a vicarious relation to the oppressed of the past serves as a pretext for contemporary pretensions to dominance.[34]

So despite the promise of a renewed self-understanding and a deeper cultural role, the efforts of those from White and Scott to Ginzburg and Schama provoked confusion and polarization among historians. Many simply turned away from the wider discussion, shaking their heads. The more combative among them—Himmelfarb, most notably—attacked the whole litany from White to Scott to Schama.[35] It was plausible for these traditionalists to worry that something still viable and useful was in danger of being undermined. But in pulling back from humanistic theory, they tended to repair to positions that were no longer defensible, in light of the wider assault on metaphysics and epistemology. The question was whether historiography necessarily rested on the loosely positivist ideal of representing a determinate past object, as the traditionalists assumed, or whether the wider cultural break afforded a new basis

33. Hayden V. White, "New Historicism: A Comment," in *The New Historicism,* ed. H. Aram Veeser (New York: Routledge, 1989), 293–302. On the implications of postmodernism for historiography, compare, for example, the accents of F. R. Ankersmit's "Historiography and Postmodernism," *History and Theory* 28, no. 2 (1989): 137–153, with those of Jane Caplan's "Postmodernism, Poststructuralism, and Deconstruction: Notes for Historians," *Central European History* 22, nos. 3–4 (September–December 1989): 260–278.

34. Dominick LaCapra, "*The Cheese and the Worms*: The Cosmos of a Twentieth-Century Historian," in his *History and Criticism* (Ithaca: Cornell University Press, 1985), 45–69. The quotation is from p. 69.

35. Gertrude Himmelfarb, "Telling It as You Like It: Post-Modernist History and the Flight from Fact," *TLS: The Times Literary Supplement,* 16 October 1992, 12–15.

for the long-standing sense that history writing is a vehicle for truth in a way that fictional writing is not. Some of those who intervened in the discussion, like Thomas Haskell, responding to Peter Novick, and Nancy Struever, responding to Sande Cohen, contributed elements for such an alternative, but those elements did not coalesce effectively.[36]

The uncertainties in historiography plugged into the wider discussion especially through the tension-ridden relationship between past and process, or how we of the present are connected with all that came before us. That relationship was at issue both in the concern about principles of selection and criteria of significance and in the concern about presentism, detachment, and the scope for truth. Much rests on why, in light of the wider eclipse of metaphysics, we might focus on the dominant processes, resulting in the actual world, and why we might resist, focusing instead on the stories of those others who lived outside, or who themselves resisted, or who were submerged by those dominant processes.

The relationship between past and process had been problematic even as history established itself as a distinct professional discipline in the nineteenth century. But from Leopold von Ranke's reaction against Hegel to Herbert Butterfield's assault on the Whigs, historians came to a loose consensus around the imperative to get at the past "on its own terms," even "for its own sake." This entailed both a self-effacing disengagement and a deemphasis on process, or the connectedness between the present and the past. To emphasize the involvement of the inquirer, or to feature those aspects of the past that served some process to the present, was to invite anachronism or a priori schematism—and to do violence to the past as contemporaries lived it.

Yet innovators like White and Scott insist that historical writing is necessarily presentist, constructivist, and political and thus entails some particular connection between the present and past. They seemed to mainstream historians too quick to play down the truth-value of historical writing, which seemed to blur with literature, on the one hand, and with political propaganda, on the other. To address the central question about the scope for truth, we need to consider the relationship between historical inquiry and action in light of the various ways we might relate to both past and process in a postmetaphysical world.

A Historical Approach to the Changing Culture of History

In the rough-and-tumble of contemporary debate, we sometimes neglect the obvious point that, whatever the questions raised about history as a mode of inquiry, our present intellectual situation is the resultant of our own intellectual

36. Thomas L. Haskell, "Objectivity Is Not Neutrality: Rhetoric vs. Practice in Peter Novick's *That Noble Dream*," *History and Theory* 29, no. 2 (1990): 129–157; Nancy S. Struever, review of Sande Cohen, *Historical Culture: On the Recoding of an Academic Discipline*, *New Vico Studies* 5 (1987): 193–195.

history. As participants in that continuing history, we have come to formulate particular ways of understanding the processes to which we ourselves belong—and thus particular ways of understanding our present possibilities. And our ways of doing so have rested on particular ways of understanding the history in which we are enmeshed.

The uncertainties and conflations noted above suggest that as a result of our reading of the history so far, our conception of cultural possibilities may be unnecessarily restrictive. And a fresh look at certain steps in our intellectual history might clarify the scope for a historical strand in a postmetaphysical culture. The clarification must be historical because the contingencies have mattered; it matters who confronted whom as metaphysics and modernity were undermined and as particular alternatives began to be offered. Any effort at historical clarification is obviously treacherous, however, because history itself, its status and the baggage it must carry, has been so centrally at issue.

Much recent thinking rests on our understanding of what happened at the juncture encompassing the breakdown of the Hegelian synthesis, the crisis of the first historicism, and our departure from the "great age of history" by the early twentieth century.[37] There seems to have been a kind of pivot at that point, but its character is hard to decipher. On the one hand, there was a reaction against the premium on historical approaches that had come to mark the nineteenth century. On the other hand, there was a kind of "inversion" leading, as Rorty has put it, to an "exaltation of flux over permanence."[38] Thinkers like Henri Bergson and Alfred North Whitehead tended toward this sort of reversal, which was to posit another metaphysics, taking duration, flux, or process as ultimately real. Others, like Edmund Husserl, Ferdinand de Saussure, and Heinrich Rickert, were so troubled by the relativistic implications of nineteenth-century historicism that they sought new modes of access to something suprahistorical, stable, and certain.

But at about the same time, Nietzsche, Croce, and Heidegger began exploring a different set of possibilities. For each, the eclipse of metaphysics or transcendence meant, as a first approximation, the historicizing of the world, of reality itself. Each embraced the historicity of things as their contemporaries did not. At issue was not simply an abstract intellectual reorientation but a new experience requiring a personal and cultural response. And though they represent a common departure, Nietzsche, Croce, and Heidegger experienced the intrusiveness of history differently, so each proposed, in response, a different mode of relating to the world as historical. Nietzsche and Heidegger explored

37. See, for example, Richard Rorty's "Nineteenth-Century Idealism and Twentieth-Century Textualism" (1980), reprinted in his *Consequences of Pragmatism (Essays: 1972–1980)* (Minneapolis: University of Minnesota Press, 1982), 139–159. See also Herbert Schnädelbach, *Geschichtsphilosophie nach Hegel: Die Probleme des Historismus* (Freiburg: Karl Alber, 1974), which posits a sequence of ultimately unsatisfactory efforts to confront the problems that first emerged with nineteenth-century historicism.

38. Rorty, *Essays on Heidegger*, 118n. Rorty found this tendency's "least common denominator" in the thinking of Nietzsche, James, and Bergson.

contrasting extremes, while Croce sought a kind of middle ground, though he had something important in common with both Nietzsche and Heidegger vis-à-vis the other.

At the same time, however, there were tensions, limitations, and contingencies in the legacies of all three thinkers, so the story hardly stops with them. In different ways, thinkers like José Ortega y Gasset, R. G. Collingwood, Michael Oakeshott, and Walter Benjamin explored some of the same terrain. But there has been particular significance to the more recent efforts of Gadamer, Foucault, Derrida, and Rorty to address many of the same issues as foundationalist metaphysics has continued to erode. In recasting hermeneutics, structuralism, and pragmatism, these thinkers confronted the dissolution of all that had seemed to make the world stable on some privileged, suprahistorical level; in the process, each took up aspects of the ambiguous legacy of Nietzsche, Croce, and Heidegger, though they did so in their own particular, contingent ways.

Croce has not been prominent in recent efforts to assess the postmetaphysical situation, but some of those responding to the inflation of history have shared his assumptions and offered comparable prescriptions. Gadamer, especially, came to represent, in recast form, some of what Croce was the first to interject into the discussion.[39] Partly because of what he learned from Heidegger, Gadamer's hermeneutics can cover some of the most glaring deficiencies in Croce, while Croce's absolute historicism can help box out certain contingent ambiguities in Gadamer.

Still, Croce and Gadamer were both prejudicially conservative in important respects, and even taken together they leave tensions and ambiguities. The story grows more interesting, but also more complex, when we add the forms of deconstruction associated with Foucault and Derrida, each of whom embraced the Nietzschean and Heideggerian legacies to show the scope for a new and radical kind of historical questioning. But though the issue has been much discussed, the area of intersection between hermeneutics and deconstruction has been especially difficult to map, partly because deconstruction has itself seemed to entail conflicting impulses. Its premium on playful or ritualistic disruption may undermine any chance for radical historical questioning to serve ongoing reconstruction.

Some of those seeking a more constructive postmetaphysical orientation

---

39. Gadamer's recasting of hermeneutics rested partly on encounter with Collingwood's logic of question and answer, which specified the present's central role in constituting a particular past and which had been developed from Crocean notions. Thus it was partly under Croce's indirect influence that Gadamer moved beyond the older understanding of "historicism," as the imperative to get at the past on its own terms or as the quest for the correct method of historical understanding. See Hans-Georg Gadamer, *Reason in the Age of Science*, trans. Frederick G. Lawrence (Cambridge: MIT Press, 1981), 45–47. In addition to Gadamer and Rorty, with whom I will compare Croce explicitly, see David Kolb's conclusion to *The Critique of Pure Modernity: Hegel, Heidegger, and After* (Chicago: University of Chicago Press, 1986), for a good example of a generally Crocean orientation in a thinker seeking to sidestep Hegel yet avoid the Heideggerian extreme.

embraced Rorty's neopragmatism, which claimed kinship with aspects of Gadamerian hermeneutics and which had an unacknowledged kinship with Crocean historicism as well.[40] And Rorty sometimes suggested that with the eclipse of metaphysics, historical orientation becomes the cultural core, that a radical kind of historical questioning might do for the culture what philosophy could not. Still, partly because of new preoccupations that open with the inflation of history, he, too, offered an ambiguous mixture, an aestheticized pragmatism emphasizing the scope for creating fictions for particular purposes, especially personal edification. Such accents compromised the renewed emphasis on historical approaches that he otherwise seemed to invite.

Although none of them merits the last word, there is much to be learned by treating Nietzsche, Croce, Heidegger, Gadamer, Foucault, Derrida, and Rorty in tandem. Together they enable us to stake out the terrain of postmetaphysical history and to assess the possibilities within it. It is worth concentrating on these thinkers even at the expense of others—W. V. Quine and Donald Davidson, for example—whose assault on foundationalist metaphysics has had implications for the status of history but who have been less explicitly concerned with wider cultural implications.[41] Those in the Anglo-American tradition have been less prone to view the break from metaphysics as fundamental to the culture and to feel its consequences in a deeply personal way. Part of what distinguishes Rorty himself is his determination to think through the wider implications of that break, and he has taken good advantage of recent Anglo-American philosophy in doing so, even as he has also attuned himself to the various Continental explorations of the postmetaphysical terrain.

The sequence from Nietzsche to Rorty has been prominent in establishing our sense of the cultural situation, yet the chips are still falling, and such contemporaries as Christopher Norris, John D. Caputo, David Couzens Hoy, Allan Megill, Brook Thomas, and F. R. Ankersmit have sought to explore the connections and implications as the discussion has continued. Our continuing intellectual history embraces their efforts—and whatever contribution this study can make. In light of the prominence that the extremes have assumed in dis-

---

40. See, for example, Christopher Butler's way of embracing neopragmatism in his *Interpretation, Deconstruction, and Ideology: An Introduction to Some Current Issues in Literary Theory* (Oxford: Oxford University Press, 1984).

41. In *Essays on Heidegger*, 110n., Rorty notes that Quine and Davidson "do not share Heidegger's sense of 'Western metaphysics' as pervasive and all-encompassing. So their polemics lack the apocalyptic tone common to late Heidegger and early Derrida." Still, the work of Davidson, especially, has been central to the recent phase of the assault on the metaphysical tradition, with its various dualisms. See especially his noted essay "On the Very Idea of a Conceptual Scheme" (1974), reprinted in his *Inquiries into Truth and Interpretation* (Oxford: Oxford University Press, 1984), 183–198, which opposes the dualism of conceptual scheme and reality, or world, or content, and the conceptual relativism that results from such dualisms. In pointing away from the notion that language necessarily distorts reality, Davidson posits the coherence necessary to conceive the postmetaphysical world as continuous and, ultimately, historical.

cussions of postmetaphysical possibilities, I will be concerned especially to identify the elements that might serve a moderate alternative and, more particularly, to show why such a moderate strand entails a constructive role for historical understanding. Those elements are to be found interspersed with more extreme responses to the world as historical, responses that turn from any constructive engagement with history and that may even undermine any premium on empirical historiography.

Helpful as it might be, however, any such constructive culture of history could not supplant, but could only stand in tension with, the array of extremes that first began to emerge in the responses of Nietzsche and Heidegger. A postmetaphysical culture of history would surely entail an unstable field of forces, and that whole field requires our attention.

We must also note that the inflation of history has bred resistance throughout the century, and even on this level the discussion continues. In some prominent instances, that resistance was relatively traditionalist and, in our terms, still metaphysical. Thus, for example, the explicitly antihistoricist ideas of Karl Löwith, Guido de Ruggiero, and Leo Strauss, based on religious or classical natural law positions. Moreover, in light of the decay of the first positivism, there were renewed attempts to ground science as a cultural core. First neo-Kantianism and then the neopositivism of the Vienna Circle developed partly in response to the cultural disarray that the intrusiveness of history seemed to entail.

The Marxist tradition proved another important source of resistance, although its relationship to the cultural direction at issue in this study has been especially elusive. Marx's departure from Hegel may seem a step from a still-metaphysical conception of history—abstract, idealist, speculative, totalist—to one that is concrete, down-to-earth, praxis-oriented, and open-ended. Yet by the 1920s, the most innovative Marxists, seeking to scrape away the limiting encrustations of materialism and economic determinism, were accenting Marxism's Hegelian underpinnings, which seemed to invite a greater role for consciousness, culture, and freedom. In this form, Marxism came to seem more open-ended and historicist. In recent discussion, moreover, critics generally within the Marxist tradition have attacked poststructuralism for its apparently antihistorical tendencies.[42]

Certainly Marxism, in principle, might present itself as radically historicist, insofar as it simply claimed to offer, through its critical account of the

42. See, for example, Perry Anderson, *In the Tracks of Historical Materialism* (London: Verso, 1983). In the United States, leftists like Fredric Jameson and Frank Lentricchia offered the most pointed arguments, in the face of poststructuralism, for the continued centrality of a historical approach. See Geoff Bennington and Robert Young, "Introduction: Posing the Question," in *Post-Structuralism and the Question of History,* ed. Derek Attridge et al. (Cambridge: Cambridge University Press, 1987), 1–11, for a good introduction to this confrontation.

historically specific constellation of capitalism, the most convincing diagnosis of present problems and prescription for solution. In competing with alternative diagnoses and prescriptions, such a Marxism would understand itself as participating in an ongoing conversation; it would remain willing to learn—and even to change with the growth of the world. But despite tendencies in this direction, twentieth-century Marxism has continued to rest on an extra dimension, the claim to a privileged, suprahistorical grasp of the a priori structure and direction of history itself. This entailed a certain way of understanding differentiation and conflict, as well as an image of wholeness, or "totality," as the culmination of history.[43] Whatever the obstacles to its practical realization, the notion of "emancipation" remained fundamental to the coherence and distinctiveness of Marxism. And emancipation meant not simply the overcoming of one historically specific configuration but a qualitative departure from the limiting structures of all of history as we have known it so far. The claim to a suprahistorical grasp of the course of history justified a claim to privilege in diagnosis and prescription that seemed to warrant devaluing opposing accounts a priori.

In the final analysis, then, what Marxism claimed to offer was not simply a historically specific critique of capitalist civilization but a particular conception of history, still deeply Hegelian. Insistence on this point, it must be emphasized, does not necessarily entail criticism of Marxism, let alone refutation; it is simply to say that even as it began to be recast by the 1920s, Marxism must be seen as resisting, not contributing to, the more radically historicist direction in twentieth-century culture.

But it might still be possible to resist the historicizing tendency by developing a modified suprahistorical framework not subject to the charges that could be brought against metaphysics and Hegelianism. Among efforts in this direction, the most prominent has been Jürgen Habermas's quest for a universal pragmatics, which was stimulated in part by the historicist relativism that seemed to lurk in Gadamer's recasting of hermeneutics. Indeed, Habermas disputed the premises of several of the major figures in this study and pinpointed what may indeed be elements of overreaction in their thinking.[44] While accepting much of the historicizing tendency, he wanted to retain the scope for critique, to specify criteria of rationality, and to save at least the ideal of

43. See John E. Grumley, *History and Totality: Radical Historicism from Hegel to Foucault* (London: Routledge, 1989), esp. pp. 62–63, 150–151, 206, for a sympathetic commentator's assessment of the ongoing ambiguities within Marxism over the question of totality and completion, as well as Martin Jay's masterly *Marxism and Totality: The Adventures of a Concept from Lukács to Habermas* (Berkeley, Los Angeles, and London: University of California Press, 1984), on the whole issue.

44. See especially Jürgen Habermas, *The Philosophical Discourse of Modernity: Twelve Lectures*, trans. Frederick Lawrence (Cambridge: MIT Press, 1987; orig. German ed. 1985). Habermas's debate with Gadamer is discussed in chap. 7, below.

emancipation. Habermas's prominence reminds us that the effort to conceive the relationship between what changes and what does not is still very much in progress. At the same time, however, his preoccupations make clear how central to our cultural experience the effort to come to terms with the historicizing tendency has been.

2

Tentative Steps into History

From Vico to Dilthey

The Question of Modern Historical Consciousness

The relationship between metaphysics and history had been at issue even before the waning of metaphysics came to seem fundamental to our cultural situation. Depending on the criterion or frame of reference, the advent of a "genuinely historical approach" or of "modern historical consciousness" can plausibly be found at various moments in our tradition, starting with the beginnings of the Renaissance. Certainly it had long been recognized that things human—institutions, laws, customs, even languages—change over time. Thus, among other things, the effort necessary to avoid anachronism if understanding across time was to be possible. Moreover, different institutions might be appropriate to different circumstances. But, as Reinhart Koselleck has shown, until the eighteenth century "history" was conceived as the container of a finite range of possibilities, manifesting or exemplifying something suprahistorical. Only during the eighteenth century did it become possible to conceive history in the singular—as encompassing all the particular histories of this and that. Thus history came to suggest, for the first time, a kind of totality. Then the French Revolution indicated that this history could be the scene—perhaps was inevitably the scene—of genuine novelty.[1]

1. Reinhart Koselleck, *Futures Past: On the Semantics of Historical Time*, trans. Keith Tribe (Cambridge: MIT Press, 1985; orig. German ed. 1979), esp. p. 58. See also Michael Allen Gillespie, *Hegel, Heidegger, and the Ground of History* (Chicago: University of Chicago Press, 1984), 12, 181 n. 24, on the comparison at issue. Gillespie accents the limits of the break that such scholars as Donald Kelley and George Huppert have found in the Renaissance.

Hans Blumenberg has outlined a historical sequence of concepts of reality that includes an analogous break at about the same time, when reality came to seem "the result of an actualization" and open to "a future that might contain elements which could shatter previous consistency and so render previous 'realities' unreal." Now our sense of what the world could entail included novelty, surprise, as never before. This new sense of reality as open to the future in itself proved a stimulus to human activity.[2]

Gradually, and relatively recently, then, it became possible in the Western tradition to conceive the world as fundamentally historical in some sense. This new historical consciousness achieved articulation as a sequence of thinkers reacted against the intellectual mainstream, reformulated with the twin Galilean and Cartesian revolutions. Though now emphasizing epistemology, that mainstream was still wound around foundationalist metaphysics. The reaction encompassed, most notably, Giambattista Vico against René Descartes, G. W. F. Hegel against Immanuel Kant, German romanticism, with its concern for historically differentiated national cultures, against Enlightenment universalism, and Wilhelm Dilthey, with his concern for the autonomy of the human studies, against the imperialism of the natural sciences. By the end of the nineteenth century, these thinkers had produced many of the categories through which we think about history even today. Still, their efforts hardly added up to a consistent countertradition. Moreover, though Vico, Hegel, and Dilthey embraced history in pioneering ways, each continued to rely on something metaphysical and suprahistorical. Thus the tensions and ambiguities in the thought of each, and thus the possibility of a more radical step.

Individuality and Completeness in Vico and Hegel

Vico showed, as Michael Mooney has put it, that if we are "to know what man is," we must grasp him "genetically, as a being in time."[3] But this insight can lead in several directions, and Vico's legacy has proven particularly complex. Some place Vico in the tradition of rhetoric, of *sensus communis*, of practical wisdom, a tradition that had developed from Aristotelian *phronesis* to Renaissance civic humanism but that by Vico's time apparently had to be refurbished in light of the claims of the newly dominant Cartesians. Others view Vico as a protohistoricist who showed that reason is not universal, that cultures are disparate individualities, that there are discrete ways of organizing worlds, none correct in some absolute sense. Poetic wisdom has an integrity of its own,

---

2. Hans Blumenberg, "The Concept of Reality and the Possibility of the Novel," trans. David Henry Wilson, in *New Perspectives in German Literary Criticism: A Collection of Essays,* ed. Richard E. Amacher and Victor Lange (Princeton: Princeton University Press, 1979), 32–33, 33n.

3. Michael Mooney, *Vico in the Tradition of Rhetoric* (Princeton: Princeton University Press, 1985), 261.

affording access to a realm of truth foreclosed to conceptual thinking. Thus Vico could serve the romantic insistence on the autonomy—and even superiority—of art in the face of universalizing rational philosophy and the developing cult of science.[4] Still, Vico himself embedded his understanding of poetry in a wider science of the human world, based on the different ways human beings use language.[5] In developing this conception, however, he offered elements for a deeper kind of historicism, accenting not the discreteness of "individualities" but the radical immanence of the whole human world, which simply grows on itself.

Vico agreed with contractualists like Thomas Hobbes and Hugo Grotius that we must start from the beginning, imagining the situation of human origins and thinking the human situation through from there. In this sense, he was not seeking simply to continue an earlier tradition of practical wisdom, common sense, and rhetoric. But Vico remained sufficiently within the protohistoricist tradition of Italian Renaissance philology to deplore the anachronism that he found characteristic of his own age, with its geometric turn of mind and corresponding deemphasis on the significance of historical difference. Explicitly in opposition to the ascendant Cartesians, he insisted on the need to avoid presentist conceits, especially the assumption that present concepts already embody whatever there is.[6]

For Vico, then, it was axiomatic that the founding act of humanity could not have been a rational social contract by people who think as we do, for we think as we do only because of all the experience we have had. The emerging or happening of the human world could only have begun with the simplest, most concrete things conceivable. At the beginning of history was an act of imagination occasioned by the thunderclap that, Vico suggested, led the feral prehumans to look up in astonishment and to see, in the living, roaring sky, a god speaking to them. Thus began the specifically human process of imagining a particular world. Vico sought to conceive the first humans as utterly immanent, able to respond to novel experience, to represent to themselves what was happening, only in terms of what they *already* "knew," on the basis of absolutely nothing but what they had experienced so far. At the beginning, they did not even have "the seat of their pants" to go by, only their own bodies; they could only imagine "metaphorically," in light of their limited bodily experience. Vico sought to envision what it must have been like for those who had to imagine what was

4. This point has been widely made but nowhere better than in several of Isaiah Berlin's essays in *Against the Current: Essays in the History of Ideas* (New York: Penguin, 1982); see pp. 80–129.

5. Thus, for example, Donald Verene found in Vico a new science of the imagination, with anticipations of Ernst Cassirer's philosophy of symbolic forms. See Donald Phillip Verene, *Vico's Science of Imagination* (Ithaca: Cornell University Press, 1981).

6. See, for example, Giambattista Vico, *The New Science of Giambattista Vico*, trans. Thomas Goddard Bergin and Max Harold Fisch (Ithaca: Cornell University Press, 1984), 60 (nos. 120, 122–123).

happening in this way—and to think through what it means that human culture began in such a way.[7]

Vico's myth of human origins, though fanciful in one sense, offered a brilliant way of conceiving the starting point naturalistically, with no appeal to some transcendent sphere. At the origins, the first humans were, to be sure, in contact with something "given"—with their own bodies, or with the thunder, so that we may still ask, what is thunder *really*? But Vico made that contact as empty as possible. The founding moment rests on metaphor, and things move contingently, by means of new metaphors, from there; all "parallel" or mimetic representation between humanity and some external "reality" is lost at the outset. Thus it is futile to conceive the human situation in terms of the familiar subject-object dualism of the modern philosophical tradition. Even the term "metaphor" is misleading, insofar as it connotes an independent reality that language either represents indirectly or misrepresents. The gap between language and reality collapses.

In the same way, there is no privileged, transcendent human subject. Human beings land running, already in motion, already caught up in creating a human world, most fundamentally by means of inherently creative language. From the start, that human world can only grow on itself by responding to itself, because there is nothing else.

Vico's myth of origins, then, enables us to grasp the world as "always already" a set of imaginative representations based on preceding experience. As far back as we can conceive, even at the beginning, there is only creative, imaginative language, so that anything we could characterize as humanity is always already caught up in a linguistically constructed world, and there is nothing outside this language. The growing human world of imaginative language is thus self-contained; it is reality itself.

It follows that we today are still doing what human beings have done from the beginning, coming to terms with new experience by imagining in terms of what we have experienced so far. The only difference is that by now a considerably more complex world has resulted, and our repertoire—our language—is correspondingly larger as a result. And that repertoire will continue to grow as we respond to the novel world that has resulted from the aggregate of human response so far. The coming to be of the human world is a single continuing event happening through the creativity of human beings in language.

Although for Vico the conceptual thinking characteristic of the "age of men" differs from the earlier poetic thinking, imagination remains fundamental because the "poverty of language" characterizes not just the human situation at

7. Ibid., 116–118 (nos. 374–378); see also pp. 37–38 (no. 62). It is worth considering Vico's reduction to metaphor and rhetoric in light of Hans Blumenberg's "An Anthropological Approach to the Contemporary Significance of Rhetoric," trans. Robert M. Wallace, in *After Philosophy: End of Transformation?* ed. Kenneth Baynes et al. (Cambridge: MIT Press, 1987), 429–458; see esp. pp. 439, 444, 456.

the founding moment. Rather, language is forever "poor"—inadequate fully to encompass and fix the world—not least because, through every new act of knowing-imagining, the world outgrows the language that has resulted so far.

Although knowledge would thus seem finite and provisional, it was crucial for Vico that we can claim genuinely to know. With his axiom of *verum-factum*, Vico meshed knowing with making; we can know what we have made. Thus while we humans may measure and describe the natural world, only God can know it, because it was He who made it. However, we can know the human world, the world resulting from history, precisely because we have made it.[8] Yet a fundamental tension marked Vico's conception, for though he had brackdescribed God, and though his account of knowing suggested that knowledge is endlessly finite, practical, and provisional, he aspired to a divine kind of knowledge, which entailed a definitive grasp of the eternal and completed.

It was crucial, to be sure, that the level of the necessary and eternal could not be apprehended directly, through the mere exercise of reason; thus Vico's assault on the rational universalism of the contractualist and the natural law traditions. Cultures develop historically as discrete individualities, so we could hope to know a finished whole only through historical inquiry. But for Vico, it was possible to discern suprahistorical structures or patterns—an "ideal eternal history"— at work in the particular phenomena of the human world. This suprahistorical dimension was the focus of Vico's new science, which specified the necessary cycle of human cultural approaches and corresponding institutions.

Although that cycle might be conceived as providential, Vico's orientation generally remained radically immanentist. What we come to know, through his new science, is not so much the will of God as "what man is." So such knowing amounts simply to mind grasping its own nature.[9] Underlying the disparate phenomena of history were a priori forms of the imagination, characterizable in terms of the rhetorical tropes and manifesting the deep structure of mind itself. By studying the progression of particular manifestations in history, we can have access to that structure.[10] This notion of mind knowing itself points toward modern structuralism, and thus, for example, Terence Hawkes began his survey of the structuralist tradition precisely with Vico. And thus Hayden White embraced Vico as he too sought to delineate a progression of cultural strategies characterizable by the rhetorical tropes.[11]

    8. Vico, *New Science*, 96–97 (no. 331). Verene, *Vico's Science*, 48, is especially good on Vico's way of moving from the verum-factum principle to the ability of thought to connect itself to itself, thereby creating intelligibility.
    9. See Verene, *Vico's Science*, 161–162, for an especially effective characterization.
    10. See Vico, *New Science*, 78–79 (nos. 241–245), 112 (no. 368), 129–130 (no. 405), 131 (no. 409), 414–415 (no. 1096), on the principles of ideal eternal history and their links to the rhetorical tropes.
    11. Terence Hawkes, *Structuralism and Semiotics* (Berkeley, Los Angeles, and London: University of California Press, 1977), 11–15; Hayden V. White, *Metahistory: The Historical Imagination in Nineteenth-Century Europe* (Baltimore: Johns Hopkins University Press, 1973).

With a slight shift in the weighting of the elements, however, Vico's thinking leads to something very different—a kind of totalizing historicism. From this perspective, the focus of interest is not on the a priori forms of the mind's imagining but on what the mind has imagined so far, the particular world that has resulted, and that is resulting still, from its particular acts of imagination. The actual course of our historical experience does not simply reveal structures of mind that are already in place but actually determines what mind can do, can be, as it proceeds.

Even insofar as we think in terms of a priori forms making possible whatever happens, it is possible to make the historical content—what has already resulted from imagination, and the basis for further imagination—so rich that the forms become relatively empty. Rather than on mind, we focus on the actual course of history because further imagining rests more interestingly on what has been imagined so far than it does on the ongoing forms of the mind's capacity to imagine. Moreover, while we ourselves can imagine as suprahistorical the mind's capacity to imagine in characteristic, classifiable ways, our conception of what those ways involves will be historically specific—part of the history being generated by our ongoing imagining—because they will reflect what has in fact been imagined by human beings in each of those ways.

As we saw above, growth by means of imagination continues even with the coming of rational thought in Vico's "age of men." Thus, as Donald Verene has emphasized, Vico's notion of ideal eternal history is itself an act of *fantasia*—in our terms, a historically specific imagining of the whole in light of experience so far, including experience of the human conceptual tools thereby elaborated.[12] This suggests that, on every level, verum-factum is a matter of knowing endlessly provisional particulars and not the relatively empty suprahistorical forms—the ideal eternal history, the cycle of structuring tropes.

From this perspective, knowing never transcends the human world but occurs entirely within it. Now understood as historically specific and provisional, knowing cannot satisfy metaphysical demands for certainty, but it is adequate to our needs, serving the ongoing making-happening of the world. We come to know the world in some particular way as we respond imaginatively to what the world has become so far, and our way of knowing it contributes to its growth, its becoming something different.

On one level, this weak, Vichian form of knowledge revives the tradition of Aristotelian phronesis, which similarly specified a provisional, practical wisdom based on human experience so far. But if we follow the more radical of the directions Vico opens up, his thinking points even beyond phronesis. History is not simply the mundane embodiment of eternal principles of effective practical conduct, understood as provisional only in their application, only because circumstances change. Rather, what had been taken to be suprahistorical

12. Verene, *Vico's Science*, 108–113.

principles appears ever more empty as it comes to seem that the world grows, is ever new, on every level.[13]

We have seen that Vico, in his quest for a new science of the human world, sought to discern suprahistorical structuring principles in the particulars of history. For Hegel, in contrast, the mundane facts and events of history are significant not as instances of suprahistorical types or as members of some class that science apprehends and classifies. Rather, each is unique, unrepeatable, and each plays an irreplaceable part in a unique process, helping make the world the particular way it is. There is no scope for transcending, through a generalizing science, this particular process to some higher, truer level.

Sympathetic students of Hegel like George Dennis O'Brien and Robert C. Solomon have accented this "individualizing" dimension in opposition to essentialist philosophy, to Enlightenment universalism, and to the culture of science.[14] But it is equally crucial that for Hegel, the individualities of history form a totality; history is a single, unified, and all-encompassing process. Moreover, that process is meaningful, significant. For Hegel, the fact that there is history, with its variability and difference, is not a mundane imperfection but is essential to what the world is and necessary for its purpose to be achieved. But this was to posit a kind of metaphysical frame, so Hegel's way of positing the world as a single history entailed a still-metaphysical dimension that Vico sometimes seemed poised to do without. Vico's conception was potentially more open-ended.

Hegel competed with Johann Gottlieb Fichte within German idealism for the terrain beyond Kant, whose epistemology, leaving an unknowable noumenon, seemed incomplete and inadequate. Hegel's solution posited history as the arena in which what there is—spirit—comes to full self-understanding, thus achieving the complete knowledge that Kant had seemed to preclude. At the same time, Hegel's experience of the era of the French Revolution, which he greeted with fervent expectation, brought home the reality of change and the possibility of genuine significance on the historical level. Perhaps the Revolution portended the redemption glimpsed in the Christian tradition, a state of fulfillment that, we only now come to realize, was to be achieved not simply at the end of time but actually *through* the historical process.

As Hegel saw it, history results from the self-externalization of spirit, which makes itself radically immanent precisely to achieve self-knowledge, to become fully conscious of itself *as* spirit, or freedom. Indeed, time is gener-

13. It is symptomatic that Mooney's failure to distinguish these possible directions leads him, by the end of his fine study, to link the tradition of practical wisdom to social science. See Mooney, *Vico*, 255, 261–263. If we emphasize that direction in Vico, the provisional rough-and-ready quality of practical wisdom is lost. Insofar as there is change in what there is to be known and what needs to be known, practical knowledge must be more radically open-ended and provisional.

14. See, for example, George Dennis O'Brien, *Hegel on Reason in History: A Contemporary Interpretation* (Chicago: University of Chicago Press, 1975), esp. pp. 78–79, 95–96, 114–115.

ated only because spirit must externalize itself in order to have the experiences necessary to come to know itself. But this means that for Hegel the historical process has a particular content and direction, given a priori. It is the process of coming to self-knowledge, which we achieve only with the completeness at the end of the process. At that moment spirit grasps not only its own essence but also the meaning of all that *has* meaning in what has happened. We understand the rational necessity of the process whereby we came to this understanding. So whereas for Hegel, in contrast to Vico, mind cannot grasp its own nature in some direct, immediate way through scientific detachment, we do achieve complete, genuine, even Godlike knowledge through the totality of the historical process.

To be sure, Hegel is open to a variety of interpretations regarding the nature of both the process and its end. Some accent the necessity, others the contingency, of the individual moments, the relationship among them, and their chronological sequence. The completeness to be attained may be conceived as relatively full and restrictive—as for those who emphasize the achievement of a particular set of political institutions—or as relatively empty and open-ended.

Sympathetic recent observers, such as O'Brien, Solomon, and even Rorty, tend to portray the Hegelian process and telos in the latter light as they play up Hegel's open-ended "historicism." Adapting Gertrude Stein, Solomon envisions us proclaiming, when we get to the end of Hegel's process, that "there's no there, there." Completeness is nothing but full awareness of the endless open-endedness of history, and thus of human freedom.[15] In the same vein, David Hoy notes that Hegel has room for such a radically open-ended conception insofar as "thought changes itself in the course of trying to understand both itself and the world."[16]

But Hegel admits only a relatively restricted measure of openness; such readings tend to jump the gun. It has become tempting to read him in this contemporary way only because of the ongoing inflation of history that has accompanied the waning of metaphysics. Even if, with Solomon, we understand the dialectical mechanism to be looser and the chronological order, the actual deployment in time, to be more contingent than has generally been assumed, a given set of experiences remains necessary for the spirit to know itself, to achieve full self-consciousness. And even if we understand the telos as a *completely* empty sort of self-knowledge, there is still an end given at the beginning, stemming from the suprahistorical necessities of spirit, and there remains

15. Robert C. Solomon, *In the Spirit of Hegel: A Study of G. W. F. Hegel's "Phenomenology of Spirit,"* 14–16, 636–637; see also pp. 190–191, 235. Although Solomon, much like Rorty, finds in Hegel what he calls a "central indecision," an "awkward and sometimes confused mixture of absolute idealism and historicism," he explicitly plays up the historicist emptiness and incompleteness throughout his study. For his characterization of the tension in Hegel, see esp. p. 239, but also pp. 4–5, 315, 360n, 498.

16. David Couzens Hoy, "Taking History Seriously: Foucault, Gadamer, Habermas," *Union Seminary Quarterly Review* 34, no. 2 (Winter 1979): 90–91.

something privileged about whatever furthers movement toward that end.[17] Because the world spirit in Hegel's conception is already, on some level, here, complete, there is an a priori frame for what happens, can happen, or can be meaningful in history.

So even as each embraced history in unprecedented ways, Vico and Hegel kept history in bounds because each operated in terms of an image of "divine" completeness. On some level, the world is complete, and suprahistorical principles on that level govern history. Completeness is required for real knowing, as opposed to the merely provisional knowledge of historical particulars that we can achieve prior to the completion of the process. In the final analysis, then, neither Vico nor Hegel offered the scope for novelty and creativity, or the scope for a radically historical approach to the world, that each, in certain of his formulations, seemed to invite.

But in inflating history as they did, they invited a new set of questions. How do we conceive the world as historical if, with the waning of metaphysics, we can no longer conceive of a frame or goal? How do we characterize a world in which contingency and endless incompleteness mix with the individuality of things? In a world with this consistency, what is the place of human being?

Historicism and Historiography after Hegel

Before those questions intruded, the first historicism emerged, adding to the cultural mix. As part of the romantic reaction against the rationalist universalism of the Enlightenment, historicism held that discrete national cultures and institutions, as the products of history, have their own integrity and value and thus are not to be judged according to some allegedly rational, suprahistorical standard. But historicism gathered force also in reaction against Hegel, who came to seem the archetype of a priori schematism, a speculative philosopher of history whose aims stood diametrically opposed to those of practicing historians. Whereas Hegel had embraced the individuality of things from one perspective, he had seemed too quick to subordinate the particular events of history to an a priori, teleological process.

Hegel had in fact reproached Barthold Niebuhr, the great pioneering historian of ancient Rome, for merely collecting facts without seeking the level of meaning, the level on which those facts make sense to us. But recent students of Hegel have shown that Hegel, as a historian, was considerably more subtle than the stereotype suggested. Indeed, he sometimes had good reason for charging that it was not he himself but his critics among the historians who were

17. This fact is evident even in Solomon's account. See Solomon, *In the Spirit of Hegel*, 229–230, 233, 475–478.

guilty of anachronism.[18] Still, it is undeniable that Hegel approached history in terms of an a priori conception of what counted; past moments were worthy of attention only insofar as they had contributed to a particular, privileged process. Those that had no place in that process were of no general interest, were even meaningless.

Reacting against Hegel, individualizing historicists denied that the significance of the particulars of history depended on their place in some privileged process and sought more genuinely to approach the past on its own terms. Ranke, especially, offered imperatives that became articles of faith for practicing historians. Rather than conceive each generation as simply a stepping-stone to the next, he insisted that "every epoch is immediate to God, and its worth is not at all based on what derives from it but rests in its own existence, in its own self. . . . [E]very epoch must be seen as something valid in itself and appears highly worthy of consideration."[19] This was to suggest that all manifestations of the human have value, are inherently of interest. And against the notion that the historian judges the past and offers practical principles to instruct the present, Ranke claimed to be seeking simply to get at the past "wie es eigentlich gewesen," as it actually happened.[20]

Virtually from the outset, however, such accents led to new uncertainties about selection and significance and about the uses of historical inquiry and the status of historical knowledge. Whatever its excesses, Hegel's approach had specified a principle of coherence and unity, as well as the kinds of historical questions that could most fruitfully be asked. But if each individual culture is in touch with God in its own way, if all manifestations of the human are significant, how do we decide what to study? By the later nineteenth century, a particular culture of history had crystallized as the array of new questions found answers that variously invoked God, science, progress, and the nation-state. But those answers were contingent and delimited, and they entailed a crucial tension between past and process as the focus of historical inquiry.

In the context of national self-assertion and nation-state building, the individuality that came to seem most pertinently at issue for history was the nation, people, or state and the development of what seemed progressive political institutions. This set of concerns afforded plausible and indeed appropriate criteria of selection, helping to give historiography an important but still delimited

---

18. Duncan Forbes, in his introduction to Georg Wilhelm Friedrich Hegel, *Lectures on the Philosophy of World History: Introduction: Reason in History*, trans. H. B. Nisbet (Cambridge: Cambridge University Press, 1975), xv–xxvi, offers a spirited defense of Hegel against much of the long tradition of criticism.

19. Leopold von Ranke, *The Theory and Practice of History*, trans. Wilma A. Iggers and Konrad von Moltke (Indianapolis: Bobbs-Merrill, 1973), 53.

20. Leopold von Ranke, "Preface: *Histories of the Latin and Germanic Nations from 1494–1514*," trans. Fritz Stern, in *The Varieties of History: From Voltaire to the Present,* ed. Fritz Stern (Cleveland: World, Meridian, 1956), 57.

cultural niche as national and generally political history. To be sure, this emphasis on national history led beyond the pluralism of Johann Gottfried von Herder and Ranke to various more chauvinistic forms of nationalist historiography by the later nineteenth century. For Heinrich von Treitschke in Germany or Whiggish historians like Thomas Macaulay and George Macaulay Trevelyan in England, history focused on the historian's own national tradition, tracing its triumphant march to its present political institutions. In this generally Whiggish guise, history tended to become a celebratory myth, helping to cement a national community.

But the Whig tradition was eventually discredited, losing out to the serene imperatives of Ranke, at least in the self-understanding of the historical profession. Practicing historians have continued to subscribe to the principles that informed Butterfield's classic critique of the Whig tradition in 1931. And this was to reaffirm the notion that the genuine historian seeks "to understand the past for the sake of the past," not for the sake of the present.[21] As proof against Whiggish excess, this imperative made sense, but it masked an array of questions about past, process, and the present uses of historical understanding.

The reaction against Hegel also raised questions about method and the status of historical knowledge. It is a commonplace that the decline of German idealism by the middle of the nineteenth century meant abandoning the effort to understand human experience or the meaning of things in some total, unified way. Particular empirical researches replaced Hegelian "speculation." Nineteenth-century historicism tended to converge with positivism in accenting value-free detachment and painstaking empirical research to get at the past "as it actually happened."[22] By the later nineteenth century, most practicing historians insisted on the scientific nature of their enterprise, which held to strict rules of evidence and inference and rigorous criteria of causation, explanation, and generalization.

But to seek acceptance within the culture of science entailed risks for historians, especially as the new social sciences began flexing their muscles by the beginning of the twentieth century. The generalizing social sciences could not do without historical data, and they might provide generalizations useful to the historian, but they threatened the disciplinary autonomy of history at the same time. The historian might simply become the sociologist's research assistant, providing the raw material, the individual cases, that the real scientist then turns into genuine knowledge.

At the same time, however, there was reason to doubt that historiography was enough like the scientific enterprise to make any synthesis of historicism

21. Herbert Butterfield, *The Whig Interpretation of History* (New York: W. W. Norton, 1965; orig. pub. 1931); see esp. pp. 16–17.
22. John E. Grumley, *History and Totality: Radical Historicism from Hegel to Foucault* (London: Routledge, 1989), 68–69, 72, is especially good on the convergence and divergence of historicism and positivism.

and positivism possible. Some, especially in Germany and Italy, sought to start with what distinguished history and science and to explore the significance of the generally romantic countertradition for the questions facing historiography.

Insofar as it took freedom, purpose, and meaning to distinguish the human sphere, historicism stood opposed to the generally positivistic approach, with its deterministic implications and its attempt to subsume particulars under general laws. But to distance history from science, the assumed paradigm of knowledge and truth, raised questions about whether historical inquiry could claim to yield a truth of its own, and if so, how—on the basis of what method. Moreover, the recognition that historians are themselves historically specific and never entirely disinterested became increasingly intrusive. Alexis de Tocqueville bumped up against the riddles surrounding his own historicity as he tackled the problem of the French Revolution in the 1850s. However, he managed to sidestep the most troubling questions as he concluded that, happily enough, his was precisely the time—just far enough removed from the events themselves—to tease out the truth of the French Revolution.[23]

Some took a further step and claimed not only that the historian is necessarily "interested" but that the historian's active involvement is essential in bringing the past to life. Johann Gustav Droysen, writing in 1868, noted that the facts do not "speak for themselves, alone, exclusively, 'objectively.' Without the narrator to make them speak, they would be dumb. It is not objectivity that is the historian's best glory. His justness consists in seeking to understand."[24] Insofar as historians are themselves historically specific, yet play this sort of active role, the study of history was in some sense part of the history being studied. Historians necessarily approach the past in terms of prior knowledge of some whole or framework, but then, presumably, gain from that inquiry some new knowledge that changes their understanding of the whole and thus the prior knowledge they bring to bear at the next moment. From this perspective, the relationship between present and past, historical inquiry and history itself, was far more complex than the positivist image of dispassionate discovery and representation could explain. This sense could seem exciting, even liberating, insofar as it invited a more creative role for the historian, but it was also disturbing. Precisely insofar as it was distinctive, historical knowledge seemed merely relative and thus subject to skepticism.

But a deeper relativism also lurked as the Hegelian framework fell away, leaving uncertainty about how the individualities of history meshed with wholeness, totality, or overarching meaning. Ranke posited a link to God, but

23. Alexis de Tocqueville, *The Old Regime and the French Revolution*, trans. Stuart Gilbert (Garden City, N.Y.: Doubleday, Anchor, 1955), 3–5. See also Linda Orr, "The Revenge of Literature: A History of History," *New Literary History* 18, no. 1 (Autumn 1986): 8, on this theme in Tocqueville.

24. Johann Gustav Droysen, *Outline of the Principles of History*, trans. E. Benjamin Andrews (Boston: Ginn, 1893; orig. German ed. 1868), 52–53.

this was conservatively to invoke a transcendent sphere that, for others, did not hold.[25] To those who found Ranke no more convincing than Hegel, science seemed to offer the most promising alternative. Historians, like other scientists, were busily discovering given facts that would eventually add up to a finished picture, which might entail one of the various developmentalist patterns that positivists from Auguste Comte to Herbert Spencer proposed. If, however, history could not follow the lead of science, those individualities seemed to stand naked, disembodied, "just one damned thing after another."

Dilthey and the Unfinished Revolution

By the last years of the nineteenth century, concern with history had introduced an array of difficult questions about individuality and totality, purpose and focus, method and the status of historical knowledge. Dilthey sought mightily to address the outstanding issues and to find a rigorous, convincing way of combining the broadly historicist ideas that had resulted from the nineteenth-century encounter with history.

Dilthey took it as axiomatic that the stuff of the human studies was distinctive and thus could not be apprehended through the methods of the natural sciences. However, the human studies had an approach of their own, and historians, though they had to apprehend disparate individualities across a temporal chasm, did come up with something worthy of the term "knowledge." In one sense, historical understanding was but an instance of understanding in general, which always entails surmounting some degree of difference, yet which goes on all the time, requiring no esoteric insight or method.[26] But Dilthey's determination to face up to the distinctive historicity of the human world meant he could not leave it at that.

Descartes's quest for an indubitable, suprahistorical starting point initiated the modern turn in philosophy; Kant offered a kind of completion by specifying the transcendent categories making knowledge possible. Explicitly in opposition to this whole tradition, Dilthey held that even the presuppositions of our thinking, even the most fundamental concepts and rules, are historical prod-

25. On Ranke's way of invoking God to keep history from collapsing into meaningless chaos, see Georg G. Iggers, *The German Conception of History: The National Tradition of Historical Thought from Herder to the Present* (Middletown, Conn.: Wesleyan University Press, 1968), 69, 77, 80.

26. Hans Peter Rickman, *Wilhelm Dilthey: Pioneer of the Human Sciences* (Berkeley, Los Angeles, and London: University of California Press, 1979), 63–69, 72–79. See also pp. 123–142, on Dilthey's attempt to lay out a "critique of historical reason," specifying how historians like Ranke come up with knowledge. I am partial to Rickman's account, but I have also profited from two other major works on Dilthey that also appeared during the 1970s: Rudolf A. Makkreel, *Dilthey: Philosopher of the Human Studies* (Princeton: Princeton University Press, 1975; 3d printing with a new afterword, 1992); and Michael Ermarth, *Wilhelm Dilthey: The Critique of Historical Reason* (Chicago: University of Chicago Press, 1978).

ucts. And while he hoped to specify, in a Kantian way, the categories involved in understanding the human world, he recognized that any such specification would be incomplete, because the categories could change, or new ones could emerge, with new experience in history.[27] So rather than appeal to a starting point free of historically specific presuppositions, we must recognize that human beings—and human knowing—are embedded in history. From the dominant perspective, of course, to admit this embeddedness seemed to undermine the possibility of genuine knowledge altogether, but Dilthey sought to turn the tables.

In opposition to Kant and his own neo-Kantian contemporaries, Dilthey held that it is not some participation in transcendental reason that makes understanding possible but the fact that the human inquirer is part of the human world to be understood. In other words, understanding is possible not because we stand above history, but because we do not. Understanding takes place essentially because mind can understand what mind has created, a notion that Dilthey seems to have taken over directly from Vico. To combine embeddedness with a claim to knowledge was to recognize the hermeneutic "circularity" involved in all understanding. The process of understanding moves back and forth, between idea and context, or between myself and the other I seek to understand. As Dilthey saw it, then, hermeneutics was no longer, as for Friedrich Schleiermacher, an approach to the understanding of texts, especially texts that might be misinterpreted, but an approach to the whole human world. And that approach was necessary not simply because the human world was involved with understanding, interpretation, and meaning, but because it was fundamentally historical, and thus never finished or complete, and because any knower was embedded in history, and thus finite.[28] In conceiving historical understanding as itself historically situated, Dilthey invited a sense of the human world as endlessly growing, on every level, growing precisely as we understand it anew from our present vantage point.

So there can be knowledge of the human world, but for Dilthey, it is never simply a copy but always a construction, a reinterpretation, by a historically specific inquirer with a particular angle of vision. Thus, though historical understanding was ordinary and unproblematic in one sense, the relativistic implications of historicity gave deeper point to the ongoing questions about the status of historical knowledge, its cultural value vis-à-vis scientific knowledge. A concern to head off skepticism affected Dilthey's priorities, leading him to focus on method and to conceive the object of historical inquiry in a particular way.[29]

Even if the point was not to make the human studies more scientific, Dilthey

27. Rickman, *Wilhelm Dilthey*, 128–130, 132–136.
28. Iggers, *German Conception of History*, 143; Rickman, *Wilhelm Dilthey*, 132, 148–149.
29. Rickman, *Wilhelm Dilthey*, 48–50, 141–142, 155.

found it essential to specify the method whereby inquiry in the human studies could be sufficiently objective to yield genuine knowledge. Properly understood, hermeneutics was itself the method of the autonomous human-historical studies. By specifying the correct form of hermeneutic interaction between the inquirer and the object of study, Dilthey hoped to show how understanding in the human studies could be objective—even subject to testing and verification. Max Weber would pick up on this side of Dilthey, seeking a more rigorous, social scientific way of meshing the understanding that Dilthey posited with causal explanation. But even Dilthey, for all his emphasis on the distinctiveness of the human studies, respected science in its sphere and hoped that dialogue between the scientific and hermeneutic approaches could reunify the culture.[30]

Moreover, Dilthey's preoccupation with relativism led him to insist that it was possible in principle to distinguish instances of the human that had been historically conditioned from those that, stemming from a common human nature, could be universally valid in some sense. On the basis of evidence from historical experience itself, it would be possible to develop a cautiously systematic anthropology.[31] And, in important measure, *that* was the fundamental purpose of historical inquiry.

Dilthey assumed, more generally, that on some level there is still a solid, stable, suprahistorical reality, which remains our ultimate interest. We cannot get at it directly, both because it only manifests itself historically and because we inquirers are historically specific and finite, but we might glimpse this still-metaphysical realm precisely by examining the diverse instances of history. In "The Dream," a lecture on his seventieth birthday in 1903, Dilthey spoke of the anxiety he had come to feel as he recognized that we can only approach human being in different, even conflicting ways, each one-sided, yet each with a measure of validity: "To contemplate all the aspects in their totality is denied to us. We see the pure light of truth only in various broken rays." Dilthey assumed that there is "a single truth," but it is hidden from us, above all by the differentiation that the fact of history itself entails. But the historical consciousness that seemed to shatter any unified conception of the world proves Janus-faced; it "saves the unity of man's soul" at the same time. By looking through our historically specific worldviews, we may still "glimpse into a final harmony."[32]

History, then, was more important than ever as a basis for human self-understanding and orientation in the world. In crucial respects, in fact, it was more important than philosophy or science, for "man does not discover what he is through speculation about himself or through psychological experiments but

30. Ibid., 154–155, 157–158, 173.
31. Ibid., 139–142.
32. Wilhelm Dilthey, "The Dream," in *The Philosophy of History in Our Time,* ed. Hans Meyerhoff (Garden City, N.Y.: Doubleday, Anchor, 1959), 40–43.

through history." In the same way, "what man is and what he strives for he only discovers in the development of his nature through the millennia; it is never spelled out in universally valid concepts, only in vital experiences which spring from the depths of his whole being."[33] In positing essences and a suprahistorical order, Dilthey wanted to be reassuring. There are still stable foundations, he was saying—but they seemed suspiciously like quicksand. As H. P. Rickman has put it, "We know there are firm foundations, but we never can be absolutely sure that we are standing on them. . . . While retaining the ideal of objective truth [we] must accept its elusiveness and live with the difficulty of disentangling the core of truth from the temporal guise imposed by the fact that the human nature on which [we] rely is itself historically moulded."[34]

So even as Dilthey embraced the insights about individuality and historicity that had resulted from the nineteenth-century confrontation with history, he was preoccupied with the need to head off, or at least to balance, what seemed their threateningly relativistic implications. Thus he ended up emphasizing method, the scope for systematic inquiry, and the possibility of glimpsing some whole or universal.

One recent authority, citing Dilthey's accent on the scope for the theoretical, systematic, and general, concludes that Dilthey "might properly be considered as one of the first architects of the program 'historical science beyond historicism.' "[35] To others, however, Dilthey was simply giving in to historicism.[36] Still others have found some of Dilthey's preoccupations unnecessary and have accented the incompleteness of his embrace of the historical. Critique of Dilthey was pivotal to, most notably, Gadamer as he sought to accept historicity and to recast hermeneutics in a more radical way.[37]

As a result of the uncertainties surrounding Dilthey's position, especially the growing preoccupation with relativism, historicism seemed to be in crisis by the early twentieth century. As usually conceived, the "crisis of historicism" culminated after World War I in Ernst Troeltsch's noble but rather tortured efforts and Friedrich Meinecke's nostalgia for the serenity of Ranke.[38] With these thinkers, the ambiguous tradition of historicism seemed to have reached a culmination of sorts. But to many, it seemed a dead end.

33. Both passages are quoted in Rickman, *Wilhelm Dilthey,* 139.
34. Ibid., 142.
35. Ermarth, *Wilhelm Dilthey,* 351–353.
36. See, for example, Gillespie, *Hegel, Heidegger,* 121–122. Gillespie cites contemporaries and later critics—and ends up endorsing the charge himself. His argument leads from this point into the explicitly antihistoricist efforts of Edmund Husserl.
37. Hans-Georg Gadamer, *Truth and Method* (New York: Seabury, 1975; orig. German ed. 1960), 192–214. In his *Dilthey,* 414–419, Makkreel defends Dilthey from the most damaging of Gadamer's charges. I return to this issue in chapter 7, below.
38. Especially symptomatic is Friedrich Meinecke's "Deutung eines Rankeswortes," in *Aphorismen und Skizzen zur Geschichte,* 2d ed., enlarged (Stuttgart: K. F. Koehler, 1952), 119–129. See also the noted study by Karl Heussi, *Die Krisis des Historismus* (Tübingen: J. C. B. Mohr, 1932).

In their different ways, the major pioneers from Vico to Dilthey had departed from the long-standing metaphysical assumption that there can be direct access to a realm where things are what they are, a realm transcending the capricious change and differentiation of history. It came to seem that to apprehend "what man is," or any comparable suprahistorical structure of reality, we cannot climb directly beyond the chaotic particulars of history by relying on rational deduction, natural law, some invariable standard or procedure, or the scientific analysis of mind or brain. Rather, we must focus on history, because those suprahistorical essences are not simply given at any one time, in any particular instance. Perhaps something along those lines will ultimately be revealed *completely* in history, as for Hegel, or perhaps we mundane, finite creatures can aspire only to glimpses of what there really is. In either case, only study of history, the particular manifestations in time, affords access to the permanent, suprahistorical grounding or generator that had always been at issue in the metaphysical tradition.

But Vico, Hegel, and Dilthey all assumed that such a stable, suprahistorical realm still exists—and remains the ultimate focus of interest. As a result, there were tensions in the thinking of each, and even taken together they left an array of questions about the relationships between the universal and the historical, between individuality and totality, and between past and present.

At first, severing history from the totalizing of Hegel had seemed liberating because it invited treating individual cultural phenomena as worthy in themselves and not merely as instruments in an overarching world-historical process. But was that to leave a mere sequence of disembodied individualities, with no link to anything universal? Rather than liberating, the historical treatment might prove critical and corrosive, exposing as *merely* historical what had seemed suprahistorical and metaphysically grounded. History seemed to dissolve the world, cutting the culture off from the universal, by disembedding the particular instance from the totality in which it had seemed to have a meaningful place. This was a tendency, even as the culture tried various ways of linking the particulars of history to something higher—the universal laws of science, the universal God of Ranke, or the universal progressive process crucial to the array of developmentalists from Hegel to Comte and Spencer. By the end of the nineteenth century, there sometimes seemed no refuge from this critical historicizing impulse; the internal criticism of positivism suggested that even the scientific world-picture was but a human construct, elaborated over time, and thus but another merely relative cultural individuality or historical product.[39]

Because the first broadly historicist revolution, from Vico to Dilthey, was

39. On the place of critical positivism in nineteenth-century thought, see Maurice Mandelbaum, *History, Man, and Reason: A Study in Nineteenth-Century Thought* (Baltimore: Johns Hopkins University Press, 1971), 13–20, 304–310, 359–362.

central to the waning of metaphysics, it has often been assumed that with it we made the break from metaphysics into history, developing what, in simpler times, we called "modern historical consciousness." But because this revolution remained under the shadow of the old metaphysics, there remained the possibility of a second step, a deeper embrace of history, eluding even that shadow. Although in retrospect we can see openings for this more radical step along the way from Vico to Dilthey, enough of the old framework survived to make it unnecessary, even inconceivable, for the thinkers we have discussed. However, tensions remained even as their efforts reached a provisional culmination in Dilthey's thinking. At about the same time, other thinkers took precisely this second step, seeking to overcome, or sidestep, those tensions.

3

The Reduction to History

New Confrontations with Time and History

The sequence of ideas from Vico to Dilthey fed into a wider cultural tendency to think in terms of change, evolution, or development by the later nineteenth century. It had come to seem, as never before in the West, that human beings are fundamentally caught up in time or history, even that "reality" itself is somehow temporal or historical. During the later nineteenth century, the metaphysical tradition, recast through the various forms of developmentalism, seemed able to encompass this new sense of things. But by the end of the century, the intrusiveness of time and history was forcing a more radical rethinking. Some sought a new means of access to the suprahistorical, while others moved in the opposite direction, taking change, time, novelty, and creativity as ultimately real. But attempts to explore the human situation on this latter basis led in radically different directions, which have not been adequately distinguished. Thus a brief sketch is essential to grasp the novelty of the common departure that we find in Nietzsche, Croce, and Heidegger.

The effort to transcend the realm of change and novelty had been central to the Western metaphysical tradition, but it became more single-minded in light of the newly intrusive historicizing tendency. To an array of thinkers by the early twentieth century, the reconquest of the suprahistorical realm had come to seem the major cultural priority. Thus, for example, the neo-Kantian Heinrich Rickert responded to the troubling diversity of historically specific value systems by positing a transcendent value realm that somehow makes possible the diverse value manifestations of the empirical world. But the most influential of these efforts were Edmund Husserl's phenomenology and the structuralism that grew out of Ferdinand de Saussure's linguistics.

By means of a newly rigorous phenomenology, Husserl sought a grounding for certainty, for knowledge independent of history, society, and even the contingent construction of the human psyche, mind, or brain.[1] He worried, then, not only about historicism but also about psychologism, or the reduction of logic and the categories of thought to the structures of the human psyche. In a sense, however, psychologism seemed so threatening only because of the broader historicist tendency, only because the mental equipment of human beings no longer seemed universal and suprahistorical, but rather to have come to be as it is in response to particular circumstances, as a contingent product of evolution in time. The package of historicism and psychologism threatened to make knowledge merely relative and thus to breed skepticism—and even, Husserl feared, some general crisis of Western civilization.[2]

At the outset of modern philosophy, Descartes had similarly sought to ward off skepticism, as had Kant, in a more sophisticated way, in response to the new skepticism of David Hume. But those efforts had come to seem inadequate, so Husserl sought a more radical approach, eschewing the presuppositions that still lurked in the thinking of his predecessors. By bracketing any notion of an actively thinking subject or an external world, any notion that what is found in consciousness refers to something else, by concentrating *only* on the phenomena that appeared in consciousness, Husserl thought it possible to isolate the necessary and indubitable structures of experience. Starting from the "transcendental ego" or purified consciousness that he believed resulted from this reduction, he sought to show that consciousness does not simply identify but confers meaning and that essences, not simply individual things, appear to consciousness. To head off solipsism, he posited intersubjectivity; only in community with others can I claim to know the world.[3]

Husserl's effort was intriguing, but critics ever since have noted its inadequacies. The attempt to bracket has seemed futile, a kind of desperate last gasp, especially because the meaning of phenomena appears in language, a historical and culturally specific product. As Leszek Kolakowski has put it, "While performing the transcendental reduction, we cannot get rid of language, and this means: of the whole cultural history of mankind."[4] Moreover, for Husserl, the particular instances are not the real focus of interest but point to essences, assumed to be given once and for all. But any such essences may be only

1. Leszek Kolakowski, *Husserl and the Search for Certitude* (New Haven: Yale University Press, 1975), 17–23, 34–35.

2. Husserl's most explicit assault on historicism is his "Philosophy as a Rigorous Science" (1910), reprinted in his *Phenomenology and the Crisis of Philosophy*, trans. Quentin Lauer (New York: Harper and Row, Torchbook, 1965). See pp. 77–79, 122–147.

3. Kolakowski, *Husserl*, 40, 61, 65, 73–77.

4. Ibid., 55–56.

provisional summations of particulars so far, which we divide up and arrange in certain ways for certain contingent purposes. And the accent on intersubjectivity suggested that knowing might be a temporal process—and endlessly provisional.

The difficulties with Husserl's approach helped convince others, most obviously Heidegger and Derrida, that any such quest for timeless certainty was misguided. It was partly in response to Husserl that Heidegger sought to encompass the historicity of human being in *Being and Time*, published in 1927, then took another step and began focusing on the historicity of being itself. Husserl sought to keep up, writing *The Crisis of European Sciences and Transcendental Phenomenology* (1936–1937) partly in response to Heidegger's initial turn. In this work, which remained unfinished on his death, Husserl fully recognized that historical self-reflection permeates the transcendental reduction; there is always an a priori "life world." Yet even as he admitted this element of variability and relativity, he continued to struggle to posit something suprahistorical.[5] There is something universal about the way any life world works, and we can get at that universal structure. Indeed, the life world can be the subject of a universalizing science.[6] And in light of the crisis Husserl believed to be developing, such a universal science, however abstract its object, was more than ever the cultural priority.

Much like Husserl at about the same time, the linguist Saussure found history so intrusive that it had to be precluded in a newly radical way if knowledge according to the broadly Cartesian ideal was to be possible. Finding inadequate the recent efforts to understand change in language in terms of development within a stable system, he reworked the relationship between the phenomenon of linguistic change and the element of system that might afford the focus for a secure science. Change comes from outside the linguistic system, from the actual use of language, which cannot be understood in specifically linguistic terms at all.[7] The actual use of language, Saussure was implicitly suggesting, was at least sometimes fundamentally creative. Any such use might change language in a way that could not have been predicted beforehand. So the use of language and change in language were bound up with a process of change over time, with history, and could not be captured in scientific knowledge.

But by writing off that diachronic dimension, Saussure decided, it would be

5. Edmund Husserl, *The Crisis of European Sciences and Transcendental Phenomenology: An Introduction to Phenomenological Philosophy*, trans. David Carr (Evanston: Northwestern University Press, 1970). See also David Carr's sympathetic exposition, *Phenomenology and the Problem of History: A Study of Husserl's Transcendental Philosophy* (Evanston: Northwestern University Press, 1974), which features the tension between Husserl's continuing attempt at a transcendental orientation and his effort "to take history seriously."

6. Hans-Georg Gadamer, *Philosophical Hermeneutics*, trans. David E. Linge (Berkeley, Los Angeles, and London: University of California Press, 1977), 190–196. See also pp. 158–164, 167–168.

7. Jonathan Culler, *Ferdinand de Saussure* (New York: Penguin, 1977), 22–41, esp. pp. 36–37.

possible to identify the structure of language at any one time, the system of relations and rules making possible any actual use of the language. He could posit such a system because he assumed a radical dichotomy of sign and signified; the structure was a self-contained system of relationships among the signs and did not depend on some relationship with the changing "outside" world. On the basis of this synchronic dimension, it would be possible to develop a science first of language, then of human cultural expression in general, laying bare the structure of the system and showing how it works, how meaning is generated by the operations of the elements in the system.

But a science of this sort was in one sense thin, eviscerated. Although a stable structure can be delineated at any one moment, change continues, and every subtle innovation in actual usage forces into being a subtly different system at the next moment in time. The linguistic system has to adjust to endless innovation; the science is perpetually swallowed up by history.[8]

Structuralism began to emerge in the late 1940s as Claude Lévi-Strauss sought to draw out Saussure's insights to develop a full-scale science of culture. Suggesting that the basic structure of language underlies an array of societal practices, Lévi-Strauss focused strictly on the signs in an effort to discern the underlying system, the gridwork of rules that enables the signs to have meaning and that, in a sense, makes possible whatever happens. A science of human being is possible, said Lévi-Strauss in 1949, precisely because we can apprehend the structure underlying the changing cultural phenomena of history.

> Anthropology cannot remain indifferent to historical processes and to the most highly conscious expressions of social phenomena. But if the anthropologist brings to them the same scrupulous attention as the historian, it is in order to eliminate, by a kind of backward course, all that they owe to the historical process and to conscious thought. His goal is to grasp, beyond the conscious and always shifting images which men hold, the complete range of unconscious possibilities. These are not unlimited, and the relationships of compatibility or incompatibility which each maintains with all the others provide a logical framework for historical developments, which, while perhaps unpredictable, are never arbitrary.[9]

As history inflated, it seemed essential to Lévi-Strauss to find something suprahistorical that could be known definitively, even if it proved to lie on this

8. See Derek Attridge, "Language as History/History as Language: Saussure and the Romance of Etymology," in *Post-Structuralism and the Question of History*, ed. Derek Attridge et al. (Cambridge: Cambridge University Press, 1987), 183–211, on the strains in Saussure's own text that resist the effort to fashion a synchronic, suprahistorical science of language. Saussure's story betrays its own rhetoricity especially where etymology is at issue; a sense of the historicity even of the key terms undermines any possibility of mastery, of getting it right. Attridge concludes that Saussure can be read *either* as an essentialist scientist *or* as a proto-poststructuralist who points the way to a deconstructive political and cultural praxis. See esp. pp. 202–204.

9. Claude Lévi-Strauss, *Structural Anthropology*, trans. Claire Jacobson and Brooke Grundfest Schoepf (New York: Basic Books, 1963), 23 (1949).

highly abstract level of rules, or patterns of relationships: "the effort to find a deeper and truer reality behind the multiplicity of apparent realities, that seems to me to be the condition of survival for the human sciences."[10]

Structuralism is widely viewed as the culmination of the modern quest for a suprahistorical science of human culture, based on the assumption that even the human sphere stems from something stable and in some sense natural. Indeed, structuralism has seemed the last gasp of that quest—before the whole enterprise turned on itself, collapsing into poststructuralism. Poststructuralists like Foucault and Derrida argued that though structuralism assumed it could view the human world from the outside, it was doing so from the inside, especially because it too was caught up in language and thus was trapped in its own characteristic modes of discourse. The sort of closed system structuralism envisioned was impossible; something keeps sticking out, eluding the attempt to fit everything together.

Concern to isolate something stable and certain that transcends history has been an enduring theme in twentieth-century thought. But the sense that time, change, novelty, and creativity had not gotten their due led other early twentieth-century thinkers in something like the opposite direction. If a metaphysics of being, givenness, or foundations no longer seemed to hold, the alternative might be to posit reality as something like flow or process or evolution.

The most influential of those exploring this direction was the French thinker Henri Bergson (1859–1941), who enjoyed a particular vogue between the publication of his *Creative Evolution* in 1907 and the beginning of the First World War in 1914. Like his near-contemporary Husserl, Bergson was "Cartesian" in the sense of bracketing the everyday world in an effort to concentrate on inner experience, or pure consciousness; only there, it seemed, could a kind of certainty be found. But Bergson thought it essential to embrace precisely what Husserl was determined to resist—dissolution into the flow of time.

Participating in the wider pragmatic move, Bergson bought the notion that mind is a practical organ, a tool for living. In our practical way of dealing with the world, it is useful—indeed, essential—that we divide the world up into discrete events and objects, that we conceive events as repeatable, that we posit stable "things" that are what they are. But the practical orientation has led us to a limiting metaphysics, which conceives stable essences as higher, more real than variable individual instances and which leads us to believe we can subsume whatever we encounter within stable categories. Indeed, those assumptions inform language itself, which is ultimately practical, mechanical.

We apprehend the deeper truth of things insofar as we turn from practical needs and linguistic categories and, through a kind of intuition, apprehend our

10. Quoted in Sanche de Gramont, "There Are No Superior Societies," in *Claude Lévi-Strauss: The Anthropologist as Hero,* ed. E. N. Hayes and Tanya Hayes (Cambridge: MIT Press, 1970), 18.

own consciousness. We thereby gain access to a certain experience of time—not time that might be divided up, segmented, and measured, but real time, pure duration (*durée*). In this mode we experience not timelessness but perfect continuity, bound up with continuing memory, which is essential to the continuity of the self.[11] But in turning inward to experience durée, we also grasp change, novelty, creativity, freedom, and individuality, all of which the practical orientation leads us to deny through reduction to stable categories. In this mode of intuition, in fact, we have immediate access to the élan vital, the eternally creative life force—which is much like God.[12]

By starting with this inward experience, we can shake free of traditional metaphysics, with its emphasis on discrete events and objects, on stable "things" related in a mechanistic way. Rather than assume that movement requires a prior moving thing, we understand that movement is real; things are temporary crystallizations.[13] Time and novelty, or creativity, are two sides of the same coin: because there is creativity, time is generated; because time is real, there is genuine creativity. And individuality is bound up with the reality of time because novelty and creativity mean that things and events are unrepeatable, unique.

Bergson might have focused on the actual world that endlessly results from the totality of human creativity and that affords a particular content to public time, or history. Instead, however, he insisted on the radical disparity between the durée accessible through intuition and the apprehension of that public world though historical inquiry. By implication, we understand history in a practical, deterministic mode. Historical inquiry remains necessary for practical orientation, but we gain access to the deeper reality of things by turning inward, away from the public historical world. So even as he sought to take time and motion seriously as never before, Bergson did not find it necessary to take history, the actual chain of particular events over time, seriously in the same way. As we will see below, it was especially at this point that Nietzsche, Croce, and Heidegger diverged, for they experienced the weight of that actual historical world in a way that Bergson did not.

With his premium on inwardness, Bergson opened the way to a new religiosity, encompassing a form of mysticism. He insisted on the special value of the mystics in our tradition and noted his own kinship with William James, who was similarly seeking to specify the forms of religious experience that

11. Leszek Kolakowski, *Bergson* (New York: Oxford University Press, 1985), 15–16, 24–25. See also Sanford Schwartz, *The Matrix of Modernism: Pound, Eliot, and Early Twentieth-Century Thought* (Princeton: Princeton University Press, 1985), 21–31.

12. Kolakowski, *Bergson*, 21, 25, 34, 46–47, 70, 73. See also Theodore Ziolkowski, *Dimensions of the Modern Novel: German Texts and European Contexts* (Princeton: Princeton University Press, 1969), 210–211, 213.

13. Kolakowski, *Bergson*, 2, 45, 95–96.

become possible in a generally pragmatist world.[14] At the same time, Bergson was at least pointing to a new suprahistorical metaphysics, a statement of what reality is. At last we might get it right—once and for all. His thinking helped inspire the "process philosophy" of the later Alfred North Whitehead, who similarly sought to reconcile continuity with novelty. Like Bergson, Whitehead started by taking events to be logically and metaphysically prior to objects; events were real, and objects depend on them—not the other way around.[15] And Bergson's sense of the whole as creative evolution accessible to human intuition pointed to Pierre Teilhard de Chardin's optimistic evolutionary cosmology.

Whether we accent mysticism or a new metaphysics of process, the outcome of Bergson's effort to jettison traditional metaphysics was relatively conventional. The tradition we will follow, starting with Nietzsche, Croce, and Heidegger, was more radical because it explicitly eschewed emphases like Bergson's.[16]

Precisely as Husserl, Saussure, and Bergson were writing, the growing preoccupation with time and history affected literature, occasioning a number of the defining themes of early modernism. Bergson was himself influential, but in turning inward to focus on subjective consciousness, the early modernist writers encountered a domain of experience that he did not explore. For what we seem first to encounter, when we turn inward, is neither a universal nor a purely personal realm but a particular historical legacy lacking necessity or strong justification. The modernists explored the modes of experience and response that became possible as the historical inflated. We can better grasp the stakes of the cultural break at issue if we look briefly at a few aspects of that modernist exploration, which make clear how deeply individual experience was implicated in the inflation of history. Experience of a merely historical world could entail a suffocating sense of confinement or a giddy sense of lightness; in response the individual might seek authenticity in opposition to the historical legacy, or aesthetic satisfaction in ordering the historical bits and pieces, or a renewed sense of oneness even in the face of the fragmentation and contingency that seemed to characterize a merely historical world.

Michel, the protagonist of André Gide's *The Immoralist* (1902), begins as a conventional historian, but he comes to understand history as layer upon layer of mere convention that covers over the authentic self he feels smoldering within him. At first his effort to peel away those layers encompasses redoing the inherited historical account, which buttresses a certain conventional mode of being but which had stemmed from merely contingent needs and desires at

---

14. See especially Henri Bergson, *The Two Sources of Morality and Religion*, trans. R. Ashley Audra and Cloudesley Brereton (New York: Henry Holt, 1935; orig. French ed. 1932).

15. See also Kolakowski, *Bergson*, 45, 101.

16. See, for example, Schwartz's lucid discussion of the difference between Bergson and Nietzsche in *The Matrix of Modernism*, 36–39.

work in his culture. By forging a different history, connecting with hidden dimensions of the past—such as the experience of the young Gothic king Athalaric—Michel could apprehend hidden aspects of himself. But Michel ultimately decides that authenticity, creativity, and fully lived experience require turning from *any* concern with the past, any mode of historical consciousness.[17]

In *The Man without Qualities*, Robert Musil explored the uncanniness that creeps into individual experience in a world that has no more substance than the historical. Ulrich, Musil's protagonist, is initially willing to let "himself be shaped by the external circumstances of life" through immersion in his historically specific context and tradition.[18] He lets others furnish his house, for example, to provide the essential connection—and limitation. But though he understood some sense of belonging to be essential, Ulrich found the relationship between the personal and the historical to be tension-ridden and ambiguous. In one sense, the historically specific culture was deeply confining, even a straitjacket, yet in another the historical world enveloping us is shallow, lacking necessity. Ulrich has caught on to the contingency and arbitrariness of it all; if the individual "is told that something *is* the way it is, then he thinks: Well it could probably just as easily be some other way." And this sense engenders "the capacity . . . to attach no more importance to what is than to what is not."[19] Thus, Ulrich manages what J. M. Coetzee has called "a certain reserve toward the real world, a living sense of alternative possibilities."[20]

But that sense does not invite commitment toward the future in a world that has come to seem light and insubstantial. Ulrich understands that for no good reason, one may connect or fail to connect with the motion of the particular world. The individual may send out ideas in all directions, "but only what produces resonance in his environment will radiate back to him and condense, whereas all the other messages are scattered in space and lost."[21] Suspended between past and future, Ulrich lives disengaged, uncommitted, hovering in "a web of haze, imaginings, fantasy and the subjunctive mode."[22]

Musil suggests that this sense of lightness emerged especially in "Kakania"—late imperial Austria. There

> one was negatively free, constantly aware of the inadequate grounds for one's existence and lapped by the great fantasy of all that had not happened, or at least

17. André Gide, *The Immoralist*, trans. Richard Howard (New York: Alfred A. Knopf, Vintage, 1970), esp. pp. 50–53, 65–66, 145–146.

18. Robert Musil, *The Man without Qualities*, vol. 1, trans. Eithne Wilkins and Ernst Kaiser (1930) (New York: G. P. Putnam's Sons, Perigee, 1980), 17. See also p. 31, on the experience of being caught up in a moving world.

19. Ibid., 12, 34. See also pp. 64–65.

20. J. M. Coetzee, "On the Edge of Revelation," *New York Review of Books*, 18 December 1986, 10.

21. Musil, *The Man without Qualities*, 64–65, 134. Musil also remarks that "at times [Ulrich] felt just as though he had been born with a gift for which at present there was no function" (p. 65).

22. Ibid., 12. See also pp. 15–17, 70.

had not yet irrevocably happened. . . . *Es ist passiert*, "it just sort of happened," people said there. . . . It was a peculiar phrase, not known in this sense to the Germans and with no equivalent in other languages, the very breath of it transforming facts and the bludgeonings of fate into something light as eiderdown, as thought itself.[23]

This is the lightness of the merely historical world. And though Musil suggested that it was experienced first in this particular context, he found it central to the modern cultural situation in general. That situation breeds a particular type, the "man without qualities," approaching the world through irony.

But there might be other ways of coming to terms with a world that seemed at once stifling and insubstantial as the historical inflated. In his famous essay of 1919, "Tradition and the Individual Talent," T. S. Eliot betrayed a concern for individuality and creativity in the face of an overwhelming tradition. Yet precisely because the past impinged on the present individual merely as bits and pieces, arbitrarily connected through the conventional historical account to which we have fallen heir, it could be confronted in a newly creative way. So rather than disengage and turn inward or settle for mere self-assertion, Eliot sought to confront the world as historical head on, making it his own by ordering the bits and pieces in an overtly aestheticist way.[24] To be sure, it "requires a ridiculous amount of erudition," as he put it elsewhere, to encompass the entire past as present, yet he yearned for precisely that wholeness, for "the only real truth is the whole truth." In *The Waste Land* (1922) he added reference upon reference, juxtaposing points of view, letting one character melt into another, in order to build the most comprehensive whole he could.[25]

For Eliot, however, there was something terrifying about the growing sense that the world can have nothing but a merely contingent human ordering. In "The Dry Salvages" (1943), he refers to

> The backward look behind the assurance
> Of recorded history, the backward half-look
> Over the shoulder, towards the primitive terror.[26]

We grasp that "recorded history" is only a flimsy human contrivance, a merely historical way of connecting ourselves to the whole. It keeps us only intermittently from the primitive, terrifying sense that our world of historical bits and

23. Ibid., 34.
24. T. S. Eliot, "Tradition and the Individual Talent," in *Selected Prose of T. S. Eliot*, ed. Frank Kermode (New York: Harcourt Brace Jovanovich, 1975), 37–44. See also Schwartz, *The Matrix of Modernism*, 181–183, 186–187.
25. Both passages quoted in James Longenbach, *Modernist Poetics of History: Pound, Eliot, and the Sense of the Past* (Princeton: Princeton University Press, 1987), pp. 174, 200. See also pp. 202, 205–207, on Eliot's "yearning for the whole truth."
26. T. S. Eliot, "The Dry Salvages," in *Four Quartets* (San Diego: Harcourt Brace Jovanovich, 1971; orig. pub. 1943), 39, lines 101–103.

pieces is fundamentally meaningless. Thus we cannot suppress "the backward half-look."

And for Eliot, in the final analysis, the satisfaction to be gained by self-consciously ordering fragments from the past did not in itself afford an antidote. By means of art, however, it might be possible to see through the fragments to the source of things or the totality of things, to achieve a species of mystical or visionary experience. James Longenbach notes that in Eliot's *The Waste Land*, "a primitive revelation of 'the whole truth' (the thunderous 'DA') is disseminated, by the process of tradition, throughout history."[27] Faith is bound up with this capacity to grasp the whole, to apprehend a divine revelation coming down through the whole tradition.

Eliot's remarkable exploration of the temporal and historical dimensions of personal experience in his *Four Quartets* led him to envision a level of timelessness, perhaps even a level prior to the bifurcation of temporal and timeless. Near the end of "The Dry Salvages," he contrasts our ongoing need to probe past and future with the "hints followed by guesses" that accompany our intimations of timelessness:

> The hint half guessed, the gift half understood, is
> Incarnation.
> Here the impossible union
> Of spheres of existence is actual,
> Here the past and future
> Are conquered, and reconciled.[28]

With the eruption of time and history, the bifurcation of temporal and timeless became more deeply problematic, leading Eliot to recast "Incarnation" itself as the overcoming or dissolution of precisely those problems. We understand traditional religious categories afresh, as the antidote to the new sense of fragmentation, irony, and primitive terror resulting from the modern break in historical consciousness.

The modernists' preoccupation with history was deeply symptomatic, but their divergent explorations left an array of open questions. Even if we assume that history is but a contingent overlay hiding some authentic self, how might that self be extricated, and what mode of life is appropriate to it in the public, merely historical world? Gide's Michel ends up tormented by his "useless freedom." His friends wonder if he will manage to reconnect with his own time and find a productive social role. For Gide, that question is central, but he provides no answer.[29]

27. Longenbach, *Modernist Poetics of History*, 227.
28. Eliot, "The Dry Salvages," 44, lines 214–219. See also Helen Gardner, *The Composition of "Four Quartets"* (New York: Oxford University Press, 1978), 57–58, 145–147.
29. Gide, *The Immoralist*, 3, 169.

Musil's Ulrich is comparable to Michel in seeking access to what is repressed, hidden, or held back as culture develops. And for him, as for Michel, what has been hidden is in some sense sexual, even in some sense evil. But is this hidden dimension historically variable and specific or always the same? If Ulrich is confronting the mechanisms of his particular culture, is there scope for historical inquiry to gain access to what had been hidden? Musil leaves us to wrestle with the relationships among art, science, history, and the conditions of ethical response, forcing us to recognize that our ways of doing so are themselves historically specific.[30]

Eliot's response betrayed some tension between the visionary artist, seeking wholeness, and the critic, aware of the historicity and finitude of any such quest.[31] He noted that life is always turned toward creation, which, in fact, is the present "interest" that enables us to bring the past to life. But he did not fully confront the sense in which any way of creatively apprehending the "entire past," even his own, might be finite, historically specific, and itself particularizing.

This Particular World

Like Bergson and the literary modernists, Nietzsche, Croce, and Heidegger sought to rethink the human situation on the basis of becoming, time, or history. But a common element in their way of conceiving—and experiencing—the intrusiveness of history set them off from their contemporaries. After a point, however, they too diverged, and their responses differed radically.

Although the recognition of change, motion, or becoming meant that things could no longer be conceived simply as what they are, it was crucial for Nietzsche, Croce, and Heidegger that the world does not simply fly apart, or collapse in a heap. Each posited a postmetaphysical, purely horizontal kind of continuity. Earlier and later, before and after, still matter; indeed, we are what we are as a result of what has come before us, and in responding as we do to the particular present situation, we participate in the coming to be of what comes after us. We are influenced, and we influence in turn. These simple postulates afforded the coherence and continuity necessary to conceive what "there is" as history, at least as a first approximation.

What mattered for all three thinkers was that some particular world is endlessly coming to be, over time. Nietzsche's assault on metaphysical notions of stable being left only sheer becoming, but becoming is not empty. Something in particular is endlessly coming to be. With the possible exception of will to power, nothing simply "is" but rather everything has become, has resulted from

---

30. David Luft, *Robert Musil and the Crisis of European Culture, 1880–1942* (Berkeley, Los Angeles, and London: University of California Press, 1980), 216–217.

31. In developing this point, I have profited particularly from Longenbach, *Modernist Poetics of History*, 209, 220–221, 237.

there is. Thus even the totality is individual—some particular way. With Nietzsche, Croce, and Heidegger, the broadly historicist current in our tradition became totalizing again, after the individualizing reaction against Hegel. But what each of them posited was a "weak," post-Hegelian kind of totality, radically contingent, lacking any suprahistorical frame or goal, and thus ever provisional and incomplete. Each sought to think through what happens to individual experience when the totality that encompasses and survives the individual comes to seem merely finite, provisional, and weak.

For Nietzsche, Croce, and Heidegger, then, experience of the eclipse of metaphysics led to a sense that we are caught up in, that we belong to, a particular total event, *this* event. My being cannot be separated from the actual present world, which is the resultant of the totality of history so far and which, unstable and tension-ridden, is endlessly being remade through the responses of present individuals, including me.

The notion of weak totality has been hard to grasp because earlier ways of understanding totality and individuality have continued to dominate the discussion. As a result, students of the period often lump together thinkers—Dilthey, Bergson, and Croce, for example—who should be distinguished. Some assume that Marxism must be central to any consideration of "totality" and history. Yet Marxian totalism remained relatively strong and teleological, so preoccupation with Marxian categories has made it difficult to think through the weak alternative. But unless we grasp the weak totalist way of conceiving the world as historical that we find in Nietzsche, Croce, and Heidegger, we cannot adequately characterize the cultural possibilities that opened with the waning of metaphysics.

History, Language, and Individual Experience

The assault on the metaphysical tradition rendered ever more problematic the notion that mind, thinking, or language connects with a distinguishable object, or outside world. Language, especially, had seemed to provide the necessary bridge between subject and object; it was a neutral medium or transparent window allowing representation of "nature," the world that existed independently of us. As notions of mirroring or representation were undermined, language became a problem; it was either too embedded or too abstract to bridge the gap any longer.

With the loosely pragmatist move, to be sure, language came to seem natural, immanent—and effective for practical purposes. But it was so merely relative to our contingent needs and questions as to cut us off from the way things really are, independently of us. This was unnerving, though there might be antidotes. For Bergson, language was a practical tool that, by abstracting, cuts off from the deeper reality of things, but precisely as we grasp the limits of

something else. While Saussure was bracketing the unruly diachronic
to make possible a synchronic science of language, Croce accented the
novelty and creativity that make language change and grow. What ul
matters is the diachronic dimension, the actual world being built up
such creative response in language. In a parallel way, Heidegger conclu
it was not radical enough simply to incorporate historicity into the sor
nomenology Husserl had done. Rather, it was necessary to concei'
"there is" as "eventing," happening, or coming to be.

So Nietzsche, Croce, and Heidegger were embracing somethin
reduction to history, but this was not simply to flip-flop, saying that in
"given" foundations or essences, what "there is" is history. "History"
an answer, which might take the cultural place of the old metaphysical a
but a new set of questions, even a new mode of questioning. What es
demanded attention were the implications of the inflating historical
range of personal experience.

To experience the world as historical entailed, first, a sense of the ut
tude of the world. As we come to believe that, on every level, the world
is only because it has *become* what it is, we feel the weight of the bland
that the world is forever becoming some particular way, as opposed t
ways that it might have become. From this perspective, even our particu
ence, or apprehension of nature, has resulted historically, as a function
historically specific questions we have asked.

This sense of particularity and finitude carried such weight becaus
metaphysical connectedness entailed contingency; any historical ou
including our own, might be conceived as idiosyncratic, even a billion-
fluke. A particular world results—apparently endlessly results—from h
yet this world has nothing necessary about it. Although Heidegger woul
to speak of "destiny," we will see that a sense of the uncanny particula
things was fundamental even to him.

If we insist on thinking in terms of a beginning, it is more like Vico'
Hegel's. History does not start with logos, some potential for wholeness
way things "are" on some level. The beginning does not afford direction,
an end, and thus tell us what we might do, or make of ourselves, so tha
we "really" are will ultimately stand revealed as the resultant of the p
itself. The beginning is simply the initiation of an open but particula
process. Rather than a logos, or form to be filled, we must imagine a sit
of dumb brutes starting from scratch, "knowing" only their own bodies,
basis of which they can only respond as best they can, once such a respo
suddenly demanded. Each response creates a new situation eliciting a
response.

But particularity does not preclude totality. At each moment, a thick bu
finite interweaving of particular individualities constitutes a totality; an
particular world, this provisional resulting of the particularities so far,

guage we begin to see how to apprehend that deeper reality in a direct, nonlinguistic way. Others went in the opposite direction and developed a science of culture—semiotics or structuralism—that claimed to lay bare the underlying system of rules enabling the signs to have meaning. But that system was apparently self-contained, so dissolving the older subject-object dualism, which language had seemed capable of bridging, merely ushered in a new, unbridgeable dualism of language and reality. The "modern" response, as mirroring and representation were called into question, encompassed the diverse efforts, from Bergson to structuralism, to specify an alternative conception, as well as the ironic sense of disjunction between language and reality that seemed the outcome for those who found us trapped in language as a self-contained system.

Another possibility was to consider the connection between language, as finite yet unstable and changing, and the coming to be of a particular world. It is striking that even Bergson did not develop this possibility, though his thinking combined the generally pragmatist insight with an emphasis on the reality of creativity, change, and novelty. He was so concerned with the sense in which language cuts us off from something that he did not focus on the way changing, growing language is bound up with the coming to be of a particular world.

By looking in precisely this other direction, Nietzsche, Croce, and Heidegger brought human being together with the actual historical world in a way that eluded the dualism of language and reality that lurked in the array of modern approaches. From their perspective, it was not enough to make the generally pragmatist point that human knowing is bound up with living and doing. The deeper challenge was to explore the sense in which human being, knowing, and language are bound up with the motion of the world, with the ongoing happening of a particular totality. And thus the distinctive effort to link human being to history, coming to be, happening, or event that characterized the effort of each to sidestep the subject-object dualism.

But once we have separated human being and world in the first place, it is hard to characterize, in a nondualistic way, the relationship between ourselves and the endless coming to be of our particular world. Nietzsche, Croce, and Heidegger each took pains to do so without falling into either side of the longstanding metaphysical dualism. We human beings are not active agents, in the strong metaphysical or modern sense, but neither are we passive instruments or contemplators. In the final analysis, there is simply no point in asking how some distinguishable, preexisting subjective consciousness arrives at knowledge of the so-called external world.[32] Nor was any of the three thinkers settling simply for another form of subjectivist idealism, conceiving language as a

32. For this point in Heidegger, see Gadamer, *Philosophical Hermeneutics*, 118–119; and Michael E. Zimmerman, *Heidegger's Confrontation with Modernity: Technology, Politics, and Art* (Bloomington: Indiana University Press, 1990), 226. On p. 122, Zimmerman notes that Heidegger, for all his assault on modern subjectivism, vacillated between "to shape or fashion a thing" and "to draw out or to disclose what is somehow already there."

projection of the world by subjectivity, though an initial reading might suggest as much. Rather, each sought to fuse human being and world so that the questions yielding the whole array of such metaphysical responses do not arise.[33] Heidegger's several characterizations of human being—as *Dasein*, or being-in-the-world, as dwelling in the house of language, as the clearing or opening for some world to come to be—were attempts to convey, sometimes rigorously, sometimes poetically, a nondualistic relationship that had already been central, though less explicit, for Nietzsche and Croce.

Indeed, although some of their accents were discordant, all three thinkers found language fundamental as the intersection between human being and the endless becoming of the particular world in time, through history.[34] Even for Nietzsche, whose assault on metaphysical truth led him to speak of lies and fictions, language does not hide what is "really" nothingness, chaos, flux, any more than it represents or copies—or cannot quite represent or copy—an independent objective world. Language is the medium through which some particular world comes to be.

Because our language is bound up with coming to be, we cannot hope to define it once and for all or confine it within stable linguistic rules. Croce's radically historicist conception anticipated Wittgenstein's brand of ordinary language philosophy in obliterating any distinction between language and speech.[35] As a system, "language" is nothing but a momentary, provisional abstraction from what speech has done up until now. Language is thus the embodiment, at any one moment, of the particular totality of our collective experience so far. Heidegger's emphasis on the originary force of language, as the way of coming to be, and his notion of language as spoken by being itself as it particularizes in history are comparable to Croce's vision of spirit endlessly taking a certain form through creative language.

---

33. See, for example, Nietzsche's way of playing down agency in *On the Genealogy of Morals*, trans. Walter Kaufmann and R. J. Hollingdale (with *Ecce Homo*), ed. Walter Kaufmann (New York: Random House, Vintage, 1967), 45–46; the subject is not conceivable apart from the doing itself. See also his assault on subjectivism in *The Will to Power*, ed. Walter Kaufmann, trans. Walter Kaufmann and R. J. Hollingdale (New York: Random House, Vintage, 1967), 267–271 (nos. 481–490), and 297–299 (no. 552).

34. Nietzsche sometimes suggested that the world is forever outgrowing what we can say about it. Language grows as it seeks to catch up, but it always remains one step behind. See especially Friedrich Nietzsche, *Twilight of the Idols*, in *The Portable Nietzsche*, ed. and trans. Walter Kaufmann (New York: Viking, 1954), 530–531. For Heidegger, in contrast, language is always ahead of us. Even for Heidegger, however, our actual speech lags behind language, so Heidegger's conception proves closer to Nietzsche's than it initially seems. See Martin Heidegger, *On the Way to Language*, trans. Peter D. Hertz (New York: Harper and Row, Perennial, 1971), 75.

35. Hayden White has made this point to good effect in his *Metahistory: The Historical Imagination in Nineteenth-Century Europe* (Baltimore: Johns Hopkins University Press, 1973), 390–391. Wittgenstein has been more often compared with Heidegger; see Ross Mandel, "Heidegger and Wittgenstein: A Second Kantian Revolution," in *Heidegger and Modern Philosophy: Critical Essays*, ed. Michael Murray (New Haven: Yale University Press, 1978), 259–270, for a helpful approach to the points at issue.

Following Heidegger's lead, Gadamer would make the overall point more explicitly still: It is precisely in coming to expression in language that being is temporalized (*sich zeitigt*).[36] The illusion that things precede their manifestation in language conceals the fundamentally linguistic character of our experience of the world. So rather than assuming a dualism, forcing priority to either world or mind, we start with the correspondence or congruence itself, which becomes concrete in our linguistic experience of the world. As we grasp what it means to be always within language, we no longer worry about something outside, transcendent, from which we might feel excluded. The problems of epistemology dissolve, the irony of separation dissipates, and we shift our focus to the horizontal dimension—the history—that is generated as language expands. It is a matter of indifference whether we say instead "that we generate as we expand the language." To understand things in a nondualistic way is to cease worrying about such distinctions.

In conceiving reality as an overarching eventing or happening, Nietzsche, Croce, and Heidegger each explicitly eschewed any strong conception of human agency.[37] Although the world becomes some particular way only as the result of what we do, history is no more the result of conscious human choice than it is of divine providence. We cannot foresee what will result from our actions, so we do not know, as we participate in the happening of it, what is being made of this moment, the resultant so far. Nor does history *become* the product of willed human agency at some point, as in one understanding of Marxism. To avoid any implication that we, as conscious subjects, make the world, or that we are the instruments of some supraindividual entity that makes the world, we sometimes seem forced to adopt contorted phrasing, especially involving passive voice, to speak of what is happening as a world results through human being and language.

But just as history is not willed human creation, neither is it some blurry, incomprehensible backdrop for personal existence. All three thinkers confronted, more systematically than the early modernists, the relationship between individual human being and the larger public or historical world. At issue for each was not simply the historicity of my personal life but my involvement with the whole endlessly provisional world that comes to be through history. And Nietzsche, Croce, and Heidegger each started, at least, by positing a relationship of congruence between human being and that world. Human being is not to be understood as *merely* finite, in contrast with infinite

---

36. Gadamer, *Philosophical Hermeneutics*, 50. See also pp. 77–79.

37. Although Croce's hostility to the culture of science led him to claim links to the humanistic tradition, he, like Nietzsche and Heidegger, eschewed Cartesian subjectivism and Hegelian notions of human self-revelation. Indeed, Croce was repeatedly attacked for playing down individual agency and the subjectivity of the person in insisting that the spirit—ultimately history itself—is the only reality. See, for example, Benedetto Croce, *Filosofia e storiografia* (Bari: Laterza, 1969; orig. pub. 1946), 144; which provoked existentialist assaults that will be discussed in chap. 5, below.

and always existing being; rather, human finitude is the other side of the world as historical.[38] There is nothing inadequate about our relationship with a world of nothing but history, so there is no call for modernist irony.

For each of the three, however, new preoccupations intrude as we adjust to such a world. In seeking to think through individual experience, each fastened on a family of "religious" categories—responsibility, anxiety, guilt, judgment, grace, redemption, innocence, the holy. At this point, however, Nietzsche, Croce, and Heidegger diverged, for an array of new possibilities seemed to open. We may feel a heightened sense of responsibility, or a sense of relief and innocence, or the need for a kind of disengagement. But for all three, the sense that personal possibilities are radically bound up with a particular place in history was fundamental.

The wave of generational thinking that Robert Wohl found characteristic of the "generation of 1914" stemmed not only from the ironies surrounding World War I but also from a growing sense that the horizons of personal experience are fundamentally historical. One result was a heightened feeling of responsibility—for seizing the opportunity that this particular moment allots me to contribute to the ongoing happening of the world. Yet the opportunity proves fragile, the moment fleeting, and most of Wohl's figures felt, by the 1920s, that they were living in disharmony with their own time.[39] Although they experienced the interpenetration of historical situation and personal possibility in a heightened way, they were not sure how best to respond. It can be argued that those of this generation proved mostly futile because they failed to ask the historical questions necessary to understand the needs and possibilities of their particular historical moment.

In probing the relationship between individual experience and history, Nietzsche, Croce, and Heidegger focused precisely on the scope for historical inquiry and understanding, though in doing so each encountered the historiographical questions that remained open by the late nineteenth century. All three eschewed the emphasis on past as opposed to process that came to characterize historiography with Ranke's reaction against Hegel. For each, historical inquiry grows from an active present response and constitutes some particular way of connecting the past to the present. Our particular ways of knowing history, of connecting past and present, participate in the resulting of the next moment. Indeed, so radically is historical knowing bound up with the reality to be known that even the long-standing distinction between res gestae and historia rerum gestarum begins to blur. The reflexive sense that in affording some particular meaning to our history we are ourselves part of the ongoing process was crucial

38. See Gadamer, *Philosophical Hermeneutics*, 215, for this characterization with respect to Heidegger.
39. Robert Wohl, *The Generation of 1914* (Cambridge: Harvard University Press, 1979), 208, 235.

to each of the three thinkers, informing their sense of their own intellectual contributions.[40]

However, to insist that historical knowing is bound up with present action seemed to surrender to precisely the relativism and skepticism that had come to seem so threatening by the later nineteenth century. And certainly it was axiomatic for each of the three thinkers that the old strong truth had fallen away. But whereas Nietzsche generally settled for a kind of perspectivism, Croce, Heidegger, and Gadamer, coming later, sought to show that it is still "truth" that happens—or can happen—as the particular world comes to be in language, including the language of historical understanding.[41] And truth is possible precisely because the inquirer is also an actor, caught up in some particular present.

So the attempt to make sense of the postmetaphysical situation led Nietzsche, Croce, and Heidegger down the same path, which diverged from the innovative modernist course of their contemporaries. But though they conceived and even experienced the new situation in analogous ways, their responses came to differ radically.

40. See Hilary Lawson, *Reflexivity: The Post-Modern Predicament* (La Salle, Ill.: Open Court, 1985), on the centrality of reflexivity in Nietzsche, Heidegger, and Derrida.

41. Jeffrey Andrew Barash, *Martin Heidegger and the Problem of Historical Meaning* (Dordrecht: Martinus Nijhoff, 1988), 218–220, 222; and David D. Roberts, *Benedetto Croce and the Uses of Historicism* (Berkeley, Los Angeles, and London: University of California Press, 1987), 137–163.

4

Nietzsche

The Innocence of Becoming

The Trouble with History

Not only is Nietzsche's contribution to the assault on metaphysics widely recognized, it is taken for granted that, as one aspect of that assault, he denigrated "history," helping to undermine the premium on historical modes of understanding characteristic of the nineteenth century.[1] Around the turn of the century, Dilthey warned against the shortsighted denigration of historical consciousness that he found in Nietzsche and the developing vogue of Nietzsche's thought.[2] From then on, Nietzsche's emphasis on self-creation, his critique of "the will to truth," his aestheticist talk of the fictions we create in order to live in the face of blank becoming—all have seemed to suggest that his thought was fundamentally antihistorical.

It is certainly true that Nietzsche inveighed against the historical sense as inimical to vitality and creativity. In *Beyond Good and Evil*, for example, he associated history with the faddish borrowing from any and all historical periods that seemed characteristic of his own century and that stood in sharp con-

1. See, for example, Jonathan Arac, "Aesthetics, Rhetoric, History: Paul de Man and the American Use of Nietzsche," in *Why Nietzsche Now?* ed. Daniel O'Hara (Bloomington: Indiana University Press, 1985), 418. For a critical perspective on Nietzsche's critique of the tradition, see Stephen Houlgate, *Hegel, Nietzsche and the Criticism of Metaphysics* (Cambridge: Cambridge University Press, 1986). Houlgate offers a Hegelian critique of Nietzsche, partly to counter Gilles Deleuze's way of embracing Nietzsche against Hegel.
2. Michael Ermarth, *Wilhelm Dilthey: The Critique of Historical Reason* (Chicago: University of Chicago Press, 1978), 318–321. See also Ernst Behler, *Confrontations: Derrida/Heidegger/Nietzsche*, trans. Steven Taubeneck (Stanford: Stanford University Press, 1991), 19.

trast to the self-affirmation he valued.[3] He had in mind, for example, the copying and emphasis on revival in architecture that later drew the wrath of pioneering modernists like Walter Gropius. But historical-mindedness covers a multitude of possibilities, and Nietzsche sensed that what remains as the metaphysical tradition dissolves is precisely history. As he experienced it, however, history in a postmetaphysical mode was anything but sustaining or reassuring.

In attacking nineteenth-century historical-mindedness, Nietzsche was not simply shifting the focus from public to private, from historical copying to individual self-creation, from historical consciousness to some subjective time consciousness or concern with one's personal past. It was the relationship between these two levels—the public-historical and the personal-individual—that he found decisive. Through the categories of his maturity—*amor fati* (loving one's fate), eternal recurrence, the innocence of becoming—Nietzsche was seeking to envision a mode of individual experience emptied of the troubling mode of historical consciousness that first seemed to follow from the waning of metaphysics.

Even as a young scholar, Nietzsche was restive with the dominant historicist imperatives of his own time, especially as embodied in philology, his own academic specialty.[4] His first major work, *The Birth of Tragedy* (1872), flew in the face of the notion that we study the past for its own sake, apart from some contemporary concern. Nietzsche sensed that historical inquiry and understanding were necessarily bound up with the living of the present inquirer. Precisely because history was not the province of a past readily distinguishable from the present, historical inquiry might have a deeper contemporary relevance than the standard justifications and imperatives suggested. As the other side of the coin, however, if history was not confined to the past, it entailed risks; it could be corrosive.

Nietzsche's untimely meditation "On the Uses and Disadvantages of History for Life" (1874) has come to be associated especially with one, relatively familiar antihistorical theme. What he found disadvantageous for life in his own time was especially a passive, vulgar-Hegelian endorsement of the actual and a sense of coming late, of living when little of moment was left to be done. In this double sense, a premium on history undermined the sense of possibility necessary for ongoing creative energy.

This baggage surrounding history was part of what troubled Nietzsche, but an emphasis on this theme has diverted attention from a preoccupation that was also evident in this early meditation and that proved deeper, dominating his subsequent intellectual quest. We moderns, Nietzsche tells us, are caught up in "the tireless unspinning and historicizing of all there has ever been." History

---

3. Friedrich Nietzsche, *Beyond Good and Evil: Prelude to a Philosophy of the Future*, trans. Walter Kaufmann (New York: Random House, Vintage, 1966), 150–152.
4. Carl Pletsch, *Young Nietzsche: Becoming a Genius* (New York: Free Press, 1991), 91, 126–127, 130–135.

dissolves everything "that possesses life," just as it had, partly through the agency of David Friedrich Strauss, the Christianity in which Nietzsche himself had been raised. And this makes for the "dismantling of all foundations, their dissolution into a continual evolving that flows ceaselessly away." There may have been something great and noble about, for example, the founding of Christianity, but between Christianity's founding and its historical success "there lies a very dark and earthy stratum of passion, error, thirst for power and honor."[5] Nietzsche experienced, in a deeply personal way, the corrosiveness of historical understanding—what it means to grasp things, perhaps even all things, as contingent historical products.

The problem was that historical inquiry reveals, not the reason for things, but the lack of reason, the sheer contingency of everything that has resulted historically. Nietzsche was clearly appalled as he began to sense that our world has resulted from nothing but history, which, in turn, is nothing but this freakish concatenation of lies, errors, and self-serving actions. History, he says, "always brings to light so much that is false, crude, inhuman, absurd, violent that the mood of pious illusion in which alone anything that wants to live can live necessarily crumbles away."[6] From this perspective, insofar as the hypertrophy of historical-mindedness threatened to undermine action, it was not because history makes us complacent but because it undermines even the foothold for commitment. Yet apparently nothing could resist the corrosive historical treatment; by Nietzsche's time, history had become a maelstrom sucking everything in. What had seemed the true world now appeared as but a layering of human contrivances in a field of sheer becoming.[7]

So the world was coming to seem nothing but history, but this was obviously not Hegel's sort of history, because the process seemed utterly without the higher-order rationality and necessity that Hegel had posited. To understand the world historically is not to grasp some justifying reason but to realize that things would not have to be this way at all. The fact that our reality has turned out, so far, to be this way and not some other way comes to seem a billion-to-one fluke, honeycombed with absurdity.

This sense of reality collapsing into the mere contingency of history remained fundamental to Nietzsche's experience and intellectual enterprise. In his notes of the mid-1880s, he remarked that "the victory of a moral ideal is achieved by the same 'immoral' means as every victory: force, lies, slander, injustice"—to which he subsequently added the marginal gloss, "unsparing honesty."[8] Such honesty compels us to recognize that the whole of our world is

5. Friedrich Nietzsche, "On the Uses and Disadvantages of History for Life," in *Untimely Meditations*, trans. R. J. Hollingdale (Cambridge: Cambridge University Press, 1983), 96–97, 108, 113. Pletsch, *Young Nietzsche*, 165–166.

6. Nietzsche, "On the Uses and Disadvantages," 95.

7. Ibid., 63–67, 100–102, 120–123.

8. Friedrich Nietzsche, *The Will to Power*, trans. Walter Kaufmann and R. J. Hollingdale, ed. Walter Kaufmann (New York: Vintage, 1967), 171 (no. 306), 171n (editor's note).

woven around such capriciousness and contingency. And he was struck with
how much is crushed, stifled, lost, as any particular world comes to be.[9]

To emphasize contingency was to dissociate origins from meaning, purpose,
reality, truth. Nietzsche's way of answering his own question in *Daybreak* is
typical: "How did rationality arrive in the world? Irrationally, as might be
expected: by a chance accident."[10] He asserted the implications most fully in
On the Genealogy of Morals.

> The cause of the origin of a thing and its eventual utility, its actual employment
> and place in a system of purposes, lie worlds apart; whatever exists, having some-
> how come into being, is again and again reinterpreted to new ends, taken over,
> transformed, and redirected by some power superior to it; all events in the organic
> world are a subduing, a *becoming master*, and all subduing and becoming master
> involves a fresh interpretation, an adaptation through which any previous "mean-
> ing" and "purpose" are necessarily obscured and even obliterated.[11]

"Genealogy" would be Nietzsche's way of analyzing what has "somehow come
into being," what has happened between that "origin" and the present. And his
premium on genealogy was not to dismiss history but to take history more seriously—radically and deeply seriously. However, because history is not some
orderly process of development implicit in the origins, but merely contingent,
accidental, capricious, there can be no shortcut to suprahistorical understanding. The genealogical understanding of anything that "is" requires painstaking
analysis.

Though some of his preoccupations were novel, Nietzsche was concerned
with history in something like the conventional sense when he wrote "On the
Uses and Disadvantages of History for Life." At issue was not just empty, neutral "becoming" but history, with a determinate content; capricious though our
history has been, it has resulted in something in particular, in this and not that.
And the fruit of historical inquiry was not some sort of fiction or "lie" but plain
old historical truth. Indeed, the problem with history was precisely that it
uncovered the historical truth of things present—a problem because the unvarnished truth proves disillusioning, nauseating, and thus inimical to further
action.

At this point, Nietzsche's antidotes to the disadvantageous effects of
historical-mindedness were relatively conventional and did not directly
address the most troubling aspects of the hypertrophy of history. He spoke of
constructing history selectively, in such a way as to enhance life; he spoke
of forgetting, by moving away from any cultural premium on empirical

---

9. See, for example, Nietzsche, *Beyond Good and Evil*, 101–102.
10. Friedrich Nietzsche, *Daybreak: Thoughts on the Prejudices of Morality*, trans. R. J.
Hollingdale (Cambridge: Cambridge University Press, 1982), 125 (no. 123).
11. Friedrich Nietzsche, *On the Genealogy of Morals*, trans. Walter Kaufmann and R. J.
Hollingdale (with *Ecce Homo*), ed. Walter Kaufmann (New York: Random House, Vintage, 1967),
77 (2d essay, sec. 12); emphasis in original.

historiography; he valued those great individuals who "do not carry forward any kind of process but live contemporaneously with each other," in an exalted dialogue across history.[12] By communing with the like-minded over time, the life-affirming individual seems to deny time and history altogether.

But Nietzsche also responded in more innovative ways, first by turning the tables and historicizing historical-mindedness itself. The nineteenth-century premium on historical understanding stemmed from a sense of coming late that was itself historically specific, not suprahistorically privileged.[13] At first, this insight seemed reassuring. Despite the nineteenth-century tendency, we apparently do not *have* to think historically and thereby experience the world as freakish and jerry-built. Once the ideal of truth is similarly historicized, the historical accounts that result from our historicizing way of accounting for things come to seem but one set among the innumerable fictions that human beings impose on empty becoming.

Emptiness and Connectedness

By the time of his "middle works," *Human, All Too Human* (1878), *Daybreak* (1881), and *The Gay Science* (1882), Nietzsche had taken this further step.[14] In *Human, All Too Human*, he announced his discovery that even belief in truth as a superior value arises only in certain historically contingent situations. So it was not simply our particular historical truths but the very idea of truth as a cultural value that could be shown up as historically specific, contingent, and subject to dissolution.

But if truth could not hold, neither could the idea of history as usually understood—connoting a world that was, on some level, sufficiently coherent and stable to admit truth. As history consumes even itself, we are left with mere flux, sheer becoming, on which human beings, in their need for the security of stable being and suprahistorical truth, impose their particular, contingent fictions. What we take to be "truths" are simply the particular fictions or illusions that have made possible our particular mode of life, that have enabled us to live—more or less well.[15]

Growing from within the particular true world we have posited, the Western ideal of truth has been central to our particular mode of life—which is not to be valued highly, according to Nietzsche's criteria. The recent emphasis on *historical* truth is but an aspect of that larger cultural strategy. It was bound up

12. Nietzsche, "On the Uses and Disadvantages," 106, 111.
13. Ibid., 101.
14. Gianni Vattimo finds philosophical postmodernity emerging precisely as Nietzsche worked into these middle works. See his *La fine della modernità* (Milan: Garzanti, 1985), 172–175.
15. "On Truth and Lie in an Extra-Moral Sense" (1873), a fragment published posthumously and reprinted in *The Portable Nietzsche*, ed. and trans. Walter Kaufmann (New York: Viking, 1954), 46–47. For examples of Nietzsche's continuing insistence on this theme, see also *Beyond Good and Evil*, 29; and *The Antichrist*, in *The Portable Nietzsche*, 639–640, 642.

with a particular way of conceiving the world—as historical and thus in terms of continuity, even rationality and necessity. In showing up the ideal of historical truth as but a particular, contingent lie, Nietzsche seemed to undercut the whole package. Whereas historical inquiry had seemed to assume a tyrannical privilege, endlessly showing the capriciousness of our world, we come to feel ourselves free to remember or forget as we choose. As part of the repertory of cultural lies, historical understanding could be assessed simply in terms of its value for "life."

Although it may first seem unnecessarily provocative, the term "lie" is a fair characterization, because in constructing fictions we are hiding from the real nothingness of flux or becoming. We want to believe that some metaphysical sanction or necessity attaches to the particular, merely contingent world that has become. In *Beyond Good and Evil*, Nietzsche asks rhetorically, "Does one not write books precisely to conceal what one harbors?" and then suggests that beneath every philosophical opinion, there is another, and another beneath that, with no stable foundation: "Every philosophy is a foreground philosophy," a surface over something richer, stranger, which, however, is also a surface, for "underneath" there is only "an abysmally deep ground behind every ground, under every attempt to furnish 'grounds.' " Ultimately, in fact, "every philosophy also *conceals* a philosophy; every opinion is also a hideout, every word also a mask."[16] As I discuss in chapter 8, deconstruction would take one of its cues from Nietzsche's emphasis on this endless concealment and exclusion.

We seem well on our way to the familiar "posthistorical" Nietzsche of discontinuity and self-creation, but at this point we encounter a fork in his response to the appalling experience of the collapse into history. By historicizing even the historical treatment itself, by dissolving everything into empty becoming and fictional contrivance, Nietzsche seemed able to deflate the particular world and to sidestep any deeper confrontation with the appallingly capricious particularity of things. But he sensed that this tack was too easy; something about the new experience of "nothing but history" continued to gnaw at him.

It was important to grasp that reality, including the present premium on the historicizing mode itself, did not have to be this way, but it *was* this way—and it mattered that it was. There may be nothing behind us but "dreadful accident," but this moment is as it is because there have been *these* accidents and not some others. Even though what "there is" is "really" only lies, it is decisive that it has been *these* lies and not some others. Though there may be great scope for creative reinterpretation, to recognize that the actual is but a provisional, unstable, contingent historical resultant does not make it go away, or enable us to lie it away. What we are left with, then, is not simply a limitless invitation to invent fictions; we necessarily begin with the

16. Nietzsche, *Beyond Good and Evil*, 229.

particular world generated by our particular lies so far, a world with which each of us is indissolubly bound up.

A number of Nietzsche's emphases during this middle period suggest his continued preoccupation with the nature of that world and the modes of experience possible within it. Even while attacking the historical-mindedness of his own time, he insisted that it was precisely a historical sense, a *deeper* historical sense, that the West had lacked—and continued to lack. In *Human, All Too Human*, he charged that "lack of historical sense is the family failing of all philosophers," who lead us to think we can infer an eternal essence from human being as it is now. "But everything has become: there are *no eternal facts*, just as there are no absolute truths. Consequently, what is needed from now on is *historical philosophizing*, and with it the virtue of modesty."[17] Nietzsche was recognizing that human being has become as it is through a particular historical process. And modesty was called for because we come to understand that our interpretation, like all the others, will not apprehend stable, suprahistorical "being" but will simply add to the history by giving a particular understanding of the resultant of that history so far.

Metaphysicians, Nietzsche went on to argue, worry about the relationship between the world of appearance and the thing-in-itself; they want to know what there *really* is, apart from the contingencies of historical circumstance. They have overlooked the possibility that what we

call life and experience . . . has gradually *become,* is indeed still fully in process of *becoming,* and should thus not be regarded as a fixed object on the basis of which a conclusion as to the nature of its originator (the sufficient reason) may either be drawn or pronounced undrawable. . . . That which we now call the world is the outcome of a host of errors and fantasies which have gradually arisen and grown entwined with one another in the course of the overall evolution of the organic being, and are now inherited by us as the accumulated treasure of the entire past—as treasure: for the value of our humanity depends on it.[18]

This passage makes it especially clear that the departure from metaphysics soon leads us to a fork in the road. On the one hand, where there once seemed suprahistorical essences that metaphysics might grasp, we now see only "a host of errors and fantasies," and we seem to have turned our backs on any cultural premium on, or perhaps even the possibility of, historical truth. But on the other hand, those errors and fantasies are the particular errors and fantasies that have produced our world—the only world we have, the world with which we must deal. And through the same process we ourselves have become the particular beings that we are. So there might be special value in understanding ourselves

17. Friedrich Nietzsche, *Human, All Too Human: A Book for Free Spirits*, trans. R. J. Hollingdale (Cambridge: Cambridge University Press, 1986), 12–13.
18. Ibid., 19–20.

and our world historically, even though postmetaphysical historical inquiry would focus on contingency and not essence and even though no complete, definitive account would be possible.

Although some have found in Nietzsche the warrant for an antihistorical emphasis on "discontinuity," he was much taken with the connectedness of things—on precisely the historical level.[19] Even after suprahistorical essences or necessities are forgotten, things cohere, q follows p and is as it is partly because p was as it was. "History" is simply this temporal coherence, this connectedness of things from one moment to the next.

Moreover, Nietzsche was struck with the fact that this horizontal interconnectedness means that things last—and thus are for keeps. In *Human, All Too Human*, he suggests "that . . . every action performed by a human being becomes in some way the cause of other actions, decisions, thoughts, that everything that happens is inextricably knotted to everything that will happen." Thus we "come to recognize the existence of an actual *immortality*, that of motion: what has once moved is enclosed and eternalized in the total union of all being like an insect in amber."[20] This notion makes sense only insofar as the world is a history, only insofar as the endless becoming is not just empty flux but takes on a particular content.

Moreover, this connectedness across time meant that our personal lives are bound up with the happening of this particular world. As Nietzsche put it in *The Gay Science*, "*The most dangerous point of view.*—What I do or do not do now is as important for everything that is yet to come as is the greatest event of the past: in this tremendous perspective of effectiveness all actions appear equally great and small."[21] And because of this insight into the permanent weight of what we do, Nietzsche could write a few years later, "I myself am fate and have conditioned existence for all eternity."[22]

Nietzsche, of course, was not shy about claiming world-historical importance for his own contribution, and his antiegalitarianism shaped his way of conceiving the implications of his insight into the immortality of what we do. But his notion that "all actions appear equally great and small" indicates that each of us, in everything we do, has "conditioned existence for all eternity." To be sure, members of "the herd" all do essentially the same things; their actions are interchangeable, so there is no drama to the action of any one of them. Yet even Nietzsche could not deny that collectively their actions add up and weigh heavily, as the impact of our long experience of Christianity amply attested. For all his emphasis on the higher types, Nietzsche grasped that the

19. See, for example, *Will to Power*, 165 (no. 293).
20. Nietzsche, *Human, All Too Human*, 97 (no. 208).
21. Friedrich Nietzsche, *The Gay Science*, trans. Walter Kaufmann (New York: Random House, Vintage, 1974), 212–213 (no. 233).
22. As quoted by Joan Stambaugh, *Nietzsche's Thought of Eternal Return* (Baltimore: Johns Hopkins University Press, 1972), 59.

mechanism through which a particular reality results is egalitarian—indeed, all too egalitarian.

So even if we think in terms of lies or fictions, it matters for all time that human beings have imposed these fictions and not some others, because subsequent fictions will respond to, and thus embody, the particular world that has resulted so far. What remains, with the collapse of metaphysics, is not mere flux or discontinuity but the total particular that results from the connectedness of things. For Nietzsche, that is the terror. And the challenge was to find a way beyond what he found appalling about the bland particularity of our merely historical world.

Reshaping the Past

With the reduction to history, we initially experience our connectedness with the past as a limitation and burden. Our present and we ourselves seem to have resulted from a past that is not freely chosen—that has, in fact, the freakish, capricious consistency of "dreadful accident."[23] Yet its weight is overpowering. Especially in *Thus Spoke Zarathustra*, Nietzsche sought to envision redemption from the weight of "it was," the unwilled past.

That effort ultimately led Nietzsche in two innovative directions. The first, accenting the scope for will, creativity, and radical historical questioning, proved congruent with a radical historicism. But something about the experience bound up with that response led Nietzsche to push beyond, to what we might call a "posthistoricist" position, a mode of individual experience emptied of genuinely historical consciousness.

The past is heavy, not airy and weightless, precisely because it was a certain way and not some other; so it will not do simply to turn away from it, laugh at it, or play with it. Says Nietzsche's Zarathustra, "A new will I teach men: to *will* this way which man has walked blindly, and to affirm it, and no longer to sneak away from it like the sick and decaying."[24] So to dissolve the burden of "it was," we must come to terms with the particular way the world has been by inquiring into it and, on that basis, specifying an understanding of the past and its connection with us that we can affirm. Nietzsche wanted to be able to say "Yes to the point of justifying, of redeeming, even all of the past."[25] In a world of nothing but history, redemption would entail understanding the whole past, in all its contingency, as necessary to the resulting of our particular present—and saying that we would not have it otherwise.

At first glance, the lack of metaphysical grounding seemed to afford unlimited scope for creative human will to reshape the past to serve this present pur-

23. Friedrich Nietzsche, *Thus Spoke Zarathustra*, in *The Portable Nietzsche*, 251, 253.
24. Ibid., 144.
25. Friedrich Nietzsche, *Ecce Homo*, trans. Walter Kaufmann (with *On the Genealogy of Morals*), ed. Walter Kaufmann (New York: Random House, Vintage, 1969), 308.

pose. Says Nietzsche's Zarathustra, "All 'it was' is a fragment, a riddle, a dreadful accident—until the creative will says to it, 'But thus I willed it; thus shall I will it.' "[26] "As creator, guesser of riddles, and redeemer of accidents," Zarathustra goes on to say, "I taught them to work on the future and to redeem with their creation all that *has been*. To redeem what is past in man and to re-create all 'it was' until the will says, 'Thus I willed it! Thus I shall will it'— this I called redemption."[27] So in this mode Nietzschean affirmation entailed actively shaping all those accidental fragments back there, including even the meaning of past lives, so that they can be understood as leading to a willed present. This is the initial thrust of amor fati—Nietzsche's formula for affirming what I understand as necessary for my life and this moment to be as they are.[28]

Since students of Nietzsche have been quick to accent the antihistorical side of his thinking, it bears special emphasis that amor fati refers not to some isolable level of the self as opposed to the larger "public" world of history. Thus Alexander Nehamas's influential reading, though superb in many respects, is one-sided in framing Nietzsche's point as self-creation/discovery, based on encounter with one's own past, conceived in isolation.[29] Nehamas's account does not do justice to Nietzsche's sense that the distinction between self and history has broken down. As the passages quoted above make clear, individual actions are for keeps, immortal, bound up with the shaping or resulting of the public, historical world, not just a distinguishable self. Conversely, any individual is but a piece of that totality, with its finitude and fatality.[30] Thus what is to be shaped and affirmed is not simply a personal past but a particular totality, the world resulting from history.

Because everything is bound up together, Nietzsche noted repeatedly, I cannot condemn anything without condemning everything; in the same way, affirmation of any single moment entails affirmation of all of existence.[31] So amor fati is not just a matter of not wanting anything about *myself* to be different; because my life is bound up with this totality, the whole capricious history has been necessary for my personal experience to be as it is. What is to be affirmed is the whole interlocking chain of "accidents" necessary for this particular world to be as it is. Nietzsche envisioned not merely some generic affirmation

26. Nietzsche, *Thus Spoke Zarathustra*, 253. See also Nietzsche, *Ecce Homo*, 308–309.

27. Nietzsche, *Thus Spoke Zarathustra*, 310; see also pp. 249–254, for the pivotal section entitled "On Redemption."

28. See *The Gay Science*, 223 (no. 276), for Nietzsche's first use of amor fati. See also Nietzsche, *Will to Power*, 536 (no. 1041); Nietzsche, *Ecce Homo*, 258, 324; and Nietzsche, *Nietzsche contra Wagner*, in *The Portable Nietzsche*, 680; which make it clear that the amor fati formula became entwined almost immediately with the idea of eternal recurrence, as I discuss below.

29. Alexander Nehamas, *Nietzsche: Life as Literature* (Cambridge: Harvard University Press, 1985), esp. pp. 157–159, 188–190.

30. See, for example, Nietzsche, *Will to Power*, 536 (no. 1041).

31. Ibid., 316 (no. 584), 165 (no. 293), 532–533 (no. 1032); Nietzsche, *Thus Spoke Zarathustra*, 435.

of "life" but affirmation of *this* life, recognizing what the this-ness involves—and has involved.

The past weighs so heavily because the fragments from back there come to us already shaped; a historical interpretation we have not chosen, and that we nonetheless take to be definitive, initially surrounds our present experience. We take it as "true," so we are not even aware it is nothing but a historical interpretation—even a reinterpretation. For Nietzsche, however, it could be taken for granted that any historical account has been constructed—contingently, even arbitrarily—as part of the resulting of the particular world. Certain reinterpretations have proven powerful enough to win out and structure the world as it has become so far. To understand the world as nothing but history is to grasp the scope for deconstructing and redoing the account we have inherited, for giving the past new meaning in light of our ways of living the present. So to dissolve the weight of "it was," we must at once inquire into the past and self-consciously deconstruct the oppressive account we have inherited.

If what lies back there is nothing but a jerry-built history, historical questioning expands and deepens, cutting all the way to the bottomless bottom. By unearthing buried layers, showing up layer after layer as merely historical and contingent, we disassemble the unchosen past into "fragments," bits and pieces that we can then reassemble as we choose, in light of the way we choose to be at present.

In a Nietzschean mode, we understand that such deconstruction leads to nothing more than a redescription. As a historical inquirer, I am not establishing the truth once and for all but simply showing up some present understanding as itself historical and replacing it with one of my own. My way of framing my inquiry and shaping its results stems from my particular purposes, my particular will to power, which entails the "imposition of one's own forms."[32] The becoming of the particular world continues as what it has become, so far, is subjected to such ongoing reinterpretation, stemming from the will to power that resides in individuals.

For all Nietzsche's emphasis on fictions and lies, however, what I need to dissolve the weight of the past is a true account of the becoming of this particular world.[33] Nietzschean will to power entails an attempt to stamp one's particular *true* interpretation on the world. Even though my particular redescription stems from my creative will, and even though no account is definitive or complete, I cannot say just anything about the past if I am to find redemption. I must genuinely confront the particular way "it was," including the particular way the past has come to weigh on me through our inherited historical account; otherwise, the scope for dissolving the weight of the past is lost. Despite Nietzsche's

---

32. Nietzsche, *Beyond Good and Evil*, 203.
33. See, for example, *The Antichrist*, 612, where Nietzsche claims to be telling "the *genuine* history of Christianity" (emphasis in original).

assault on the "will to truth" and his emphasis on creative fictions, willful lying or fancy affords no redemption. And we do know the difference. Try it.

But though some of Nietzsche's accents presuppose a weak, radically historicist conception of truth, he was not in a position to explore the scope for such a dimension in a postmetaphysical culture. Preoccupied as he was with the assault on metaphysical truth, he did not make the distinctions necessary to explain what such a weaker truth might entail, why we can come up with it, how it stems from will yet differs from willful fiction or fantasy.

What Nietzsche did, however, was to carry out such radical historical questioning himself, especially in *On the Genealogy of Morals*, which seeks to understand how we in the West have become as we are, with our particular moral categories and the hangups that have resulted from them. In his own contingent way, he sought genuinely to understand the particular historical reality that has resulted from those buried contingencies. He focused on dimensions of the Western tradition that genuinely troubled him, that had real consequences for his life. And it was crucial that he come up with an account he could genuinely believe in, could take to be true. So his account was deeply serious, not fanciful or playful.

Such historical questioning is central to *Beyond Good and Evil* as well. In an important sense, in fact, Nietzsche's whole enterprise was an effort of historical excavation to dissolve the weight of "it was," the particular tradition that had imposed this particular mode of being on him—and us. And with the cultural reconstitution that has accompanied the eclipse of metaphysics, Nietzschean genealogy has seemed ever more central as an approach to the world as historical. It frees human creativity by showing the historical contingency of what had come to seem suprahistorical and natural.

Nietzsche's first way of positing redemption from the weight of "it was" thus entailed an active and apparently ongoing engagement with history, including a premium on historical questioning to serve creative world-making. But somehow this loosely historicist response elicited troubling concerns about responsibility and guilt, judgment and punishment. So Nietzsche's accents changed as his confrontation with the world as historical deepened.

What Nietzsche began to envision has proven extraordinarily difficult to characterize because he was explicitly seeking to avoid the customary dualisms of freedom-determinism, active-passive, and innovation-repetition. Willed creative response remained, but it was to be experienced and understood—in relation to the totality of things—in a new way. Nietzsche sought to make history, which had seemed to demand our endless active engagement, go limp, so that individuals would come to experience themselves as a piece of fate, flowing with the totality. This response may be characterized as posthistoricist because it presupposes the reduction to a merely particular history yet seeks to avoid the experience that Nietzsche's initial, generally historicist response seemed to entail. It was with his second response that Nietzsche reached the obscure categories of his maturity—eternal recurrence and the innocence of becoming, which gave a deeper meaning to amor fati.

Affirming the Particular Totality

Somehow even affirmation of the whole past was not enough for redemption, so Nietzsche pushed on to formulate a more radical form of affirmation, adding eternal recurrence to amor fati, thereby expanding what is to be affirmed and altering the relationship between the individual and the totality. With the addition of eternal recurrence, the future as well as the past is drawn into the present moment, and the world to be affirmed becomes the finite totality of a closed system.[34] As a result, we no longer feel ourselves to be making the future as we act in our particular ways. But why did Nietzsche find it so important to draw the future into the finite totality? What did he find troubling about the historicist tension of his first response?

We saw that redemption, with the first formulation of amor fati, entails recasting the capricious accidents of the past into products of one's own will. But this suggested that the work of redeeming the past is never finished, because more dreadful accident is at work in the process whereby each moment becomes the next. To experience the world in this way thus seemed to yield an imperative of ongoing action, a restless effort to keep creating, from the fragments of the past, a situation that I can fully affirm. Moreover, we noted that Nietzsche's emphasis on interconnectedness means that everything we do has history-making implications. There is nothing but the horizontal, endlessly provisional world of human redescription and response. Under these conditions, I might feel a heightened sense of responsibility for what I do, including my ways of shaping the past, and even feel myself subject to judgment for how well I do it. Orientation to the future breeds uncertainty, guilt. I have never quite done enough; even insofar as I forge a new situation from the dreadful accident of the past, the moment constantly slips away from me.

To achieve redemption, then, it could not be sufficient merely to redescribe the past in the process of affirming the present, in the way that Nehamas has emphasized.[35] It is not enough that I experience every present moment as the culmination and justification for all that has ever been. Redemption requires that I experience every present moment as complete, so that there is nothing else that needs to be done. At every moment, I must feel such reconciliation with the whole that there is no scope for, no need for, future-oriented projects to *further* change the meaning of the past, now to include the moment just completed. Thus the future must be drawn into the present moment that I affirm.

---

34. Nietzsche, *Will to Power*, 536 (no. 1041).
35. See, for example, Nehamas's characterization in *Nietzsche*, 160–162, where, despite some significant ambiguity, openness to the future is accented.

But what must the world be like, or what world would we have to posit, for this to be possible?

Nietzsche introduced eternal recurrence, or eternal return, in August 1881 in a famous passage in *The Gay Science*, after hinting at it earlier in the same volume.

> *The Greatest Weight.*—What if some day or night a demon were to steal after you in your loneliest loneliness and say to you: "This life as you now live it and have lived it, you will have to live once more and innumerable times more; and there will be nothing new in it, but every pain and every joy and every thought and sigh and everything unutterably small or great in your life will have to return to you, all in the same succession and sequence—even this spider and this moon-light between the trees, and even this moment and I myself. The eternal hour-glass of existence is turned upside down again and again, and you with it, speck of dust!"
>
> Would you not throw yourself down and gnash your teeth and curse the demon who spoke thus? Or have you once experienced a tremendous moment when you would have answered him: "You are a god and never have I heard anything more divine." If this thought gained possession of you, it would change you as you are or perhaps crush you. The question in each and every thing, "Do you desire this once more and innumerable times more?" would lie upon your actions as the greatest weight. Or how well disposed would you have to become to yourself and to life *to crave nothing more fervently* than this ultimate eternal confirmation and seal?[36]

Nietzsche found this notion novel, prophetic, exhilarating; he consistently portrayed it as the highest possible formulation of affirmation—and as the core of his mature thinking. Yet the category has bedeviled commentators. Some find it a cosmological principle, others a mode of selfhood. Allan Megill suggests that it makes no significant sense at all.[37] Yet it was clearly a way of confronting the world as a total history, and it needs to be understood in terms of the reduction to history at issue for us in this study.

Most commentators agree that eternal recurrence is not to be taken as a literal cosmological principle, involving the actual recurrence of everything, even though this might seem to follow if we posit the infinity of time and the finitude of matter/energy. As Nehamas has argued, what matters is the notion's psychological significance, its implications for individual experience. Nietzsche envisioned a new approach to life, lived *as if* eternal recurrence were the case. He valued the mode of life that could grasp and desire eternal recurrence, not

36. Nietzsche, *Gay Science*, 273–274 (no. 341); emphasis in original. See also the editorial note by Walter Kaufmann, p. 273 n. 71. In addition, see Peter Bergmann, *Nietzsche: "The Last Antipolitical German"* (Bloomington: Indiana University Press, 1987), 136–137.

37. Allan Megill, *Prophets of Extremity: Nietzsche, Heidegger, Foucault, Derrida* (Berkeley, Los Angeles, and London: University of California Press, 1985), 101–102.

the dubious cosmology that would underpin it. Nor does Nietzsche's use of eternal recurrence require any such cosmology.[38]

But though it is not a cosmological principle, eternal recurrence is a conception of the totality of things. And Nehamas, in concluding that "the eternal recurrence is not a theory of the world but a view of the self," concentrates excessively on the level of personal experience and individual psychology at the expense of that sense of totality.[39] It is crucial that the sense of self that Nehamas associates with eternal recurrence was the outcome of several steps, starting with Nietzsche's early experience of history as a particularizing totality. Indeed, Nietzsche's archetypal experience of nothing but history gives point to the idea of eternal recurrence and explains his insistence on its decisive importance. In fastening on the notion, Nietzsche was responding, most immediately, to the preoccupations that came to the fore with his generally historicist response.

In one of his unpublished fragments, Nietzsche suggested that all possible combinations are tried out, and some commentators have understood eternal recurrence in these terms, wondering what the point is, what difference it could make. Read this way, the notion would take all the sting out of "it was." But even in this passage, Nietzsche concludes that the world is "a circular movement of absolutely identical series."[40] What matters is the particularity of the sequence, in which the combination at each moment affects all subsequent moments. And elsewhere Nietzsche insists explicitly that the world *lacks* the capacity for infinite transformations.[41] Thus, as Ivan Soll has emphasized, eternal recurrence cannot mean that all possible combinations are realized; rather, what is ultimately at issue is one eternally recurring series.[42] Nietzsche's emphasis was on the eternal recurrence of *the same*, as opposed to the other, or the whole array of possibilities.[43] What matters is the *this*-ness, the particularity.

38. Nehamas, *Nietzsche*, 142–154. See also Laurence Lampert, *Nietzsche's Teaching: An Interpretation of "Thus Spoke Zarathustra"* (New Haven: Yale University Press, 1986), 259–260, on why Nietzsche sometimes cast the notion in quasi-scientific terms.

39. Nehamas, *Nietzsche*, 150.

40. Nietzsche, *Will to Power*, 548–549 (no. 1066).

41. See especially ibid., 546–547 (no. 1062).

42. Ivan Soll, "Reflections on Recurrence: A Re-examination of Nietzsche's Doctrine, *Die Ewige Wiederkehr des Gleichen*," in *Nietzsche: A Collection of Critical Essays*, ed. Robert C. Solomon (Garden City, N.Y.: Doubleday, Anchor, 1973), 328–330. Lampert, in *Nietzsche's Teaching*, 255–257, similarly emphasizes that Nietzsche envisioned affirming things in their particularity.

43. Compare Pierre Klossowski, "Nietzsche's Experience of Eternal Return," trans. Allen Weiss, in *The New Nietzsche: Contemporary Styles of Interpretation*, ed. David B. Allison (New York: Dell, Delta, 1977), 109, 117–118. While arguing convincingly that eternal recurrence dissolves the weight of what we do, Klossowski suggests that a new universe of possibilities opens at every moment—an accent that does not do justice to the initial dismal sense of finitude. In contrast, Gilles Deleuze, whose work was even more central to the emergence of "the new Nietzsche" in France during the 1960s, seems to make the notion unnecessarily formal when he accents the endless repetition of the throw of the dice itself, as opposed to the series that results when some particular number comes up with each throw. The continued throwing of the dice is simply ongoing

The sequence, in other words, is a particular way, and there is a sense in which the world, though endlessly becoming, is complete as a finite particular.

Eternal recurrence means, most obviously, that history has no goal or end. So not only are we to do without God and a transcendent heaven; there is also no prospect of the completion and deliverance that Hegel and Marx imagined. Nietzsche even took a second step and warned against placing too much stock in the discovery that there is no goal; it is too easy to infer that the newly discovered aimlessness of the world has been intended, that mechanisms have been set up *to prevent* the world from reaching a goal or final state of "being." The discovery of no goal might even be taken to have been the goal.[44]

We might assume at first that in precluding any sort of goal, Nietzsche wanted both to expose the "weakness" that requires such illusions and to buttress human creativity at every moment. But in fastening on eternal recurrence, he was seeking to *preclude* novelty and creativity, in order to make the world—this particular world—a closed system. His shrill denial of novelty and creativity seems curious at first because it is hard to square with some of his other emphases. When attacking metaphysics and ideals of suprahistorical truth, he consistently held that human beings create a world, as opposed to discovering a world already there, and this emphasis can be found even in his later works. The reduction to history, with the corollary that "I myself am fate and have conditioned existence for all eternity," seems to entail precisely the novelty and creativity that Nietzsche sometimes took pains to deny.[45]

At the same time, however, Nietzsche had long sought to play down individual agency and human creativity in some of his passages. In *Human, All Too Human*, for example, he insisted that the most valuable creations just happen, ultimately as part of the circular fatality of the world, requiring no anxiety about agency or creativity on the part of human beings.[46] He increasingly found it necessary to fight the idea of the world as created, even the very idea of creation.[47] In *The Gay Science*, he warned that even after the death of God, various shadows of God remain, lurking especially in our notions of novelty and creativity. Those shadows will "cease to darken our minds" only when we have

---

particularizing; to point to that throwing is simply to say that change or becoming continues. But this is already a given. With the idea of eternal recurrence, Nietzsche was responding to the finite totality of the chain of results, not simply positing the endlessness of particularizing. Indeed, the dice throw, derived from *Thus Spoke Zarathustra*, is a misleading analogy because the reconfiguring of the world at every moment starts not from scratch but from the outcome of the last throw. See Deleuze's *Nietzsche and Philosophy*, trans. Hugh Tomlinson (New York: Columbia University Press, 1983; orig. French ed. 1962), 22–29, esp. pp. 26–27. See also Ronald Bogue's clear and balanced exegesis in his *Deleuze and Guattari* (London: Routledge, 1989), 27–32.

44. Nietzsche, *Will to Power*, 546–547 (no. 1062).

45. See above, p. 65. See also *Beyond Good and Evil*, 117, 136, for examples of Nietzsche's ongoing emphasis on the scope for willed human creation.

46. Nietzsche, *Human, All Too Human*, 97 (no. 210).

47. Nietzsche, *Will to Power*, 546–550 (nos. 1062–1067).

managed fully to de-deify the world, so Nietzsche began explicitly denying novelty and creativity: "Let us beware of thinking that the world creates new things."[48] In a note from 1885, he observed that "the world, even if it is no longer a god, is still supposed to be capable of the divine power of creation, the power of infinite transformations." We think this way partly by habit, but Nietzsche implied that "all those who would like to force on the world the ability for *eternal novelty*" were simply trying to assume the mantle of creator that had once belonged to God. Nietzsche even appealed to "the recently attained preponderance of the scientific spirit," which contrasts with the religious, god-inventing spirit, to buttress his vision of the world as a closed system, lacking the capacity for eternal novelty.[49]

At first, Nietzsche's denial of both goal and novelty-creativity makes the human situation, and the world itself, as dismal as possible. Because there is nothing but this closed circle of dreadful accidents, he could say of the world in 1888, "It lives on itself: its excrements are its food."[50] The world just is, is here, not in the old metaphysical and suprahistorical sense, but rather as the finite totality of a particular history. To feel the weight of this dismal fact is to face the nauseating particularity of the world that Nietzsche experienced, in a halting way, in "On the Uses and Disadvantages of History for Life." The mode of eternal recurrence intensifies the original experience of the collapse into history, initially making that experience even more appalling. Now we come to experience reality as, for all time, this way—this particular closed system and not some other. Moreover, just as the possibility of deliverance or fulfillment falls away, neither can there be nothingness or oblivion. We are confined to this particular horizontal world forever.

Although Nietzsche clearly thought in terms of a circle, an identical series, a weaker version of eternal recurrence helps dramatize his point. The future can hold no more than what can result from this moment, itself merely a particular resultant. Any possible future will thus embody this freakish present moment, which, in that sense, recurs forever. The thing is here forever, as a closed system—this particular closed system. Combining endlessness and completeness, cementing limitation and finitude, eternal recurrence completes the reduction to a particular history, making it as radical and thoroughgoing as possible.

Redemption lies in fully experiencing this reduction but then going on to a mode of life in which the nauseous experience of limitation dissipates. I must be able genuinely to say that I would not have it otherwise, in full knowledge of the sort of stuff that went into making this moment what it is, in full knowledge that it has had nothing but its own excrement to feed on. And I fully under-

48. Nietzsche, *The Gay Science*, 167–169.
49. Nietzsche, *Will to Power*, 546–547 (no. 1062).
50. Ibid., 548 (no. 1066).

stand that novelty is precluded, so this moment, excrement and all, recurs forever. To affirm this moment, I must be able to affirm the whole thing because I experience this moment—in all its appalling finitude—as the culmination of everything, past *and* future, because even the future has no more significance, holds no more for us, than to come back round to this. "My consolation," said Nietzsche, "is that everything that has been is eternal."[51]

What is to be affirmed, then, is not simply the past that resulted in this present but the whole closed system of which this present moment is a necessary part. Only in the mode of eternal recurrence does the experience of amor fati become total. It goes without saying, however, that for Nietzsche, such affirmation of the whole contingent, particular world was only for certain hardy spirits; the weak would be unable even to fathom it.[52]

The mode of completeness that Nietzsche posited differed radically from Hegel's precisely because Hegel's still-metaphysical apparatus had dissolved, leaving nothing but history. For Nietzsche, the present is a culmination, but a weak and recurring culmination, not the necessary end of a teleological process. Moreover, *every* moment is a culmination, each finite and particular, yet each a microcosm of all that ever has been and ever will be. At the same time, it is crucial that every moment is a culmination as opposed to a stepping-stone; thus every moment can be experienced as an end in itself. Nietzsche could thereby envision a world, a mode of living, "without goal, unless the joy of the circle is itself a goal."[53] And he noted explicitly that to live in the mode of eternal recurrence is to make possible, even in this world of endless becoming, the completeness we once associated with stable being: "To impose upon becoming the character of being—that is the supreme will to power. . . . That *everything recurs* is the closest *approximation of a world of becoming to a world of being*:—high point of the meditation."[54]

At the same time, Nietzschean completeness does not mean the "wholeness" that Hegel and others have sought to envision, as an antidote to our alleged, much lamented fragmentation and alienation. Nietzsche was seeking to grasp what redemption would mean when we have come to understand that we are *not* becoming whole or complete selves, that there is no such prior form for us to fill. What is required is not action on the world to add to it, to have more experiences, to develop one's self, but simply a new mode of experiencing what there already is. In a crucial sense, in fact, we are to be redeemed precisely from the assumption of inadequacy and incompleteness, from the gnawing sense that one can, one must, always do *more* to overcome the lack, in response to the fact that the particular episodes of our finite world have still *not* made us "whole" or "complete." The mode of affirmation that now

51. Ibid., 548 (no. 1065).
52. Ibid., 35–39 (nos. 55–56).
53. Ibid., 550 (no. 1067).
54. Ibid., 330 (no. 617); emphasis in original.

becomes possible means that we no longer experience the finitude and particularity of the world—and thus of ourselves—as a limitation.

In one sense, then, the accent on eternal recurrence, and the attendant denial of novelty and creativity, is simply to warrant full experience of the present moment—as entirely sufficient. But in concentrating everything into the present through a post-Hegelian kind of completeness, Nietzsche was quite explicitly responding to an experience that newly opened with the reduction to history—and that he found negative. The transcendent God had long seemed the creator of the world and the judge of human beings. With the death of that God, the idea of the world as created remained, but in the merely historical world, creation seemed to result from ongoing human activity.[55] Having inherited or usurped God's creative attributes, we feel responsible for what the world becomes. Indeed, the endless openness of the merely historical world imposes a heightened sense of responsibility—a sense that entails anxiety and the possibility of guilt and judgment. In the mode of eternal recurrence, in contrast, there is nothing that needs to be done, so we are free not only from resentment of the past but also from the guilt that remained as a shadow across the world even with the eclipse of metaphysics.

The idea of eternal recurrence enabled Nietzsche to imagine a situation of playful innocence, the "innocence of becoming," a telling phrase that he used at several key points in his mature writings, most notably in a striking section of *Twilight of the Idols*: "Becoming has been deprived of its innocence when any being-such-and-such is traced back to will, to purposes, to acts of responsibility: the doctrine of the will has been invented essentially for the purpose of punishment, that is, because one wanted to impute guilt." "Today," Nietzsche continued, "we immoralists are trying with all our strength to take the concept of guilt and the concept of punishment out of the world again," most immediately in opposition to the theologians, who "infect the innocence of becoming by means of 'punishment' and 'guilt.' " But how can our continuing experience of guilt and punishment be dissolved? What must we be able to say of the world if we are to feel innocence instead?

> That no one *gives* man his qualities—neither God, nor society, nor his parents and ancestors, nor he himself. . . . No one is responsible for man's being there at all, for his being such-and-such, or for his being in these circumstances or in this environment. The fatality of his essence is not to be disentangled from the fatality of all that has been and will be. . . . One is necessary, one is a piece of fatefulness, one belongs to the whole, one is in the whole; there is nothing which could judge, measure, compare, or sentence our being, for that would mean judging, measuring, comparing, or sentencing the whole. But there is nothing besides the whole. That nobody is responsible any longer, that the mode of being may

55. Ibid., 546–547 (no. 1062).

not be traced back to a *causa prima*, that the world does not form a unity either as a sensorium or as "spirit"—that alone is the great liberation: with this alone is the innocence of becoming restored. The concept of "God" was until now the greatest objection to existence. We deny God, we deny the responsibility in God: only thereby do we redeem the world.[56]

With everything already "here," we experience ourselves not as creating the world but as happening with the world. Thus Nietzsche's Zarathustra inveighs against "for"—purposiveness or instrumentality—in our experience of what we do: "Unlearn this 'for,' you creators! Your very virtue wants that you do nothing 'for' and 'in order' and 'because.' You shall plug up your ears against these false little words."[57] The purposelessness of living in the mode of eternal recurrence undercuts the imperative to make a *different* future that would result from an experience of tension with the resultant of history so far. And with no scope for purposive agency, there is no scope for responsibility, guilt, or judgment.

Even in *The Gay Science*, Nietzsche linked the idea of purpose with the notion of accident in a way that foreshadowed his mature vision of redemption: "Once you know that there are no purposes, you also know that there is no accident; for it is only beside a world of purposes that the word 'accident' has meaning."[58] As purposiveness drops out, then, the mechanisms through which some particular world comes to be in history no longer seem appalling and oppressive; I no longer experience the happening of the world as "dreadful accident." I can thus affirm and feel one with the whole.

In the mode of eternal recurrence, "becoming" of course continues, but we simply happen with the circular event of the world, feeling ourselves "eternal" as we do. And though action continues as well, it comes to be experienced as innocent play, even dance, as opposed to responsible, purposive, history-making creation. Thus Nietzsche's reference to " 'play,' the useless—as the ideal of him who is overfull of strength, as 'childlike.' "[59]

Especially in his late work *The Antichrist*, Nietzsche explored what it would mean to feel eternal in a merely historical world. Relishing the paradoxical twist of his argument, Nietzsche insisted that "heaven" is no longer something to come but a mode of present living and acting for every moment. And Jesus had exemplified the glad tidings by living in "the kingdom" of this mode; in experiencing each moment as eternal and complete, he had been the terrestrial embodiment of redemption, not merely the promise of a redemption to come. Redemption is now; heaven is here.[60]

56. Friedrich Nietzsche, *Twilight of the Idols*, in *The Portable Nietzsche*, 499–501. See also Nietzsche, *Will to Power*, 402–403 (no. 765).
57. Nietzsche, *Thus Spoke Zarathustra*, 403.
58. Nietzsche, *The Gay Science*, 168.
59. Nietzsche, *Will to Power*, 419 (no. 797). See also Nietzsche, *Ecce Homo*, 258, on "play."
60. Nietzsche, *The Antichrist*, 607–609, 614–616.

The experience Nietzsche envisioned in *The Antichrist* entails something like responsibility, but not for history. The only responsibility is of the higher types for value, by being or living in a life-affirming way.[61] They are responsible not for doing anything in particular, through history-making action, but for *being* in a certain way, for living and experiencing in a certain way. Doing will follow, but it will be innocent, because, again, with every moment a culmination, there is nothing more that needs to be done.

Nietzsche's mature categories enabled him to posit a world in which, despite the reduction to history, we do not experience our actions as "making history," as helping to create the world, to determine what it becomes. As action becomes a kind of innocent play, the sense of weight, responsibility, and endless tension with the world dissipates. Even though I "have conditioned existence for all eternity," I am simply a necessary part of the whole fatality that is in a crucial sense already complete.

In the same way, there is no premium on knowing any particular chunk of history to help us respond to the present in a purposive way, in the mode of "making history." If I affirm all that has happened, I feel no call to ask about, or to deconstruct, any particular part of it. I can simply play with the relics of the past as I dance with the happening of the world.

It is crucial, however, that even in this final phase Nietzsche was not proposing that we simply ignore the world as history, turning from it to concentrate on present living as an end in itself. At each moment, I fully understand all that it means for reality to be historical, all that it means for this world to be as it is. Yet what matters to me is not my involvement in the ongoing history but my affirmative experience of the eternal present. As the world flattens into nothing but history, redemption requires a "posthistoricist" mode of experience that resists and transcends the totalizing historicism that first seemed to follow from the eclipse of metaphysics and that portended the anxious responsibility, guilt, and judgment that Nietzsche feared.

Nietzsche's Triple Legacy

The deepest thrust of Nietzsche's thinking does indeed prove ahistorical or antihistorical in implication—but not because he turned from nineteenth-century modes of historical-mindedness to emphasize self-creation. Rather, his mature strategy stemmed from a sustained effort to come to terms with the new, more all-embracing experience of the world as historical that imposed itself with the waning of metaphysics. Without this experience of the reduction to history, and the attendant sense of belonging to this particular finite totality,

---

61. Ibid., 646. For a related theme, see *Twilight of the Idols*, 555, where Nietzsche argues that greatness pertains to a particular mode of human being, not to effects or public uses.

categories like amor fati, eternal recurrence, and the innocence of becoming would hardly be meaningful at all. Yet Nietzsche kept coming back to these themes, almost obsessively.

No doubt the preoccupations that led Nietzsche to them reflected his particular biographical circumstances. His father was a Protestant pastor who died when Nietzsche was only five years old. Nietzsche was under intense family pressure to follow his father into the ministry, yet he lost his faith altogether in his teens. Thus, to some extent, surely, his concern with responsibility, guilt, and innocence. But the point is not to reduce Nietzsche's thought to the accidents of biography. Such biographical idiosyncrasies meant simply that Nietzsche felt with a particular intensity a new set of preoccupations that were coming more widely to the fore. Thus his response has proven archetypal.

At the same time, however, we have seen that Nietzsche's quest for posthistoricist innocence was the last of several ways he responded to the collapse into history. And what he bequeathed to the subsequent effort to specify the terms of a postmetaphysical culture has proven a contradictory, tripartite legacy. His initial aestheticist response, accenting fictional redescription, has contributed to the tendency to blur the distinction between history and fiction. Because there is no final, determinate way the world is, the world comes to seem a fictional text subject to endless reinterpretation stemming from the creative will that resides in individuals.

But even as he emphasized fictions, Nietzsche fastened on the other side of the coin as well: the connectedness of things meant that some particular world endlessly results from the concatenation of individual response. And he showed why we might seek to know—truly know—the world that has resulted from our particular lies and fictions as we respond to it with new creative fictions of our own. In this sense, Nietzsche worked beyond aestheticism to his second, radically historicist response, which accents the scope for deconstructing that world through genealogy, a form of historical inquiry that serves ongoing action. By showing that all our ways of being are subject to such genealogical inquiry, he radically expanded the focus—and potential import—of historical inquiry.

But it is equally important that Nietzsche did not stop with this radical historicism but pushed on to a third strategy, centering on the quest for innocence. Although the resulting orientation was extreme, this quest was plausible, and it initiated an ongoing concern with individual experience in the face of an intrusive, suffocating history. A purely historical world has seemed to offer new scope for play, dance, laughter, and self-creation, and exploration of such possibilities has proven essential to the ongoing mapping of the postmetaphysical terrain.

Distinguishing the aestheticist, historicist, and posthistoricist directions in Nietzsche's thought enables us not only better to grasp the thrust of each but also to box out the blurring and overreaction that his legacy has also occasioned. Yet the distinctions are difficult because the three strands coexisted in Nietzsche's mature thinking and because they have gotten further intertwined as the Nietzschean legacy has been disseminated.

Nietzsche's quest for innocence was one response to the new experience of nothing but history, but Croce and Heidegger moved in very different directions in response to much the same new sense of the world.

5

Croce

History as Thought and Action

Croce's Uncertain Legacy

In the 1880s, precisely as Nietzsche was writing his mature works, Benedetto Croce began the intellectual quest that led to what he labeled absolute historicism. Like Nietzsche—and Heidegger a bit later—Croce lost his Christian religious faith as a young man, and his sense that the old religion was in irreversible decline fundamentally shaped his sense of the cultural challenge. Indeed, he believed his generation had the historically specific task of replacing the old religion, and he understood his own intellectual enterprise as a contribution to that effort.[1] For him, as for Nietzsche and Heidegger, traditional religion was bound up with a dissolving metaphysics, so he too ended up an overtly antimetaphysical thinker who took it for granted that there could be no suprahistorically privileged grasp of things, no foundation, framework, or goal for human being.[2]

But whereas Nietzsche and Heidegger ended up proposing extreme strategies in response to the loss of transcendence, Croce sought a kind of middle ground. In addition to opposing still-metaphysical claims to authority, he sought to head off what he found to be the overreaction that threatened with the eclipse of metaphysics. The vogue of Nietzsche during the first decade of

1. Benedetto Croce, "Frammenti di etica" (1915–1920), reprinted in *Etica e politica* (Bari: Laterza, 1967), 167–168. See also Benedetto Croce, *Cultura e vita morale: Intermezzi polemici* (Bari: Laterza, 1955), 35 (1908), 166–167 (1911); and Benedetto Croce, *Ultimi saggi* (Bari: Laterza, 1935), 223–224 (1926).
2. In criticizing "antihistoricist" claims to suprahistorical privilege and all residues of metaphysical thinking, Croce was as explicit and consistent as either Nietzsche or Heidegger. See, for example, Croce's noted essay "Antistoricismo" (1930), in *Ultimi saggi*, 251–264.

the century seemed but one indication of an unwelcome tendency toward irrational extremes, some of which invited playful self-indulgence, others, morbid self-preoccupation. To counter such extremes, Croce sought to refurbish certain traditional cultural components; indeed, he fastened on "history" to specify a way of conceiving both knowing and doing in a postmetaphysical world.[3] We can know the world as history, and history is what we need to know, given what the world is. Moreover, it is history that we make when we act, building onto every present moment, each of which is nothing but the resultant of all human actions so far.

Such notions seem bland and tame alongside those of Nietzsche and Heidegger, so it has been easy to miss Croce's radicalism and originality. Even during the first half of the century, when he was among the best-known intellectuals in the Western world, the essential thrust of his intellectual enterprise was hard to pin down. To some he was a systematic, neo-Hegelian philosopher; to others, primarily an aesthetician and literary critic; to others, a historian, moralist, and organizer of culture. Then, by the later 1940s, Italians began to consider him passé as they looked for fresh ideas after Fascism.[4] Many embraced Antonio Gramsci's innovative form of Marxism as a way beyond the Crocean framework. Gramsci's critique of Croce in his posthumously published *Prison Notebooks* helped cement the notion that Croce invited a premium on abstract speculation or mere understanding as opposed to concrete action.[5] Indeed, Croce seemed to stand for a passive, conservative acceptance of whatever results from history. Moreover, he had apparently been a retrograde humanist whose influence had kept Italy from developing a modern scientific culture—and especially from embracing social science.

As the new discussion in the humanities gathered force in Western culture by the 1960s, Croce seemed safely neglected. Young Italians seeking to come to terms with the likes of Nietzsche and Heidegger assumed they should move as far from Croce as possible. Yet there was something anomalous about

3. Thus Croce's emphasis on "history as thought and action," the literal and unproblematic translation of the title of *La storia come pensiero e come azione* (Bari: Laterza, 1966), first published in 1938 and translated into English by Sylvia Sprigge as *History as the Story of Liberty* (New York: W. W. Norton, 1941).

4. See David D. Roberts, *Benedetto Croce and the Uses of Historicism* (Berkeley, Los Angeles, and London: University of California Press, 1987), 1–22, 260–265, on the vicissitudes of Croce's reputation. In addition, see the gloomy assessment of Croce's decline by the most distinguished of the younger Croceans, Raffaello Franchini, in his *Intervista su Croce*, ed. Arturo Fratta (Naples: Società Editrice Napoletana, 1978). On the fortunes of Croce's work in the United States, see David D. Roberts, "La fortuna di Croce e Gentile negli Stati Uniti," *Giornale critico della filosofia italiana*, ser. 6, 14 (May–December 1994): 253–281. For an indication of Croce's earlier international prominence, see Donald T. Torchiana's account of his influence on Yeats: "Yeats and Croce," in *Yeats Annual No. 4*, ed. Warwick Gould (London: Macmillan, 1986), 3–12.

5. For the essentials of Gramsci's case against Croce, see *Quaderni del carcere*, 4 vols. (Turin: Giulio Einaudi, 1975), 2:1225–1226, 1240, 1271, 1327, 1435, 1477.

Croce's dramatic eclipse, a fact recently emphasized by René Wellek, the distinguished historian of literary criticism. Wellek observed that in movements influential since Croce's death, from Russian formalism and structuralism to hermeneutics and deconstruction, Croce "is not referred to or quoted, even when he discusses the same problems and gives similar solutions." Yet Croce, for Wellek, was arguably the most erudite and wide-ranging figure in the history of criticism.[6]

Even a cursory look, from the perspective that becomes possible with the waning of metaphysics, suggests that Croce came to be neglected for dubious reasons—and that he might fruitfully be reconsidered. Whereas he had indeed been an early critic of the new social sciences, the social scientific approaches he sought to preclude were precisely those that were falling into disrepute in wider intellectual circles a generation later.[7] Between the wars, moreover, his radically antipositivist approach to historiography attracted innovative historians like Charles Beard and Carl Becker, who found exciting his way of addressing precisely the issues of presentism, relativism, and truth that have again been central in recent years. In the final analysis, however, even supporters like Beard found Croce's approach *too* radical and provocative, and Croce's historiographical thinking was not fully digested at that point.[8] To be sure, his name came up as a matter of course in historiographical discussions even as late as the 1960s, but by then he was generally lumped with R. G. Collingwood, a misleading juxtaposition, because certain of Collingwood's best-known themes—reenactment, for example—are not really Crocean.[9] Once the focus of historiographical discussion shifted with the publication of White's *Metahistory* in 1973, Croce virtually disappeared altogether.

This was curious because White had begun his career as a Croce partisan,

6. René Wellek, *A History of Modern Criticism*, vol. 8, *French, Italian, and Spanish Criticism, 1900–1950* (New Haven: Yale University Press, 1992), 187, 189.

7. See, for example, Richard J. Bernstein, *The Restructuring of Social and Political Theory* (Philadelphia: University of Pennsylvania Press, 1976); and Stanislav Andreski, *The Social Sciences as Sorcery* (New York: St. Martin's, 1973), on the growing recognition of the limits of the social sciences as they had crystallized by the 1960s.

8. On the relationship between Croce and Beard, see Ellen Nore, *Charles A. Beard: An Intellectual Biography* (Carbondale: Southern Illinois University Press, 1983), 156, 158–162, 165, 192. Although Beard more enthusiastically embraced Croce, Becker more fully grasped what Croce was up to. Compare especially their respective presidential addresses to the American Historical Association: Carl L. Becker, "Everyman His Own Historian" (1931), reprinted in Becker, *Everyman His Own Historian: Essays on History and Politics* (New York: F. S. Crofts, 1935), 233–255; and Charles A. Beard, "Written History as an Act of Faith" (1933), *American Historical Review* 39, no. 2 (January 1934): 219–231. The debt to Croce was explicit in each.

9. The nature and extent of Collingwood's debt to Croce has periodically been subject to controversy. See Alan Donagan, review of Louis O. Mink, *Mind, History, and Dialectic: The Philosophy of R. G. Collingwood*, *History and Theory* 9, no. 3 (1970): 363–375, esp. p. 364, for a sense of the issues. Croce offered his own assessment in 1946, after learning of Collingwood's death in 1943; see *Nuove pagine sparse*, 2 vols. (Bari: Laterza, 1966), 1:35–53.

even proclaiming "the abiding relevance of Croce's idea of history" in an article published in 1963.[10] Croce figured prominently even in *Metahistory*, but there White portrayed him as the sterile culmination of nineteenth-century historiographical traditions.[11] By severing history from the search for usable general knowledge, Croce was voiding it of present political import and confining it to the haven of art. Moreover, White viewed Croce as deemphasizing action in favor of passive acceptance based on retrospective understanding. Yet it had been Croce's pioneering, radically antipositivist way of relating present action and historical inquiry that had excited those like Becker and Beard a half century before.

Croce was long viewed, in Italy and elsewhere, as a neoidealist system builder, operating within an essentially Hegelian framework. In the four works of his "Philosophy of the Spirit," especially the *Logic* and the *Philosophy of the Practical* of 1908, he established philosophical categories that he continued to invoke for the rest of his life. This seems to suggest a premium on systematic philosophy, established once and for all. But Croce came to insist that no philosophy, including his own, could be definitive. Indeed, his repeated attacks on system building and any pretense of definitive philosophy are among the most striking features of his thought.[12]

Croce was seeking, among other things, to understand the role philosophy plays in a world without the foundations, essences, rules, or structures that philosophy had tried to establish. Even his relatively systematic *Logic* was an attempt radically to recast logic and thereby to show what truth comes to mean in an ever-provisional world of particular instances. Ernst Cassirer noted with disapproval in 1913 that "[Croce's] whole doctrine, even though it proclaims logic as the basic science, in fact turns out to be an unlimited historical relativism in which change is studied so to speak for its own sake, in which no objective-logical enduring factors of any kind are discerned or set off."[13] Cassirer understood that Croce's was no ordinary logic; it was rather a kind of giving in to history, and Cassirer himself wanted no part of it. For Croce, philosophy would always be with us, but it would always be ad hoc and provisional—hardly foundational. Croce, then, was less concerned to establish his own philosophical system than to explore the limits of any such effort; he was

10. Hayden V. White, "The Abiding Relevance of Croce's Idea of History," *Journal of Modern History* 37 (June 1963): 109–124.

11. Hayden V. White, *Metahistory: The Historical Imagination in Nineteenth-Century Europe* (Baltimore: Johns Hopkins University Press, 1973), chap. 10; see especially pp. 378–379, 397–400. See Roberts, *Benedetto Croce*, 345–349, 376 n. 41, 410–411 nn. 45 and 48, for a fuller critique of White's treatment of Croce than is possible here.

12. See, for example, Croce, *Cultura e vita morale*, esp. pp. 248–253 (1922), but also pp. 262–263, 279–280, 292–300. In addition, see Roberts, *Benedetto Croce*, 90–98, for a fuller discussion of this issue.

13. Ernst Cassirer, "Erkenntnistheorie nebst den Grenzfragen der Logik," *Jahrbücher der Philosophie* 1 (Berlin, 1913): 34. See also John Michael Krois, *Cassirer: Symbolic Forms and History* (New Haven: Yale University Press, 1987), 10–11.

among the first to suggest that there is no privileged, foundationalist role for philosophy to play.

Croce has persistently been typed as a philosophical idealist, but though his debt to the idealist tradition is undeniable, he eventually concluded that "idealism" was a term to be abandoned and proposed that his own position be labeled "absolute historicism" instead.[14] The point was not to specify another metaphysics but to grasp the sense in which, to use more contemporary phrasing, "nothing is unambiguously and decidably what it is."[15] How might we conceive a world that is forever coming into being, that is forever provisional and incomplete? The philosophical concerns that had given rise to idealism as one response were simply no longer at issue.

Croce, then, portrayed himself as a radical historicist, yet major Italian students of European historicism like Pietro Rossi and Fulvio Tessitore have attacked Croce while embracing the German tradition of individualizing historicism, from Herder and Ranke to Dilthey and Meinecke.[16] Because Croce criticized that tradition and embraced a species of totalism, these critics have found it easy to lump him with Hegel and the system builders of philosophical idealism. So it is hardly surprising that Croce's thinking has proven elusive—and easily misconstrued.

A Postmetaphysical Historicism

Renewing the most cogent theme in this long tradition of criticism, Tessitore charges that Crocean historicism was simply the culmination of the abstract reason of the Enlightenment; history is the history of reason, with everything explained and the irrational excluded.[17] Given Croce's way of embracing the familiar categories at issue, this characterization seems plausible at first. Croce did emphasize the coherence and even rationality of history, accents that seemed suspect even in the 1940s, in light of events, and that may now seem utterly spurious, in light of our concern with contingency, discontinuity, and rupture. He even advocated "faith in history." But Tessitore's line of criticism is profoundly misleading, given our tendency to understand the central categories in Hegelian, still-metaphysical terms. With the break discussed in chapter 3, such notions became utterly different in cultural implication.

Croce was fully abreast of the debates about history that brought Wilhelm Dilthey, Wilhelm Windelband, and Heinrich Rickert to the fore in Germany

14. Benedetto Croce, *Discorsi di varia filosofia*, 2 vols. (Bari: Laterza, 1959), 2:15–17 (1945).

15. The phrase is from John D. Caputo, *Radical Hermeneutics: Repetition, Deconstruction, and the Hermeneutic Project* (Bloomington: Indiana University Press, 1987), 249.

16. See, for example, Pietro Rossi, *Storia e storicismo nella filosofia contemporanea* (Milan: Lerici, 1960), 303–305, 309–311, 314; and Fulvio Tessitore, *Dimensioni dello storicismo* (Naples: Morano, 1971), 74–82, 87–95, 105–111.

17. Fulvio Tessitore, "Brevissime note su Croce e lo storicismo," in *Benedetto Croce trent'anni dopo,* ed. Antonino Bruno (Rome: Laterza, 1983), 261–264.

by the late nineteenth century. But once he had forged the essentials of his response, he felt he had gone beyond the terms of those debates—as in important respects he had.[18] Croce's absolute historicism was a synthesis, or *Aufhebung*, of the Hegelian sense of totality and the opposing accent on individuality in German historicism. Thus he came to characterize his historicism as absolute, in contrast to the individualizing German version.

A sense of the particularity of things—the import of the concrete individual case—had led Croce to produce the paper of 1893 that first made his reputation, "History Subsumed under the General Concept of Art."[19] Against the loosely positivist insistence that history had to be a science if it was to count as knowledge, he argued that history is not a form of science, seeking to derive lawlike generalizations with predictive power, but a form of art—art, however, understood idiosyncratically, as the mode of knowledge of particulars. His initial emphasis stemmed from a sense that reality *is* particular and thus in some sense historical.

In his subsequent work, Croce went further, turning the cultural tables by arguing that though science is essential to us, its laws and generalizations are only rough-and-ready abstractions from particular cases, based on questions we have formulated for practical purposes. To assume that science gets at stable laws, categories, or essences was the height of metaphysics. Up to a point, of course, this argument paralleled that of many of Croce's contemporaries, from Bergson to the pragmatists. But Croce was taking an extra step into a radical historicism; our ways of understanding the human world cannot be scientific because they are aspects of the ongoing creation, or coming to be, of something new, which endlessly makes necessary a renewed understanding even of what there already was.

But even as he emphasized individuality, creativity, and novelty, Croce understood that the old questions about the whole or totality did not simply disappear; rather, they had to be confronted afresh. He found his way of doing so especially through encounter with Hegel, whom he treated systematically in a once-famous essay published in 1906 and to whom he returned repeatedly throughout his long career.[20] Although Croce's debt to Hegel was considerable, his departure from Hegel was just as important, as he never ceased to emphasize.

18. Daniela Coli, *Croce, Laterza e la cultura europea* (Bologna: Il Mulino, 1983), 77–80.

19. "La storia ridotta sotto il concetto generale dell'arte" (1893), in Benedetto Croce, *Primi saggi* (Bari: Laterza, 1951), 1–41. See also Mario Corsi, *Le origini del pensiero di Benedetto Croce*, 2d ed. (Naples: Giannini, 1974), 23–25, 50–51, on the importance of the particulars of local history for the young Croce.

20. Now the lead essay in Benedetto Croce, *Saggio sullo Hegel seguito da altri scritti di storia della filosofia* (Bari: Laterza, 1927; orig. pub. 1913), it was translated into English by Douglas Ainslie as *What Is Living and What Is Dead of the Philosophy of Hegel* (London: Macmillan, 1919). For Croce's mature sense of his own relationship to Hegel, see especially *Il carattere della filosofia moderna* (Bari: Laterza, 1963; orig. pub. 1941), 38–53. See also Raffaello Franchini, *Croce interprete di Hegel e altri saggi filosofici*, 3d ed. (Naples: Giannini, 1974), 3–51.

For Croce, Hegel's way of positing the totality as a single history had been essential, but Croce anticipated much of French postmodernism in denying that anything like Hegel's grand master story was at work in that total history. Hegel's conception rested on unwarranted teleological assumptions, and much of what he had sought to relate dialectically in fact remains distinct. The challenge was to posit a post-Hegelian totality, to conceive that single history as radically open, without following some necessary dialectic, without telos, and thus without any dominant thread given a priori by what spirit *is* on some level. With Croce's synthesis, the totality becomes concrete and mundane, particular and forever incomplete.

Croce found his way beyond the dichotomy between Hegel and historicism by developing one possibility in the legacy of his Neapolitan predecessor, Giambattista Vico. Croce invoked Vico throughout his career, claiming that only in our time, with the eclipse of metaphysics, could we begin to appreciate the most radical implications of Vico's thinking.[21]

For several decades it has been de rigueur in Vichian studies to attack Croce's alleged idealist deformation of Vico, based on the assumption that Croce was a Hegelian affording privilege to conceptual thought.[22] There *was* something Hegelian in Croce's understanding of Vico, and his way of adapting Vico led him to miss some of what Vico had to say. Still, Croce was not so much deforming Vico as pursuing one of the several directions Vico had opened; from Croce's perspective, in fact, Vico himself had fallen into inconsistency because he had not pushed hard enough in that direction.

Croce fully understood the revolutionary import of Vico's "poetic" conception of thought, and he took over wholesale Vico's notion of the autonomy of the creative imagination, or *fantasia*.[23] For Croce, imagination is the original, creative power of spirit; it does not simply afford images *of* something—something already here—but gives form to mind and life, to thinking and acting. To be sure, Croce insisted on an ongoing role for the rational concept as well but not in a Hegelian way, folding fantasia within a concept conceived as higher, truer. In Croce's hands, the concept simply does not have the "Hegelian" function vis-à-vis the imagination that critics assume it must. Fantasia or poetry comes first and is never overcome altogether; the fact that it wells up continually is one measure of the endless openness and creativity of the world. But we are forever making a kind of rational sense of the world too, through a

21. In addition to Croce's *The Philosophy of Giambattista Vico* (New York: Russell and Russell, 1964), published in Italian in 1911 and published in an English translation by R. G. Collingwood in 1913, see Benedetto Croce, *Filosofia e storiografia* (Bari: Laterza, 1969), 353–354 (1947), for a much later example of his insistence on the centrality of Vico.

22. Such hostility to Croce informs two of the best full-length studies of Vico in English, Donald Phillip Verene's *Vico's Science of Imagination* (Ithaca: Cornell University Press, 1981), esp. pp. 23, 68–69, 217; and Michael Mooney's *Vico in the Tradition of Rhetoric* (Princeton: Princeton University Press, 1985), esp. pp. xi, 26–29.

23. Benedetto Croce, *Estetica come scienza dell'espressione e linguistica generale* (Bari: Laterza, 1958; orig. pub. 1902), pp. 242–244, 254–256, 489.

distinguishable cognitive faculty. Croce ended up positing an endless "circle" of related but distinguishable forms of the spirit, or facets of human being, so that neither imagination nor cognition can be conceived as higher. Rather, each is equally essential to human being and to the endless coming to be of the world. And each is eternal.[24]

What Croce found in Vico was a way of understanding reality as history— and history as totality—but without Hegel's metaphysical and teleological framework. Vico's radical way of bracketing nature leaves us with only the concrete human world, the world that results as human beings respond through their imaginative, creative language to what has resulted so far. Adapting Vico, Croce posited not telos, or even progress, but only neutral growth; what we do can only respond to—and grow upon—the resultant of what has been done before. In this sense, past actions endure even as something new results from what we do. The "reason" at work in history is nothing but this coherence, which is sufficient for there to be some particular world. We have seen that Nietzsche posited the same fundamental connectedness through time.

For Croce, then, it was axiomatic that at every moment a world has resulted from history, a world open to human understanding; we can look back and see how it came to be this way and not some other way. Indeed, we perceive a species of necessity to its becoming. But this is simply to say that the history had to be this way for there to be this world and not some other, not that the history had to be this way in some metaphysical sense.[25] The present world has no metaphysical sanction, no suprahistorical legitimacy. It has only a bland historical sanction: there has resulted—so far—this particular world, the one in which we must operate.

Croce was well aware that in positing this sort of rationality in history he was not saying very much—certainly not what we long thought we needed to be able to say. But there is simply not much that can be said in advance, in a suprahistorical way, about the substance or content of history. What ultimately matters is what happens, what results from the sum of what we do. At the same time, however, what he said was not trivial but opened the way to a certain, relatively productive kind of postmetaphysical culture.

Part of what Croce found in Vico was a way of positing the creativity and novelty that seemed essential to a world that was perpetually incomplete. If we ponder the endless growth of the world through human response, we conclude that what there is, is creative—and indeed may be conceived as a single creative

24. For Croce's derivation of the circle of distinct categories, two pertaining to knowing or mental activity and two to acting or practical activity, see *Logica come scienza del concetto puro* (Bari: Laterza, 1967; orig. pub. 1908), 49–50, 52–53; and *Filosofia della pratica: Economia ed etica* (Bari: Laterza, 1963; orig. pub. 1908), 199–207. See also Roberts, *Benedetto Croce*, 77–83, 98–105.

25. See Roberts, *Benedetto Croce*, 117–137, for a fuller discussion and the relevant references to Croce.

spirit. To many, however, any reference to "spirit" suggests metaphysics in its most ethereal and futile form. But Croce had reason to insist that to posit a single spirit, growing in, through, and *as* history, was the most appropriate way of characterizing what "there is" in a radically concrete and antimetaphysical way.

The spirit does not operate apart from differentiated, historically specific human beings. Rather, it is nothing but us. We are all finite embodiments of the spirit, and as such, we all participate in the process through which a particular world endlessly comes to be. Each individual is creative, but our creativity must respond to the present resultant of history, or the total activity of the spirit so far, and we necessarily interact with others as we respond. Thus the creation of reality in history is a suprapersonal task, not of any one individual, but of the universal spirit, or *dio-creatore*, immanent in all individuals.[26] In that sense, the question of agency falls away; it is a matter of indifference whether we speak of the creation, the happening, or the coming to be of the world. Ultimately, the Crocean spirit is nothing but the particular world, which grows on itself as the creativity that resides in differentiated, individual human beings responds to the resultants of prior creative responses. The world is a single creative happening that we belong to, that we *are*.

Though his reliance on the term "spirit" breeds confusion, Croce's way of relating totality and individuality anticipated recent efforts to do without the strong Cartesian self. His approach can be compared, for example, with that of Gilles Deleuze, who explored "the playful fold of the self" in an effort to posit something like individuality, and even some scope for novelty, without positing a self distinguishable from the universe enveloping it.[27] In one sense, the Vichian Croce never embraced in the first place the assumptions that led to the "sovereign ego" and the other aspects of modern philosophy that thinkers from Nietzsche to Rorty have taken such pains to reject. So Croce found it relatively easy to deny a self conceivable apart from the happening, or coming to be, of this particular world.

In his effort to conceive the world in postmetaphysical terms, Croce shared several of Nietzsche's steps, and he seemed at first to offer an aestheticist vision inviting comparison with the aestheticist side of Nietzsche.[28] For Croce,

26. See, among many examples, Croce, *Filosofia e storiografia*, 250–255 (1947); Croce, *Carattere*, 209–210; and Benedetto Croce, *Teoria e storia della storiografia* (Bari: Laterza, 1973; orig. pub. 1917), 93–98.

27. Ronald Bogue, "Foucault, Deleuze, and the Playful Fold of the Self," in *Mimesis, Play, and the Self*, ed. Ronald Bogue and Mihai Spariosu (Albany: State University of New York Press, 1994).

28. The slippery term "aestheticism" must be used with care. Thus, for example, René Wellek notes that the tendency to associate Croce with aestheticism is misguided; in abolishing "the distinction between art and any act of intuition," Croce was in fact a major source of the revolt against "aesthetics" in literary studies. See Wellek's *The Attack on Literature and Other Essays* (Chapel Hill: University of North Carolina Press, 1982), 101. Though I am using the troublesome term, my emphases here are precisely congruent with Wellek's. Because the aesthetic inflates, "aesthetics" is not simply a delimited branch of philosophy or a special concern of literary critics.

as much as for Nietzsche, there is no "true world" that we can copy or represent, nor are there stable suprahistorical values that tell us what to do. The coming to be of a world rests on the capacity of human beings to say "thus I would have the world be"—and to act accordingly. The world at every moment results from the interaction of all our efforts to impose our own form, interpretation, or truth.

To be sure, Nietzsche, in some of his moods, accented the special role of the most creative individuals, while Croce emphasized the mundane process of interaction itself, leaving us with a kind of liberal pluralism and humility.[29] The outcome of our interaction always transcends the intention of any one actor; ongoing history-making is a collaboration. Yet even this difference is less important than it seems because, as noted in the last chapter, Nietzsche recognized that the present world had resulted from mechanisms that were all too egalitarian.

For Croce, human response is "moral" insofar as it stems from "care" for what the world becomes. Nietzsche, in contrast, valued response that is "beyond good and evil," no longer subject to the categories of our particular morality, which he found life-debasing. But up to a point even this difference is only one of terminology and accent. The ethical impulse that Croce emphasized aims to free up human creativity—and thus converges with the Nietzschean imperative of life enhancement. Crocean freedom is the freedom to respond creatively; Nietzschean power is the capacity to shape creatively. Nietzsche accented our continual striving for ever more power as we seek to impose our own interpretations on the world.[30] Croce accented our continual striving for ever more freedom by overcoming obstacles to our creativity; freeing up creativity is the reverse side of the ongoing growth of freedom.

Still, in the final analysis, Croce's emphasis on history as thought and action contrasts sharply with Nietzsche's emphasis on fictions and quest for innocence. In fact, each set of responses makes clearer the basis of the other.

Knowing the World as History

As we have seen, Nietzsche seemed first to suggest that because the world is only empty becoming, it is radically open to whatever form human beings impose on it. Our particular world rests on a dominant understanding of the past that is simply the particular fiction, or "lie," that has resulted so far from

29. See, for example, Friedrich Nietzsche, *The Will to Power,* trans. Walter Kaufmann and R. J. Hollingdale, ed. Walter Kaufmann (New York: Vintage, 1968), 277 (no. 513), for Nietzsche's insistence that "the powerful" create the laws and categories. For Croce's repeated emphasis on world-historical modesty, see "Frammenti di etica," 151–153; *Carattere,* 209–210; and *Discorsi di varia filosofia,* 1:297 (1942). See also Roberts, *Benedetto Croce,* pp. 216–220, on the humility and pluralism that informed Croce's recasting of liberalism.

30. Nietzsche, *Will to Power,* 267 (no. 481), 367 (no. 689).

generally hidden human purposes. Even as he accented the scope for radical "genealogical" inquiry, Nietzsche suggested that in writing my particular history I am simply imposing my particular fiction, serving my wider effort to make possible a particular mode of life.

Questions about detachment and objectivity have bedeviled historians off and on for more than a century, but the wider eclipse of metaphysics has recently deepened their bite. As noted above, Croce was one of the first to confront this set of issues in a radically antipositivist way. Indeed, his approach was so radical that he seemed extreme and threatening to some contemporaries.[31]

Although accents and terminology have differed, Croce was squarely on the side of those from Nietzsche to Derrida who have sought to conceive an alternative to the long-standing assumption that language represents an independently existing reality. Indeed, his starting point was more explicitly aestheticist than Nietzsche's. In his *Aesthetic* (1902), the book that made him famous, Croce adapted insights from Vico and German romanticism to posit a radically antipositivist view of the world, based on imaginative language as the cutting edge of the growing spirit. Worlds come to be in language, which is inherently poetic and creative.[32] And for Croce, as much as for Nietzsche, historical questioning is a moment in a process of world-making that stems ultimately from the will of individuals to make the world a certain way.

In reacting against positivism, Croce was as eager as Nietzsche to jettison the ideal of a determinate historical truth to a fixed past. There is no historical "thing-in-itself," he insisted, no past "as it actually happened" that might be discovered and rendered once and for all.[33] What the past was, and is, is not fixed or given, but, just as for Nietzsche, endlessly open and thus endlessly slipping, shifting. What it was depends on what it becomes, and what it has become so far is what it is for us. In that sense, there is no "past" but only the history that is generated as we make some present sense of the documents available to us at present—and of the present resultant of all previous attempts to forge some particular understanding. As Croce put it in 1939, we "interrogate the past in order to make of it the basis for present action, and the past that was thought in this way was never finished and stable, but always in movement and change, and it is inseparable from our present, which, too, is restless

31. See, for example, A. F. Pollard, "An Apology for Historical Research," *History* 7 (October 1922): 161–177, which seeks to defend empirical historiography against the explicitly Crocean position of Ernest Barker in "History and Philosophy," *History* 7 (July 1922): 81–91. Troubled by the apparent extravagance of Croce's formulations, Pollard misconstrued Croce's thrust, which was not to undercut the autonomy of history, as Pollard worried, but to make new sense of it.

32. Croce sought to be provocative, insisting, for example, that two identical words do not exist, that each word is a work of art, that "language is perpetual creation." See Croce, *Estetica*, 16–17, 60, 164.

33. Benedetto Croce, "Contributo alla critica di me stesso," in *Etica e politica*, 350; Croce, *Teoria e storia della storiografia*, 43–48; and *La storia come pensiero e come azione*, 122.

and does not subside in achieving solutions but rather indefatigably poses new problems that will give rise to new solutions."[34]

Such emphases seem at first to undermine any notion that historical questioning can, or needs to, get at truth. But though historical knowing for Croce can only be partial, interested, and provisional, he still insisted that what results from genuine historical inquiry is a particular truth, as opposed to some imaginative or useful fiction. Those who emphasized fiction, even "metaphor," remained under the shadow of metaphysics, with its image of representing a world already there. They were not radical enough to see what "truth" might mean in a postmetaphysical mode. But how could historical knowledge be possible when the world to be known is forever growing out from under us and when we ourselves, as would-be historical knowers, are historically specific and finite?

Croce made such a splash in Italy during the first decade of the century because he appealed to young, avant-garde intellectuals who, like their contemporaries elsewhere, were discovering Nietzsche at the same time. Croce and Nietzsche seemed to point in the same direction, away from positivist determinism and toward the scope for human beings, as free and creative "artists," to shape the world anew. At first, then, these young intellectuals thought they could have Croce *and* Nietzsche. But by 1910 they had grown disillusioned with Croce, who seemed to take back with the second hand what he had given with the first. As he worked beyond the *Aesthetic* to his more fully developed *Logic* and *Philosophy of the Practical* of 1908, Croce began insisting on the terms of his moderate alternative, partly to head off what he felt was the tendency toward irrational excess in the responses of his erstwhile followers. Rather than conceive life, the self, or the world as "literature," radically open to human aesthetic will, Croce was a spoilsport who imposed a kind of mundane discipline, on two levels.

First, we must respond to the particular world that has resulted from history so far, so that whatever we do, if it is to become real at all, will grow in a continuous way on what has already resulted. In a sense, we do remake the world by means of creative language, but in Croce's hands the scope for inventing new worlds by redescribing the past proved not to have all the heady consequences it first seemed to. We are not able to reinvent the world afresh simply by redescribing the old one, or by inventing a new language; we cannot leap out of our particular history or tradition. A particular world has resulted—and continually results—from the interaction of the creative responses of each of us. And we can only go on doing what we have always done, responding to that particular world, thereby adding to a continuous history, or coming to be.

34. Croce, *Carattere*, 100; see also p. 213, as well as Croce, *Logica*, 171–172; and Croce, *Teoria e storia della storiografia*, 306–307. Compare the similarly antipositivistic argument of Peter Munz in *The Shapes of Time: A New Look at the Philosophy of History* (Middletown, Conn.: Wesleyan University Press, 1977), 204–205, 220–221, 226, 230–231.

So though we are always engaged in inventing a new language, it is a mundane and collective process, bound up with our response to the world that has resulted from the interaction of earlier responses. We may be as willful, as radical, as we like—and then see what happens.

Second, because we must respond to a world with a particular shape, we are well advised to know that world in a cognitive way, by using our heads, and this necessarily requires disciplined—though hardly disinterested—historical inquiry. Such knowing enhances our chance to connect with the world, so that we might help mold the next moment.

Although there is an irreducible aesthetic or creative element in our initial response to the world, Croce insisted that a distinguishable cognitive faculty comes into play when we seek to understand, which entails knowing the world as history. We misconstrue our cultural possibilities if, with our new sense that language is creative, we fail to grasp the ongoing point of that distinction. In one sense, Croce simply took for granted Vico's principle that we can know what we have made—the human world as opposed to nature, which only God can genuinely know. Knowing the world as history is one of the attributes of the spirit, one of the things human beings do, and "truth" is simply what happens when we approach the world in a certain way. For Croce, much as for Heidegger and Gadamer a bit later, human beings are open to the happening of truth. Indeed, human being must be understood as *the* opening for the happening of truth.

But knowing is only one of the things we do, and Croce was not claiming that any single work of history provides unvarnished truth or knowledge. Historical inquirers are themselves finite, individuated historical actors, with particular concerns and commitments; they operate in the practical as well as in the cognitive mode when they produce their histories, which are always partial and "interested." So how do we know if any particular historical account is true or not? Indeed, why should we seek truth in the first place, when we might seek power or some practical advantage? At issue is how the act of knowing and the capacity for truth relate to the practical side of the human spirit—and through it to the world of action.

Just as the knowing or theoretical side of what human beings do can be divided, in a rough-and-ready way, between the aesthetic and the cognitive, the practical side can be divided into the ethical and the useful. For Croce these are the four things human beings do, the four attributes of the spirit, and each of them is at work in historiography. Croce initially emphasized the distinction among these four categories, partly in opposition to utilitarianism, Marxism, and pragmatism, with their various reductionist tendencies. But the four categories were related as well, and Croce tried out various ways of conveying that relationship without ever finding a completely satisfactory solution. In his earlier works, he posited a circular relationship, but he gradually began featuring interconnections among the four categories, even assigning privilege to the ethical by the 1920s.[35] This made it clearer that the scope for knowing and truth is bound up with action, our mode of practical involvement with the world. But from the start, Croce had emphasized that practical considerations—both the useful and the ethical—are at work in the construction of any historical account.

Seeking to influence the culture's self-understanding, historians order their material in the way that makes their argument as convincing as possible. More generally, a desire to make the story interesting, or aesthetically pleasing, or morally edifying, or readily publishable, may affect the final form of the historical account. In each such case, the component of the practical that seeks "utility" has been at work. Partly because of such considerations, then, any actual work of history will be not pure historical truth but a messy mixture. Indeed, Croce could have accepted much of White's argument that the various ways of forming a coherent, convincing story from a given set of facts reflect characteristic rhetorical strategies that stem, in part, from the will of the inquirer.[36] But even though any actual history will have practical elements, it will also, if it is genuine history, contain a component of truth, and thus there are cognitive criteria for distinguishing among historical accounts.

The scope for truth, too, is bound up with the practical—its ethical side, our care for what the world becomes. Croce insisted that genuine historical inquiry, as opposed to a bloodless antiquarianism, is not disinterested but stems from some contemporary concern. Indeed, "all history is contemporary history," because it is some such concern that leads the present inquirer to pose some particular historical question and thereby to forge some particular connection with what went before.[37]

In explicit contrast to Ranke, who seemed engaged, as Croce put it, in the fine art of embalming a corpse, Croce understood the focus of history to be not some past moment apprehended for its own sake, then fixed once and for all, but some process, one of the endless ways the present has resulted from the past. Each of the endless succession of present moments is a new vantage point from which the historical inquirer illuminates, even constitutes, one of the infinite array of such processes.[38] So rather than render the past "thing in itself," each historical inquiry participates with others in the ongoing happening or coming to be of some particular historical understanding. Our collective act of establishing some particular understanding is itself part of the ongoing process; the historical account is part of the history it studies.

35. See, for example, Croce, *Teoria e storia della storiografia*, 311; Croce, *Carattere*, 114–116, 223–225; and Croce, *Filosofia e storiografia*, 169–170 (1947), for the notion that historical inquiry is moral when it is genuinely open to truth.

36. See especially Croce, *Teoria e storia della storiografia*, 29–30.

37. See ibid., 4–7, 10–12, 16, 99–106, for the overall argument. See also Croce, *Cultura e vita morale*, 265 (1924); and Croce, *La storia come pensiero e come azione*, 11–12.

38. For Croce's critique of Ranke, see *La storia come pensiero e come azione*, 65–67, 73–88. See also Croce, *Teoria e storia della storiografia*, 304–305.

Whereas for Hegel we discover the privileged content of history after making it, for Croce there is no a priori form to history determining a privileged content. But the reaction against Hegel does not undermine any scope for differentiation and articulation, so that everything in history is simply valuable "for its own sake." A particular, unstable hierarchy of significance endlessly results as we ask the particular historical questions we do, based on our contemporary concerns, and as we interact in an effort to persuade others of our answers. At every moment we decide what is privileged anew.

Because historical inquiry is immersed in an endless process, Croce was the first to admit that historical knowledge lacks what long had seemed the defining attributes of historical truth. But for two crucial reasons, this need not yield the giddy playfulness or the anxious vertigo it might initially seem to. The first reason concerns our practical need for truth to make our way in the world. The second concerns the process of interaction, or unacknowledged collaboration, from which truth results.

Croce sought explicitly to turn the tables on pragmatism by insisting that truth is possible precisely because of the practical stakes of our inquiries.[39] In asking historical questions, we try to illuminate the present in its historical genesis, because we are caught up in practical situations in which we want to act effectively. We cannot say just anything as we construct our historical account, because our present has resulted from a past that has been a particular way and not some other way. Insofar as we genuinely seek to learn, we open ourselves to truth. The outcome, however, can only be a partial, provisional truth, not the definitive truth we long thought we needed—and thought we got by copying a stable, finished past.

Although Nietzsche himself did not develop them, his practice as a genealogical historian offered scope for the distinctions that Croce took care to specify. Nietzsche's interpretation of the emergence of our Judeo-Christian moral tradition was passionate and deeply interested, intended to illuminate aspects of present experience in order to foster a different mode of life. But in delving into that history, Nietzsche sought genuinely to learn something about the bizarre course of things that had resulted in this actual present, with its particular hang-ups and neuroses. He proved a powerful historian precisely because his present purposes demanded *not* an utterly fanciful and capricious creation but his particular true reading of the coming to be of our particular world.

When Croce addressed the relationship between our ethical capacity and historical inquiry, his first concern was to head off the sort of moralism that obstructs learning and truth. Thus he distinguished genuine history from moralistic history, or "oratory," intended to exemplify prior moral principles or to support a prior political stance. At the same time, Croce insisted that historical

39. Croce, *Carattere*, 176. See also Roberts, *Benedetto Croce*, 153–154.

understanding is useful only in a preliminary way: it prepares action but cannot determine it—cannot specify a particular course of action. In this sense, the practical and the ethical side of the practical remain autonomous. But Croce also recognized that it is ultimately the ethical dimension of human being that leads us to relate to the world in such a way that truth becomes possible. Insofar as, to adapt Heidegger's category, we care about the world, we seek genuinely to learn about it so that we can better affect what it becomes.[40] It is this openness in inquiry that yields truth as opposed to entertainment or propaganda, willful fantasy or edifying fiction. Genuine historical inquiry serves the happening of truth because it is itself a moral act.

Any such premium on truth may appear prim and old-fashioned, even limiting and authoritarian, when compared to the recent, loosely Nietzschean emphasis on fiction and metaphor, which seems to invite openness and creativity. But Croce came back to the question of truth, and the distinction between historical knowing and fiction, partly because he had sidestepped the dualism of language and reality that had led us to posit "metaphor" in the first place. From a Crocean perspective, those playing up metaphor have not fully escaped the metaphysical notion of an independent, extralinguistic reality; language seems ever more fundamentally metaphorical as its capacity to mirror or represent that reality directly becomes increasingly doubtful. Croce's postmetaphysical conception has no place even for the shadow of that independent world; no hidden residue of a thing-in-itself remains. So language for Croce is not metaphorical, standing in indirect relationship with an independent reality, but more radically and fundamentally creative. And much of his effort was to show how that creativity meshes with the scope for truth in a postmetaphysical world.

Croce understood that though truth remains possible, we may sometimes prefer edification, for example, even in our approach to the stuff of history. As noted above, an array of practical interests, other than the need for truth, may inform any particular historical account. However, historical understanding in the overall culture stems not simply from the efforts of isolated individual inquirers but from a process of interaction. Individual historians may be as willfully creative as they choose, but their impact will depend on the capacity of their work to persuade others, who are seeking to make sense of some actual situation. At every moment, the resultant of the totality of historical questioning is an unstable composite, inviting further questioning and revision. Truth happens as a continuous process through the unacknowledged collaboration of the universe of historical inquirers.

40. Croce, *Teoria e storia della storiografia*, 311; Croce, *Filosofia e storiografia*, 169–170 (1947); and Croce, *Carattere*, 223–225. See also Roberts, *Benedetto Croce*, 283–285, on the complex relationship between ethical concerns and the scope for truth. Croce recognized that an element of "oratory," even political polemic, will inform every historical account; see, for example, Benedetto Croce, *Indagini su Hegel e schiarimenti filosofici* (Bari: Laterza, 1967), 125 (1949). Much of Croce's own historical writing betrays such an oratorical element.

In positing a middle ground, Croce was seeking to show that the departure from metaphysics did not have to yield the relativism that threatened to undermine any confidence in historical truth. Relativism afflicts us, Croce insisted, only if we assume our aim is to apprehend a stable thing-in-itself back there in the past, then find that we never manage to fix things once and for all.[41] As we come to understand historical truth as particular and provisional, happening through an ongoing interaction among historical accounts, the conditions for relativism simply dissolve.

However, questions remain about the quality of the process of interaction through which historical truth *may* happen. Before addressing those questions, we must probe more deeply Croce's account of the world of action, especially his way of conceiving action as history-making. It is on that level that his divergence from Nietzsche is most dramatic.

Experiencing Action as History

We have seen that Croce insisted on the endless interaction of the theoretical and practical sides of what we do, so the scope for knowing and truth is bound up with practice, the world of action. Indeed, though we continue to know the world afresh, the whole movement of the spirit is toward action. But in considering practice, Croce took another step, giving a particular spin to his understanding of what we do. What happens through our actions is the endless remaking of the world in history. Purely contemplative thinking or understanding, even if possible, would be evanescent, unreal, because it would not enter history, contributing to that ongoing remaking. In a Crocean mode, then, we experience what we do as shaping the world for keeps. Thus Croce's emphasis on "the immortality of the act," the cumulative weight of our actions in the endless coming to be of the world.[42]

Nietzsche and Croce started with a comparably radical way of embedding human being in the endless history through which the world keeps becoming some particular way. For each, our present is nothing but the resultant of the whole past, and what we do shapes the future, conditioning reality, as Nietzsche put it, for all eternity.[43] Moreover, each denied that we might attune ourselves to some higher, extrahistorical dimension and thereby feel out of phase with our merely historical world, even though history depends on mechanisms that may seem cruel and that may, on occasion, entail a feeling of futility for the

---

41. Croce, "Contributo," 350; Croce, *Teoria e storia della storiografia*, 43–48; and Croce, *La storia come pensiero e come azione*, 122. See also Roberts, *Benedetto Croce*, 150–151.

42. Croce's emphasis on the immortality of the act and its corollary, the premium on individual vocation, is most striking in his "Frammenti di etica"; see esp. pp. 22–23, 25, 99–101, 123. See also Roberts, *Benedetto Croce*, 174–182.

43. Joan Stambaugh, *Nietzsche's Thought of Eternal Return* (Baltimore: Johns Hopkins University Press, 1972), 59.

individual. Indeed, each posited a kind of identification with the world as history and pointed toward a mode of affirmation, as opposed to alienation and the "absurd" sense of not belonging in this apparently cruel and futile world. Although we are "merely" historical creatures, we need not experience ourselves as inadequate or incomplete. In meshing with the world as history, we are congruent with all there is.

For both Nietzsche and Croce, this congruence undermines any basis for making moral judgments about anything that has happened historically. We come to feel instead the necessity of all there has been for there to be this moment, which we cannot coherently deny, for to do so would mean denying ourselves and thus the very possibility of such negation. Croce insisted that even our negative judgments presuppose the resultant of history so far, even as they help to change it.[44] Nietzsche made much the same point as he deplored the claim "to judge history, to divest it of its fatality, to discover responsibility behind it, guilty men in it." Seeking to uncover the sources of this attitude, he suggested that losers who could not bear their own lives needed "a theory through which they can shift the responsibility for their existence, for their being thus and thus, on to some sort of scapegoat." This was a mode of ordering characteristic of dissatisfied individuals who, as the culture came to experience itself as radically historical, could do no better than to blame history itself for the fact that their historically specific lives had not turned out well.[45]

But Nietzsche and Croce were subject to different preoccupations, and their modes of affirmation led to quite different conceptions of the cultural priorities. Indeed, Nietzsche posited eternal recurrence and the innocence of becoming partly to box out the sort of relationship with the world that Croce proposed a few years later. The Nietzschean sense of completeness dissolves the historicist tension that leads to a premium on action informed by historical understanding. History becomes a mere scaffold or foundation for self-justifying individual experience, even self-creation. We experience what we do as innocent play as opposed to weighty, history-making action.

Croce went in the opposite direction, emphasizing both endless openness and the cumulative weight of what we do. A purely historical world entails precisely the endless creativity and novelty that Nietzsche, in his later works, took pains to deny. The world is forever unfinished, and we feel its incompleteness as a call to further creative response in action. So my sense of affirmation means not that I settle for the particular world that has resulted so far but that I feel sufficiently at one with it to care for it, to feel some responsibility for what it will become next.

That sense of responsibility demands ethical response—response that is not merely self-serving—but it also calls my cognitive capacities into operation.

44. Croce, *Carattere*, 100–101, 208–209.
45. Nietzsche, *Will to Power*, 400–401 (no. 765).

Croce was determined to specify a measure of rationality, a cognitive moment in action, partly in response to the increasing emphasis on will, passion, or myth in the culture of his time. Rather than respond on the basis of moral passion alone, we seek to understand the present moment, through inquiry into its historical genesis, so that we might more effectively act upon it.

The sense of responsibility that informs action as history-making contrasts directly with the innocence that Nietzsche sought to imagine. And when compared with Nietzsche's radical effort to work "beyond good and evil," Croce's emphasis on ethical response, like his emphasis on truth, appears safe and conventional at first. But Croce's historicist reduction had radically transformed the ethical category. Ethical response does not involve the application of transcendent, suprahistorical values; it is simply one of the defining attributes of human being. As individuated embodiments of the spirit, we all establish right, good, justice in the particular situations we face, thereby adding to what "justice" has come to encompass so far. Such response is "ethical" precisely insofar as it results from our care for the world, our sense of responsibility for it—insofar as we want what we do to last, affecting what the world becomes.

But though Croce's way of invoking the ethical was postmetaphysical and historicist, Nietzsche still had reason to head off any such conception. The mode of eternal recurrence dissipates any experience of the world as incomplete and inadequate and the consequent sense of responsibility. The world at every moment is complete, perfect; there is nothing else that needs to be done. Even insofar as my actions will change the actual, I do not act in order to change it. As Crocean weight disappears from action, so does the shadow of judgment and guilt. Thus the mature Nietzsche could imagine action as innocent play.

Croce could have said, with Nietzsche, that "my consolation is that everything that has been is eternal."[46] But the sense for Croce was profoundly different. In a world without transcendence, I take comfort that what I do lives on after me, helping to make reality a particular way at all subsequent moments, forever. Thus what ultimately matters, what is ultimately real, is what I do, not my subjective experience, not what I go through as I decide what to do. The meaning of what I do is bound up with the larger, ongoing coming to be of this particular world.

Partly because he deemphasized sheer individual experience in this way, Croce drew fire from Italian existentialists like Nicola Abbagnano, who accused him of downplaying the subjectivity of the person, even of submerging the living, suffering individual into a blandly benign process.[47] But Croce repeatedly

46. Ibid., 548 (no. 1065).
47. See, for example, Nicola Abbagnano, *Critical Existentialism*, trans. Nino Langiulli (Garden City, N.Y.: Doubleday, Anchor, 1969), 1–18. See also Antonio Santucci, *Esistenzialismo e filosofia italiana* (Bologna: Il Mulino, 1959), 17–23, 68–77, 160–227, on Abbagnano and the existentialist critique of Croce.

denied the charge of insipid optimism; for the individual, being caught up in the happening of a particular history was closer to tragedy than to idyll.[48] Although he understood that responsibility entails anxiety for the individual, Croce saw no point in dwelling on that anxiety, and he denied that anxious personal experience was somehow privileged or ultimate. Such accents invited morbid self-preoccupation *as opposed to* a premium on responsible, history-making action. But even so, Croce was as forceful as Nietzsche or the later existentialists in probing the implications of the loss of transcendence for individual experience.

In Croce's world, desire for the immortality that only history can offer helps structure our lives. We want to affect what the world becomes, and we fear the sense of futility we feel when our actions fail to connect with the growing world. So we seek a vocation that enables us to focus our efforts and maximize our chance to respond effectively.[49] Moreover, whereas Nietzsche sought to get out from under priests, theologians, the long shadow that Christianity still cast across the world, Croce sought explicitly to reformulate Christian categories as he accented human responsibility for the ongoing growth of the world in history. Indeed, his absolute historicism was very nearly a new "religion of history," based on this recasting not only of immortality but also of providence, grace, faith, prayer, and even God for a horizontal, postmetaphysical world.

"Grace," for Croce, is the individual's participation in the overall power of the spirit; "providence" fits some particular action to the historically specific moment, making that action effective.[50] The individual may even "pray" for the grace necessary to act effectively and thereby mesh with history. And it is "faith in history," faith that what we do will interact with the contributions of others to have the desired impact on the future, that most fundamentally surrounds Crocean action.[51] In entrusting what we do to history, we hope that those who come after will use our legacies well, just as we feel under obligation to use well what the past has bequeathed to us.

Again, however, it is crucial that our cognitive capacities come into operation, complementing these religious impulses. Even my choice of an overall vocation depends partly on my historical grasp of the world in which I find myself. As was true of the generation of 1914 in Robert Wohl's account, inadequate historical understanding impedes the connection between individual and present and breeds a feeling of futility.[52]

If we feel ourselves responsible, are we then subject to judgment in Croce's

48. Croce, *Carattere*, 119.
49. Croce, "Frammenti di etica," 99–101, 123; Benedetto Croce, *Conversazioni critiche*, ser. 4 (Bari: Laterza, 1951), 201–202 (1923).
50. Croce, "Frammenti di etica," 93–94. See also Benedetto Croce, *History of the Kingdom of Naples*, trans. Frances Frenaye (Chicago: University of Chicago Press, 1970; orig. Italian ed. 1925), 248; and Benedetto Croce, *Terze pagine sparse*, 2 vols. (Bari: Laterza, 1955), 1:97–98; as well as Roberts, *Benedetto Croce*, 179–181.
51. Croce, "Frammenti di etica," 106; Croce, *Filosofia della pratica*, 173–174; Croce, *Teoria e storia della storiografia*, 325–327. See also Roberts, *Benedetto Croce*, 180–182, 190–198.
52. See above, chap. 3, p. 56.

religion of history—along the lines Nietzsche feared? Even though he accented ethical responsibility in a way Nietzsche did not, for Croce, too, there is an important sense in which what we do is innocent. Insofar as my action is an ethical response to the world, it is not subject to second-guessing according to some external, transcendent standard, for there is nothing but me at this moment to establish the moral response to this particular situation.[53] This is true whatever becomes of my response, whatever the world makes of it. Thus Croce's insistence that past actions simply are not subject to moral judgment.

Our actions are, however, subject to what Croce called historical judgment, and that would be sufficient to worry Nietzsche; even for Croce it adds a layer of anxiety in each of us as we act. Historical judgment seeks to determine what some action was—whether it was moral or not—and how it entered history.[54] Insofar as my action stemmed from laziness, or a desire for edification, or a selfish concern with my own immediate advantage, it was not ethical. Such amoral utility may even have compromised my effort genuinely to inquire, seeking to learn; the resulting deficiencies in my understanding may have compromised the effectiveness of my action, even rendered it futile. So the historian who refuses risk, settles for propaganda, or curries the favor of reviewers, invites later condemnation. Even if my action is a pure, authentic existentialist gesture, it can be condemned insofar as I failed to prepare it through historical inquiry.

For Croce, then, there is no transcendent or last judgment, but my acts and even my vocation itself are endlessly subjected to the provisional judgment of history, which is all there is to determine the meaning of what I have done. In one sense, history is the harshest of judges, because it lacks the capacity to forgive or absolve. At the same time, however, the meaning of what I have done, its place in reality, can always be made different—by means of subsequent action, even by others after my death.

Nietzsche was actively seeking to avoid even such a horizontal mode of judgment, which he felt betrayed the legacy of Christian categories. Croce, however, did not deny that Christian categories were still at work in his way of conceiving judgment, responsibility, and the scope for creative ethical response in action. Indeed, he implicitly admitted what Nietzsche charged: It was through Christianity that we came to have this sense of creativity and responsibility; the notion of creative moral spirit derives precisely from the idea of God and the world as created by God.[55] And our sense of being subjected to judgment for how we stand, or act, vis-à-vis the whole, now become history, inevitably follows.

In adapting Christian categories, Croce was seeking to enhance the

53. See especially Croce, *Carattere*, 100–101, 208–209.
54. Croce, *Filosofia della pratica*, 60–64; Croce, *Logica*, 175–177; Croce, *Teoria e storia della storiografia*, 77–80.
55. Friedrich Nietzsche, *The Gay Science*, trans. Walter Kaufmann (New York: Vintage, 1974), 167–169; Nietzsche, *Will to Power*, 546–547 (no. 1062).

plausibility of his historicist way of conceiving individual experience in a world that was, just as Nietzsche had assumed, fundamentally post-Christian but that, nonetheless, could not deny the particular—Christian—way it had been. Though we have come to recognize its contingency, and though we might now wish to reject parts of it, Christianity, too, is immortal. And thus Croce's claim, in a controversial article of 1942, that "we cannot but call ourselves Christians" (*non possiamo non dirci "cristiani"*).[56]

Is Nietzsche, then, the more innovative and postmodern of the two thinkers? It may seem so at first, because Croce invoked religious categories like grace and providence that Nietzsche was willing to do without. But it was Nietzsche who longed for, and posited, redemption, a restoration of innocence. Croce did not feel the same need for redemption because he was less traumatized by the religious categories centering around sin and judgment. Each thinker was a pioneer in the post-Christian confrontation with the enduring legacy of Christianity in our tradition, and neither need be taken as privileged or more advanced.

Commitment and Collaboration, Humility and Faith

If they are to become real and enter history, our actions interact with others, and none of us can foresee the outcome, which always transcends the intention of any one actor. So for Croce, we operate in a dual mode, understanding that ongoing growth rests on the creative responses of individuals like us but also that no individual, even the "greatest," is sufficient. We are all collaborators in the endless happening of our particular world in history. Thus Croce sometimes found it necessary to insist that the maker of the world is ultimately the whole spirit—that the spirit is the only agent.[57] But this does not mean we individual actors are but shadowy manifestations of spirit, as critics have long charged.[58] It is simply to say that the individual is bound up with the growing whole—and thus is inconceivable in isolation.

This line of thinking was the basis of Croce's recasting of liberalism during the 1920s. At any one moment, each individual embodies part of the potential of the world, so the political system must invite the committed responses of everyone to the present situation. Those political commitments will differ, and the differences are irreducible. Croce argued in 1923, for example, that each of us will respond to a given situation differently, according to our tempera-

56. Benedetto Croce, "Perché non possiamo non dirci 'cristiani,' " in *Discorsi di varia filosofia*, 1:11–23 (1942). See also Roberts, *Benedetto Croce*, 205–206.

57. Croce, *Filosofia e storiografia*, 144 (1946). See also Roberts, *Benedetto Croce*, 406, n. 3, on the use that has been made of this passage.

58. The distinguished student of historicism Pietro Rossi has made this charge repeatedly. See, for example, his "Max Weber and Benedetto Croce," trans. Keith Tribe, in *Max Weber and His Contemporaries,* ed. Wolfgang J. Mommsen and Jürgen Osterhammel (London: Allen and Unwin, 1987), 459–464.

ment, our hopes and fears, the situation we feel within us, the commitments to which we feel tied, the faith we have in certain men and certain things.[59] Thus in our political interaction—and ultimately in all interaction—everybody counts, nobody is to be explained away. Our sense of being finite participants in a history-making process of interaction engenders the broadly liberal humility, pluralism, and tolerance that balances our individual commitments.

We feel kinship and collaboration not only with our contemporaries but also with all those who came before us, those whose responses have resulted in our world, the world entrusted to us. Croce made the point in a striking passage in 1930.

> Whoever opens his heart to the historical sensibility is no longer alone, but united with the life of the universe, brother and son and comrade of the spirits that formerly labored upon the earth and that live in the work that they completed, apostles and martyrs, ingenious creators of beauty and truth, decent and humble people who spread the balm of goodness and preserved human kindness; and to all of them he makes entreaty, and from them he derives support in his efforts and labors, and on their lap he aspires to rest, pouring his labor into theirs.[60]

Although some individuals have a disproportionate influence in certain spheres, for Croce, we are *all* historical actors, making some contribution to the ongoing growth of the world. And we understand that our world is the resultant of nothing but the sum of the actions of all those who came before us, that we have fallen heir to their collective legacy. This sense of kinship stimulates each of us to do our part, to pick up and transform, through our own present action, the world that they bequeathed to us. Insofar as we care, we feel ourselves under obligation to use their legacy well.

But we feel the anxiety of responsibility as we decide how to respond to that legacy and pass it on, transformed, to those who will follow. Moreover, even insofar as we have sought to maximize the effectiveness of our actions by understanding the present historically, we cannot know what will happen to what we do. So we also feel anxiety about how our response will enter history, whether the future will use it well. In our darker moments, our efforts seem futile and our commitment wavers. But the sense of kinship and ongoing collaboration helps nurture the faith that sustains us as we go on doing what we have always done, now with a different understanding of what is happening as we do so. There is scope for faith in nothing but history itself. I commit myself and act because I have faith that what I do will join with what you do to create a next moment that will respond, in ways neither of us can foresee, to the limitations of this moment and thereby yield a richer next moment.

This way of combining a sense of slippage and risk with a faith that, as we

59. Croce, *Cultura e vita morale*, 250.
60. Croce, *Ultimi saggi*, 263–264 (1930).

entrust our acts to the future, we have not labored in vain is the core of the Cro-cean sensibility. And Croce experienced it in a deeply personal way. In con-cluding his *Philosophy of the Practical* in 1908, he noted explicitly that because there can be no definitive philosophy, the philosopher labors knowing that his work will promptly be superseded. But faith in history overcomes the resulting feeling of futility: "Every philosopher, at the end of his research, discerns the first uncertain lines of a new philosophy—that he, or someone else, will pursue. With this modesty—which stems from the nature of things, not from my per-sonal sentiment, and which is also faith in not having thought in vain—I end my work, offering it to the well disposed as an instrument of labor."[61] Although he was combative and sometimes arrogant in interacting with his cultural oppo-nents, Croce emphasized his own historical specificity and finitude throughout his career.[62]

This reflexive self-consciousness might have led Croce to one of the playful extremes that have become prominent within the postmetaphysical cultural uni-verse. But he posited action as history-making partly to head off such extremes. So rather than accent slippage and the scope for self-deconstruction or inno-cent play, Croce featured the cumulative weight of what we do, the responsible labor that serves ongoing world building. As merely human constructions, our works are always finite, incomplete, readily deconstructible, but they partici-pate in the continuing coming to be of our particular world. Thus Croce under-stood his own work as a contribution to that ongoing construction, an invitation to question, to labor further.

Each side of the Crocean coin was essential for the cultural middle ground he was seeking. Because the world is *only* a history, what I say is not definitive; but *as* a history, the world is sufficiently coherent to invite ongoing questioning and work. Each of us is only a collaborator, but it is crucial that there is scope for collaboration and that the world is endlessly remade through the interac-tion of all we do.

Still, Croce's emphasis on the history-making process of interaction raises questions about the quality of that process, the scope for distortion that it might entail. Croce considered the possibility of such distortion, but he concentrated on the self-serving "utility" in the individual's response to the world. In dis-tinguishing the two sides of the practical spirit, he showed that the useful may interfere with the ethical, thus compromising my willingness to learn. Egotis-tical interest, including mere laziness, may lead me to cling to the familiar or to my own prejudices.

But Croce had little to say about societal or contextual forms of distortion. Thus, during the early 1940s, when the opportunity to begin devising a post-

61. Croce, *Filosofia della pratica*, 406. See also Croce, *Logica*, 187–189; and Roberts, *Benedetto Croce*, 98, 181.
62. See, for example, Croce, *Cultura e vita morale*, 205–209 (1916).

Fascist politics engendered an especially rich discussion in Italy, he was widely criticized for ignoring the distorting impact of socioeconomic inequality and injustice.[63] His insistence on the sense in which everyone is free—and is thus to be taken seriously—seemed at once abstract and complacent. In fact, Croce had an important point to make, but the terms of debate in the highly charged atmosphere of the 1940s led him to turn from certain questions that were becoming ever more intrusive with the emergence of modern mass politics. Yet these were questions that had to be addressed if he was to make his point effectively.

Although he accented the freedom of all individuals and the worthiness of all political commitments, Croce sometimes stuck in qualifiers that suggested the possibility of qualitative differentiation: *if* you act with purity and humility of heart, he said, *if* you are honest; *if* you act with a pure mind, in obedience to an inner command.[64] But this was to leave an opening for—to take the most obvious example—the Marxist concept of ideology, as one account of the impurity in certain political commitments. Croce failed to push on to think more deeply about commitment, interaction, and distortion because in the climate of recrimination in Italy after Fascism, variations on such Marxist categories were being widely used to dismiss those with opposing views. Troubled by the facile use of the ideology concept, Croce simply reaffirmed his long-standing neoliberalism, emphasizing the freedom of individuals and showing how commitment can mesh with humility in our broadly political interaction.[65] But more had to be said about distortion and about what it means to take our opponents seriously. How can we remain humble if we believe we have identified a systematic source of impurity in the commitments of our opponents— a source they themselves do not recognize?

Still, though it was seriously incomplete, Croce's historicist conception had significant implications for the process of interaction. He did not deny that injustices and inequalities were at work in contemporary political interaction. He had long emphasized that there are obstacles to human freedom and that overcoming those obstacles is an imperative—indeed, the central ethical imperative. But the climate of the 1940s, especially, led him to accent the collaborative nature of that process and the humility that ought to surround our individual contributions to it. In the modern political world it becomes ever more tempting to explain away the political commitments of those with whom we disagree—by reducing them to economic interests, for example, or by

63. See especially Guido Calogero, *Difesa del liberalsocialismo ed altri saggi*, rev. ed. (Milan: Marzorati, 1972), 34, 78–80, 102–103, 257–261. See also Roberts, *Benedetto Croce*, 224–237.

64. Croce, *Etica e politica*, 191; Croce, *Nuove pagine sparse*, 1:358; Benedetto Croce, *History of Europe in the Nineteenth Century*, trans. Henry Furst (New York: Harcourt, Brace and World, 1963; orig. Italian ed. 1932), 362.

65. See Benedetto Croce, *Scritti e discorsi politici (1943–1947)*, 2 vols. (Bari: Laterza, 1973), 2:422–423 (1947), for an indication of his hostility to the ideology concept.

claiming they have been distorted by the surreptitious coercion of the media. Thus it becomes all the more important to recognize that political commitments are irreducibly different. To insist that everybody counts was to deny that some—the rational experts, the enlightened elite—can climb to some purified level, transcending the finitude of everyone else, and specify rules, decision procedures, or what counts as undistorted communication. Though I may find distortion in the views of my adversaries, I take them seriously enough to argue with them, and I have faith in the outcome of our interaction. Indeed, as Croce liked to insist, even if I could be dictator of the world and impose my own view, I would prefer to rely on the outcome of that interaction, the judgment of history.[66]

Rather than posit a goal or image of freedom, justice, and undistorted communication, Croce emphasized that distortions recur endlessly. At each moment we are hammering out what freedom is, and requires, in light of historically specific circumstances. This is the sense in which history for Croce is "the story of liberty."[67] And as the world grows, our capacity for freedom expands—but only by overcoming ever-new obstacles. Present distortion is simply another historically specific challenge. And we act to free up human being at every moment, not in the hope we might at last achieve complete human freedom, but simply to maximize the scope for creative response to the present so that the history can continue.

Even if the earlier criticism of Croce for antiscientific humanism now seems irrelevant, his emphasis on the ongoing construction of the world in history may at first suggest the sort of subjectivist humanism that Heidegger, especially, has taught us to deplore.[68] But Croce's way of relating human being to the whole entailed only a humble humanism—without the hubris that underlies the modern satisfaction with technological manipulation. Nor did Croce posit human being as a self-identical or transcendent subject, somehow in the process of becoming what it is through history. He accented collaboration and humility as he posited action as history-making partly because he, too, was seeking to undercut the hubris of subjectivism.

Although Croce came to be neglected by the 1960s, others echoed his emphasis on action as history-making as they sought to navigate between the old metaphysics and the extremes that became prominent with its eclipse. For example, Václav Havel, specifying the scope for action within Communist

66. Croce, "Frammenti di etica," 151–153; Croce, *Carattere*, 209–210; Croce, *Discorsi di varia filosofia*, 1:297 (1942).

67. See, for example, *La storia come pensiero e come azione*, 225, where Croce links liberty to the human ethical capacity, which seeks to free up the human creativity necessary for the ongoing growth of the world.

68. The tendency to conflate humanism, historicism, and technology is especially clear in Karl Löwith, "Nature, History, and Existentialism" (1952), reprinted in his *Nature, History, and Existentialism and Other Essays in the Philosophy of History*, ed. Arnold Levison (Evanston: Northwestern University Press, 1966), 17–29.

Czechoslovakia by the 1970s, sounded Crocean themes as he sought a middle ground between an outmoded Marxism and a debilitating sense of absurdity. As we find ourselves forced to abandon the possibility of human mastery of history, we may feel that history is impenetrable and that what we do is futile. Havel insisted that, on the contrary, "we all contribute to making [history]. The good and the bad things that we do each day are a constituent part of that history. Life does not take place outside of history, and history is not outside of life." The "hope" that Havel went on to outline is almost precisely Crocean "faith in history."[69] Even as we lose our faith in, or stomach for, the old sort of mastery of history, there is still a weaker, provisional sort of coherence and meaning, and we are all bound up with it. For Havel, as for Croce, what is ultimately at issue is how we experience ourselves in terms of our open-ended history.

Even E. P. Thompson sounded a Crocean note in discussing the ongoing process through which we make meaning of the past. "In the end," Thompson observed, "we also will be dead, and our own lives will lie inert within the finished process, our intentions assimilated within a past event which we never intended. What we may hope is that the men and women of the future will reach back to us, will affirm and renew our meanings, and make our history intelligible within their own present tense. They alone will have the power to select from the many meanings offered by our quarreling present, and to transmute some part of our process into their progress."[70] Thompson, like Croce, was inviting us to understand what we do in terms of an ongoing history; we can only entrust what we do to those who will come after, just as we are responsible for the world entrusted to us.

Croce's Limits

With his emphasis on history as thought and action, Croce warranted a particular range of experiences, but his quest for a moderate position made him quick to preclude more extreme responses to the world as historical that merit a place in a postmetaphysical culture. Plausibly concerned that his contemporaries were too quick to indulge in irrationalism and wallow in *Angst*, he actively downplayed the Nietzschean premium on individual self-creation, and his framework affords little room for the responses of an array of subsequent thinkers, from Albert Camus to Richard Rorty. Because these thinkers paid greater attention to the mere capriciousness of the historical world and to the

69. Václav Havel, *Disturbing the Peace: A Conversation with Karel Hvížďala*, trans. Paul Wilson (New York: Vintage, 1991), 180–181, 189–190. See also Havel's title essay, translated by Paul Wilson, in Václav Havel et al., *The Power of the Powerless* (Armonk, N.Y.: M. E. Sharpe, 1985), 29–30, 41.

70. E. P. Thompson, *The Poverty of Theory and Other Essays* (New York: Monthly Review Press, 1978), 42.

sense of futility or suffocation it may entail for the individual, each suggested, as Croce did not, that individuality or selfhood must be forged in tension with history, even to spite it.[71]

In the same way, Croce actively denied any scope for the religious "open-ness to the mystery" that Heidegger thought we might achieve by attuning our-selves to the sending of the particular world in history, to "coming to be" itself. The only mystery for Croce is the unknown, which is simply what has not yet happened—or simply the future.[72] Openness to the mystery could be nothing more than the faith and commitment necessary to participate as the future comes to be. As we will see in the next chapter, however, Heidegger suggested that we might find new modes of religious experience by relating to the world as historical in a way that eschews the active, history-making orientation char-acteristic of Croce's historicism. From a Heideggerian perspective, Croce was simply overreacting, unnecessarily precluding even a new religiosity as he helped bury the old.

Not only did Croce ponder the place of historical inquiry in a postmeta-physical world but he wrote history himself, in response to the challenges of his own historically specific context. Most notable are the four full-scale works he published between 1925 and 1932, starting with the *History of the Kingdom of Naples* and concluding with the *History of Europe in the Nineteenth Century*. These were exercises in what Croce called ethical-political history, which reacted against historical determinism by tracing the thread of free human response. But Croce's emphasis on leading political ideals tended to be overtly elitist and to preclude analysis of the structural factors conditioning the responses of ethical-political agents. Thus his histories seem bloodless and one-dimensional, especially when compared with the innovative social history of the last half-century or so, which has moved beyond politics and articulated ideas to focus on ordinary people and everyday experience. To be sure, his insistence that we approach *every* historical actor as a free, creative moral agent remains useful as a check to the widespread historiographical tendency to take socioeconomic class as privileged and, more generally, to insist on quasi-reductionist modes of explanation. But his neglect of structural factors makes his works at best one-sided. It was unfortunate that his growing opposition to Marxism led him to turn from his earlier way of conceiving Marxist cate-gories—historical materialism, class, ideology—as canons of historiographi-cal interpretation, affording a useful range of questions.[73]

71. I compare Croce and Camus in my *Benedetto Croce*, 189–198.

72. Croce, *Filosofia della pratica*, 175–176; Croce, *Ultimi saggi*, 223–224 (1926). Among Italians growing up within a generally Crocean framework, Aldo Capitini offered the most effective critique of Croce's tendency to restrict unnecessarily the scope for alternative, post-Christian forms of religiosity. See Aldo Capitini, *Religione aperta*, 2d ed. (Venice: Neri Pozza, 1964), 72–73, 98–100, 178–185.

73. Benedetto Croce, *Materialismo storico ed economia marxistica* (Bari: Laterza, 1968; orig. Italian ed. 1900), 74–75, 109–110. See also Roberts, *Benedetto Croce*, 44, 289–290.

But in deeper ways, as well, Croce's historiographical practice seems to compromise the more central cultural role for history that he advocated. Although the array of things that can be historical, and that can only be understood through historical inquiry, seems to expand to infinity as metaphysical foundations dissolve, Croce's way of conceiving reality as history entailed a limiting form of presentism, so his conception seemed to end up restricting, rather than expanding, the range of historical questioning.[74] The premium was to understand the present in its historical genesis, to know what it is—the better to be able to act on it. What matters in any past moment are the seeds of the next, or what by now has resulted in our present world. What is lost, forgotten, or "held back," as the spirit grows in history, simply "is not," so the present moment, as the resultant of the whole past, embodies all that remains living of the past. Although Croce afforded wide scope for us to give new meaning to the past, his way of concentrating the whole past into each present moment precluded the potentially more fruitful relationship between us and those who came before us that Gadamer would later posit, partly by adapting Heidegger. Whereas Gadamer accented the scope for genuine dialogue between present and past, the Crocean approach has long seemed closer to mere monologue.

Croce was determined to deny some "modern predicament," and he had plausible reasons for foreclosing the histrionic breast-beating to which "modern man" has been prone. There is nothing special about our situation; there is no "pathology of modernism." But Croce's determination to play down crisis led him to conceive the whole course of history as a relatively smooth continuity, without ruptures and thus without buried layers that subsequent historical inquiry might unearth. For both Nietzsche and Heidegger, in contrast, there is something quite special about our time, and very radical historical questions—questions literally inconceivable before—become possible, and necessary, as a result. Whether or not we find Nietzsche or Heidegger convincing on this score, Croce seems to have been too quick to preclude such possibilities—and the scope for radical historical questioning that would follow.

In some of his moods, Croce himself surely knew better, as when he saw the historically specific task of his generation to replace the old religion. Though every generation presumably faces its historically specific tasks, some such tasks are deeper than others; Croce's own generation faced a crisis or rupture, and to understand it surely required a new and deeper kind of historical questioning, of precisely the sort that Nietzsche and Heidegger opened up. Yet Croce did not seem even to encourage such questions, let alone formulate them himself.

74. Although the appropriate criticism does not depend on a Marxist or radical framework, Gramsci got close to the problem when he stressed that Croce's works on nineteenth-century Europe and liberal Italy conservatively left out the revolutionary moment. See Gramsci, *Quaderni del carcere*, 2:1316–1317. See also pp. 1326–1328, 1480, in the same volume.

Because philosophy can only follow history in the Crocean universe, Croce maintained that the philosophers in our tradition have not all been dealing with the same big problems but have responded in an ad hoc way to the confusions that have resulted from historically specific situations.[75] However, this way of relating philosophy to history means not only that philosophy cannot have been foundational in the usual metaphysical sense, specifying foundations that are already there. It also denies that philosophy can have played a foundational *function* in our tradition—the function it has played for Heidegger or Collingwood or Ortega y Gasset. For each, philosophy was historically specific, even contingent, but once established, the particular philosophy constituted a kind of channel shaping the culture's subsequent possibilities.[76] Because Croce did not conceive the function of philosophy in the same way, he did not afford the same scope for unearthing such buried layers through radical historical questioning.

But though Croce did little to expand historical questioning in practice, his absolute historicism helps us understand the expansion that has in fact taken place and the constructive cultural role it can play. The moment of Crocean response, then, must be considered in tandem with others, some competing, some complementary. As I have emphasized, Croce's quest for a moderate direction places him between the competing extremes of Nietzsche and Heidegger. Still, for all their differences, the responses of Nietzsche and Croce had something important in common; each confined our experience to this particular world, a world that results from nothing but history. Heidegger's response, in contrast, led to a kind of disengagement from our world, the particular sending of being in history to which we belong. From a Heideggerian perspective, in fact, Nietzsche and Croce were twin representatives of the nihilism that threatened to envelop Western culture now that metaphysics had run its course.

75. Croce, *Teoria e storia della storiografia*, 131–132, 152–153; Croce, *Ultimi saggi*, 219–220 (1926).
76. See especially R. G. Collingwood, *An Essay on Metaphysics* (Oxford: Clarendon, 1940); and José Ortega y Gasset, *The Origin of Philosophy*, trans. Tony Talbot (New York: W. W. Norton, 1967).

6

Heidegger

Historicism, Disengagement, Holiness

Heidegger and the Reduction to History

Although Martin Heidegger has been central to recent humanistic discussion, there has long been disagreement about the import of his intellectual legacy. To some, he has appeared conservative and obscurantist, with his "jargon of authenticity," his seemingly fatalistic emphasis on "destiny," and his apparent nostalgia for "Being" with a capital "B."[1] Recent criticism has emphasized his association with Nazism and, what many find more troubling, his "silence" afterward, his refusal to accept responsibility, to admit he had made an error. Heidegger's link to Nazism has made his thinking seem at least suspect, perhaps irrelevant, perhaps evil.[2] To others, however, Heidegger has long

---

1. Among the most influential of Heidegger's critics was Theodor W. Adorno, one of the most prominent members of the Frankfurt school. See especially *The Jargon of Authenticity*, trans. Knut Tarnowski and Frederic Will (Evanston: Northwestern University Press, 1973); and *Negative Dialectics*, trans. E. B. Ashton (New York: Seabury, Continuum, 1973), esp. pp. 128–131, where Adorno links Heidegger's accent on "historicality" to a loss of tension with the actual, to "the naked affirmation of what is anyway—the affirmation of power." See also Peter Gay, *Weimar Culture: The Outsider as Insider* (New York: Harper and Row, Torchbooks, 1970), 81–84, for a hostile account in a widely read study by a distinguished cultural historian.

2. The literature occasioned by the recent interest in Heidegger's association with Nazism is already voluminous and cannot be discussed in detail here. It is generally recognized that the appearance of Victor Farias's *Heidegger and Nazism*, first published in France in 1987, and translated into English by Paul Burrell, Dominic di Bernardi, and Gabriel R. Ricci, forced the issue to the forefront. See the review essay by Thomas Sheehan, "Heidegger and the Nazis," *New York Review of Books*, 16 June 1988, 38–47, on the initial phase of the controversy; and Luc Ferry and Alain Renaut, *Heidegger and Modernity*, trans. Franklin Philip (Chicago: University of Chicago Press, 1990), 1–54, on the controversy Farias's book occasioned among those interested in Heidegger in France. See also "Symposium on Heidegger and Nazism," ed. Arnold I. Davidson, *Critical Inquiry*

111

appeared not conservative but radical, an indispensable figure in the break from metaphysics and the "modernity" that seems ever more insidiously wound around technology in a way that he uniquely may illuminate. And even with the furor over Nazism, some continue to insist that we have something essential to learn from him, despite his deplorable political choice and his insensitivity in the aftermath.

One way of coming to grips with Heidegger's thinking, especially the obscure works of his maturity, is to start with the sense in which he, like Nietzsche and Croce, was responding to the newly intrusive experience of the world as historical.[3] Heidegger became preoccupied with history early in his career, and his determination to think through the historicity of things and the place of human being in a merely historical world fueled his intellectual quest, leading to several distinguishable approaches. The last of them seems to teeter on the edge of vacuousness, but it proves significant as a response to precisely the collapse into history that preoccupied Nietzsche and Croce. Heidegger's mature response, however, was radically opposed to each of theirs.

It is possible to address Heidegger on this level without hiding or minimizing his support for Nazism. In fact, both his adherence to Nazism and his seemingly evasive posture afterward were central to the process whereby he reached his mature orientation to the actual historical world. Yet his initial political commitment was surely naive, and his whole approach to Nazism manifested the worst sort of national chauvinism. Heidegger started by thinking Germany was special and that Nazism embodied a uniquely German capacity to respond to the modern crisis. But then, once Nazism had failed, he portrayed it not as German after all—but as Western, all too Western. His orientation was self-serving on both counts. If we seek a political guide or moral exemplar, we must look elsewhere.

But it would be shortsighted to view Heidegger's political response as a warrant to dismiss him altogether. The hopes he placed in Nazism, and the lessons he drew from its undeniable failure, stemmed from a deeper experience that remains part of our own. He was a pioneer in exploring postmetaphysical possibilities, but he started with an extreme, even apocalyptic sense of the modern cultural situation. He came to recognize that the hopes he had

---

15, no. 2 (Winter 1989): 407–488. For the subsequent phase, see Thomas Sheehan, "A Normal Nazi," *New York Review of Books*, 14 January 1993, 30–35; and Michael Rosen, "Heidegger in Question," *TLS: The Times Literary Supplement*, 24 June 1994, 4–6.

3. Among recent studies on Heidegger, Jeffrey Andrew Barash, *Martin Heidegger and the Problem of Historical Meaning* (Dordrecht: Martinus Nijhoff, 1988), has most systematically traced the impact of concerns about history, historicity, and historical reflection in the development of Heidegger's thinking. As Barash notes, the place of history in Heidegger's thought has received little systematic study; though Heidegger's initial preoccupation with historicity is obvious, it is widely seen as pointing in nonhistorical or antihistorical directions. See pp. 2–3, 7, 12–13 (n. 3), chap. 3.

invested in the apocalyptic politics of Nazism had been misplaced, but he hardly concluded from the triumph of the Communist East and the capitalist West that everything was fine after all. Rather, he ended up relentlessly apolitical. And in positing a mode of disengagement from the world of history-making political action, he was able to explore, as no one had before, certain cultural possibilities that remain within the postmetaphysical mix even today. We need to understand both the sense of the world that led to the Heideggerian extreme and the orientation that finally settled out from his several attempts to specify an appropriate response.

Virtually from the outset, a sense of loss informed Heidegger's intellectual enterprise. It stemmed first, most obviously, from the eclipse of the traditional religion, for Heidegger had been raised a Catholic and spent six years in Jesuit secondary schools before beginning preparation for the priesthood at the archdiocesan seminary at Freiburg in 1909. But he took courses at the Albert Ludwig University in Freiburg at the same time, and after two years, in 1911, he gave up the idea of becoming a priest and left the seminary to concentrate on philosophy at the university.[4]

Heidegger had begun to sense that something more encompassing even than the "death of God" had to be addressed. As he asked how our religious experience had become bound up with that sort of God in the first place, he shifted from religious-theological to philosophical issues, focusing on the Western metaphysical tradition. That tradition seemed increasingly suspect in some circles because of the inroads of time, becoming, historicity, evident in thinkers like Nietzsche and Dilthey, each of whom Heidegger encountered at an early age.[5] In important respects, in fact, it had been the inflation of history that had dissolved the once-meaningful religious categories of our tradition. Otto Pöggeler has nicely characterized the way religious and historical concerns came together to dominate Heidegger's career: "As a born theologian, but one who became homeless, Heidegger turned against the historians and philologists who changed a present and future task (with Hölderlin, the task once more

---

4. Thomas Sheehan, "Heidegger's Early Years," in *Heidegger: The Man and the Thinker*, ed. Thomas Sheehan (Chicago: Precedent, 1981), 4–5. See also Heidegger's autobiographical sketch, "My Way to Phenomenology" (1963), in his *On Time and Being*, trans. Joan Stambaugh (New York: Harper and Row, Torchbooks, 1972), 74–82.

5. Thus, for example, Michael E. Zimmerman, in *Heidegger's Confrontation with Modernity: Technology, Politics, Art* (Bloomington: Indiana University Press, 1990), 146, notes that Heidegger, influenced by Dilthey, saw being not as eternal but as finite, temporal, historical. In the same way, Theodore Kisiel finds a "quasi-Diltheyan, counter-Husserlian shift from psychology to history" as the key to phenomenological investigation as Heidegger saw it by the end of 1919. See Kisiel's *The Genesis of Heidegger's "Being and Time"* (Berkeley, Los Angeles, and Oxford: University of California Press, 1993), 121. Even earlier, in a 1915 sketch of his own intellectual development, Heidegger discussed how he had come to recognize the central importance of history, after his initial antipathy to it. The document is quoted in Hugo Ott, *Martin Heidegger: A Political Life*, trans. Allan Blunden (New York: Basic Books, 1993); see pp. 85–86.

to speak of the divine) into informing us about a cultural and literary history already over and done with."[6]

So as the transcendent God faded and the metaphysical tradition increasingly appeared suspect, a kind of retrospective historical understanding seemed all that was left to us. And Heidegger was acutely aware that he himself was coming of age at a particular point in the history of the West, with its particular philosophical and religious traditions. Much like Croce, he believed that it fell to his generation to address the religious issue anew, to find a way, as Michael E. Zimmerman has put it, to "restore meaning to a world from which God seemed increasingly absent."[7] But religious renewal was necessarily bound up with philosophical critique and confrontation with the historicity of things.

As a student first of Rickert, then of Husserl, who replaced Rickert at Freiburg in 1916, the young Heidegger had occasion to know at first hand the leading German attempts to respond to the widespread concern with historicism and its apparent crisis. In his dissertation on Duns Scotus, completed under Rickert's direction in 1916, Heidegger sought to combine neoscholasticism with Rickert's way of positing a transcendent sphere of values; at this point, there still seemed a fixed human nature and a foundation for truth. But during the years from 1918, when he began teaching as a Privatdozent at Freiburg, until 1923, when he won a regular position at the University of Marburg, he began to feel that the challenge of history and historicity had to be confronted in a more thoroughgoing way. He found a common inadequacy in Dilthey, in his mentors Rickert and Husserl, in his near-contemporary Karl Jaspers, and even in leading German Protestant thinkers; none seemed prepared fully to face up to "history."[8] In their different ways, all were clinging to foundations, to grounding, partly out of the assumption that only thus could relativism and skepticism be headed off.

History and historicity had to be taken more seriously, but Heidegger also found something inadequate about the existing historical culture, because modern historiography had developed under the shadow of metaphysics. Practicing historians made our relationship with history "safe" by positing a past that is at once radically distinguished from the present and over and done with, a fixed object. Paradoxically, then, the mainstream historical approach kept us from the sense in which our living is bound up with the particular history in which we find ourselves—into which we have been thrown.[9] To depart from

6. Otto Pöggeler, "Neue Wege mit Heidegger," *Philosophische Rundschau* 29 (1982): 48 (n. 6), as quoted in David Kolb, *The Critique of Pure Modernity: Hegel, Heidegger, and After* (Chicago: University of Chicago Press, 1986), 240.

7. Zimmerman, *Heidegger's Confrontation*, 21.

8. Barash, *Martin Heidegger*, chap. 3, argues convincingly that the years 1918–1923 marked a radical turning point for Heidegger, precisely because the preoccupation with history now came to the fore. See also David Farrell Krell, General Introduction to Martin Heidegger, *Basic Writings*, ed. David Farrell Krell (New York: Harper and Row, 1977), 7–8, 13, 20–21.

9. Barash, *Martin Heidegger*, 143, following Heidegger's *Anmerkungen zu Karl Jaspers "Psychologie der Weltanschauungen"* of the early twenties. See also p. 222.

metaphysics and to take history more seriously might mean raising the stakes of our historical inquiries and intensifying our sense of responsibility for what the world becomes.

At the same time, however, Heidegger echoed some of the concerns that had informed Nietzsche's "untimely essay" on history almost a half-century before. Especially in the "methodological introduction" to his 1920–1921 course on the phenomenology of religion, Heidegger found something problematic about the implications of the modern historical sensibility for individual experience. The sense that history was inflating to absorb everything—so that anything I might do, like everything else, will simply pass into history—seemed to make the world ephemeral and light, undercutting creativity.[10] Thus the point of confronting history more deeply was not simply to establish the autonomy of history and certainly not to specify a distinctive method. History was too important to be cut loose or left on its own. For Heidegger, as for Croce, the key was somehow to bring philosophy and history together, but in a post-Hegelian way.

Heidegger came to share many of the premises about the historicity of things, even the notion that what "there is" can only be some particular history, that helped shape the thinking of Nietzsche and Croce. Moreover, Heidegger fully grasped the cultural point, even the fatality, of the new axis that the responses of Nietzsche and Croce established. But he strained to think beyond them because he found something appalling in the apparently anthropocentric historicist outcome that responses like theirs portended for the culture. Whereas Nietzsche and Croce affirmed the actual and our confinement to it, Heidegger, in his later thinking, sought a kind of disengagement from the course of the actual, so that a new kind of religious dimension might become possible in light of the collapse into history.

"The problem of being" that preoccupied Heidegger seems incredibly abstract on first encounter; indeed, his sense that we are caught up in an ever-deeper "forgetting of the question of being" may well seem utterly vacuous to us. But from a Heideggerian perspective, our inability to feel the weight of such matters is itself a major indication of the debased, "needful" quality of our own time. And for Heidegger, "the problem of being" was explicitly bound up with the concerns about history and historicity that, as we have seen, had become important cultural themes by the first decade of the century.

As a preliminary, we might say that as it imposes itself on us now, the problem of being is that "it" is not all here—on any level. Until very recently in our tradition, the question of being had seemed to concern the "whatness of beings." We start with the things that are and then seek their grounding—something stable, permanent, the condition of their being as they are. It is only on

10. Ibid., pp. 154–156, 159; see also p. 161 n. 18, on the situation of the unpublished transcription of these lectures from Heidegger's 1920–1921 course on the phenomenology of religion.

this level, we assume, and not on the level of variable and transitory individual beings, that we get at the way things *really* are, the level of ultimate reality. What we seek, then, is the essence of things, the being that underlies mere beings. But this has meant that we think of being on the basis of beings, and because of this particular perspective we understand being—being shows itself to us—"in and as a transcending."[11] So the erection of a transcendent sphere was the reverse side of the break into metaphysics in the Western experience.

In our tradition, it became almost impossible to conceive of being without or apart from beings, the particular things of the world that . . . that what? That "are," we first say, but things have begun to change when we find ourselves saying instead, "that have come to be." With the intrusion of historicity or history, the problem changes from the "whatness" to the "thereness" of beings. We have begun to experience the reduction to history, and this for Heidegger is both troubling and promising. On the one hand, with the loss of any sense of grounding, of any transcendent framework, we seem to fall into a nihilism based on technological manipulation—and portending some definitive forgetting of "being," some definitive foreclosure of religious experience. On the other hand, the eclipse of metaphysics means that we might open ourselves to a new mode of experience, encompassing a new experience of the holy.

Heidegger might have said, with Cézanne, "I am the primitive of the way I have discovered," because his quest led him onto terrain that had never been explored in our tradition. Merely to find the language, to let a new way of saying take form, was excruciatingly difficult. As Heidegger put it in 1947, "Thinking does not overcome metaphysics by climbing still higher, surmounting it, transcending it somehow or other; thinking overcomes metaphysics by climbing back down into the nearness of the nearest. The descent, particularly where man has strayed into subjectivity, is more arduous and more dangerous than the ascent."[12] We need somehow to wake up to what is right before us, yet somehow hidden: "we need the ability to wonder at what is simple, and to take up that wonder as our abode."[13] We need to "step back," to make possible a new experience of what is so close that it is difficult to see, to hear, to say.

Although he remained preoccupied with the same cluster of concerns over his long career, Heidegger's effort to respond led to three distinguishable stages or approaches. They overlapped in certain respects, and his mature approach presupposed his earlier insights and categories. In retrospect we can discern elements of all three even in the introduction to *Being and Time*, written after the text was completed, but the dynamic of Heidegger's way of trying them out affected the overall shape of his thought—and thus his subsequent legacy.

11. Martin Heidegger, "Letter on Humanism," trans. Frank A. Capuzzi and J. Glenn Gray, in *Basic Writings*, 216–217.

12. Ibid., 231.

13. Martin Heidegger, *Early Greek Thinking*, trans. David Farrell Krell and Frank A. Capuzzi (San Francisco: Harper and Row, 1984), 104.

Being and Time and After

Heidegger's first approach, in his *Being and Time* of 1927, was radical and novel in one sense, conventionally philosophical in another. Even as he reacted against his mentor, Husserl, he took over not only Husserl's phenomenological method but also something of Husserl's sense of cultural priorities. At this point Heidegger assumed that some sort of universal phenomenological science was possible—and what was most needed.[14]

Earlier approaches to the problem of being had been too abstract, so Heidegger adapted Husserl's phenomenological method in an effort to begin with concrete human existence instead. By attending without presuppositions to the "things themselves," to naked human experience, it should be possible to identify the pervasive categories or structures "underlying" a variety of experiences, grounding them and making them possible.[15] Such structures lie on the "ontological" level, beneath the level of phenomenological or merely "ontical" description of what is in fact the case. So Heidegger's inquiry in *Being and Time* was still "transcendental" in seeking to specify the conditions necessary for such and such to be possible.

But Heidegger started with a radically different set of phenomena, or experiences, than Husserl had. Indeed, he reacted strongly against Husserl's theoretical, ahistorical view of consciousness. Our natural viewpoint is not as an observer but as "being-there," *Da-sein*, thrown into some particular situation. Knowing is not transcendent and detached but embedded and fundamentally practical.

To identify the transcendent conditions or underlying structures was to encounter especially the temporal character of human being and the instrumental character of human activity. In adapting Husserl's phenomenology, Heidegger was seeking to develop a rigorous philosophy of human being in its historicity, a fundamental ontology wound around the inherent finitude and particularity of human existence. In a sense, Heidegger was offering a painstaking analysis of some of what Nietzsche and Croce had simply taken for granted. No longer could we think things through by starting with some sovereign ego or transcendent consciousness, or with the a priori subjectivity of the subject. Human being is fundamentally being-there, Dasein, thrown into some historically specific situation and projected, with it, into the future.

Although Heidegger hoped to proceed from this fundamental ontology to a

14. Martin Heidegger, *Being and Time*, trans. John Macquerrie and Edward Robinson (New York: Harper and Row, 1962; orig. German ed. 1927). See also Heidegger, "My Way to Phenomenology," and John D. Caputo, *Radical Hermeneutics: Repetition, Deconstruction, and the Hermeneutic Project* (Bloomington: Indiana University Press, 1987), 83.

15. Karsten Harries, "Fundamental Ontology and the Search for Man's Place," in *Heidegger and Modern Philosophy: Critical Essays,* ed. Michael Murray (New Haven: Yale University Press, 1978), 66. See also John M. Anderson, Introduction to Martin Heidegger, *Discourse on Thinking* (New York: Harper and Row, Torchbook, 1969), 15–16.

new understanding of being, his analysis in *Being and Time* operated especially on the level of individual experience. We as individuals all find ourselves within some historically specific situation, which affords the horizon from within which we live our lives. And we are never complete but always projected into the future. Yet for the individual, the future is not endlessly open but finite, to be closed by death.

Because we are temporal and finite, our choices are for keeps. We find ourselves to be creatures who care for the world, for others, and for our own place in the scheme of things. But we are also subject to the anxiety that Heidegger, in *Being and Time*, found to be the core human experience. Such anxiety is not fear of anything in particular but simply the reverse side of care, our involvement with and concern for the world.[16] The immediate imperative that followed from this overall understanding of the human situation was authenticity on the individual level. Authentic existence grasps its own historical specificity, projection, and finitude and takes responsibility for itself in light of that understanding.

The categories like anxiety, authenticity, and commitment that emerged from Heidegger's analysis in *Being and Time* became popular during the forties and fifties with French existentialism, which resulted especially from Jean-Paul Sartre's way of adapting Heidegger. But Heidegger's subsequent career made it clear that the existentialist reading obscured his deepest purposes.[17] Care remained fundamental, but as Heidegger moved beyond *Being and Time*, he no longer emphasized the personal anxiety that attends being toward death.

Although his phenomenological analysis of being-there constituted an important break in Western thought, Heidegger in *Being and Time* was still doing philosophy in a traditional, suprahistorical mode. His manner of questioning was "transcendental," in the sense that he was approaching the matter at hand as a detached observer, from the outside. Even if we fully embrace historicity, accepting it as constitutive of human being, we can specify an ontology sufficiently fundamental to get at the ahistorical structures of human being.

But even as he was writing *Being and Time*, Heidegger came to sense that a new ontology was not the cultural priority. He had shown that human being in general is being-there, but what mattered was that *we* are *here*, in this historically specific situation of darkening and loss. To specify a fundamental ontology, however rigorously, was still too abstract to respond to the experience of loss that had stimulated his quest from the beginning—and that even pervaded *Being and Time*. Rather than a new kind of philosophy, a new way of approaching history seemed necessary. Moreover, much like Croce at the end

16. See Heidegger, *Being and Time,* secs. 40, 53, and 62, on anxiety; and secs. 39–44 and 65 on care. See especially sec. 44 on truth.

17. Hans-Georg Gadamer, *Philosophical Hermeneutics*, trans. David E. Linge (Berkeley, Los Angeles, and London: University of California Press, 1977), 124–125, 139–141, is especially good on the sense in which emphasis on the existentialist element in *Being and Time* concealed Heidegger's real aims.

of his *Philosophy of the Practical*, Heidegger recognized that there will be something historically specific *even* about any determination of the structures. Thus the reflexivity that forced Heidegger to ask: why *these* accents *now*?[18]

Much has been written about the *Kehre*, or "turn," in Heidegger's thinking by the later 1930s, and though there is disagreement about the sharpness of the break, there is general agreement about the new direction it involved.[19] For Gianni Vattimo, for example, it was to move from a plain on which there is only "man," or finite, thrown, individual human being, to a plain on which there is principally being. And the "being" at issue was somehow historical, or coterminous with its history. For Zimmerman, Heidegger turned from the structure of Dasein to focus on the historical play of being itself. Thus authenticity, for example, pertained not to individuals and their decisions but to entire historical epochs and cultures.[20]

The new imperative was to consider "the history of being"—and this implied two levels of analysis. On the one hand, Heidegger wanted to probe the general sense in which being is historical and to consider what is necessary for that to be the case. On the other hand, he was concerned with the particular history in which we ourselves are caught up—the history that had resulted, so far, in *this*. In Heidegger's move beyond *Being and Time*, the general or theoretical concern came together with the more immediate, even personal concern; examination of being as historical converged with examination of the present situation of forgetting and loss that had resulted from our particular history.

Being and History, Our History and Nihilism

Even in specifying, in *Being and Time*, that historicity is constitutive of individual human being, Heidegger was implying something about being itself and its relationship to the history that impinges on us as individuals.[21] If human being is this, if individual experience is this, then what can we say about the world, the particular world that comes at us and to us, affording the horizons within which we live our lives? As his focus changed, Heidegger began drawing out certain implications from his analysis of the structure of Dasein. What needed to be understood was not so much the anxiety of personal experience

18. For examples of the reflexivity and sense of historical specificity prominent in *Being and Time*, see pp. 19, 21, 28, 32, 35. See also Zimmerman, *Heidegger's Confrontation*, pp. 143, 147–148.

19. John Caputo, for example, plays down the sharpness of the break in his *Radical Hermeneutics*, 85–86, arguing that the sources of Heidegger's own "radical hermeneutics" were already evident in *Being and Time*. For Heidegger's own retrospective, which links the Kehre to the holding back of pt. 1, div. 3, of *Being and Time*, see "Letter on Humanism," 207–208, 235–236.

20. Gianni Vattimo, *La fine della modernità* (Milan: Garzanti, 1985), 182; Zimmerman, *Heidegger's Confrontation*, 147–148.

21. Barash, *Martin Heidegger*, 231, points toward this understanding of Heidegger's "turn" from the quest for a fundamental ontology. See also Ott, *Martin Heidegger*, 179–183, on Heidegger's divergence from Husserl.

but the collective, supraindividual dimensions of finitude, projection, and care.

Being and Time brought individual human being together with others in some historically specific situation or collective historicity, which Heidegger characterized as *Geschick* (destiny). Human being entails belonging to some tradition, which is particular by definition. The moment of individual choice is a particular *historical* moment in which Dasein confronts the particular historical possibilities it has inherited. Thus, as Caputo has put it, "Dasein's temporalizing (*Zeitigung*) is historicizing, and its historicizing is cohistoricizing in and with its 'generation.' "[22] And in *Being and Time* Heidegger explicitly linked care to authentic historicality. Moreover, the analysis of Dasein in *Being and Time,* showed that human being is the "there" in which being can appear.[23] Human being is a clearing for the coming to be of a particular world in history.

In emphasizing the "belonging together" of human being and coming to be, Heidegger was dissolving the old dualistic separation between human being, mind, or language, on the one hand, and the world, reality, or "what is," on the other—just as I discussed in chapter 3. Only by "moving away from the attitude of representational thinking," he insisted in a 1957 lecture, can we do as we must and start with neither being nor man but with their relationship.

> Man's distinctive feature lies in this, that he, as the being who thinks, is open to Being, face to face with Being; thus man remains referred to Being and so answers to it. Man *is* essentially this relationship of responding to Being, and he is only this. . . . Being is present and abides only as it concerns man through the claim it makes on him. For it is man, open toward Being, who alone lets Being arrive at presence. Such becoming present needs the openness of a clearing, and by this need remains appropriated to human being. . . . Man and Being are appropriated to each other. They belong to each other.[24]

This relationship is such that what "there is" is history. Whatever there is has come into being in this openness or clearing. Such coming into being is a kind of particularizing—coming into being *as something in particular*, as finite, as this and not that. Thus Heidegger would come to emphasize that a holding back or withdrawal accompanies every coming to be, every sending of being, a notion that will be crucial for us in what follows.

22. Caputo, *Radical Hermeneutics*, 87–89; the quote is from p. 89. Caputo goes on to note that "it is just this historical dimension of authentic Dasein, the historicity which is essential to authenticity, that is often overlooked in the usual renderings of *Being and Time*." See *Being and Time*, 41, 436–447, for indications of Heidegger's interest in the generation as a form of cohistoricizing.

23. Heidegger, *Being and Time*, pp. 436–447; Zimmerman, *Heidegger's Confrontation*, xxii, 21. As will become clearer below, the question was not how entities appear or disclose themselves—the question that leads to a preoccupation with technology—but how particular worlds come to be in history.

24. Martin Heidegger, *Identity and Difference*, trans. Joan Stambaugh (New York: Harper and Row, 1969; orig. German ed. 1957), 31–32.

In moving beyond *Being and Time*, Heidegger began positing history as total-ity in the post-Hegelian mode discussed in chapter 3. The coming to be of a his-torical world is a single event or happening, a destiny or destining (Geschick), but destining is not to be conflated with fate (*Schicksal*), some sort of inevitability or unalterable course. Heidegger was not positing some predetermined logic of his-tory, Hegelian or otherwise.[25] The history of being, the coming into the open, is a sending or giving in language: "Words and language are not wrappings in which things are packed for the commerce of those who write and speak. It is in words and language that things first come into being and are."[26] So language does not represent some preexisting reality but rather discloses, or allows to come to be. And thus language is not simply one human capacity among others: "Rather, lan-guage is the house of Being in which man ek-sists by dwelling, in that he belongs to the truth of Being, guarding it."[27] Language, then, is fundamental both to what we are and to the coming to be of whatever comes to be.

Concerned with the impasse to which Dilthey's thinking had led, Heidegger sought fully to embrace, as Dilthey had not, the inflation of hermeneutics that was a corollary of the inflation of history. What was ultimately at issue, in the hermeneutic emphasis on the ongoing growth of the tradition in language, was not how we know or understand but what there is to be known or understood, what the world must be like.[28] Conversely, insofar as hermeneutics took on ontological weight, the epistemological issue needed to be radically recon-ceived—and might dissolve altogether. What we need is not some method for achieving a true representation of a previously existing reality. We simply need to understand that truth—some particular truth—happens with coming to lan-guage. Truth is neither correspondence nor coherence but a disclosure, depend-ing on human being and its place in the world.[29] Yet truth hardly seemed inevitable; the present outcome of our own tradition seemed to entail some-thing like error instead.

25. See especially Martin Heidegger, *The Question Concerning Technology and Other Essays*, trans. William Lovitt (New York: Harper and Row, Torchbook, 1977), 24, on destiny as sending. For a particularly cogent discussion of the distinction between destiny and fate, see Richard A. Bernstein, *The New Constellation: The Ethical-Political Horizons of Modernity/Postmodernity* (Cambridge: MIT Press, 1992), 107.

26. Martin Heidegger, *An Introduction to Metaphysics*, trans. Ralph Manheim (New Haven: Yale University Press, 1959; orig. German ed. 1953, based on lectures from 1935), 13.

27. Heidegger, "Letter on Humanism," 213. See also Martin Heidegger, *Poetry, Language, Thought*, trans. Albert Hofstadter (New York: Harper and Row, Colophon, 1975), 73–74; and Mar-tin Heidegger, *On the Way to Language*, trans. Peter D. Hertz (New York: Harper and Row, Peren-nial, 1982; orig. German ed. 1957), 133.

28. Caputo, *Radical Hermeneutics*, 61–62. As Caputo puts it, hermeneutics was no longer a matter of epistemology but took on ontological weight.

29. Ernst Behler, *Confrontations: Derrida/Heidegger/Nietzsche*, trans. Steven Taubeneck (Stanford: Stanford University Press, 1991), 34–35, is good on the sense in which truth for Hei-degger happens through human being, understood as a historically specific clearing, but not through human agency. Behler here follows especially Martin Heidegger, *Nietzsche*, vol. 3, *The Will to Power as Knowledge and as Metaphysics*, trans. Joan Stambaugh, David Farrell Krell, and Frank A. Capuzzi (San Francisco: HarperCollins, 1991), 187–188.

The more dispassionate, theoretical side of Heidegger's concern with the temporality of being was entwined from the start with a more personal side, stemming from his experience of the present as debased and inadequate. Being is not historical in some general, abstract sense but always a particular history. So the "history of being" that we must ponder is our particular history, and this had resulted, so far, in a cultural situation that entailed a certain experience for Heidegger—and, it seemed obvious, not for Heidegger alone. Because the theoretical issue could not be separated from the sense of crisis that had stimulated his quest from the start, Heidegger no longer sought to be detached, objective, even "scientific" after *Being and Time.*

Indeed, Heidegger's new mode of inquiry included a strongly reflexive dimension. His own manner of questioning was part of the larger phenomenon, bound up with our particular historical experience in the West, that he was seeking to address. Only now, at this moment in our history, could these questions have imposed themselves.[30] And because he had worked through what seemed the best thinking of his time, Heidegger could plausibly believe that his own inquiry and the sense of loss that prompted it were of general cultural import—indeed, were the culmination, so far.

Because something precious appeared to have been lost to us, Heidegger persistently charged that the present cultural situation was one of nihilism, stemming from forgetting: "To forget being and cultivate only the essent—that is nihilism."[31] But what precisely are we forgetting, or losing, as we come to focus exclusively on the world that has actually come to be? Because nihilism, in one formulation, entailed a loss of experience of "the holy," our first impulse may be to understand it in terms of the "death of God." But virtually from the start Heidegger felt himself confronting something more basic than the failure of a particular, once-convincing idea of God to convince any longer. Nihilism stemmed from a deeper tendency that, among other things, had led us to invest our experience of the holy in a God that was bound to seem one being among others—and that thus could grow stale, wither, and die. The invention of that sort of God had simply been a step in the forgetting that was the real basis of nihilism. The nihilism of our time, Heidegger came to argue, is manifested in science and technology, on the one hand, and in anthropocentrism, humanism, and historicism, on the other.

The metaphysics that had decisively informed our experience in the West was what first required attention. Indeed, "metaphysics is the historical ground of the world history that is being determined by Europe and the West."[32] Heidegger worked through that tradition again and again, most notably in the four lecture courses on Nietzsche that he offered at Freiburg from 1936 to 1940 and that became the basis of his four-volume *Nietzsche,* first published in 1961.

30. Heidegger, *Introduction to Metaphysics,* 44–45.
31. Ibid., 202–203.
32. Heidegger, *The Question Concerning Technology,* 109.

The metaphysical tradition entailed an ever more overtly manipulative and technological mode of relating to things. But this was ultimately because of the progressive forgetting of the distinction between presencing and presence, coming to be and existing. In response to our experience of the groundless "presence" of things, we seek some ahistorical grounding. We name presencing, so it becomes a thing, even as we take it as a grounding or foundation.

> As soon as presencing is named it is represented as some present being. Ultimately, presencing as such is not distinguished from what is present: it is taken merely as the most universal or the highest of present beings, thereby becoming one among such beings. The essence of presencing, and with it the distinction between presencing and what is present, remains forgotten. *The oblivion of Being is oblivion of the distinction between Being and beings.*[33]

In a sense, metaphysics had been the consequence, not the cause, of forgetting, because only insofar as we forget do we seek a transcendent "grounding" for what is, by seeking the being of beings. The forgetting of being involves a forgetting of how the things that are came to be. Our language makes it all "present," but secondhand, everyday, so that the original force, the primordial bite, is lost. And as the metaphysical framework crystallizes, we become enmeshed in logic, cause and effect, and a conceptual and representational approach to language.

Although the present situation of nihilism was the culmination of the whole tradition, it stemmed most immediately from the break into modernity and subjectivism with Descartes. Despite some continued reliance on the Christian God, Cartesian subjectivism made human being the foundation as never before; the real obeys the principles that govern the human mind.[34] Needing an alternative to the certainty of revelation, Descartes posited a human subject that decides what is knowable and that actively constitutes what is known.

With Kant, still more explicitly, the autonomous human subject plays a decisive role in constructing a meaningful world. Hegel's identification of the real with the rational took this subjectivism a step further. Though his direction was profoundly different from Hegel's, Husserl by the early twentieth century similarly ended up with subjectivity, or consciousness, as the matter of philosophy, now brought fully to presence.[35] No more than Hegel could Husserl have raised the question of how there can be presence as such.

Although Husserl had most immediately occasioned Heidegger's effort in

---

33. Heidegger, *Early Greek Thinking*, 50. See also Martin Heidegger, "The End of Philosophy and the Task of Thinking," in *Basic Writings*, 374. Zimmerman, *Heidegger's Confrontation*, chap. 11, offers an especially effective summary of Heidegger's account of the history of Western metaphysics.

34. Martin Heidegger, "The Age of the World Picture," in *The Question Concerning Technology*, 128, 132–134, 147–153. See also Ferry and Renaut, *Heidegger and Modernity*, 58.

35. See Heidegger, "The End of Philosophy," 380–383, 389, on Hegel and Husserl as culminations of subjectivism. See also Barash, *Martin Heidegger*, 262–266.

Being and Time, Heidegger came to view Nietzsche as the nihilistic culmination of the whole tradition, including its final subjectivist phase. With Nietzsche, the Cartesian God, the Kantian thing-in-itself, and the Hegelian absolute
spirit all fell away; being itself is precluded, is reduced to nothing. The human
subject was limited by nothing outside itself, and nothing remained but sheer
will, willing nothing but itself, seeking power for its own sake. The Nietzschean outcome revealed the meaninglessness of the whole metaphysical tradition, and it threatened to preclude definitively the renewal or recovery that
Heidegger was seeking. Heidegger's questions about being simply could not
be formulated from within the Nietzschean framework.[36]

When translated into the world of practice, modern subjectivism led to the
end of metaphysics and the triumph of science. As the empirical sciences split
off from philosophy, establishing their independence, philosophy was left first
with a temporary vestigial role, subservient to science, but then began to disappear altogether.[37] By Heidegger's own time, science had come to seem the
universalizing culmination of the whole philosophical tradition in the West.
Thus Gadamer stresses Heidegger's insight "that science originates from an
understanding of being that compels it unilaterally to lay claim to every place
and to leave no place unpossessed outside of itself."[38]

With the triumph of science, we can relate to the world only in one highly
restricted way, so even when we approach our own history, for example, we
insist on cause-and-effect explanation, precluding other modes of understanding.[39] The world comes to seem a collection of objects, available as instruments
for the human subject to measure and control. Thus the modern cult of technology and the manipulation of things that technology, conceived broadly, made
possible. The emergence of this all-encompassing technology is the practical
corollary of the completion of metaphysics. History reduces to the self-momentum
of technology as it becomes ever less possible to argue that technology is an
instrument for human ends. With the culmination of our metaphysical tradition,
then, we move toward "the planetary imperialism of technologically organized
man," bringing about a total and uniform technological rule over the earth.[40]

36. Martin Heidegger, *Nietzsche*, vol. 4, *Nihilism*, trans. Frank A. Capuzzi (San Francisco:
HarperCollins, 1991), 202–203; Martin Heidegger, "The Word of Nietzsche: 'God Is Dead,' " in
The Question Concerning Technology, 107–112. Behler's account of Heidegger's confrontation
with Nietzsche is particularly helpful; see *Confrontations*, 17–48.
37. Heidegger, "The End of Philosophy," 374–378.
38. Hans-Georg Gadamer, *Reason in the Age of Science*, trans. Frederick G. Lawrence (Cambridge: MIT Press, 1981), 163.
39. See Zimmerman, *Heidegger's Confrontation*, 80–81, on the difference between cause-
and-effect explanation and the disclosure Heidegger envisioned. See also Bernstein, *The New Constellation*, 93–97, 104.
40. Heidegger, "The Age of the World Picture," 152–153. See also Martin Heidegger, *Discourse on Thinking*, trans. John M. Anderson and E. Hans Freund (New York: Harper and Row,
Colophon, 1969; orig. German ed. 1959), 43–57; Heidegger, "The Word of Nietzsche," 77–79;
Zimmerman, *Heidegger's Confrontation*, 172–173, 186, 201; and Michael Allen Gillespie, *Hegel,
Heidegger, and the Ground of History* (Chicago: University of Chicago Press, 1984), 124, 128.

The present situation was thus paradoxical in the extreme. Although metaphysics had been the problem in one sense, its end did not in itself promise liberation but rather entailed nihilism and the danger of a definitive forgetting. Still, the end of metaphysics constituted a kind of hinge or pivot, making possible a new kind of questioning, including Heidegger's own. Moreover, the present extreme—the "heedlessness" that he found the peculiar greatness of the modern age—makes possible the preparation, at least, of something else for the future.[41] But what else could there be, and how, more specifically, are we to prepare for it?

In his middle phase, roughly 1933 to 1945, the years of the Nazi regime in Germany, Heidegger responded in two complementary ways, actively addressing each end of our metaphysical tradition. He sought to work back through the tradition to retrieve what had been lost, but he also found scope for political action to overcome the present and bring about a new, nontechnological orientation. Only as both these approaches proved dead ends did he begin to outline the very different response of his mature third phase.

The Scope for an Active Response

Especially during 1933–1934, at the outset of Hitler's regime, Heidegger believed that Nazism, as a new, radically oppositional form of politics, could address the present crisis and bring about a more satisfactory relationship to modern technology.

With his gloom about creeping control and manipulation, Heidegger was part of an ongoing romantic current, especially powerful in central Europe and evident, for example, in the "negative totality" theme to be found in Max Weber, the young Georg Lukács, and much of the Frankfurt school.[42] This current stood opposed to another that was prominent at the same time—in the German Bauhaus, for example. The opposing sides agreed that history was moving in a particular direction, summed up as "modernization" or "Westernization" and involving increasing rationality, efficiency, and control through technology. But their evaluations differed profoundly. For Gropius and the dominant current at the Bauhaus, the antidote to our misgivings was to abandon futile nostalgia and to take full advantage of the modern machine age to form the basis for a new tradition. Among those who read "modernization" in a negative way, some could still find hope in the Hegelian-Marxian promise of reintegration to overcome the fragmentation of modernity, attributed to liberal capitalism. But for Heidegger, as for Nietzsche and Croce, any hope for that sort of fulfillment through history was part of what had fallen away.

---

41. Heidegger, "The Age of the World Picture," 153.
42. I have learned much from John E. Grumley's account of this current in his *History and Totality: Radical Historicism from Hegel to Foucault* (London: Routledge, 1989), though it seems to me that Grumley and others have been too quick to associate totalist historicism with the radical tradition and its quest for total emancipation.

However benign its intentions, Marxism could only be part of the problem, not the solution.

In Weimar Germany's new conservatism, to which Heidegger's diagnosis owed much, concerns about modernization and technology mixed with anti-Marxist, antidemocratic, and anti-"Western" emphases. Although not all those involved with the new conservatism cast their lot with Nazism, many did, on the basis of a contingent political judgment. Heidegger was among them. Nazism seemed different, a genuine alternative to all that was alienating in the dominant modernizing direction.

Although he explicitly rejected the Nazi appeal to biology, race, and natural force, Heidegger believed Nazism capable of creating a "regional" culture—the space for an alternative to the mainstream technology and everydayness that he found embodied in both the United States and the Soviet Union.[43] Different cultures are caught up in different ways in the wider historical destiny of the West; only Germany, where doubts about modernity were most pronounced, could nurture an active political antidote. By renewing contact with Western cultural roots that had somehow remained more accessible in Germany, Heidegger himself could help Nazism understand its mission. On that basis, the Nazi regime could open the way to a different human relationship to entities, letting them appear in a nonmanipulative way.

Even his detractors admit that Heidegger quickly became disillusioned with Nazism in practice. As early as 1934, he concluded that Hitler's regime was heading in the wrong direction, strengthening technology.[44] But far from repudiating the new German politics, Heidegger continued to believe that his own intellectual enterprise was somehow congruent with the real core, the "inner truth and greatness," of Nazism. And he remained convinced that the Germans were especially open to what he was attempting to do. In this sense his disillusionment by the midthirties was superficial; the real break came only with the definitive defeat and disintegration of Nazism in 1945. From that point he became more resigned about technology, and he pulled back from even the possibility of political response.

During the Nazi years, Heidegger began to argue that certain German-language poets—Friedrich Hölderlin, especially, but also Rainer Maria Rilke, Georg Trakl, and Stefan George—afforded an antidote to the culture of technology. The poetry of each seemed to elude the stale, objectified language of the modern era and to manifest a deeper need—and an openness to something new. More generally, Heidegger fastened on art as "originary," creative,

43. Ferry and Renaut, *Heidegger and Modernity*, 24, 46. Jacques Derrida, *Of Spirit: Heidegger and the Question*, trans. Geoffrey Bennington and Rachel Bowlby (Chicago: University of Chicago Press, 1989; orig. French ed. 1987), probes Heidegger's way of repairing to "spirit," as opposed to a naturalistic biological determinism, in his embrace of Nazism.
44. Zimmerman, *Heidegger's Confrontation*, 76, 80.

uncaused—and thus as closer to being itself than the manipulative, flattened-out language of everyday use.[45]

So artists, especially poets, might play a special role in a destitute time, but Heidegger also discerned a role for thinkers like himself to question our tradition in a fresh way. By working back through the layers of our history, it might be possible to "destroy" or deconstruct the whole history of metaphysics, enabling us literally to recover what we have forgotten or lost.[46]

Even in planning part two of *Being and Time*, Heidegger envisioned something like such a "destruction of the history of ontology." He would work back first to Kant, then on to Descartes's departure from Scholasticism, and finally to Aristotle, all with reference to concepts of time. But though it was outlined in the introduction, written after a portion of the book was completed, part two never appeared.[47] Within the framework of *Being and Time*, any such inquiry could only have been ancillary, showing why the various stages of our philosophical tradition had never given us a fundamental ontology. But as our relationship with our own history came to seem more complex, and as fundamental ontology no longer seemed the priority, the imperative of historical inquiry took on a different resonance, a deeper bite. As philosophy contracted and history inflated, deconstructing the tradition became a naked, stand-alone enterprise, itself the priority.

Even in *Being and Time*, however, Heidegger's way of positing the world as historical suggested the possibility—and value—of penetrating all that is through deconstructive historical questioning. Insofar as we understand our world in an authentically historical way, we step back from the givenness of the present; we undermine the immersion in "what is" and the hypertrophy of the "they," or *das Man*, that accompany everydayness: "the temporality of authentic historicality . . . *deprives* the 'today' of its character as present, and weans one from the conventionalities of the 'they.' "[48] By continually bringing the world to historical consciousness, then, we resist our tendency to take the world

45. Martin Heidegger, "The Origin of the Work of Art" (1935), in *Poetry, Language, Thought*, 17–87. Much of Heidegger's notion of art as originary recalls Vico and Croce; note, for example, Zimmerman's characterization in *Heidegger's Confrontation*, 79–80, 229. But whereas Heidegger suggested that poets play a special role in coming to be, especially in the present situation of incipient nihilism, Croce accented the poetic moment in *all* human response. Although some are obviously more creative than others, there is no bifurcation between the prosaic everyday and the privileged poetic. Thus the growth of the world through creative human response involves everyone—and is continuous. Any suggestion that some special poetic creativity or insight might occasion a qualitative break is mere nostalgia. Derrida's critique of Heidegger stemmed partly from a comparable denial of any neat distinction between the artistic and the prosaic; the world is all of the same consistency, and it happens in essentially the same way all the time.

46. Behler, *Confrontations*, 29–30, shows that the "destruction" Heidegger envisioned was essentially the "deconstruction" that Derrida would later develop.

47. Heidegger, *Being and Time*, 41–49 (Introduction, II, 6).

48. Ibid., 443–444. See also James DiCenso, *Hermeneutics and the Disclosure of Truth: A Study in the Work of Heidegger, Gadamer, and Ricoeur* (Charlottesville: University Press of Virginia, 1990), 49.

as given. For the Heidegger of *Being and Time*, however, this insight was an aspect of authenticity, not the key to a strategy that might enable us, at this historically specific moment, to challenge our destiny and in some sense undo the present.

As his priorities changed, Heidegger thought more deeply about the scope for historical questioning. The need to respond to nihilism might enable human beings, for the first time in our tradition, to ask truly radical historical questions, leading to the actual deconstruction of the whole metaphysical tradition and the recovery or retrieval of what that tradition had hidden from us. What was not possible in the epoch of Kant or Descartes now becomes possible for us.

By 1935, when he presented the lectures at the University of Freiburg later published as *An Introduction to Metaphysics*, Heidegger was emphasizing the scope for this sort of radical historical inquiry. And he was especially attentive to the fact that our historically specific situation seemed to demand this line of questioning, insofar as only now had we become possessed by the feeling that "the essent"—everything that actually is—might not be what it is and as it is.[49] Only with the reduction to history, in other words, does it become possible to conceive the whole of our tradition—"everything"—as contingent and ungrounded.

Heidegger envisioned working back through the epochs of Western metaphysics, deconstructing or undoing them, attending to what had *not* been asked, *could* not have been asked, to what had "concealed itself" as this tradition had unfolded. In principle this approach might invite a kind of dialogue, enabling us to bring out possibilities heretofore hidden within our tradition, possibilities that had not yet come to fruition. Temporal separation and our historically specific need might enable us to attune ourselves, for example, to what remained unthought, did not come to language, for the early Greeks.[50] Gadamer would follow that direction, though in a particularly conservative spirit, as we will see.

Heidegger's own aims, however, were more grandiose, reflecting his more apocalyptic sense of the situation. The deconstructive enterprise had to be doubly radical, getting to the root of the problem by going all the way back, then achieving a definitive overcoming by uprooting the tradition. In light of the present situation of darkening and loss, Heidegger was not interested in an ongoing dialogue that would merely enrich or expand that tradition.

In striking contrast to his later emphasis on disengagement, "releasement," and passive "thinking," Heidegger's language in *An Introduction to Metaphysics* was confident, even aggressive. Although the priority was now a form of history and not philosophy, there still seemed the possibility of a definitive

49. Heidegger, *Introduction to Metaphysics*, 28–29.
50. DiCenso, *Hermeneutics*, 69, 72, is especially good on this issue.

solution or qualitative break. Our present aim, Heidegger proclaimed, was "to stand on the very ground from which logic rose and to overthrow it (as the dominant perspective for the interpretation of being)." Through his deconstructive inquiry, we could move "toward a true transcending of nihilism."[51]

If the whole tradition entailed forgetting and loss, each step from Plato to Nietzsche must have carried us ever further from some more desirable experience of being, the world, ourselves. So it seemed that there must have been a time *within* our tradition when we experienced what we have now lost, or knew what we have now forgotten. The forgetting that had led to the present nihilism must have stemmed from a particular mistake at some point—a mistake that started our descent into metaphysics. Aiming, as he put it, to "win back our roots in history," Heidegger set out in *An Introduction to Metaphysics* to reconnect with that moment.[52] We could thereby retrieve from within our tradition the more desirable relationship to being that had been lost.

Generally, when adopting this approach, Heidegger took the advent of Platonic metaphysics, positing a timeless transcendent sphere, as the pivotal moment.[53] Bound up with that metaphysical turn was the advent of logic and a conceptual understanding of language. From this perspective, it seemed that the pre-Socratics, standing before the break into metaphysics, must have enjoyed a richer, more desirable experience. So the imperative was to work back through Plato to Anaximander, Parmenides, and Heraclitus, to listen for what they might tell us, to attune ourselves to their fuller experience of being.

Because language was the vehicle for coming to be, Heidegger's deconstructive inquiry was heavily etymological in thrust. He sought to peel away the subsequent encrustations to recover what he took to be the original meanings of such key terms as *alētheia, logos,* and *physis,* then to show how that original meaning, embodying a fresher, more desirable experience, had gradually been forgotten as changes in their meaning entailed a certain loss of resonance or connotation. For example, "truth" started as *alētheia,* unconcealment, and lost something as it gradually became correspondence or correct representation.

Even if this effort at peeling away and unearthing does not yield a definitive retrieval, it might at least afford us messages from the early Greeks or glimpses of what had been lost. But whatever the precise outcome, the imperative seemed to be to reconnect with an earlier phase within our tradition.

Heidegger's emphasis on such reconnection has drawn considerable

51. Heidegger, *Introduction to Metaphysics,* 188, 203. See also p. 117 for the basic imperative.
52. Ibid, 39. See also Sandra Lee Bartky, "Heidegger and the Modes of World Disclosure," *Philosophy and Phenomenological Research* 40, no. 2 (December 1979): 215, on the sense in which we get further away with each phase.
53. See "The Age of the World Picture," 131, and "The End of Philosophy," 375, 386, for examples of Heidegger's tendency to take Plato as the pivot into metaphysics.

criticism. Although Derrida, for example, derived his deconstructive strategy partly from Heidegger, he found Heidegger too hung up on nostalgic retrieval.[54] For Derrida, as for Croce, no moment is ever as dramatic as Heidegger conceived our own to be—or the break into metaphysics to have been. Moreover, Heidegger was still metaphysical in positing a single, unified history of the West when, from Derrida's perspective, there is really only a plurality of dispatches flying off in all directions. Derrida's eagerness to conflate history with metaphysics may have kept him from grasping the basis for Heidegger's insistence that we belong to a finite totality, a unified history. But Derrida convincingly pinpointed the "nostalgia" in Heidegger's emphasis on reconnection or retrieval.

Still, though Heidegger remained nostalgic for the freshness of an earlier time, he pushed on to the obscure response of his maturity at least partly because he came to feel some of what Derrida had in mind in criticizing nostalgia and retrieval. Indeed, Heidegger came implicitly to admit that to posit the full experience of being at some moment *within* our tradition—or within history at all—was only nostalgic myth-making. Even if we did manage to attune ourselves to them, the early Greeks cannot be our masters, teaching us how again to experience being and "the holy." For one thing, it no longer seemed that they had enjoyed some plenitude or esoteric wisdom that has come to be denied to us. For another, our temporal distance from them came to seem more important; all the history between them and us—including the subjectivism, technology, and nihilism—is part of us, is central to the way being has come to shine in us. We are caught up in the destiny of the West in a different way than the Greeks, so they can have no direct lessons for us.

In Heidegger's mature works, we no longer hear the aggressive tone, the pretense of critical overcoming or definitive retrieval, that is to be found in *Introduction to Metaphysics*. Rather than seek actively to overcome metaphysics, we simply turn away from it: "To think Being without beings means: to think Being without regard to metaphysics. Yet a regard for metaphysics still prevails even in the intention to overcome metaphysics. Therefore, our task is to cease all overcoming and to leave metaphysics to itself."[55]

Despite his sense of loss, Heidegger ultimately could not find a stopping point, anything with which to reconnect, within the tradition. Even if we work back past Aristotle and Plato all the way to Parmenides and Heraclitus, we never find the point where we can say, "here is where they went wrong." So it

---

54. Caputo, *Radical Hermeneutics*, 165–166, 169–170, follows the Derrida critique with sympathetic discernment. See also Zimmerman, *Heidegger's Confrontation*, 258–259. For the core of Derrida's case, see Jacques Derrida, *Margins of Philosophy*, trans. Alan Bass (Chicago: University of Chicago Press, 1982; orig. French ed. 1972), 31–67. Though accenting Heidegger's still-metaphysical tendencies, Derrida recognizes that distinctions among Heidegger's accents and phases are necessary; see esp. p. 65.

55. Heidegger, *On Time and Being*, 24. See also Heidegger, "Letter on Humanism," 210.

was hardly the point to blame those who had seemed key historical agents—Plato, or the Romans—for mistakes deflecting us from what had seemed the proper path, a path that we, after a disastrous detour, at last might rejoin. Although he continued to believe that the pre-Socratics had been closer to something that we moderns have forgotten, they were always already in the process of losing it.[56] A kind of "slippage"—to adapt Derrida's category—was in operation from the start and is part of the deal. There has always been some concealing, some holding back.

In "The End of Philosophy and the Task of Thinking," first published in 1966, Heidegger admitted explicitly that thought about the opening itself, about coming to be per se, could be found at no time in the past: "Presence as such, and together with it the opening granting of it, remain unheeded. Only what *alētheia* as opening grants is experienced and thought, not what it is as such." Moreover, Heidegger had to agree with critics who had pointed out that even Homer, well *before* the pre-Socratics, used "truth" not as unconcealment but as correctness and reliability. Thus, said Heidegger, "we must acknowledge the fact that *alētheia*, unconcealment in the sense of the opening of presence, was originally experienced only as *orthotēs*, as the correctness of representations and statements." So we cannot claim there had been a change in the concept of truth within our tradition, from unconcealment to correctness, corresponding to or representing what is present.[57]

Heidegger also insisted that to indicate, from our present perspective, what remained unthought in the tradition was not to criticize that tradition; it was not by chance or carelessness that we had experienced only what unconcealment had granted, only what had in fact come to be. Withdrawing, or holding back, is essential to *alētheia* or unconcealment.[58] In the same way, Heidegger concluded just after the war that the oblivion of the distinction between being and beings, presencing and what is present, was not simply a consequence of a human mistake or failure. On the contrary:

> Oblivion of Being belongs to the self-veiling essence of Being. It belongs so essentially to the destiny of Being that the dawn of this destiny rises as the unveiling of what is present in its presencing. This means that the history of Being begins with the oblivion of Being, since Being—together with its essence, its distinction from beings—keeps to itself. The distinction collapses. It remains forgotten. Although the two parties to the distinction, what is present and presencing, reveal themselves, they do not do so *as* distinguished. Rather, even the early trace of the distinction is obliterated when presencing appears as something present and finds itself in the position of being the highest being present.
>
> The oblivion of the distinction, with which the destiny of Being begins and

---

56. Heidegger, "The Age of the World Picture," 147. See also Zimmerman, *Heidegger's Confrontation*, 259.
57. Heidegger, "The End of Philosophy," 388–391. The quoted passages are on p. 390.
58. Ibid., 388, 390.

which it will carry through to completion, is all the same not a lack, but rather the richest and most prodigious event: in it the history of the Western world comes to be borne out. It is the event of metaphysics. What now *is* stands in the shadow of the already foregone destiny of Being's oblivion.[59]

In a crucial sense, then, the West was on its way to metaphysics from the start. Immediately, presencing itself becomes present—we name it, it becomes a thing. So the distinction is hidden, is on its way to being forgotten. There is a hiding, a holding back, from the moment there is our particular world at all, from the moment our event begins. As with the myth of human origins that Vico posited, humanity started already in motion, on the run; humanity was always already in a language that is inherently particularizing, that at once discloses something and precludes or keeps something from coming into being at the same time. The concealing or forgetting that leads to metaphysics defines the particular event, or giving, or sending, of the whole Western world.

So even as he continued to focus on the coming to be of the Western tradition, paying particular attention to the early Greeks, Heidegger came to insist that the point was not to recapture the Greeks, or to try to understand them better than they understood themselves, but to think the unthought occurrence, the clearing itself.[60] It fell to us not simply to retrieve something that had been lost or hidden but to think in ways never before possible in the West.

Heidegger continued to return to the early Greeks, but no longer with the strong objective that marked *An Introduction to Metaphysics*. He noted that the forgotten distinction between being and beings "can invade our experience . . . only if it has left a trace which remains preserved" in our language. It is likely that the distinction was more fully illuminated in early language; thus, in part, the continuing premium on going back. But even early in our tradition, the distinction between being and beings had not been designated as such. So no longer did Heidegger place the same premium on etymology, to peel away subsequent corruptions to recover the original meanings of key words, the right meanings once there and forgotten. Thus he warned, for example, that "an appeal to the meaning of *alētheia* accomplishes nothing and will never produce anything useful."[61]

Even in *Introduction to Metaphysics* Heidegger's aim of historical recovery meshed uneasily with some of what he suggested about nothingness, which was essential to what had to be confronted: "To press inquiry into being explicitly to the limits of nothingness, to draw nothingness into the question of being—this is the first and only fruitful step toward a true transcending of nihilism."[62] As Gadamer has emphasized, Heidegger found nothingness central to what metaphysics had hidden in our tradition.

59. Heidegger, *Early Greek Thinking*, 50–51 (1946).
60. Heidegger, *On the Way to Language*, 39; Heidegger, *Identity and Difference*, 52.
61. Heidegger, *Early Greek Thinking*, 51, 103.
62. Heidegger, *Introduction to Metaphysics*, 203.

Heidegger revealed the essential forgetfulness that dominated Western thought since Greek metaphysics due to the embarrassment caused by the problem of nothingness. By showing that the question of being included the question of nothingness, he joined the beginning to the end of metaphysics. That the question of being could represent itself as the question of nothingness postulated a thinking of nothingness repugnant to metaphysics.[63]

To come to terms with the nothingness hidden by metaphysics was not simply to undo some early Greek mistake; rather, it was to come to terms, in a more general way, with the sense in which being is historical. By formulating the reduction to history in rigorous terms, we might better understand the present debasement—and begin to discern what might come after it.

Nothingness had been at issue for Heidegger even in the phase of fundamental ontology, accounting for the freedom and openness of Dasein as *Eksistence*.[64] Things are not just here but come to be. And they can only come to be in some "clearing," which is empty, nothing, thus affording the space for things that formerly were not, to be, to stand out. Such a clearing is always some specific place, some historically specific moment, the scene of human being-there. But nothingness was implicitly at issue also because of what "coming to be" seemed to involve—a particular sending or shining that is at the same time a concealing.

Heidegger's way of treating nothingness as he moved beyond *Being and Time* made it clearer that confrontation with the reduction to history had been the other side of his departure from metaphysics all along. Nothingness is bound up with both particularity and contingency, or lack of necessity. Its import, always sidestepped in our tradition, now had to be and could be confronted—precisely because of the reduction to history. As Heidegger emphasized, we come to feel the resonance of the "rather than nothing" in the basic question, "why is there anything at all, rather than nothing?" To add the possibility of nonbeing, nothingness, is to raise quite a different question than simply "why are there essents?" We now grasp as essential to the essent "the problematic fact that it might also *not* be what it is and as it is." Indeed, the essent reveals itself in this possibility. "Our questioning," the questioning that only now becomes possible and necessary, "opens up the horizon, in order that the essent may dawn in such questionableness." In the perspective of our questioning, the essent wavers between nonbeing and being—"it has never caught up with or overcome the possibility of nonbeing."[65]

With the reduction to history, in other words, we experience the whole of the actual, the essent, the world that has come to be, as merely contingent and

63. Hans-Georg Gadamer, *Truth and Method* (New York: Seabury, 1975; orig. German ed. 1960), 228.

64. Martin Heidegger, "What Is Metaphysics?" (1929), in *Basic Writings*, 105–106.

65. Heidegger, *Introduction to Metaphysics*, 28–30.

historical and thus riddled with nothingness—with, again, "the problematic fact that it might also *not* be what it is and as it is." Nothing that is, is necessary in some absolute sense. And things never simply are as they are, because they are bound up with absences, with all that every sending, or actualization, precluded. Because of nothingness, the essent is particular; coming to be is some particular history. What needed to be considered, Heidegger came to feel, was not so much the particulars of our history, the actualizing steps of Plato and Aristotle and their successors, but the world as historical and the place of human being, ourselves, in the happening of the actual world.

Just as he pulled back from his emphasis on deconstructive historical questioning, Heidegger gave up all hope for an active political response after World War II. Even he could not deny that Nazism had failed; indeed, it had proven all too modern in its embrace of technology.[66] Yet he was evasive and dishonest in discussing the disastrous outcome of Nazism and the role he himself had played during the Nazi years. Much of his stance was narrowly self-serving, and he seemed unwilling to face up to the risks of the global, apocalyptic thinking, with its tendency to devalue present human life, that had led him to invest his hopes in Nazism.

Still, Heidegger's silence reflected his larger sense of the present historical situation and the possibilities it afforded. On this level, he had reason to be unapologetic, unregenerate, even after the failure of Nazism; he found no reason to conclude that either or both of its political competitors, American liberal capitalism or Soviet communism, had been right after all. The triumph of the United States and the Soviet Union signified a deepening of the embrace of technology, while the failure even of the Nazi-led German revolution indicated that there could be no alternative through active politics. So Heidegger simply went his own way, avoiding the explicit discussion of Nazism and his own role that would, from his perspective, simply have given comfort to the political embodiments of contemporary nihilism.

With the failure of both the deconstructive and the political approaches, Heidegger came to believe that the reign of technology was not nearing its end but was only just beginning.[67] Under the circumstances, political action—even purposive action of any kind—can only yield more of the same. So Heidegger's sense of apocalyptic possibility gave way to a still-deeper sense of confinement.

66. Ferry and Renaut, *Heidegger and Modernity*, 60–71, 76–80. See also Heidegger's " 'Only a God Can Save Us': The *Spiegel* Interview," trans. William J. Richardson, in *Heidegger*, ed. Sheehan, esp. p. 61. The interview dates from 1966, but it was held by agreement for posthumous publication; it appeared in *Der Spiegel* on 31 May 1976, just after Heidegger's death. In addition, see Jeffrey Herf, *Reactionary Modernism: Technology, Culture, and Politics in Weimar and the Third Reich* (Cambridge: Cambridge University Press, 1984), on the tensions in the Nazi relationship to modern technology.

67. See, for example, Martin Heidegger, *What Is Called Thinking?* trans. J. Glenn Gray (New York: Harper and Row, Colophon, 1968; orig. German ed. 1954), 160, where he refers to "this era, when Europe's modern age is just beginning to spread over the earth and be consummated."

Out the Other Side of Historicism

Disillusioned with our history and its outcome and having abandoned any hope for history-making action, Heidegger might have turned from history altogether. But instead he deepened his consideration of history in an effort to open the way to a new relationship to the world as historical as such.

Heidegger continued to believe that our historical moment is pivotal, especially because of the unique danger that technology entails. But with his third phase he sought to probe beneath the effects of technology to pinpoint its very essence and thereby to make clearer why technology was the "greatest danger." Because technology is uniquely all-embracing, it conceals revealing itself; its reign threatens a definitive forgetting of how things—the world itself— comes to be. But precisely because the reign of technology reduces things in this way, recognition of what technology entails can serve the turning at the hinge. And what would follow would not be simply a more appropriate relationship to entities, or even a different relationship to technology per se, but a different experience of destining itself, of coming to be as history.[68] Such a different experience opens the way to a different relationship to the world as historical as such—and thus to "being" itself.

In some of his statements even after 1945, Heidegger still found the cultural priority to be learning to use technology appropriately, letting entities be rather than forcing them into our molds. But generally, after the failure of his second approach, he became more temperate in his assessment of technology and the whole Western tradition from which it had emerged. Technology is our destiny; it cannot be stopped, overcome, or uprooted.[69] Yet even as we accept technology as fundamental to what we now are, we might find a way of relating to it that does not affirm it, participate in it, or carry it forward. Our situation at the hinge, then, came to seem more paradoxical than ever; we can be released from the grip of technology only insofar as we recognize we are in its grip, accepting it as our destiny, and leave aside any compulsion to master or overcome it.

As the first step, then, our priority shifts from overcoming technology to simply understanding its essence.[70] But to understand its essence is to

---

68. It seems to me that even the best recent accounts do not make sense of what Heidegger was doing in pulling back from any active response to the technological outcome of "the West." For example, Zimmerman, *Heidegger's Confrontation*, 226–227, 259, and Bernstein, *The New Constellation*, 100, 107–115, offer superb characterizations yet still leave us wondering about the point. Because we tend to share Heidegger's preoccupation with technology, we may assume that the technological issue—how entities appear—is decisive, but we need to move from technology to destiny to history to historicism to make sense of Heidegger's quasi-religious response, which cannot be understood simply as a nostalgia for nearness.

69. See Heidegger, *Discourse on Thinking*, 50–51, for the basic point, but see also p. 54 for the suggestion that we can and should use technology more appropriately. In addition, see Zimmerman, *Heidegger's Confrontation*, 220.

70. "Martin Heidegger in Conversation with Richard Wisser," in *Martin Heidegger and National Socialism: Questions and Answers,* ed. Günther Neske and Emil Kettering (New York: Paragon House, 1990), 84–85. This is from a 1969 interview.

understand the way we belong to it, the way we are caught up in it as our particular history, the way we belong together with our history. So rather than focus on technology itself, how we use it, or even how we might overcome it, we step back to focus on the way we are bound up with it, as destining, or coming to be as our particular world, our particular history.[71] We begin to grasp destining as particularizing, opening and foreclosing possibilities, and we begin determining the relation of human being to a world that is necessarily finite, confining, *nothing but* some particular history.[72] From there, we can begin to find a way of relating to the world as historical *in general*, a relationship to the way we belong to a particular history, a relationship to the confinement itself.

Heidegger's thinking about art moved in a parallel direction after 1945. He still suggested a privileged role for poets, and he remained interested in art as nontechnological and as the vehicle for genuine novelty. But the scope for art blurred as Heidegger's accents changed with his third response.[73] The key was not to attune oneself to particular artists who might point beyond the present debasement but to think the essence of art as uncaused worlding. To think about art was thus an aspect of thinking about the world as sheer coming to be. So even insofar as he continued to accent art, Heidegger's concern was to think through the world as historical as such.

Once it became clear what the essence of technology entailed, Heidegger found the danger not so much in technology per se but in "historicism," which was emerging as the dominant way of experiencing ourselves and conceiving what "there is" in our nihilistic world. To find a way, at the hinge, to pivot into something else was to discern an alternative to the historicist way of relating to the world as nothing but history.

In 1946, Heidegger insisted that "historicism has today not only not been overcome, but is only now entering the stage of its expansion and entrenchment. The technical organization of communications throughout the world by radio and by a press already limping after it is the genuine form of historicism's dominion."[74] A few years later he noted that we are caught up in an irresistible process of frenzied ordering; and thus the danger that "all revealing will be consumed in ordering, and that every thing will present itself only in the unconcealedness of standing-reserve."[75] In other words, our way of subjecting everything to purposive, history-making action threatens to become all-encompassing and to preclude definitively any alternative.

Historicism for Heidegger was the outcome of the whole chain linking meta-

---

71. On this point, especially, Bernstein is superb; see *The New Constellation*, 100, 107–115.

72. Heidegger, *The Question Concerning Technology*, 24–35. See also Heidegger, *What Is Called Thinking?* 31–32, where Heidegger finds decisive "the relatedness of man to what we call history."

73. Heidegger, *The Question Concerning Technology*, 34–35.

74. Heidegger, *Early Greek Thinking*, 17.

75. Heidegger, *The Question Concerning Technology*, 31–34.

physics, subjectivism, and technology. By one measure "reality" in our era reduces to what can be objectified, known, and manipulated by the human subject; by another, "reality" is generated as such manipulation takes place. Either way, we come to conceive reality as the ongoing making of the world in history, through willed human response. With the notion that human being makes the world, we have a universalizing anthropocentrism, or humanism, and finally the anthropocentric historicism that Heidegger associated especially with Dilthey.[76] By the twentieth century, the world reduces to an object of human will, and everything appears to us to be available for manipulative technology. The being of an entity lies simply in presenting itself in accordance with the categories imposed by the historical epoch.[77]

The forgetting of being had always meant that we can see only beings, but in the earlier epochs of our tradition, we had thought we could somehow discern, if necessary by peering through those particular beings, being, conceived—again—as the grounding, the transcendent condition, the ultimate reality of things; that was what metaphysics had always meant. The advent of historicism had been fundamental to the eclipse of metaphysics, though it had been a halting process. Even Dilthey had thought we still might apprehend something stable and suprahistorical as we peer through the particulars of our fundamentally historical world.

But after Dilthey, with the step we saw in Nietzsche and Croce, historicism was coming to mean taking the particulars of our actual history—the ontic—to be ultimate reality, to be everything. With the eclipse of our metaphysical tradition, in other words, we have become able to focus only on the things that actually are, the individual things that, we now come to understand, have come to be in time, through history. Let us recall Heidegger's definition of nihilism, quoted above: "To forget being and cultivate only the essent—that is nihilism." And Heidegger explicitly linked nihilism to the collapse of being into what comes to be in history: "The essence of nihilism lies in history; accordingly, in the appearing of whatever is as such, in its entirety, Nothing is befalling Being itself and its truth, and indeed in such a way that the truth of what is as such passes for Being, because the truth of Being remains wanting."[78]

If we ask, as our metaphysical tradition still leads us to, what in the final analysis "there is" in light of that reduction, we can see only the human making or agency or will that seems to bring the particulars of reality into being, whether it is characterized in Nietzschean terms, as will to power, or in Crocean terms, as post-Hegelian spirit. Nietzsche had given voice to the developing

76. Heidegger, "The Age of the World Picture," 133–134, 140.
77. Here I follow Zimmerman, *Heidegger's Confrontation*, 226–227, where his discussion comes closest to the dimension at issue here. Although he does not consider the historical dimension as such, Zimmerman helps us understand that this sort of reduction to history was central to what Heidegger felt must be headed off.
78. Heidegger, "The Word of Nietzsche," 109.

sense that human beings are in some sense making the world—through sheer will to power—and that beyond the particular world resulting from contingent human response there is nothing at all.[79] But whether we refer to Nietzschean will to power or to Crocean creative spirit is secondary. Each is a way of flattening everything into the actual particular history.

Even as Heidegger, in his later writings, continued to portray Nietzschean will to power as the nihilistic culmination of Western metaphysics, he deepened his understanding of Nietzsche's mature strategy. Now Heidegger did greater justice to the sense in which Nietzsche had been seeking to respond to precisely the reduction to "becoming" that had helped start Heidegger, too, on his particular intellectual path. Indeed, Heidegger grasped, perhaps better than anyone before him, how the idea of eternal recurrence and the ideal of innocent total affirmation emerged from Nietzsche's effort to envision what would be necessary to dissolve the gnawing resentment of "it was," the fact of a past not subject to my will, that was creeping into human experience with the waning of metaphysics.[80] Nietzsche was responding to a new sense of finitude, of confinement within a particular destiny, that first breeds a desire for revenge against time. But even insofar as Nietzsche was not simply positing another metaphysics, his mature response was appalling to Heidegger, for it entailed affirming the actual particular, the essent, and precluding any opening to something else.

The tendency of contemporary historicism, then, was to compress all of being into the actual historical course of things, leading us to believe that this particular line of past, present, and future is all there is. As the world reduces to these three dimensions, we may, with Nietzsche, laughingly affirm the particular reality that has become through history, or, with Croce, stoically plod along, building more history onto the old as we do so. What matters from a Heideggerian perspective is that, either way, we settle for a restricted, even one-dimensional, mode of experience. We no longer even grasp the possibility of an orientation, a human place, that might open to something else, another dimension, perhaps an object or source of religiosity.

Historicism, then, was the more general danger, encompassing technology. Yet historicism was essential to our destining, the outcome of our history so far, and a historicist age opens up a new possibility, beyond what had been possible under the earlier reign of metaphysics. Thus, again, the sense that our present situation is a kind of hinge. But the point was not simply to recognize,

79. See *Nietzsche*, 3:167–168, where Heidegger links eternal recurrence to the actual multiplicity of beings, understood as the phenomenological side of will to power. In insisting on eternal recurrence, Nietzsche was reducing the world to that multiplicity.

80. Heidegger, *What Is Called Thinking?* 48–73, 85–86, 90–93, 97–98, 103–105. See also Heidegger, *Early Greek Thinking*, 22–23. Robert S. Gall, *Beyond Theism and Atheism: Heidegger's Significance for Religious Thinking* (Dordrecht: Martinus Nijhoff, 1987), is good on Heidegger's critical use of Nietzsche; see esp. pp. 19–20.

once we understand that we can expect no privileged messages from within our tradition, that the message is that there is no message, that there is no privileged epoch but only particular finite histories.[81] That would be to settle for the reduction to history—and might then invite either the Crocean or the Nietzschean responses. The key for Heidegger was fully to grasp the reduction as the outcome of the eclipse of metaphysics yet *not* settle for contemporary historicism as the outcome.

At issue was the human relationship to the world as historical. Relatively late in the history of metaphysics, Hegel brought the relationship between being and history to center stage for the first time, but the Hegelian way of subordinating the realm of temporality and change to stable being had not held up. And, as Heidegger saw it, the culture was still picking up the pieces. What we first need to ponder, after Hegel, is that the particular sendings of being do *not* add up to wholeness or completeness.[82]

At the same time, however, Heidegger found the mainstream historical culture that had crystallized after Hegel to misconstrue our relationship with history and the past.[83] In one sense, of course, the relationship to history reflected in contemporary historiography simply manifested the fundamentally manipulative, technological quality of our nihilistic age. Seeking security, we objectify the past, the better to control it, to make it safe. We gain the illusion of explanatory power by forcing the past into an all-encompassing network of cause and effect. Even as we impose our present categories and standards onto the past, we tend to cut it off from us, distinguishing it sharply from the present. History, said Heidegger, is taken to be about the past, so we assume the tradition it encounters "lies behind us—while in fact it comes toward us because we are its captives and destined to it. The purely historical view of tradition and the course of history is one of those vast self-deceptions in which we must remain entangled as long as we are still not really thinking."[84] By itself, then, historiography does not enable "us to form within our history a truly adequate, far-reaching relation to history."[85] The point, then, was not to eschew encounter with history but to develop a different relationship with it.

Opening the way to that relationship required a deeper understanding of what is entailed in the coming to be of a world in history. So with his new

81. Here I depart from Caputo, *Radical Hermeneutics*, 181, 185.

82. Heidegger, *Identity and Difference*, 47–49. See also Bartky, "Heidegger and the Modes of World Disclosure," 232, on Heidegger's departure from Hegel.

83. In *The Question Concerning Technology*, 38–39, Heidegger argues explicitly that our present ways of understanding history only obstruct what is essential—"to think the essence of the historical from out of destining." In *What Is Called Thinking?* 32–33, Heidegger notes that "by way of history, a man will never find out what history is."

84. Heidegger, *What Is Called Thinking?* 76. See also Martin Heidegger, *What Is a Thing?* trans. W. B. Barton, Jr., and Vera Deutsch (Chicago: Henry Regnery, 1967), 43; Heidegger, "The Age of the World Picture," 122–123; and Barash, *Martin Heidegger*, 279–280.

85. Heidegger, *Early Greek Thinking*, 17–18. See also pp. 100, 122–123.

orientation by the later 1940s, Heidegger sought to specify how past, present, history, and human being come together in a world that lacks the grounded necessity of metaphysics and that is always only something in particular, not everything, not complete. But once being or presencing could no longer be conceived as a thing or ground, the terminology became treacherous indeed. Heidegger tried out various, often idiosyncratic ways of characterizing what being as history involves, referring, for example, to worlding, based on the distinction between earth and world, and to the regioning of that which regions. But though the terminology varied, he pinpointed two essential features.

First, Heidegger came to accent the "epochal" character of being, taking over a term adapted from the Greek *epochē*, made familiar by Husserl, as holding back. Being holds back precisely as it actualizes itself as "there is" something. Using the double meaning of the German *Es gibt* as "there is" and "it gives," Heidegger showed that when "there is" something, there has been a giving, or sending. Being as *Es gibt* means that precisely as it gives/there is some particular actuality, being holds back: "As it reveals itself in beings, Being withdraws."[86] This holding back is to be understood in a double sense. The sending itself is concealed; we "see" only the actual that has come to be. But giving/holding back also entails endless particularizing; what comes to be is always some particular way as opposed to some other that it might have been.[87] At any one moment, in other words, only something comes to be, not everything. Holding back is essential for something in particular to come to be. Even within the framework of earth and world that he posited in the mid-1930s, Heidegger specified that entities belong to the earth and cannot be reduced to the event of their appearing within a historical world. Earth never fully presents itself in any world.[88]

In *Being and Time,* Heidegger sought to show that human being, and ultimately language, affords the clearing, the space for being to "shine" in some particular way. In his later works he insisted more explicitly that language, as the medium for coming to be, necessarily conceals or holds back precisely as it enables something to become present: "Language is the lighting-concealing advent of Being itself."[89] Being and humanity are forever coming together, interfacing in language in some particular way.

We can only say that unconcealment is the coming into appearance, as a

86. Heidegger, *Early Greek Thinking*, 26. Sandra Lee Bartky's translations of this passage—"Being withdraws as it reveals itself in what-is"—is in some ways preferable. See her "Heidegger's Philosophy of Art," in *Heidegger*, ed. Sheehan, 266. On the theme of giving and holding back, see also Heidegger, *On Time and Being*, 9–10; and Heidegger, "Letter on Humanism," 214.

87. Heidegger, "The Age of the World Picture," 145–147. Heidegger refers, for example, to "always as this particular unconcealment" and notes that "presencing is determined from out of unconcealedness in its particularity."

88. Heidegger, "Origin of the Work of Art," 39–57. See also Zimmerman, *Heidegger's Confrontation*, 226.

89. Heidegger, "Letter on Humanism," 206; see also pp. 205, 213.

particular something, of that which presences, but Heidegger cautions us that our customary grammatical understanding of language leads us to think in terms of "an It that is supposed to give, but that itself is precisely not there." So we must "abandon the attempt to determine 'It' by itself, in isolation, so to speak. But this we must keep in mind: The It, at least in the interpretation available to us for the moment, names a presence of absence."[90] If we insist on the obvious distinction, then being is better conceived as the sending/holding back as opposed to the "it" that sends/holds back as something comes to be. Thus, as Heidegger put it, "The unconcealedness of beings—this is never a merely existent state, but a happening."[91] But the dimension Heidegger was after cannot be adequately named, because any such naming, even in the preferable participial form, tends to make it a thing, another particular essent.

Still, in portraying unconcealment as a happening, Heidegger was recognizing that temporality is essential to the shining of being as particular. And part of what required attention was that somehow this empty temporality turns out to be historical. Even in the face of this temporalizing, things cohere, relate to each other, so that being shines or gives itself as some particular *history.*

In his important lecture of 1962, "Time and Being," Heidegger said explicitly that he was after a kind of fourth dimension, distinguishable from the three dimensions of temporality—past, present, and future:

> The unity of time's three dimensions consists in the interplay of each toward each. This interplay proves to be the true extending, playing in the very heart of time, the fourth dimension, so to speak—not only so to speak, but in the nature of the matter. True time is four-dimensional. But the dimension which we call the fourth in our count is, in the nature of the matter, the first, that is, the giving that determines all.[92]

This giving gives in such a way, as "nearing nearness" or "gathering nearness," that past, present, and future cohere—in some certain way. Heidegger sought to characterize the matter by juxtaposing contradictory attributes—nearing and distancing. The giving is such that past, present, and future are near enough that the things given do not fly apart into chaos but distant enough that they do not collapse into one another to form a stable, finished, immobile unity. Thus Heidegger could say that the " 'nearing nearness' . . . brings future, past, and present near to one another by distancing them. For it keeps what has been, open by denying its advent as present."[93] Gathering nearness affords continuity and coherence; the world slips and at any moment is never fully what it "is," but it responds to itself as it does so. Thus there is at once the coherence and the

90. Heidegger, *On Time and Being*, 17–18.
91. Heidegger, "Origin of the Work of Art," 54.
92. Heidegger, *On Time and Being*, 15.
93. Ibid., 15. I have added the comma to the translation of the second sentence. See the discussion on pp. 15–16 for the overall point.

measure of openness and change necessary for the giving or shining of being to be a history.

With this line of questioning, Heidegger was looking through what we seem to be left with, our merely historical world, to ask what things must be like for this to be what there is. On the basis of the resulting insights, he hoped to tease his way through the historicist emphasis on the actual history to a new kind of openness to the giving itself. And from there we might begin to discern a more fruitful way of experiencing ourselves in relationship with what happens, is happening.

But if a kind of openness becomes possible now, Heidegger's way of portraying the whole history of the West as a single "propriative event," or *Ereignis*, has seemed to some critics to be unnecessarily confining. If we are to grasp the basis of Heidegger's quest for a new openness, and what such openness might entail, we must take care to understand the finitude he associated with human belongingness to a particular history.

In his stimulating *Critique of Pure Modernity*, David Kolb finds something too restrictive in Heidegger's way of emphasizing the single event or epochal granting of the West, because it means a "unified content," "a unified meaning to structure the space opened to us," so that we must think of the "world as a whole constituted by a unitary granting of presence." Against Heidegger's way of restricting us to that single event, Kolb insists that "there is no end to what we can say."[94] He thereby points toward the constructive, non-Heideggerian cultural orientation that becomes explicit in his concluding chapter. But this set of emphases keeps Kolb from seeing why Heidegger might find other priorities within the framework of groundlessness and finitude that Kolb and Heidegger both take for granted.

Kolb's way of characterizing the single and unified Ereignis, the event to which we belong, does not convey all that Heidegger found significant about the sending of being as a particular history. The point is not simply that some privileged content limits us unduly; rather, whatever we say will be part of a particularizing, will belong to the continuing of this particular event.[95] Our whole world—any world—is a particular event, continuing to grab us, involve us, compel our belonging. Our involvement may entail the multiplicity, the "infinite analysis," that Kolb advocates, but Heidegger was struck with the sense in which whatever results from our multiple responses will be more of the same history, the eventing of this particular world. The particularity is thick enough to allow whatever we could possibly say, but no matter what we say, the eventing remains particular. The finitude and confinement operate on a higher level than Kolb's characterizations suggest. Thus the kind of openness Kolb advocates cannot address the finitude and confinement that Heidegger posited.

94. Kolb, *The Critique of Pure Modernity*, 245, 249, 256, 261.
95. Ibid., 249, 251–252.

Only insofar as we grasp this higher-level finitude, and how it might be experienced, can we understand what a corresponding kind of openness might entail. Heidegger was seeking a relationship to that finitude that would allow us to experience something other than the mere continuance of the particular event. He was suggesting there was some deep value in that *as opposed to* the response that Kolb advocates. But why? And how do we get at it, open ourselves to it?

Attuning Ourselves to the Sending

With Heidegger's third approach, we still engage our particular history or tradition but now in the curiously passive mode he called "thinking."[96] In light of his earlier, more aggressive accents, we may assume that this approach entails contemplation, even a resigned acceptance of our particular destiny. But the orientation Heidegger envisioned cannot be characterized in our usual terms. It is not simply contemplative, though it is meditative. It is not passive but active, involving a restless continuing conversation with our tradition. It entails not affirmation but disengagement.

The thinking Heidegger advocated stands opposed, most obviously, to the instrumental or purposive thinking that he claimed had dominated our tradition at least since the early Greeks. In his "Letter on Humanism," written just after World War II, he made the point especially in opposition to Sartrean existentialism, but his target could as easily have been Nietzsche or Croce. To experience the essence of the mode of thinking he envisioned and to carry it out, "we must free ourselves from the technical interpretation of thinking. The beginnings of that interpretation reach back to Plato and Aristotle. They take thinking itself to be a *technē*, a process of reflection in service to doing and making." Heideggerian thinking, then, eschews action in the conventional sense of "working or effecting"; it does not aim to affect the horizontal world of history, by making more history. Still, thinking for Heidegger is a form of action, indeed, the highest form, because it "lets itself be claimed by Being so that it can say the truth of Being."[97] In this sense, Heideggerian thinking is meditative as opposed to instrumental or representational, serving action upon this world.[98] At the same time, however, it is active and restless; we do not simply contemplate something over and done with but keep working back through our tradition.

In doing so, we attend first to what had remained unthought, to what was concealed as being was sent in the particular way it was. Emphasizing the preciousness of the unthought, Heidegger advocated

96. See Heidegger, *Identity and Difference*, 41, on the need to return to the tradition, to what has already been thought.

97. Heidegger, "Letter on Humanism," 193–194, 204.

98. Heidegger, *On the Way to Language*, 74.

letting every thinker's thought come to us as something in each case unique, never to be repeated, inexhaustible—and being shaken to the depths by what is unthought in his thought. What is unthought in a thinker's thought is not a lack inherent in his thought. . . . The more original the thinking, the richer will be what is unthought in it. The unthought is the greatest gift that thinking can bestow.[99]

In accenting the unthought, Heidegger envisioned *unthinking* the course of the actual so that we might attend to the interplay of giving and holding back. The purpose was not to undo anything in particular, nor was it to retrieve something lost. Nor are we seeking access to something formerly precluded that, when now brought to actuality, initiates a different future.[100] Nor is the ongoing encounter to be conceived as the dialogue that might bring out the richness of possibility for creative transformation and further growth, as with Kant's "strong misreading" of Plato.[101]

Turning in the other direction, any such emphasis on the unthought might seem to warrant blurring the distinction between what did not become actual and what did—and perhaps to invite play. Thus Michael Allen Gillespie worries that Heidegger's emphasis on the unthought means rising "above the constraints imposed by the demand for historical accuracy."[102] Gillespie emphasizes that we must grasp what actually *was* thought before what was left unthought can be penetrated. In fact, however, Heidegger recognized that we need to confront the actual, what did in fact become our tradition. And we still must open ourselves to the happening of truth as we do so, even though our aim is not some positive reconstruction, let alone the quest for a radical rupture in the tradition that Gillespie attributes to Heidegger. It remained crucial that there has been *this* actual particular destining; there is no warrant for fanciful play or for willful fictions to recast the tradition based on present needs. Nor does Heidegger invite the "enjoyment" that Vattimo finds in Heideggerian thinking, making Heidegger too much like Nietzsche.[103]

The key is rather that by attending to the unthought we grasp the endless concealing or holding back and thus the sense in which coming to be is a shining or particularizing, a sending of being as this particular world. We manage to step back and disengage from the whole of our particular event. And in doing so, we attune to the giving, the particularizing itself, the way things come to be. Typically, Heidegger characterized what this entails in various ways, some using recognizable philosophical categories, some utterly idiosyncratic. We

99. Heidegger, *What Is Called Thinking?* 76–77.
100. Compare Gillespie, *Hegel, Heidegger,* 167–168, 172–174, which makes Heidegger too conventionally revolutionary.
101. Heidegger, *What Is Called Thinking?* 77.
102. Gillespie, *Hegel, Heidegger,* 167–168.
103. Vattimo, *La fine della modernità,* 182–186, on "pensiero di fruizione."

think the difference between being and beings and the oblivion of the difference.[104] We "let ourselves into releasement to that which regions."[105] However the aim is characterized, we think through our history simply to listen and thereby to experience the sending itself. The resulting *Gelassenheit*, releasement, allows us access to a mode of experience until now precluded in our tradition.

In Heidegger's third phase, then, no particular moment is decisive; everything is flattened out, and things go limp. Caputo has summed it up nicely: "The task of thinking is not to be taken in by any particular historical configuration but to make the step *back*, to see in any particular historical meaning a giving of that which withdraws and hence to experience that giving-withdrawing itself, to experience it as such."[106] And we can attune ourselves to this dimension *only* by rummaging through our particular history, "unthinking" its particulars as Heidegger specified. We cannot simply turn away from history or contemplate the actual, the essent.

If we think dualistically, there is still "something" suprahistorical that reveals itself in history, but it is crucial that Heidegger had departed from both Hegel and Dilthey in the way discussed in chapter 3. Our historical experiences are merely particular sendings; they do not coalesce to reveal or to realize "being" as a totality—in the way that history proves the self-revelation of spirit for Hegel. For Heidegger, as for Dilthey, we focus on our particular history because *these* particulars, *these* be-ings, *these* truths are all we have to think through. But in Heidegger the point has become profoundly different even than for Dilthey because, with the full embrace of the reduction to history, there is no longer some stable ground, hidden by history and our own historicity, that we might glimpse even as we focus on the particulars of history. Rather, we attune to the sending, understanding that it is empty: it "is" only as history. By attending to how things come to be in history, we experience ungroundedness, the sheer happening of this and not that, the free creativity hidden with our insistence on cause-and-effect explanation.

Having taken for granted that being can no longer function as a grounding and having found it impossible to deny that the actual historical is in one sense all there is, Heidegger was seeking encounter with the "something else" that had to be at work in the coming to be as history.

---

104. See especially the crucial passage in Heidegger, *Identity and Difference*, 49–52.

105. Heidegger, *Discourse on Thinking*, 77–79. It is explicit here that releasement is *not* simply a mode of presencing that we allow things and that stands opposed to the dominant technological way.

106. Caputo, *Radical Hermeneutics*, 204. In the final analysis, however, the point of Heideggerian thinking is not that "one realizes that there is nothing but the play of the epochs," as Caputo puts it on pp. 204–205, for this would be very nearly the nihilistic outcome for which Heidegger was determined *not* to settle. The point is that even as we fully feel the reduction to "nothing but . . . ," we also experience "something else," another dimension.

Everyday opinion sees in the shadow only the lack of light, if not light's complete denial. In truth, however, the shadow is a manifest, though impenetrable, testimony to the concealed emitting of light. In keeping with this concept of shadow, we experience the incalculable as that which, withdrawn from representation, is nevertheless manifest in whatever is, pointing to Being, which remains concealed.[107]

In seeking to open to this "incalculable," Heidegger hoped to renew the scope for religious experience in a world reducing to nothing but history. This dimension seemed to open just beyond the postmetaphysical experience of history that he shared with Nietzsche and Croce. The religiosity that Heidegger envisioned was not only posttheological but posthistoricist. There could be no return to transcendence, but neither was it enough simply to grasp historicism as absolute and this particular as *our* destiny. On the contrary, the key for Heidegger was to grasp historicism as our truth, but then to respond by taking the step back or "beyond," making room again for the holy.[108]

Just after World War II, Heidegger lamented that "being is still waiting for the time when it will become thought-provoking to man." And he worried that present tendencies seemed to preclude the kind of preliminary thinking and experience that would form the basis for fresh thinking about what we might mean by "God."

How can man at the present stage of world history ask at all seriously and rigorously whether the god nears or withdraws, when he has above all neglected to think into the dimension in which alone that question can be asked? But this is the dimension of the holy, which indeed remains closed as a dimension if the open region of Being is not lighted and in its lighting is near man. Perhaps what is distinctive about this world-epoch consists in the closure of the dimension of the hale [*des Heilen*].[109]

The particular sending of "the West" was in danger of closing in on itself in one-dimensionality, confining itself to technology, historicism, the universe of experiences that Nietzsche and Croce had posited. This would be to preclude definitively *any* genuinely religious experience, any experience of the holy.

But it remained true that at this historicist hinge in our tradition, there is scope for a new openness as well. Although poets like Hölderlin had helped prepare the way, it fell to Heidegger himself to conceive a posthistoricist religiosity. And only in light of the broadly historicist challenge did his way of

107. Heidegger, "The Age of the World Picture," 154.
108. Compare the implication of Vattimo, *La fine della modernità*, 184, that the key is precisely to grasp historicism as absolute. Vattimo makes the point as part of his overall effort to synthesize Heidegger and Nietzsche. See also Gall, *Beyond Theism and Atheism*, esp. pp. 25–30, which argues convincingly that the religious dimension in Heidegger's thinking is not to be appropriated by theology—as those like Rudolf Bultmann and Heinrich Ott were wont to do.
109. Heidegger, "Letter on Humanism," 202–203, 230.

asking the question of being, feeling the weight of the matter, become possible and necessary in the West. As the whole of being seemed to flatten into the actual historical dimension, feeding on its own excrement, it became possible to experience the absolute historicity of things, to feel the interpenetration of nothingness and actuality. On that basis it became possible to think through what is entailed in the sending of being as history and, from there, to suggest a new way of experiencing the human relationship to the sending of being.

Although Heidegger's way of thinking through history to the giving itself is essentially meditative, it is crucial that the Heideggerian orientation is restless and reflexive. We can never say what needs to be said once and for all. We never reach a goal or end that would enable us to contemplate an extrahistorical dimension, at last apprehended in pure form.

Because whatever we think or do will be part of our particular history, the way we hold open, even the way we apprehend the fourth dimension, will be particular, historically specific. Thus Heidegger's cautionary note in his lecture "Time and Being."

> Always retained in the withdrawing sending, Being is unconcealed for thinking with its epochal abundance of transformations. Thinking remains bound to the tradition of the epochs of the destiny of Being, even when and especially when it recalls in what way and from what source Being itself receives its appropriate determination, from the "there is, It gives Being."[110]

Even when we manage a sense of how being is given, we are bound to our particular tradition and do so in a particular way—not in a universal, complete, final way. Even in recognizing and experiencing being as particularizing, we do not abstract ourselves from our particular destining. Heidegger was always aware of the tension, but attending to that tension was central to his mature approach.[111] Thinking is reflexive; I think about the fact that my own thinking is historically specific, that in thinking *this* I belong to the tradition I am thinking about.

The fact that there is no rest is ultimately a corollary of the fact that what there is, is a history. But at the same time, we are constantly in danger of being swallowed up in a confining historicist nihilism. Thus the curious mode of argument in Heidegger's later works. To keep things from congealing, he kept adding new terms, trying to say it in a different way, suggesting the need for a

---

110. Heidegger, *On Time and Being*, 9–10.

111. This paradox and tension must be emphasized against any notion that the later Heideggerian step back to think Ereignis as such in itself constituted an ending-beginning. Compare the implication of Werner Marx in his 1979 introduction to the new edition of his classic *Heidegger and the Tradition* (Evanston: Northwestern University Press, 1982; orig. German ed. 1961), xl–xli. The fact that concealment no longer conceals itself is a new beginning in one sense, but in Heidegger's terms what it begins is historicism. Heideggerian disengagement is a *response* to that historicism, stemming from a longing for an alternative to it.

still more basic line of questioning. Yet things never came to rest; the same questions kept returning, to be reformulated. Heidegger was explicit about the need to keep on the move: "Our task is unceasingly to overcome the obstacles that tend to render such saying inadequate." We must be ready "to let our own attempts at thinking be overturned, again and again, by what is unthought in the thinkers' thought."[112]

There was no end in sight to the confrontation with Parmenides, for example, but this endlessness, rather than a failing, is simply a corollary of incompleteness. Rather than fixing Parmenides once and for all, we continually question him anew, on the basis of new experience, precisely as Heidegger himself was doing.[113] We do not expect any definitive answers from the Greeks, or anyone else. In emphasizing this restless and reflexive encounter, Heidegger offered not some definitive solution but a kind of ritual, which might serve as an ongoing cultural component for a postmetaphysical world, a component based on one possible—though surely extreme—way of responding to the world as historical. Such ongoing ritual seems attractive especially when political response, even the apocalyptic response of Nazism, can only yield more of the same.

But Heidegger suggested that such ritualistic disengagement might serve a deeper purpose, as a way to hold things open for something else, a new dispensation, a different history. Although we cannot hope to overcome, for example, the confusion that Greek categories have bequeathed to us, Heidegger insists that "the attempt to heed this confusion steadfastly, using its tenacious power to effect some resolution, may well bring about a situation which releases a different destiny of being."[114]

In some of Heidegger's characterizations, such steadfast heeding seemed to suggest, again, that we can only wait passively. In his famous *Der Spiegel* interview of 1966, held for posthumous publication, he concluded, "Nur noch ein Gott kann uns retten" (Only a god can save us).[115] But we prepare ourselves for a different sending by actively thinking through our history, attending to the holding back, so that we disenthrall ourselves from our actual destiny. It is thus that we hold ourselves open for an upsurge of the holy, a different experience, even a different dispensation.[116]

112. Heidegger, *On Time and Being*, 24; Heidegger, *What Is Called Thinking?* 77. See also Heidegger, *Discourse on Thinking*, 52–53; and Heidegger, "Origin of the Work of Art," 55–57. In addition, see David Halliburton, *Poetic Thinking: An Approach to Heidegger* (Chicago: University of Chicago Press), 182; and Walter Bieml, *Martin Heidegger: An Illustrated Study*, trans. J. L. Mehta (New York: Harcourt Brace Jovanovich, Harvest, 1976), 8–9, on the restlessness of Heidegger's approach.
113. Heidegger, *Early Greek Thinking*, 100–101, 105–106.
114. Ibid., 25.
115. Heidegger, " 'Only a God Can Save Us,' " 57.
116. See Heidegger, "Letter on Humanism," 216, 218, on the idea of a new "dispensation" and the preparation required for it.

There is little for us to say about what that might entail. For now we cannot escape the spatial metaphors and linguistic dualisms that have led us to conceive God and the holy as we have, in terms of such concepts as immanence and transcendence. But even radical immanence is not given once and for all. The point, then, is not that the new God or gods will or will not be transcendent; the dichotomy itself would fall away with a different sending in language.

Yet when compared to what we used to take religious experience to involve, Heidegger's attuning and waiting offers only a pale, limited experience of the holy, a pathetic religiosity, because it seems utterly without positive content. But that is all that is possible for us now, in light of the actual resulting in nihilism, in a historicist world feeding on its own excrement. Still, this new way of experiencing the holy may prove richer than it seems, and it might hold things open for a new giving involving a still richer experience.

On the basis of its posthistoricist dimension, Heideggerian religiosity can be distinguished both from earlier religious emphases and from newer forms of mysticism spawned by the intellectual displacement. As noted briefly in chapter 3, Henri Bergson, like Heidegger, was seeking a kind of posttranscendent religiosity, but what Heidegger envisioned was more radical precisely because it was also posthistoricist. Attuning to the giving-sending is not the same as attuning to the nonrational life force, which is conventional in comparison—and easily becomes a new metaphysics, as we saw. For Bergson, the challenge was to rescue religiosity from science, not from history, while for Heidegger, science had already dissolved into history. The challenge, then, was closer to rescuing religiosity from history, to making way for a new religiosity even in light of the reduction to history.

In a sense, Heidegger was inviting simply an "openness to the mystery," but it is crucial that, because it was posthistoricist, the Heideggerian stance is also distinguishable from mysticism as usually understood.[117] Such openness rests on a restless and reflexive thinking of the particular history, as opposed to mere feeling, to intuition of something else, or to some mushy oneness presumed to transcend history and historicity. Heidegger's emphasis on openness stands in instructive contrast with the accents of literary modernists like Ezra Pound and T. S. Eliot, who became interested in mystical or visionary experience in light of the hypertrophy of history.[118] Unlike these writers, Heidegger did not seek to see through the particulars of history to oneness or wholeness; it is precisely such oneness or wholeness that is not there. But once

---

117. In a number of works Caputo has compared Heidegger with the mystical tradition—generally to Heidegger's disadvantage. See especially the concluding chapter to Caputo, *Radical Hermeneutics*, but see also pp. 185–186, for indications of tension in Caputo's interpretation. See also John D. Caputo, *The Mystical Element in Heidegger's Thought* (New York: Fordham University Press, 1986).

118. James Longenbach, *Modernist Poetics of History: Pound, Eliot, and the Sense of the Past* (Princeton: Princeton University Press, 1987), 212–213.

we have fully experienced that absence, *then* what can it mean to open ourselves to the mystery? It involves an experience of the difference as such, of
particularity itself—of the obvious become uncanny. We open ourselves to the
mystery only by approaching our particular history in a new, posthistoricist
way.

But if continuing engagement with our history distinguished Heidegger's
quest for a new religiosity, is it fair to charge, with Rorty and Derrida, that he
was trapped by the terms of the philosophical tradition and that, whatever his
pretenses to the contrary, he simply added another layer to it?[119] Although Heidegger occasionally equated the thinking he advocated with philosophy, it is
crucial that such thinking does not seek transcendental conditions or definitive
solutions. Thus Heidegger's characterization in his "Letter on Humanism":
"The thinking that is to come is no longer philosophy, because it thinks more
originally than metaphysics—a name identical to philosophy." And such thinking abandons any pretense that it will "become wisdom itself in the form of
absolute knowledge," as Hegel had envisioned. Rather, "thinking gathers language into simple saying."[120]

Contrary to Derrida, Heidegger was not seeking some metaphysical key to
unlock the secret meaning of being.[121] His aim, rather, was to specify what a
broadly religious experience would entail once we recognize that there are no
such keys or secrets. Critics like Rorty and Derrida have not done justice to
the point of Heidegger's posthistoricist concern with coming to be as particularizing. Thus they fail to grasp why, even in a postmetaphysical mode, one
might choose *not* simply to turn from the tradition or use it playfully, for edification. And they fail to grasp the scope for relating to that tradition without
simply continuing it, the scope for disengagement through ongoing, restless
encounter.

To be sure, Heidegger still envisioned something like the reappropriation
of a lost or alienated essence of "man," so he seems subject to the old ideal of,
or nostalgia for, wholeness.[122] The present is debased partly because we do not
experience ourselves in the "right" way, in terms of the appropriate relationship

119. According to Rorty, Heidegger's "pathetic notion that even after metaphysics goes, something called 'Thought' might remain . . . is simply the sign of Heidegger's own fatal attachment to
the tradition." See Richard Rorty, *Consequences of Pragmatism (Essays: 1972–1980)* (Minneapolis: University of Minnesota Press, 1982), 52–54. Rorty's most critical characterizations date from
the 1970s, but though his account of Heidegger soon became more nuanced, he continued to find
Heidegger unnecessarily attached to the philosophical tradition.

120. Heidegger, "Letter on Humanism," 242. See also Karsten Harries, "Heidegger as a Political Thinker," in *Heidegger and Modern Philosophy*, 326, for an effective characterization of the
novelty of Heidegger's mature approach. In addition, see Heidegger, *What Is Called Thinking?*
79, for an example of his occasional tendency to blur "thinking" and philosophy.

121. Here I follow David Couzens Hoy's helpful account of Derrida's problem with Heidegger. See Hoy, *The Critical Circle: Literature, History, and Philosophical Hermeneutics* (Berkeley,
Los Angeles, and London: University of California Press, 1982), 78.

122. Heidegger, "Letter on Humanism," 199–200, 204, 219–220.

to being. In this sense, we are estranged from ourselves, from what we really are. In overcoming nihilism we would overcome such estrangement and experience what is truly our relationship to being.

But these imperatives no longer have the conventional meaning. For one thing, Heidegger well understood that in talking of the "essence" of human being he was using language that was still metaphysical and thus inherently limiting and misleading. We can only start with such metaphysical language, since we have only this particular repertoire of ways of saying.[123] The deeper point, in any case, is that overcoming such estrangement in Heideggerian terms means nothing like completeness or wholeness. It yields only a sense of ourselves as a clearing, with the clearing, as the term suggests, an emptiness, like a screen on which something can be projected.[124] We do not discover what we have been striving to be, and we really "are," once and for all. We simply experience ourselves as the openness for letting be.

Heidegger attacked the whole array of humanisms, from Roman to Christian to Marxian to Sartrean, that took the "humanity" of humans as a given, as "determined with regard to an already established interpretation of nature, history, world, and the ground of the world, that is, of beings as a whole." Every humanism, said Heidegger, is either grounded in a metaphysics or is itself made to be the ground of one. He used humanism pejoratively, then, because it seemed a major vehicle of the essentialism and subjectivism of our metaphysical tradition. But he took care to emphasize, at the same time, that "man" is not to be viewed as simply one thing or being among others; human being is special in the scheme of things. Indeed, he said, "humanism is opposed because it does not set the *humanitas* of man high enough."[125]

In pushing through historicism to a religious dimension, Heidegger opened up one set of possibilities while concealing others. And thus he invites especially Richard J. Bernstein's objection that the "saving power" he was seeking should encompass praxis, phronesis, action in the public realm.[126] In fact, Heidegger's perspective was so extreme that it allowed virtually no differentiation among human actions; what matters is the sense in which mechanized agriculture and mechanized killing in gas chambers are the same. Even the public action Bernstein envisions would prove to rest on the same sort of manipulation.

123. Ibid., 202, 205.
124. See ibid., 221, and Heidegger, "Origin of the Work of Art," 52–53, for examples of Heidegger's many references to human being as a clearing or emptiness.
125. Heidegger, "Letter on Humanism," 201–204, 210, 222, 224–227; the quotations are from pp. 202, 210.
126. In *The New Constellation*, 120–136, Bernstein accents Heidegger's way of precluding any such scope for action in the public realm. Especially in his key discussion on pp. 132–133, Bernstein does not do justice to Heidegger's quest for an apolitical religious alternative. But though I depart from Bernstein on this issue, it is crucial to my overall argument that Heidegger's extreme response does not exhaust the possibilities.

In investing his hopes in Nazism, Heidegger was provincial and naive, but he learned from the failure of Nazism, and he shared in the wider political disillusionment of our era as he did so. Because of the dramatic disasters, especially, but also because of the more mundane features of our political experience, even the notions that Bernstein invokes—praxis, the public sphere—have come to seem threadbare. Although it derived from his contingent encounter with Nazism, Heidegger's mature position has resonance partly because it responds to the larger experience of our culture, which had invested greatly in the scope for political action with the eclipse of metaphysics but which encountered limits and frustrations by the end of the twentieth century. Heidegger sought to explore what lies beyond the limits of action, what happens at the point where actions are leveled out, where all they can do is produce more of the same.

But as Bernstein emphasizes, such prominent students of Heidegger as Hans-Georg Gadamer and Hannah Arendt diverged sharply from Heidegger himself on this score. Each denied that the basically Heideggerian framework required any such definitive abandonment of the hope for constructive public action. Indeed, each found it possible to reconceive the political sphere on the basis of certain of Heidegger's insights.

So Heidegger does not merit the last word, but together with Nietzsche and Croce he helped establish a web of possibilities in response to the eclipse of metaphysics and the reduction to history. More recent encounters with the world as historical have operated within the new terrain these three thinkers blocked out.

7

Gadamerian Hermeneutics

Belonging to a Growing Tradition

Interlude: Pathways in a New Terrain

As the outcome of their pioneering encounters with the world as historical, Nietzsche, Croce, and Heidegger left a set of ideas that continues to influence our sense of postmetaphysical possibilities. Their intellectual legacies were inevitably fissured, so subsequent thinkers could borrow selectively from them and combine components in new ways. We have seen, for example, that though Nietzsche and Heidegger ended up deemphasizing historical inquiry to serve reconstruction, each may show, as Croce did not, how historical questioning might expand and become more culturally significant.

In the final analysis, however, Nietzsche and Heidegger were indeed "prophets of extremity," and Croce was self-consciously moderate. The common extremity lay in eschewing the bland emphasis on knowing and making history that we find archetypally in Croce. But the two extremes were in crucial respects opposite, even mutually exclusive, and attention to the difference indicates that Nietzsche and Heidegger each had something in common with Croce vis-à-vis the other. So whereas the moderate-extremity axis is sometimes essential, other axes are also at issue within the new space the three thinkers opened up.

This point must be emphasized because of the ongoing tendency to accent what Nietzsche and Heidegger have in common, even to interject a Nietzschean Heidegger into the cultural mix. A sense that the cultural priority is to undercut still-metaphysical claims to privilege, or to specify a single postmetaphysical alternative, has fed this tendency.[1] If we take the eclipse of metaphysics for

---

1. This tendency to paint a particularly Nietzschean Heidegger is evident in three thinkers to whom I am particularly indebted, John Caputo, Gianni Vattimo, and Richard Rorty. Of the three, Caputo is the most concerned to head off still-metaphysical positions; see John D. Caputo,

granted and, as a first approximation, conceive the postmetaphysical space as triangular, we can attune ourselves to a more complex array of possibilities as we move to subsequent thinkers. We can place the ongoing tendency toward extremity in clearer perspective and better grasp the scope for a moderate alternative.

More specifically, two of the most influential subsequent strategies, Gadamerian hermeneutics and poststructuralist deconstruction, each owed a major debt to Heidegger, yet the relationship between them has been problematic, even antagonistic. Before assessing their place in the ongoing exploration of the world as historical, we will find it helpful to pinpoint two sets of prejudicial conflations, each of which we can identify by separating Nietzsche and Heidegger, then looking at what each has in common with Croce. Such comparisons suggest the scope, first, for a mode of identification with the actual that does not involve subjectivist hubris and, second, for a mode of care that makes possible the happening of a postmetaphysical form of truth.

Heidegger's condemnation of his own time was so sweeping that he conflated still-metaphysical with competing postmetaphysical positions. Thus he tended to take all forms of humanism or anthropocentrism as metaphysical and to preclude modes of identification with the actual that are postmetaphysical and weak. Certainly Nietzsche and Croce, in their different ways, were anthropocentric and humanistic in a way that Heidegger was not. Each suggested that the world that comes to be in history results from human response, and each posited a mode of "affirmation" or identification with our particular history, in contrast to the postmetaphysical "alienation" that led Heidegger to his premium on disengagement. Yet in neither case did this affirmative anthropocentrism rest on the sort of subjectivist privilege that Heidegger associated with *any* form of anthropocentrism or humanism.

Heidegger's critique of "valuing" manifests his tendency to preclude such postmetaphysical alternatives:

> Every valuing, even where it values positively, is a subjectivizing. It does not let beings: be. Rather, valuing lets beings: be valid—solely as the objects of its doing. . . . [T]hinking in values is the greatest blasphemy imaginable against Being. To think against values therefore does not mean to beat the drum for the valuelessness and nullity of beings. It means rather to bring the lighting of the truth of Being before thinking, as against subjectivizing beings into mere objects.[2]

Radical Hermeneutics: Repetition, Deconstruction, and the Hermeneutic Project (Bloomington: Indiana University Press, 1987), 204–205. Vattimo synthesized the two thinkers as the basis of his own postmetaphysical *pensiero debole*; see especially *La fine della modernità* (Milan: Garzanti, 1985), 177–186. Though Rorty, in contrast, distances himself from Nietzsche and Heidegger, he accents their common quest for the "historical sublime"; see *Contingency, Irony, and Solidarity* (Cambridge: Cambridge University Press, 1989), 105–109; see also pp. 65, 97n, 99–102.

2. Martin Heidegger, "Letter on Humanism," trans. Frank A. Capuzzi and J. Glenn Gray, in *Basic Writings*, ed. David Farrell Krell (New York: Harper and Row, 1977), 228. See also Martin Heidegger, "The Age of the World Picture," in *The Question Concerning Technology and Other Essays*, trans. William Lovitt (New York: Harper and Row, Torchbook, 1977), 142, on the development of "values" from subjectivity.

In one sense Heidegger's charge applies archetypally to Nietzsche and Croce, who held that human beings give the world the only value it has—indeed, that they bring worlds into being as they evaluate. It is equally crucial, however, that neither Nietzsche nor Croce appealed to "values" and that each eschewed the subjectivist dualism that turns beings into mere objects.

For Nietzsche and Croce, as for Heidegger, it is through human being that things come to be a certain way, but unlike Heidegger, they posited evaluating as constitutive of that human being and its special role in the coming to be of anything at all. As we have seen, Nietzsche and Croce each sought to side-step subjectivism by dissolving the subject into some larger happening; evaluating is simply an aspect of that larger happening. Heidegger, viewing the options dualistically, had no room for the difference; an emphasis on human evaluating, he assumed, is no less metaphysical than an appeal to transcendent values or subjectivist grounding.

Heidegger deplored the contemporary tendency to make historical understanding serve contemporary purposes as yet another instance of the calculative reasoning and objectification characteristic of this age of technology. This charge applies to Nietzsche's invitation to redescribe the past for present purposes, but it was aimed especially at the notion, widely associated with Croce by Heidegger's time, that contemporary purposes underpin historical inquiry. But Croce's position does not carry all the anthropocentric, subjectivist baggage Heidegger had in mind. Croce explored what Heidegger precluded, the scope for a relationship to our own history that is purposive without objectifying and without inviting cause-and-effect explanation.

Although this side of his thinking remained undeveloped, Croce insisted on growing spirit as the only reality partly to eschew subjectivism and objectification. And he sought to counter the cultural ascendancy of science and technology, much as Heidegger did, because by positing a world of static, given objects, as opposed to an endless coming to be through human being, the culture of science misconstrued our relationship to what is happening. Thus Croce explicitly eschewed causal explanation and denied that a historical account could be definitive and certain.

Genuine historical inquiry in a Crocean mode stems from an orientation much like Heideggerian care. Insofar as we care for the world, we approach the past not, as Heidegger charged, to objectify it, to make it controllable and safe, but to learn, to understand our kinship with what came before and our belongingness to the same history. To be sure, historical interpretation is an instance of power: individual inquirers question history in a particular way, and they seek, through the particular interpretations that result, to influence the wider cultural self-understanding. But these historians understand their accounts as contributions to the growing historical culture. The purposiveness that informs historical inquiry is simply one aspect of the particularizing, one mechanism whereby the happening of the world continues in a certain way. Croce's orientation entailed humility, not the hubris that Heidegger associated with humanism.

Heidegger forced Nietzsche's doctrine of will to power into the sequence of metaphysical positions, then linked Nietzschean will to the restlessness of modern technology. Although he had plausible reasons to reject Nietzsche's overall orientation, Heidegger was not doing justice to the postmetaphysical force of Nietzsche's thinking.[3] Nietzsche spoke of will to power in order to characterize what is left with the eclipse of metaphysics, once there is no ground, no way things are, but only endless particularizing. Although he was the quintessential anthropocentrist in one sense, Nietzsche gradually came to balance his emphasis on human agency with the more passive accents of his maturity, especially amor fati and eternal recurrence. These made it clearer that in reducing everything to will to power Nietzsche was not seeking to posit strong human agency or some stable subject that makes objects of beings; rather, he wanted simply to indicate what "there is" if, even in the absence of metaphysical grounding, some particular world continually comes to be through human being. Just as for Heidegger himself, it is only through human being that any such worlding happens.

In the final analysis, "power" for Nietzsche is simply the glue or coherence necessary for a world to keep coming to be; *will* to power links human being to the ongoing particularizing that characterizes this endless becoming. "Will to power" simply names the capacity or attribute that brings human being together with this ongoing particularizing. There can be some particular outcome only as the continuing resultant of the ongoing concatenation of the actions that stem from the will to power of differentiated individuals, each desiring to impose his or her own form on the world. In the final analysis, the sense of fullness and the openness to innocent play that Nietzsche envisioned are anything but the blind striving, with will seeking power as an end in itself, that Heidegger attributed to him.

Nietzsche, with his particular preoccupations, accented the scope for a special caste of individuals, whose will to impose their own form is bound up with their quest for self-creation, but Croce's way of conceiving ongoing worlding, or coming to be, is comparable. Although his language was different, Croce fully shared Nietzsche's sense that there is "power," the glue that enables the world always to have some particular shape, and that it stems from creative will as arrayed in differentiated individuals. Will to power underlies the action, including persuasion, through which the world is endlessly remade. But Croce was at once more "egalitarian" and less apocalyptic than Nietzsche. On the one hand, he explicitly attacked any "great man" theory of history as he accented the history-making implications of all human actions; thus his widely misconstrued notion that the only agent is the whole spirit. On the other hand, he

---

3. For a good brief dissection of the arbitrariness in Heidegger's reading of Nietzsche, see Alan D. Schrift, "Violence or Violation? Heidegger's Thinking 'about' Nietzsche," in *The Thought of Martin Heidegger*, ed. Michael E. Zimmerman (Tulane Studies in Philosophy, vol. 32; New Orleans, La.: Tulane University, 1984), 79–86.

stressed the sense in which the process of worlding, or coming to be, is going on all the time, resulting in whatever actuality there is.

Attention to what Nietzsche and Croce have in common highlights the limits of Heidegger's way of conflating technology, subjectivism, and anthropocentrism. The package of anthropocentrism, humanism, affirmation, and power can be postmetaphysical and weak.

At the same time, however, the tendency to bring Nietzsche and Heidegger together obscures the scope for developing a major theme in Heidegger in a more moderate direction. Here again, asking what the extremist, now Heidegger, has in common with Croce helps bring that possibility to the forefront.

Caputo gives Heideggerian thinking a Nietzschean spin, as a stimulus to the ongoing play that he finds the essential postmetaphysical strategy, necessary to head off the authoritarian, still-metaphysical tendencies that continue to lurk in the culture. In the final analysis, however, Caputo found the key to this strategy not in Heidegger but in Derrida, who, he felt, had extracted and developed the genuinely antimetaphysical side of Heidegger. Caputo portrayed Gadamer, in contrast, as moving in the opposite direction, taking elements of Heidegger back toward metaphysics and authority.[4] But Caputo's way of placing Heidegger between Nietzsche and Derrida does not do justice to all the postmetaphysical dimensions of Heidegger's legacy. And Caputo's way of positing "play" as the only alternative to authoritarianism precludes Gadamer's way of developing Heideggerian insights in a less extreme, more constructive, but still postmetaphysical direction.

Croce and Heidegger differed from Nietzsche in positing care for the world as opposed to the self. And whereas Nietzsche invited pragmatic fictions to serve self-creation, Croce and Heidegger showed the scope for truth to the particular history on the basis of that care for the world. Although with different ends in view, Croce and Heidegger were each concerned to show what truth means and how it happens in postmetaphysical circumstances. In accounting for the possibility of truth, each accented the place of human being, especially human language, in the coming to be of some particular world in history. With his notion of human being as the clearing for some particular sending of being in language, Heidegger deepened the Vico-Croce way of sidestepping the old subject-object dualism. Language is a vehicle not for representing a prior reality but for the happening of a truth, understood not as correspondence but as disclosure.

To be sure, Heidegger would have had no interest in finding common cause with Croce against Nietzsche, and his concern for disengagement militates against any constructive use of his insights. But it is possible to draw Heidegger's way of conceiving human being, language, truth, and coming to be in a

---

4. Caputo, *Radical Hermeneutics*, 111–119. In the concluding chapter I consider the concerns that led Caputo to cast deconstruction and hermeneutics as he did.

more affirmative, constructive direction without lapsing into subjectivist anthropocentrism.

Although Croce's presentism did not entail mere anachronism or the subjectivist humanism that Heidegger deplored, Heidegger's charge that historiography tends to close off the past to what does not conform to present standards carries some weight against Croce—and suggests the need for a Heideggerian complement. Whereas Croce's way of conceiving history afforded privilege to what leads to the next moment, to actualization, Heidegger accented the endless interplay of giving and holding back as the particular world comes to be in history. The more complex relationship to history that Heidegger invited proves to have more room for surprise, challenge, risk.

Although Heidegger pointed the way to a novel mode of historical questioning on that basis, his priorities led him in a different direction. But, as it happened, that insight was subsequently developed in both Gadamerian hermeneutics and poststructuralist deconstruction. In light of the different, even incompatible, accents of these currents, it has been difficult to see how they might come together in a constructive way.

Heidegger, Gadamer, and Croce

Gadamer studied with Heidegger and remained a Heideggerian in important respects throughout his career. But as Heidegger was seeking to step back and disengage from the actual, Gadamer adapted aspects of the Heideggerian framework to reconceive the human way of belonging to some particular tradition. He noted the extremity in the responses of both Nietzsche, with his "anguished enthusiasm," and Heidegger, with his "eschatological pathos." But those extremes "found a counterpoise in the continuity of a linguistically interpreted order of life that is constantly being built up and renewed in family, society, and state."[5] Although he shared Heidegger's distaste for modern technology, Gadamer found Heidegger too apocalyptic. Rather than portray the Western tradition as a darkening or forgetting, he emphasized the openness of our tradition to continuing growth through a "fusion of horizons," or dialogue between present and past. Even with the dissolution of all metaphysical props, there is some measure of communication and solidarity, moral response and truth, as what we do endlessly results in a common world.[6]

---

5. Hans-Georg Gadamer, *Reason in the Age of Science*, trans. Frederick G. Lawrence (Cambridge: MIT Press, 1981), 58.

6. In "A Letter by Professor Hans-Georg Gadamer" (1 June 1982), Appendix to Richard J. Bernstein, *Beyond Objectivism and Relativism: Science, Hermeneutics, and Praxis* (Philadelphia: University of Pennsylvania Press, 1983), 264, Gadamer makes this point succinctly and forcefully. A collection of Gadamer's essays on Heidegger has recently been published as *Heidegger's Ways*, trans. John W. Stanley (Albany: State University of New York Press, 1994). For Gadamer's reflections on his own intellectual development, see his *Philosophical Apprenticeships*, trans. Robert R. Sullivan (Cambridge: MIT Press, 1985).

Like Heidegger, Gadamer responded to the apparent inadequacies in Dilthey, but whereas Heidegger ended up turning from hermeneutics altogether, Gadamer set out to recast the hermeneutic tradition as he sought a more constructive response to the reduction to history. The result was what Gadamer called "philosophical hermeneutics," offered in systematic form in his masterly *Wahrheit und Methode* in 1960, published in English as *Truth and Method* in 1975.

Because Gadamer's understanding of the relevant historical lineage was parochially German, he emphasized Dilthey and Heidegger and barely mentioned Croce. But in seeking a moderate postmetaphysical orientation accenting continuity and growth, he was moving from Heidegger back in the direction that Croce had opened up. For Gadamer, as for Croce, to sidestep metaphysics and to resist the modern cult of science and technology did not have to leave us with extremes like Heidegger's. Much like Croce, Gadamer discerned an intermediate orientation focusing on the ongoing happening of a particular history, or tradition, that does not simply limit us but nourishes us and that has not, for all Gadamer's hostility to modern technology, leveled out into sameness in the twentieth century. For both Croce and Gadamer, there is much that we might do in a postmetaphysical world, and what we do has history-making weight.

The effort to rethink cultural proportions in light of the eclipse of metaphysics led Croce and Gadamer each to circumscribe science and philosophy and to think more deeply about the world as historical, because history seemed to inflate as science and philosophy were circumscribed. Like Croce, Gadamer insisted that science does not transcend situatedness or historical specificity as it makes one, derivative kind of sense of historically specific instances; rather, it operates within the overall hermeneutic and historicist framework. Not surprisingly, Gadamer found a kinship with Thomas Kuhn and accented the hermeneutic implications of Kuhn's well-known emphasis on the role of paradigms in the development of the natural sciences.[7]

More specifically, the immediate target for Gadamer, as for Croce, was not science per se but social science, which threatened to dominate the human studies at the expense of the historical-hermeneutic approach. Gadamer sought not simply to contrast the two approaches but to show that social science is itself hermeneutic.[8]

Croce and Gadamer were both seeking to go beyond Dilthey and the first historicism, but the ongoing ambiguities surrounding historicism have impeded exploration of the area of overlap between the two thinkers. Although

7. Hans-Georg Gadamer, *Philosophical Hermeneutics*, trans. David E. Linge (Berkeley, Los Angeles, and London: University of California Press, 1977), 39–40; Gadamer, *Reason*, 164, 166–167. See also Georgia Warnke, *Gadamer: Hermeneutics, Tradition and Reason* (Stanford: Stanford University Press, 1987), 40, 137.

8. Gadamer, *Reason*, 167; Hans-Georg Gadamer, "Hermeneutics and Social Science," *Cultural Hermeneutics* 2 (1975): 310.

Gadamer probed the relationship between hermeneutics and historicism, he, like most, limited his focus to the individualizing historicism of the nineteenth century, which found its major philosophical expression in Dilthey. And Gadamer's philosophical hermeneutics rests on an effective critique of that position. But Gadamer's critique does not apply to Croce, whose way of making historicism absolute had much in common with Gadamer's way of recasting hermeneutics.

The overlap between Gadamer and Croce was obviously not a matter of direct influence, although Croce, through his influence on Collingwood, had some indirect impact on Gadamer, who recognized an intellectual debt to Collingwood.[9] But neither is the point simply that Gadamer happened to parallel Croce. The key is that Gadamer's encounter with Heidegger enabled him to develop "history" as an alternative to the culture of science from a different angle than Croce's. Indeed, he analyzed systematically much that Croce had simply taken for granted and specified mechanisms that remained obscure in Croce's thinking.

However, Gadamer was subject to limitations of his own, and up to a point Croce helps us to counter them without lapsing back into metaphysics or falling into irrationalism. Thus Crocean and Gadamerian ideas prove complementary. Yet there remains something limiting even about the historicist-hermeneutic synthesis that their ideas invite. A convincing moderate, constructive alternative to the culture of extremity needs to draw from other thinkers as well.

Belonging to History

Like Nietzsche, Croce, and Heidegger, Gadamer took it for granted that we are fundamentally historical creatures, but, as he saw it, the task of thinking through the cultural implications of the fundamental historicity of human being remained incomplete. Those who first began to see the world as historical, especially Vico, Hegel, and Dilthey, had not managed radically to confront the implications of the fact that we are fundamentally part of the history we seek to know.

In Dilthey's thinking, the concerns of individualizing historicism had led to a renewed encounter with the hermeneutic tradition. And for Gadamer, that convergence had been essential, yet inadequate. The hermeneutic turn had been necessary because understanding and interpretation came to seem problematic during the nineteenth century. In accounting for the problem, Gadamer paid lip service to the possibility of masking, or false consciousness, to which Marx,

---

9. Gadamer discusses his debt to Collingwood in *Reason*, 45–47, 106. He referred to Croce occasionally, though not in an entirely consistent way. Within a few pages of his *Truth and Method* (New York: Seabury, 1975; orig. German ed. 1960), he associated Croce first with Hegel but then with an extreme subjectivism in reaction against positivism; see pp. 464, 467.

Nietzsche, and Freud drew our attention, but his dominant accent was on the growing sense of the import of temporal distance, which seemed an obstacle to historical understanding.[10] Because the original meaning was not immediately accessible, the danger of misinterpretation apparently lurked, so the challenge was to overcome the distance, bridging the gap between present and past.

To some extent, it seemed sufficient simply to invoke our common humanity or psychology to indicate an intuitive ability to empathize with other persons. But a special effort—even a special method or skill—was required to rethink the past thought, to reenact the creative act, to relive the earlier experience. Gadamer showed how hermeneutics, in Dilthey's hands, became the teachable skill or method for that kind of empathy, or psychologistic understanding. It entailed objectivity as well as psychological involvement, for it was necessary, to the extent possible, to rethink or reenact using *their* categories, as opposed to our own. Thus the confusing legacy of the first historicism, which seemed to invite involvement in a way that positivism did not but which still insisted on a kind of detachment and objectivity.

As Gadamer saw it, the psychologistic approaches of Schleiermacher and then Dilthey led to "the impasses of historicism," yet these had stimulated Heidegger to offer a more convincing understanding of the relationship between temporality and human existence.[11] On that Heideggerian basis a renewed understanding of hermeneutics, truth, and understanding itself became possible. At issue in the relationship between present and past was something more fundamental than epistemology; the key was not to specify a method or to explain how understanding across time takes place. What needed to be understood was the larger happening that such understanding serves and the human place in, or relationship with, what is happening.

Yet though Gadamer found Heidegger's contribution crucial, Heidegger had turned away from hermeneutics, so it had fallen to Gadamer himself to pursue this line of thinking. Hermeneutics had earlier been the special concern of esoteric domains like translation, biblical exegesis, or the interpretation of legal texts, which sought to understand something remote and which thus seemed to involve special problems of interpretation. But Gadamer tells us that with the reduction to history, "when the historical tradition in its entirety up to the present moment moved into a position of similar remoteness," hermeneutics inflates to become all-encompassing.[12] As the whole world came to seem historical, the past as such came to seem alien, distant, different, and a new "experience of estrangement" resulted. By the time of the first historicism, that

10. Gadamer, *Truth and Method*, 264. See Gadamer, *Reason*, 104, for his reference to "modern suspicion."
11. Gadamer, *Truth and Method*, pp. 264, 358, 460–491. See also David Couzens Hoy, *The Critical Circle: Literature, History, and Philosophical Hermeneutics* (Berkeley, Los Angeles, and London: University of California Press, 1982), 11–12.
12. Gadamer, *Reason*, 97. See also p. 99.

experience was becoming a major cultural preoccupation, but even Dilthey had not managed to deal with it. Still thinking in terms of subject-object dualism, he had fallen into the misplaced imperative of detachment.

What was essential for Gadamer, then, was to sidestep that dualism through a deeper understanding of our way of belonging to our own history. In seeking to reconceive the connection between present and past, Gadamer found Collingwood's logic of question and answer helpful, but even Collingwood had not done justice to the active, creative quality of present inquiry and to the open-ended, dialogical nature of the encounter between past and present.[13]

Seeking to clarify his purposes in 1965, in the foreword to the second edition of *Truth and Method*, Gadamer emphasized that he had not offered a general theory of interpretation or an account of its method or methods. His focus had been on something more basic—on what understanding involves in a historical world. Rather than posit transcendent subject and fixed object, we must conceive understanding as a process entailing reciprocity and reflexivity. In peering into some past moment, we relate not toward some fixed object "but toward its effective history—the history of its influence; in other words, understanding belongs to the being of that which is understood." Because all understanding is active interpretation, what had seemed "the object" grows as it is understood. And what had seemed "the subject" is not detached or aloof; rather, our own presuppositions are at issue as we understand, because what there is to be understood is the tradition through which we have become this particular way, through which our particular questions and categories have emerged. To take seriously the finite nature of one's own understanding is to "take the reality of history seriously."[14] In opposition to Dilthey and the notion that history is an object for the human subject, Gadamer insisted that "in fact history does not belong to us, but we belong to it."[15]

As it becomes all-encompassing and philosophical, then, hermeneutics is no longer a teachable skill or method but, first, an account of how understanding happens in light of difference and, ultimately, an account of how the world grows as understanding happens in some particular way.[16] It shows us not how to avoid misinterpretation in the face of the passage of time but how ongoing interpretation fills the passing time, creating a particular world in the process. Not only are historical inquiry and understanding themselves historically situated but it is partly because we understand or receive the past in this particular way, and not some other, that the future is as it is. For Gadamer, then, we present individuals are fundamentally finite and particular, but we project into the

13. See Gadamer, *Truth and Method*, 333–341, on Collingwood's logic of question and answer. This discussion makes clear how the category helped Gadamer but also how its limits showed him what remained to be specified.

14. Ibid, xix–xxiii. The quotations are from pp. xix, xxiii.

15. Ibid., 245.

16. Gadamer, *Reason*, 129–131, makes his case against Schleiermacher and Dilthey with particular clarity.

future on the basis of an infinite dialogue with the past, across time. The tradition, the world itself, endlessly grows as a result.

In following this line of reasoning, Gadamer was explicitly seeking to deepen Vico's dictum that we can know history because we have made it. Georgia Warnke effectively summarizes Gadamer's point:

> The way in which we anticipate the future defines the meaning the past can have for us, just as the way in which we have understood the past and the way in which our ancestors have projected the future determines our own range of possibilities. Thus, for Gadamer, Vico's formula entails that we understand history not simply because we make it but also because it has made us; we belong to it in the sense that we inherit its experience, project a future on the basis of the situation the past has created for us and act in light of our understanding of this past whether such understanding is explicit or not.[17]

For Gadamer, then, the distance between present and past is not "a yawning abyss" to be overcome through some special effort or technique. Rather, temporal distance makes some particular historical understanding possible—most basically because it "is filled with the continuity of custom and tradition, in the light of which all that is handed down presents itself to us."[18] In other words, a continuing process links us to the past moment because we find ourselves within a growing tradition of understanding those at that moment and of experiencing our relationship with them. No matter how radical our revisions, our way of understanding what they did can only grow from—and belong to—that tradition of understanding.

Crucial though this continuity is, however, it is equally important that continuity carries change. Because we have come later, we understand the past differently, in a sense better, than it understood itself; we can gauge the results of what those before us did—and thus determine the meaning, so far, of what they did. In Gadamer's terms, "it is a hermeneutical necessity always to go beyond mere reconstruction," so it falls to us to add the next layer of meaning by questioning and apprehending the tradition from the vantage point of this historically specific moment.[19] Thus it cannot be the aim of historical inquiry, or the key to historical understanding, to reconstruct the original or to apprehend the subjective intent of the historical actor. The point is not reenactment, Collingwood's famous imperative, which Gadamer criticized effectively, finding it incompatible with the radical historicism Collingwood claimed to profess.[20]

---

17. Warnke, *Gadamer*, 39.
18. Gadamer, *Truth and Method*, 264–265.
19. Ibid., 337.
20. Ibid., 149, 468–469. See also Gadamer, *Philosophical Hermeneutics*, 103; and Hoy, *Critical Circle*, 41. For Collingwood's notion of reenactment, see R. G. Collingwood, *The Idea of History* (New York: Oxford University Press, Galaxy, 1956), 282–302; this is the section entitled "History as Re-enactment of Past Experience."

For Gadamer, as for Croce, a corollary of this deeper, postmetaphysical way of belonging to history was a more central role for historical inquiry. But historiography had to abandon the conventional imperatives, which made the historians their own worst enemies. Gadamer reacted against Dilthey much as Croce had attacked Ranke—for merely embalming corpses. Those earlier thinkers had assumed that historical truth required detachment, that the past had to be apprehended "for its own sake." In light of such imperatives, the culture had come to take it for granted that history deals with the past *as opposed to* the present; history was cut off from present life and made safe, as though confined to a museum. For both Gadamer and Croce, in contrast, historical understanding inflates in importance precisely because we understand it as bound up with a present that is endlessly projected into the future.[21]

For both, moreover, this projection means that we seek to understand history for interested, practical reasons. Thus each has drawn charges of arbitrary presentism; indeed, each seems first simply to be giving in to the relativism that had threatened with the first historicism. Yet Gadamer and Croce each insisted that bringing subject and object together in a single open-ended history dissolves the problem of relativism and makes postmetaphysical sense of truth.

It is striking that Gadamer, writing in 1971, found it necessary to make in virtually identical terms the point about relativism that Croce had made in 1915. The relativism bound up with the reduction to history is dangerous, Gadamer insisted, only insofar as we continue to think in terms of "the standard of an absolute knowledge," which suggests there is some vantage point from which we might know something completely and definitively.[22] But we abandon any such standard as we accept history as the only reality. Knowledge can only be provisional, finite, particular—but in the absence of any absolute standard, it is not merely relative in the usual sense. And it still may be true.

In accenting the scope for truth in a purely historicist world, Gadamer, like Croce, was opposing those cultural tendencies that have led to the recent premium on pragmatic fictions or edification. But though the two thinkers made analogous points, Gadamer, drawing on Heidegger, usefully supplemented Croce's argument. At the same time, Gadamer made Heidegger's insight about the happening of truth more concrete. Truth can occur as some particular world comes to be, because of the human mode of involvement with that coming to be in history. Truth is a function of our care for the world, for what it becomes. Thus for Gadamer, as for Croce, it is precisely the "interest" of the finite present inquirer, stemming from this projection into the future, that makes truth possible: "Precisely through our finitude, the particularity of our being, which

21. Gadamer, *Truth and Method*, xxi–xxiii. See also Jürgen Habermas, *Philosophical-Political Profiles*, trans. Frederick G. Lawrence (Cambridge: MIT Press, 1983), 192–194.
22. Hans-Georg Gadamer, "Replik," in *Hermaneutik und Ideologiekritik,* ed. Karl-Otto Apel (Frankfurt: Suhrkamp, 1971), 299. See also Warnke, *Gadamer*, 130.

is evident even in the variety of languages, the infinite dialogue is opened in the direction of the truth that we are."[23]

Even as they insisted on the interestedness of our inquiries, Gadamer and Croce both found it equally important to emphasize the other side of the coin, and they posited very similar ways of distinguishing interests or prejudices that serve the happening of truth from those that impede or distort it. For truth to occur, there must be a willingness to be challenged, a desire to learn, a need to know—all to enable the world to continue to grow through history.[24] The care of the inquirer underpins that need, enabling what emerges to be a truth, as opposed to one of the contraries. For Gadamer, as for Croce, the fact that there are genuine practical stakes is the basis for truth.

The scope for truth is thus bound up with a certain way of belonging, a certain mode of identification with the actual. Each thinker sought to show why we might "respect" our present, as the outcome of our particular tradition so far, even while showing that such respect invites not passive acquiescence but creative response. We identify with the present world sufficiently to care for it, to feel responsibility for it, and to respond to it, thereby changing the outcome, making the tradition grow. Such identification and care entail a sense of the weight of what we do, which is for keeps, because the happening of history endlessly gathers our responses together and thereby expands the tradition.

Confinement and Openness

But belonging to a particular tradition can entail a sense of suffocation or claustrophobia, and thus the aestheticist premium on private autonomy and self-creation that has been one major response to the reduction to history. More generally, the emphasis of both Croce and Gadamer on continuity and tradition in a context of nothing but history has led each thinker to be accused of a prejudicial conservatism. To counter such charges, each went out of his way to accent openness and the scope for novelty. The key, for each, was to specify a moderate way of combining finitude, weight, and totality, on the one hand, with openness, novelty, and creativity, on the other. Up to a point, their way of doing so convincingly addresses the sense of suffocation and the charge of conservatism. But their efforts do not exhaust the issue and thus, in part, the ongoing plausibility of more extreme responses.

23. Gadamer, *Philosophical Hermeneutics*, 16.
24. Objecting to Richard Bernstein's characterization, Gadamer insisted that there is no scientific guarantee of truth, no method for achieving it; there is only a moral basis for disciplining inquiry so that truth results. See his "Letter," appended to Bernstein, *Beyond Objectivism and Relativism*, 263. See also Warnke, *Gadamer*, 40–41, 87, 89. In addition, see Hoy, *Critical Circle*, 52–53, 67–68, on Gadamer's understanding of what "objectivity" might mean once we realize that it cannot mean what the culture of science led us to believe it meant.

It is certainly true that for both Croce and Gadamer, a postmetaphysical culture has to get used to confinement to a finite totality. Because we belong to our particular history, we can only accept the truth of our tradition, in the sense that we can only start with what has resulted so far. Even our determination to question and perhaps change grows from within the tradition. Moreover, whatever we do, if it becomes real at all, will connect with and continue that tradition. We can only participate in the happening of a finite event, which is in one sense all there is.

Gadamer insisted explicitly that our tradition or history is a weak totality: "The idea of the whole is itself to be understood only relatively. The totality of meaning that has to be understood in history or tradition is never the meaning of the totality of history."[25] It is never exhaustive, never brings to completion the interaction—the dialogue—between present and past. Thus for Gadamer, as for Croce, it is crucial that though we are delimited or channeled by what we have been, we are not fixed; the finitude of historical situatedness does not mean that our horizons are closed. Each of them showed how change, novelty, and growth result from the interaction of present human being with the tradition that has resulted from the past.

Gadamer responded explicitly to the novel sense of determination by an unchosen past and confinement to a closed culture that informed Nietzsche's "On the Uses and Disadvantages of History for Life."[26] To counter such preoccupations, Gadamer accented change and movement, openness and the scope for novelty; he denied he was suggesting that some closed horizon encircles a culture or "that cultural tradition should be absolutized and fixed."[27] Rather, those horizons move with us; ongoing questioning of our tradition produces an ongoing expansion of horizons. As Gadamer saw it, Nietzsche's sense that historical consciousness was somehow deleterious to "life" stemmed precisely from the way the culture, under the hegemony of science, had come to misconstrue the human relationship with history, producing an unwarranted alienation from it.

Just like Croce, then, Gadamer viewed the fact that we are fundamentally historical creatures to be an invitation to a creative encounter with our tradition, an encounter that leads to ongoing growth. And like Croce, Gadamer took it for granted that the completeness Hegel envisioned is inconceivable, so the dialogue is infinite; "self-understanding is always on the way," never finished.[28] There is no thing-in-itself whose meaning or truth we either finally attain or never quite attain.

25. Gadamer, *Truth and Method*, xxiii.
26. Ibid., 271–274.
27. Gadamer, *Philosophical Hermeneutics*, 31; see also pp. 56–58, for a key passage on novelty and growth. In addition, see Warnke, *Gadamer*, 81–82, 90–92, 96–97.
28. Gadamer, *Reason*, 103, 105.

Echoing points that Croce made half a century before, Gadamer stressed that we continually modify the tradition as we respond to changed circumstances: "Through every dialogue something different comes to be."[29] He emphasized the growth even of language; the meanings of words grow every time they are used in concrete situations. Knowing a language does not mean knowing fixed meanings but participating in this endless growing-happening of language. In the same way, each application of a law is an interpretation, a performance—and fashions a new reality.[30] Even as he advocated reconnecting with the Aristotelian tradition of phronesis, or practical philosophy, which had been marginalized with the ascendancy of the natural sciences, Gadamer emphasized that our problems are different because of the new layers that are forever being added to the world.[31] We can learn from that tradition, but we will have to refashion it to make it relevant to us.

But to accent openness and novelty against the implication of suffocating finitude was only half the battle. The reduction to history invites the opposite preoccupation as well and thus the opposite extreme in response. If the world is endlessly moving and changing, we might feel not suffocation but a sense of weightlessness, lightness, even futility. Things fly off in all directions; nothing lasts. This sense of things has contributed to the playful side of the aestheticist premium on self-creation. Thus Gadamer balanced his emphasis on openness by insisting that the moment of "gathering," of coming back together, of coming to consensus, of building up a common world, also recurs endlessly. These emphases complement the Crocean themes of faith in history and the immortality of the act, which were similarly intended to specify the enduring weight of what we do.

Because the new preoccupations stemming from the reduction to history pointed in opposite directions, both Croce and Gadamer had to navigate between Scylla and Charybdis, accenting both belonging and openness, both weight and creativity, in their quest for postmetaphysical moderation. Thus their positions have proven hard to characterize—and have been easily misconstrued.

Gadamer's emphasis on openness did not convince critics like Jürgen Habermas and Karl-Otto Apel, who found in his accents a prejudicially conservative acquiescence in the authority of the particular tradition. Habermas's

---

29. Gadamer, *Philosophical Hermeneutics*, 56–58. The quotation is from p. 58; see also the reference to "ever new" on p. 57. In this context, it is worth noting that Gadamer explicitly recognized a kinship with Wittgenstein; see especially *Reason*, 164–166; but also *Philosophical Hermeneutics*, 126–127, where he accents the parallels between Heidegger and Wittgenstein.

30. Gadamer, *Reason,* 126. For comparable accents in Croce as early as 1902, see Benedetto Croce, *Estetica come scienza dell'espressione e linguistica generale: Teoria e storia* (Bari: Laterza, 1958), 16–17, 60, 160–165, 522–524.

31. Gadamer, "Hermeneutics and Social Science," 313–314.

criticisms sparked a lively debate with Gadamer by the latter 1960s, one of the most notable in the humanities since World War II.[32]

Up to a point, Habermas accepted the Gadamerian emphasis on the primacy of dialogue, in opposition to the pretenses of "monological self-certainty." He even admitted that at present "the false claim to universality made by criticism" may pose a greater danger than the Gadamerian emphasis on the authority of tradition.[33] But Habermas was bothered by the implication, which we find in both Gadamer and Croce, that there is *nothing but* that dialogue, which operates within, yet endlessly reconstitutes, some particular tradition. For Habermas, it would be fine to operate within the authority of tradition "if we could be certain that each consensus arrived at in the medium of linguistic tradition has been achieved without compulsion and distortion." But our tradition—any tradition—may be woven around such distorting coercion. And Habermas worried that Gadamer, in emphasizing consensus and the truth of the tradition, was removing from scrutiny a sphere of prereflective agreement that might include precisely such distortion. If we settle for Gadamerian hermeneutics, we have no "general criterion" enabling us to determine when such distortion is at work, when "we are subject to the false consciousness of a pseudo-normal under-standing."[34] In other words, Gadamer seems to allow no scope for pulling back from immediate hermeneutic interaction to a higher level on which the rules or criteria governing the dialogue itself might be discovered or established.

So Habermas assumed that we need something extra—some "general crite-rion"—involving "the meta-hermeneutic awareness of the conditions for the possibility of systematically distorted communication." And in fact, he main-tained, something of the sort has been implicit all along. We inevitably presup-pose a "theory of communicative competence," including what undistorted communication would entail, in our interaction with others. Indeed, it is not the particular tradition that binds us together, making communication possible, but precisely the ideal or regulative principle of undistorted communication, which we hope to realize in the future. That principle entails "the formal anticipation of an idealized dialogue" that would produce "unforced universal agreement."[35]

32. For a succinct and powerful statement of Habermas's critique of Gadamerian hermeneu-tics, see Jürgen Habermas, "The Hermeneutic Claim to Universality," trans. Josef Bleicher, in Josef Bleicher, *Contemporary Hermeneutics: Hermeneutics as Method, Philosophy and Critique* (Lon-don: Routledge and Kegan Paul, 1980), 181–211, esp. pp. 191, 202–209. See also Albrecht Wellmer, *Critical Theory of Society*, trans. John Cumming (New York: Herder and Herder, 1971), 41–51, for a comparable effort to show the limits of Gadamerian hermeneutics from the standpoint of the critical theory that has developed from the Frankfurt school to Habermas. For examples of Gadamer's countercritique of Habermas, see *Philosophical Hermeneutics*, 26–38, 41–42. Two exemplary accounts of the Gadamer-Habermas debate are Martin Jay, "Should Intellectual His-tory Take a Linguistic Turn? Reflections on the Habermas-Gadamer Debate," in *Modern Euro-pean Intellectual History: Reappraisals and New Perspectives,* ed. Dominick LaCapra and Ste-ven L. Kaplan (Ithaca: Cornell University Press, 1982), 86–110; and Hoy, *Critical Circle*, 117–128.
33. Habermas, "Hermeneutic Claim," 209.
34. Ibid., 191, 205. See also Warnke, *Gadamer*, 129–130.
35. Habermas, "Hermeneutic Claim," 206–207.

Such a regulative principle had only been implicit up to now, but Habermas found it imperative to develop it in a rigorous theoretical way, to counter the cultural tendencies that he associated with the hypertrophy of hermeneutics. Thus, in his own mature work, he sought to show how we might "deduce the principle of rational discourse from the logic of everyday language and regard it as the necessary regulative for any actual discourse, however distorted it may be." According to that principle, "truth would only be guaranteed by *that* kind of consensus which was achieved under the idealized conditions of unlimited communication free from domination and could be maintained over time."[36] Thus, as Warnke has summarized Habermas's strategy, "systematic and ideological distortions in the self-understanding of a society are to be uncovered by moving beyond hermeneutics to a critical theory of society which takes its bearings from a model of communication in which all parties affected are able to examine disputed claims on an equal basis with equal chances to perform all kinds of speech acts and without fear of force or reprisal."[37]

Some of Habermas's characterizations simply did not do justice to Gadamer, who emphasized repeatedly that the "truth of tradition" is weak and provisional. The tradition is always tension-ridden and incomplete, and this weakness is a built-in invitation to criticism. So though we find ourselves already shaped by conventional norms, those norms are in constant process of transformation, not beyond criticism and fixed. A Gadamerian framework can encompass whatever critique of present distortions that Habermas, or anyone else, can muster. Nor was Gadamer assuming the present consensus is free of distortion, or has developed without force. Indeed, he stressed that "unacknowledged presuppositions are always at work in our understanding." We enter into dialogue across time partly to bring them to light. Thus dialogue entails adventure, danger, but also the possibility of growth in our self-awareness.[38]

At the same time, Gadamer turned the tables and criticized Habermas for overemphasizing the scope for rational or theoretical reflection at the expense of hermeneutic dialogue. For Gadamer, as for Croce, it is sometimes necessary to repair to a higher, more theoretical level and consider rules, criteria, or "what counts as" such and such. But the insight to be gained on that level is itself historically specific and provisional. What counts as coerced or enlightened, distorted or undistorted, gets hammered out in the ongoing hermeneutic interaction, like everything else. As Croce always insisted, history itself is the only judge—an endlessly provisional judge.

For Gadamer, then, Habermas was too quick to retreat to some "meta-hermeneutic" level, as if "the principle of rational discourse" or what counts

36. Ibid., 202–207.
37. Warnke, *Gadamer*, 129–130.
38. Gadamer, *Reason*, 109–111; the quoted passage is on p. 111. Compare Habermas, "Hermeneutic Claim," 207.

as ideological distortion was outside the realm of hermeneutic discussion. Habermasian critique has its place in the dialogue—but not a privileged place based on some claim to reason. "My objection," said Gadamer, "is that the critique of ideology overestimates the competence of reflection and reason. Inasmuch as it seeks to penetrate the masked interests which infect public opinion, it implies its own freedom from any ideology; and that means in turn that it enthrones its own norms and ideals as self-evident and absolute."[39]

Critics like Lawrence Hinman have found a fundamental ambiguity in Gadamer's way of speaking of truth while eschewing any prescriptive dimension or discussion of method; if Gadamer is not simply to accept whatever happens, he surely requires some basis for distinguishing instances of understanding that are true.[40] And in specifying the scope for truth, Gadamer seemed to claim, if not a privileged method, at least such criteria of distinction. Hinman recognizes that the key for Gadamer was ultimately to decide what counts in specific instances, not to establish some broad theoretical principle. Yet Hinman, like many of Gadamer's critics, implicitly demands some decision procedure so that we can say with certainty that p is true and q is not.

Gadamer's point, however, was that truth is possible, that it happens, though we have no such decision procedures in a postmetaphysical world. Because we cannot be certain what counts in any particular instance, the discussion continues. Still, a relative consensus is continually established at the same time—a consensus sufficient to enable a discussion to follow, as opposed to a mere cacophony. To grasp the adequacy of this weak framework, with its particular way of bringing human being together with history, is essential to the moderate postmetaphysical position.

In short, Gadamer found the ongoing process of coming to agreement sufficient to take the place of what had seemed a universal framework derived through rational reflection. Critics like Richard Bernstein, who demand to know from Gadamer "the basis for our critical judgments," fail to do justice to Gadamer's way of showing that though there can be no "critical standards," we have an adequate framework for further discussion and disagreement.[41] Instead of the "guarantee of truth" that Habermas found still necessary, we have ongoing history, bound up with endless hermeneutic interaction. To be sure, history initially seems a very thin reed, but for Gadamer, as for Croce, the fact that we are left with history means that we need not lapse into irrationalism, aestheticism, pragmatism, or a debilitating relativism when we abandon the claim to suprahistorical criteria.

---

39. Gadamer, "Hermeneutics and Social Science," 314–315; the quotation is from p. 315. See also Gadamer, *Philosophical Hermeneutics*, 31.

40. Lawrence M. Hinman, "Quid Facti or Quid Juris? The Fundamental Ambiguity in Gadamer's Understanding of Hermeneutics," *Philosophy and Phenomenological Research* 40, no. 4 (June 1980): 512–535.

41. Bernstein, *Beyond Objectivism and Relativism*, 155.

Yet Gadamer, like Croce, saw the danger of such an overreaction, and he, too, found it necessary to repair to a relatively theoretical level to head it off. Rejecting the notion, which he attributed to the culture of science, that we can simply apply a theory elaborated a priori, Gadamer emphasized that any such theoretical enterprise starts from the world of practice. Under some circumstances, practical needs require that we stand back and, through a kind of philosophy or theory, examine the terms of contemporary practice.[42] Up to a point, Habermas himself claimed to be doing no more than this. But he also seemed to suggest that such theory could be qualitatively different from the practical interaction that led to it. Gadamer, like Croce, was more reflexive, more willing to recognize the historically specific practical basis even of the most theoretical of his own inquiries. Those inquiries were not pure or transcendent but simply part of the ongoing dialogue and contest.

And though some people may be better at such theorizing than others, a theoretical vocation does not establish a privileged group, set off from everyone else. It is striking that both Gadamer and Croce, for all their alleged conservatism, insisted that everybody counts, in opposition to any claim that rational, enlightened experts can, by means of purified theoretical reflection, climb to a higher level, transcending the historicity and finitude of the others, and specify rules, decision procedures, or what counts as undistorted communication.[43]

But even if Habermas, from a Gadamerian perspective, overstated the scope for theoretical reflection, he raised plausible questions about how we might identify distortions hidden in the unspoken assumptions—the consensus—of a particular tradition. Habermas worried that unless such distortions could be pinpointed from a theoretical perspective, they would remain beyond the reach of questioning. We said that Gadamerian hermeneutics is more open-ended than Habermas's characterizations suggest. More specifically, Gadamer seemed to point to a mode of historical inquiry that might illuminate what had been taken for granted and remained unspoken in our tradition. To show the scope for such radically unsettling historical questioning would seem to address precisely Habermas's central concern. Yet Gadamer seemed to pull back from this line of argument and to *over*emphasize the moment of agreement, the authority of tradition, and the ongoing reestablishment of consensus, at the expense of the scope for questioning and criticism, or even disagreement and conflict. We noted that Croce's understanding of the range of historical inquiry seems comparably restricted.

For both thinkers, the present is the edge of a living, creative tradition that grows partly by making new sense of itself. But Croce and Gadamer each fell

42. Gadamer, *Reason*, 131.
43. Ibid, 148; Gadamer, *Philosophical Hermeneutics*, 41–42, 93; and Gadamer, "Hermeneutics and Social Science," 312, 316. See also Warnke, *Gadamer*, 127, for an excellent discussion of Gadamer's anti-elitism in the context of his debate with Habermas.

into ambiguity in addressing the central questions that follow—about the present's relationship to what came before and about the place of that relationship in the ongoing growth of the world. Up to a point, however, their different accents prove complementary. Gadamer shows the way beyond the presentist limitation in Croce, whereas Croce overcomes an essentialist and prejudicially conservative tendency in Gadamer.

Concealment and the Fusion of Horizons

In positing an absolute historicism, Croce opened everything up to historical inquiry in one sense, but he tended to limit the historiographical focus to what in fact became actual; what matters in any past moment are the seeds of the next, so what had been forgotten or "held back" simply "is not." Because the present moment embodies all that remains living of the past, his conception did not afford scope for the potentially unsettling dialogue between present and past that Gadamer later posited.

It was especially Gadamer's way of developing a major theme in Heidegger that enabled him to cut deeper at this crucial point. With his emphasis on concealment or holding back as the other side of coming to be in history, Heidegger introduced a tension missing in Croce—in Gadamer's terms, "a relentless inner tension between illumination and concealment."[44] Gadamer found that tension fundamental, and it fell to him to draw out its implications for historical questioning in a way that Heidegger did not.

I have shown that in the final analysis Heidegger fastened on this tension as part of his quest for a quasi-religious disengagement, not to participate in the further growth of the actual. But even insofar as he, too, invited historical questioning, he indicated only a restricted range. Because he reduced the history of the West to the history of metaphysics, the historical questions that mattered were ultimately questions about philosophy. And within the history of philosophy, Heidegger was preoccupied with the Greek beginnings of our tradition.

Gadamer made more of the fact that concealment accompanies *every* disclosure, so that the whole past is riddled with tension. Thus what opens for historical questioning is not simply some particular step or chain of steps but the totality of what there is, because the "unthought," the "other" of coming into being, is diffused through the whole of what came before. And for Gadamer the openness of the whole past to questioning is crucially bound up with our present possibilities, our openness to the future. The fact that every actualizing has entailed a holding back means that we do not embody all that remains liv-

---

44. Gadamer, *Reason*, 104–105. See also Gadamer, *Philosophical Hermeneutics*, 203, 208, 226.

ing in what came before us. And though what is concealed is forgotten and hidden, it is not lost altogether.[45] So whereas Heidegger stepped back, Gadamer concentrated on the "forward" motion and growth made possible by the present's active encounter with the complex tradition, which entails this endless tension or interplay between "becoming actual" and holding back.

From a Gadamerian perspective, Croce's less dialogical conception did not make convincing sense of the ongoing growth of the world. It was not enough to say that we start from a contemporary concern and change the meaning of the past as we question history afresh. Rather, growth is possible precisely because concealment or holding back has left absences or holes in the past. Gadamerian dialogue entails attention to that "unthought," to what did not become actual; our present involvement enables us to reconnect with it, thereby allowing challenge and growth. It is especially in this sense that temporal distance is itself productive. Growth brings about a new perspective that, in turn, enables us to bring hidden assumptions to light and thus to move, yet again, beyond what we have become. Thus Gadamer's insistence that "the historical knowledge of the past sets us before the totality of our human possibilities." Tradition involves "a mediation of ourselves with our real possibilities engulfing us—with what can be and what is capable of happening to and becoming of us."[46]

Croce had simply posited the creative spirit as a kind of cutting edge, needing to look backward to discern how the present had come to be as it was, not to connect with creative possibilities that lay back there, inherent in history itself. For Gadamer, in contrast, the "presence" of such possibilities meant that our relationship with the tradition entails not simply the *expansion* of horizons that Croce posited but a genuine *fusion* of horizons.[47] As the term "fusion" implies, it is the combination of the particular present with a past that is always *more* than the actual that makes possible ongoing novelty and growth—that makes the tradition itself a creative, growing thing. In this sense, the Heideggerian dimension led Gadamer to a historicist reduction more radical than Croce's, whose way of identifying the creative spirit with history seems arbitrary by comparison.

To be sure, Croce, unlike Gadamer, was radical enough to avoid positing a distinguishable past altogether. And just as he sought to avoid the Scylla of a past "thing-in-itself," he also tried to steer clear of the Charybdis of subjectivism, dissolving the past into the meaning that we of the present, this actual moment, make it have *for us*. Thus, in part, his refusal to embrace "actualism," the radical variety of philosophical idealism that his onetime collaborator

45. Gadamer, *Philosophical Hermeneutics*, 203, 208.
46. Gadamer, *Reason,* 166–167. See also Gadamer, *Truth and Method*, 258–267.
47. See especially *Truth and Method*, 272–273, 336–338, 357–358, for Gadamer's central notion of fusion of horizons.

Giovanni Gentile began espousing just before the First World War.[48] But there remained tensions in Croce's way of positing the difficult relationship between spirit and what has resulted from the prior activity of spirit, between us and the growing tradition. From a Crocean perspective, what had seemed the stable past proves unstable because we, as creators, endlessly change its meaning, even though we are constrained by the "documents," artifacts that come to life only through present interpretation. With Gadamer, in contrast, we come to see that the past is not fixed simply because of what it means, in light of Heidegger, for the world to be historical, for being to give itself as some particular history. Gadamer fused human being with history and made history itself creative more radically than even Croce had managed to do.

In the same way, Croce's way of accounting for the creative tension, the dissatisfaction with the present that leads us to question the past in the first place, seems mysterious, even transcendent, because it simply posits the moral impulse as one of the attributes of the spirit. To be sure, the Heidegger-Gadamer reference to care is similar, but with Gadamer, drawing from Heidegger, the creative tension becomes more firmly immanent, more obviously bound up with the ongoing sending as a particular history. It is not simply because we are creative, because its meaning changes *for us*, that the past is not fixed. Again, it is not fixed because of what "it is"—because of what it means, in light of Heidegger, to be a history. In identifying creativity more with human being or spirit than with history itself, Croce was indeed more conventionally humanistic than Heidegger and Gadamer. He was less able to conceive the world as a sheer happening to which we belong.

Although Croce invited a deeply reflexive sense of the historical specificity of any inquiry, including his own, Gadamer's reflexivity was deeper. The categories at work when we probe the past are not only historical products but are themselves at risk in historical inquiry. Thus Gadamer's dictum that "true historical thinking must take account of its own historicality."[49] This reflexivity led Gadamer to accent the risk, danger, and adventure involved in broadening our self-knowledge and horizon through hermeneutic interaction.[50] In positing a more genuinely dialogical relationship between the present and what came before, Gadamer showed how historical questioning can surprise and challenge as it never quite could for Croce.

---

48. The resulting schism between Croce and Gentile proved one of the most notable in twentieth-century intellectual history. For the key statements, see Benedetto Croce, *Conversazioni critiche*, ser. 2 (Bari: Laterza, 1950), 67–95; and Giovanni Gentile, *Saggi critici*, ser. 2 (Florence: Vallecchi, 1927), 11–35. For an introduction to the terms of the dispute, see my *Benedetto Croce and the Uses of Historicism* (Berkeley, Los Angeles, and London: University of California Press, 1987), 105–116.

49. Gadamer, *Truth and Method*, 267. Georgia Warnke's translation is preferable: "A really historical thought must also think its own historicity." See her *Gadamer*, 69.

50. Gadamer, *Reason*, 109–110.

Gadamer, then, gave hermeneutics a potentially critical or radical dimension even as he denied any scope for criticism based on theoretical, suprahistorical criteria. Hermeneutic dialogue with our past brings our presuppositions to light, thereby making self-criticism possible.[51] All the present norms that shape us are open to such questioning, which, in principle, may cut to the deepest layers in our tradition.

In light of charges from critics like Derrida and Caputo, it must be emphasized that such an encounter can be radical and unsettling without being "apocalyptic," pretending definitive retrieval or the recapture of some lost primordiality. It is possible to expose the contingency and historicity of ever deeper layers in our tradition without any pretense of reaching the bottom or reappropriating some lost essence. In pulling back from Heidegger's extreme strategies, Gadamer was content to work *within* the particular tradition, serving its ongoing happening and growth. Thus, for example, once we have been through the era of subjectivity, science, and technology, there can be no question of merely reconnecting with phronesis or any other aspect of the Greek past. What is possible, again, is a creative fusion of horizons, an encounter with the past that destabilizes our present and enhances our possibilities for the future.

The Authority of Tradition

But though Gadamerian hermeneutics seems to open the way to a wider range and a more radical kind of historical questioning, Gadamer's accents proved relatively conservative, so the implications of his thinking have been hard to sort out. He himself placed little premium on deconstructive inquiry and instead stressed that as horizons move we are involved in a process of coming to agreement, of reaching a consensus. Indeed, language is itself the process of coming to agreement, of building up a common world.[52] Up to a point, this emphasis is essential to a moderate, constructive orientation within a postmetaphysical framework. Ragged though the tradition always is, provisional though every agreement is, the ongoing fusing of horizons brings human responses—conversations, criticisms, disagreements—back to the tradition as that tradition itself grows. In carrying the argument in this direction, Gadamer was simply emphasizing the moment of "gathering," or coming back together, rather than the ongoing disruption, in the endless growth of the tradition through fusion of horizons. The conservative accent can easily be balanced by the radical or critical one that Gadamer's own framework seems to invite.

But so great was Gadamer's emphasis on the renewal of consensus and "the rehabilitation of authority and tradition" that he sometimes seemed actively to

---

51. Ibid., 135; Gadamer, *Philosophical Hermeneutics*, 93–94.
52. See, for example, Gadamer, *Reason*, 166; and Gadamer, *Truth and Method*, 158.

preclude the moment of criticism, conflict, and unsettling historical questioning.[53] And thus some have found his thinking to be *prejudicially* conservative. The question is whether Gadamer is simply ambiguous, or whether, in the final analysis, he remains caught up in a metaphysically grounded authoritarianism.

Although his dominant emphasis was on openness and ongoing growth, Gadamer's way of recasting the scope for truth sometimes tended toward an ahistorical essentialism that seems to undercut that emphasis. He seemed to posit a true meaning, a thing in itself, that we might get at—or at least glimpse—through the growth of the tradition. Thus, for example, he suggested that there comes a point when we are sufficiently removed from some past moment to establish its meaning once and for all. But after claiming that temporal distance "lets the true meaning of the object emerge fully," he quickly emphasized that "the discovery of the true meaning of a text or work of art is never finished; it is in fact an infinite process."[54]

At other points Gadamer went further in implying that our past, or history, has an essence that stands in tension with any particular vantage point, including our own. He warned that because we necessarily approach the past in terms of what we already know, "it is constantly necessary to inhibit the overhasty assimilation of the past to our own expectations of meaning. Only then will we be able to listen to the past in a way that enables it to make its own meanings heard."[55] As a warning against vulgar presentism, this is surely unobjectionable, but the reference to "its own meanings" implies that the past has a certain way of being of its own that we human beings, with our finite vantage point and historically specific purposes, necessarily compromise or violate. Discussing the productive quality of temporal distance, Gadamer suggested the possibility of grasping the "true content" and "true significance" of human creations, of letting their "real nature" appear, "so that the understanding of what is said in them can claim to be authoritative and universal."[56] In the same vein, Gadamer's emphasis on the "classical" suggested that a privileged, correct understanding gradually emerges within the tradition.[57] Rather than inviting us ceaselessly to question, to engage our unstable past in dialogue, Gadamer seemed to want us simply to submit to the authority of tradition.

This prejudicially conservative tendency has made it difficult to take advantage of Gadamerian hermeneutics to develop a constructive alternative to the

53. The conservative accents were not compatible with Gadamer's dominant emphasis on the change, novelty, and growth that follow from ongoing response and dialogue. For example, his pivotal discussion in *Truth and Method*, 245–253, esp. p. 249, is anything but conservative in implication. Warnke finds Gadamer's conservatism a kind of overlay that need not follow from his recasting of hermeneutics; fusion of horizons can include disagreement and "distantiation." See Warnke, *Gadamer*, 136–138.

54. Gadamer, *Truth and Method*, 265.

55. Ibid., 272.

56. Ibid., 265.

57. Ibid., pp. 253–258, esp. p. 255. See also Warnke, *Gadamer*, 105–106, 189 n. 50.

culture of extremity. Indeed, the ambiguities in Gadamer's way of linking truth to tradition have made it easy for critics to conflate *any* reference to truth with a claim to metaphysically grounded authority. Thus, for example, Caputo's assumption that the truth Gadamer finds embodied in the tradition is essentially metaphysical, that the tradition is a vessel of some completed truth to be glimpsed.[58] Caputo's reading of Gadamer contributed to his tendency to view a playful aestheticism as the only alternative to metaphysics.

Although Croce, too, has been viewed as prejudicially conservative, he did not fall into Gadamer's quasi-essentialist muddying. His greater radicalism at several key points helps us grasp the contingency of Gadamer's prejudicially conservative side.

Croce was more radical, first, in denying a distinguishable past. There is history, but there is no "past," with its own essence; Gadamer's suggestion that we "listen to the past in a way that enables it to make its own meanings heard" is simply nonsensical from a Crocean perspective. Thus Croce afforded more scope for the crucial element of ongoing creative tension with the particular tradition. That tension leads us first to question history in an effort to learn, but it also affords the possibility of responding critically to the present on the basis of what we learn. With Croce's conception, the critical bite is built in and ongoing.

Moreover, because each of us is a bit different, each of us brings out something different through creative encounter with what came before. So whereas Gadamer accented ongoing coming to agreement, Croce showed that *dis*agreement is built in as well. The growth of the tradition rests on an ongoing contest among those different responses. For Croce, there is also "coming to agreement," but the consensus is always ragged, unstable, merely provisional. We are always caught up in a process of producing a *new* provisional consensus.

It is also clearer in Croce than in Gadamer that the process of renewing the consensus entails concrete changes in societal practice. Indeed, whereas Crocean historicism is an invitation to ongoing action, Gadamer sometimes seemed to delimit or undermine the scope for action, to make history a matter of folding within a preexisting tradition *as opposed to* extending that tradition through history as action.

Croce's more balanced way of combining criticism and agreement, change and tradition, helps us understand that the Gadamerian way of linking the happening of truth with the growth of the tradition can be resolutely postmetaphysical, despite Gadamer's own sometimes ambiguous or prejudicial characterizations. In our dialogue with the past, we seek some particular truth

58. Caputo, *Radical Hermeneutics*, 111–112. See also pp. 210–211, where Caputo suggests that Gadamer "presupposes an existing schema, a world already in place." Whereas Gadamer does posit an existing world in one sense, it is not "in place" in the metaphysical sense—fixed, stable, complete. Rather, it is only an unstable, growing historical tradition open to endless dialogue and reinterpretation.

of the tradition, and as some such truth emerges through dialogue, the particularizing of that tradition continues. The becoming true is merely historical; the truth that results is provisional, incomplete, weak.

Gadamer seems to have eschewed accents like Croce's partly because he shared Heidegger's determination to box out anthropocentrism, with its implication of technological manipulation, objectification, and hubris. In emphasizing projection into the future, Gadamer, like Croce, was suggesting that a contemporary concern underlies historical inquiry, but rather than consistently associate such inquiry with history-making action, he suggested that historical questioning from many points of view gradually enables some essence of things to come to light. As Gadamer has it, the tradition being built up is more fixed, and thus more confining, than it was for Croce.

By taking Croce and Gadamer together, it is possible to develop a historicist hermeneutics that can withstand many of the charges of prejudicial conservatism that can be raised against each thinker, taken individually. But even a synthesis of their two positions does not overcome the sense that there was something too complacent in the thinking of both.

Caputo compares Gadamer's conservative emphasis on resolution and agreement unfavorably with Heidegger's premium on ongoing questioning and deconstruction.[59] Although Caputo may be overdoing the radical, deconstructive side of Heidegger, it is true that Heidegger was a major source of the deconstructive impulse that became central by the 1970s and that stands in crucial tension with Gadamer's emphasis on the moment of coming to agreement.

Gadamer did not develop that deconstructive potential, and his accents suggest a greater premium on continuity and agreement than is necessary. Croce's reasons were different, but he too tended to preclude the depth, rupture, and crisis that would open the way to deconstructive questioning and critical dialogue. Within recent discussion, the contingent conservatism in Gadamer has been especially important in nourishing the suspicion that any accent on consensus, continuity, and history in a postmetaphysical mode entails conservative, even "authoritarian" implications.[60]

To be convincing, then, a postmetaphysical moderation needs a more explicitly radical or critical dimension than we find even in a synthesis of Croce and Gadamer. Collingwood took a step in that direction in his *Essay on Metaphysics,* which focused on the particular, contingent presuppositions that will be found underpinning any culture—and that that culture itself will take to be absolute.[61] Such presuppositions can be apprehended through historical scrutiny; such, indeed, becomes the task of "metaphysics," which is to be understood simply as one, particularly radical, form of historical questioning.

59. Ibid., 81–82, 96–97, 111–114.
60. See, for example, Christopher Norris, *The Contest of Faculties: Philosophy and Theory After Deconstruction* (London: Methuen, 1985), 25.
61. R. G. Collingwood, *An Essay on Metaphysics* (Oxford: Clarendon, 1940).

Collingwood has influenced contemporaries like Quentin Skinner and Stephen Toulmin who have similarly sought, in light of wider cultural changes, to deepen our understanding of our encounter with our own past.

However, it was especially the deconstructive approach, worked out in very different ways by Foucault and Derrida by the early 1970s, that promised to balance Gadamer's emphasis on coming to agreement and the authority of tradition. But because it developed especially through encounter with Nietzsche and Heidegger, deconstruction also included elements of both plausible extremity and overreaction. Thus its implications—and its scope for meshing with Gadamerian hermeneutics—have remained uncertain.

8

Deconstruction

The Uses and Limits of Perversity

Deconstruction and the Cultural Displacement

Deconstruction, associated especially with French poststructuralism, was the intellectual fashion of the 1970s and 1980s, though it elicited considerable hostility, as well as fervent partisanship. To detractors, it seemed prejudicially radical, unwittingly conservative, or merely nihilistic. By the early 1990s, some of its themes had become almost commonplace, though its day seemed to have passed. Critics grew more aggressive, portraying deconstruction as discredited, its earlier vogue as an embarrassment, to be explained in terms of the idiosyncrasies of French intellectual life and American literature departments.[1] However, just as deconstruction had not merited the privileged, all-encompassing role some had claimed for it, neither could it be convincingly dismissed as a mere fad. As a broad impulse, it had a deeper historical significance—and ongoing value. But even those who sought to place deconstruction in historical perspective did not agree about its center of gravity and wider cultural implications.

Used most rigorously, "deconstruction" characterized the current that developed from Jacques Derrida's understanding of texts, but the term was often

---

1. Quentin Skinner, for example, observes that deconstruction "has only recently been discredited," in "The Past in the Present," *New York Review of Books*, 12 April 1990, 39. Quoting Leo Bersani, John Ellis notes the "arrogant frivolity" of the constant antibourgeois posture of French intellectual life, but he also traces deconstruction to the French context of the mid-1960s, especially to the rigidities of the French university system. In that context, he suggests, the deconstructionist concern with "authoritarianism" had some basis, but in the more pluralistic United States, the radical antiauthoritarianism of intellectuals embracing deconstruction was merely facile, though it expressed diffuse discontents, especially with the state of literary studies. See John M. Ellis, *Against Deconstruction* (Princeton: Princeton University Press, 1989), 83–84.

applied in a looser way to encompass Michel Foucault and other French post-structuralists. Foucault and Derrida differed, and each found reason for some pointed criticism of the other. After Derrida charged that Foucault, in *Madness and Civilization*, had been too much the conventional historian in his way of using evidence and the narrative form, Foucault attacked Derridean deconstruction as a rhetorical bag of tricks.[2] Such sniping helped persuade others that sympathy to one of the two entailed antipathy to the other.

Despite important differences of emphasis, Foucault and Derrida had much in common, and they can usefully be treated in tandem. They turned from structuralism for analogous reasons, and in doing so each accepted fundamental terms of what I have called the reduction to history. In response, each sought to develop a radical strategy—Foucault especially through encounter with Nietzsche, Derrida partly through encounter with Heidegger.

A certain willful extravagance has marked both strands of deconstruction; thus, in part, the recent hostile reaction. Moreover, some of the most astute critics charged that deconstruction was simply an apocalyptic recasting of relatively familiar themes. John Searle and Richard Rorty have emphasized that among philosophers, at least, there are few foundationalists to be found, so if the Derridean brand of deconstruction is no more than antifoundationalism, it is not very exciting.[3] Derrida's unraveling of Husserl is congruent with the other assaults on the quest for certainty, or foundations, or a transcendent standpoint, that have marked the long revolution in philosophy over the past century or so.

By the late 1980s, moreover, the fruits of the deconstructive approach had come to seem predictable and unenlightening. Rorty refers to the "dreary and repetitious discovery of tiresomely familiar 'inherent strains and contradictions' " that came to mark deconstructive criticism in the United States.[4] There

2. Jacques Derrida, "Cogito and the History of Madness," originally a lecture delivered in 1963, reprinted in his *Writing and Difference*, trans. Alan Bass (Chicago: University of Chicago Press, 1978), 31–63. Foucault's response, first published in 1972, is translated by Geoff Bennington as "My Body, This Paper, This Fire," *Oxford Literary Review* 4 (1979): 9–28. On the dispute between the two thinkers, see Ann Wordsworth, "Derrida and Foucault: Writing the History of Historicity," in *Post-Structuralism and the Question of History*, ed. Derek Attridge et al. (Cambridge: Cambridge University Press, 1987), 116–125. Defending Derrida from Foucault's counterattack, Wordsworth denies that Derrida's mode of deconstructive questioning can be dismissed as textual reductionism or mere "pedagogy." See also Christopher Norris, *Derrida* (Cambridge: Cambridge University Press, 1987), 214–221.

3. Richard Rorty, *Essays on Heidegger and Others* (Cambridge: Cambridge University Press, 1991), 109–112, 125. Rorty here endorses an influential review essay by Searle, discussed below. Attempting to account for the extravagance of Derridean deconstruction, Rorty charged that Derrida had overemphasized the extent to which claims to closure are at work in the culture. In the same vein, Rorty argued that Derrida was simply making the familiar anti-Cartesian point, to be found, for example, in both Peirce and Wittgenstein, "that meaning is a function of context, and that there is no theoretical barrier to an endless sequence of recontextualizations" (p. 125).

4. Ibid., 107. In the same way, R. B. Kershner asked, "How many times can we demonstrate that a given text is 'decentered,' or that it undermines its own apparent unity and referentiality, before acute boredom sets in? Derrida himself has avoided this trap, but it has proven more difficult for his epigones to do so." See R. B. Kershner, "Dances with Historians," *Georgia Review* 45, no. 3 (Fall 1991): 599.

was something comparably tedious in the way historians bégan routinely invoking Foucault and his understanding of power and knowledge. Even when critics distinguished the masters from the epigoni, they often disagreed over how the masters themselves were to be taken. Was Derrida offering rigorous arguments, or was he essentially an ironist in his approach to the philosophical tradition?[5] Was Foucault to be taken seriously as a historian, or was he trying to subvert historical understanding itself?

Foucault and Derrida each reacted against the vogue of structuralism, with its quest for a new science of culture. Structuralism was trapped in its own historically situated modes of discourse, so it was a casualty of the eclipse of metaphysics and the reduction to history.[6] But their encounter with the structuralist enterprise remained central, affording a distinctively French angle that enabled Foucault and Derrida to expand our sense of the postmetaphysical terrain.

Deconstruction, understood loosely, is bound up with the recent expansion

5. Even Geoffrey H. Hartman and Jonathan Culler, two of the most influential proponents among American literary scholars, disagreed sharply. Hartman accented the irony in *Saving the Text: Literature/Derrida/Philosophy* (Baltimore: Johns Hopkins University Press, 1981). In *On Deconstruction: Theory and Criticism after Structuralism* (Ithaca: Cornell University Press, 1982), Culler criticized Hartman for failing to take seriously enough the rigor of Derrida's argument. While recognizing that Derrida had made noises of both sorts, Rorty endorsed Hartman's reading and found Culler too anxious to find theorems that literary critics could then apply. See Rorty, *Essays on Heidegger*, 119, 128. Rorty's treatment of Derrida as "a kind of writing" prompted criticism from one of Derrida's most persistent and lucid partisans, Christopher Norris, who played up instead what he took to be Derrida's distinctively philosophical bite. See especially Norris's "Philosophy as *Not* Just a 'Kind of Writing': Derrida and the Claim of Reason," in *Redrawing the Lines: Analytic Philosophy, Deconstruction, and Literary Theory,* ed. Reed Way Dasenbrock (Minneapolis: University of Minnesota Press, 1989), 189–203, and Rorty's response in *Essays on Heidegger*, 107–118. Although both Rorty and Norris wanted to distinguish Derrida from the bulk of his American literary followers, their accents differed even as they did so. Rorty found the thinking of Paul de Man, rather than that of Derrida himself, at the root of the excesses and confusions in American deconstruction. Norris, in contrast, valued the rigorous unmasking that he found in de Man, yet he was contemptuous of "what passes for 'deconstruction' among American literary intellectuals." Whether "deconstruction" was taken to be a method for textual interpretation or an invitation to loose, unphilosophical free play, he found the American version to be "distinctly alien" to Derrida's own concerns. See Norris, *Derrida*, 14, 18–20, 159; and Christopher Norris, *The Contest of Faculties: Philosophy and Theory after Deconstruction* (London: Methuen, 1985), 9–10, 15, 70–77, 85–96. The most influential effort in English to take Derrida seriously as a philosopher has been Rodolphe Gasché, *The Tain of the Mirror: Derrida and the Philosophy of Reflection* (Cambridge: Harvard University Press, 1986). In addition, see Rorty's critical but respectful account of Gasché in *Essays on Heidegger*, 121–128, and Gillian Rose, *Dialectic of Nihilism: Post-Structuralism and Law* (Oxford: Basil Blackwell, 1984), for an influential critique of Derrida's apparently philosophical categories.

6. Geoff Bennington and Robert Young suggest that the "post" of poststructuralism reintroduces history; see their "Introduction: Posing the Question," in *Post-Structuralism and the Question of History*, ed. Attridge et al., 1–2. Key documents in the break from Lévi-Strauss and structuralism were Derrida's "Structure, Sign, and Play" (1966), reprinted in Derrida, *Writing and Difference*, 278–293; and Roland Barthes, *S/Z*, trans. Richard Miller (New York: Hill and Wang, 1974; orig. French ed. 1970). Barthes had earlier influenced Derrida, but he seems to have been at least partly under Derrida's influence at this point, when he eschewed the reductionism of structuralist narratology and began exploring, even celebrating, the openness that resulted from the dissolution of the author as the ultimate authority. See Norris, *Derrida*, 219, 242; and Norris, *Contest of Faculties*, 28–29.

of the historiographical focus. Ever more of what we are seems to have been historically constructed, so virtually anything may be subjected to historical unearthing and thereby shown to be merely a contingent historical outcome, as opposed to natural, given, grounded. Such deconstruction may be reconstructive in its cultural aims. In the case of gender, for example, to show that a present configuration that had seemed natural was in fact historical is to allow a new way of making cultural sense of sexual difference. By the early 1990s, the scope for such deconstruction had become a commonplace. A spate of books excavated the constructed, historically specific element in everything from Africa to accuracy to homosexuality.[7] As an ongoing cultural possibility, such deconstructive historical inquiry might afford the critical moment necessary to balance the hermeneutic strand, understood as the search for consensus, as the moment of bringing back together, in the wake of disagreement and criticism.

Foucault and Derrida serve that enterprise in some respects, yet each found something else more important. In devising their deconstructive strategies, they were responding to the kinds of preoccupations that led Nietzsche and Heidegger to their posthistoricist extremes, and in some ways they expanded possibilities along the axis that Nietzsche and Heidegger had established. However, French deconstruction also included an element of overreaction that tended to compromise the reconstructive possibility *and* to blur the point of the posthistoricist extremes. Whatever the reasons, Foucault and Derrida have been more widely viewed as antihistorical thinkers than as thinkers serving a renewed culture of history. So how do the historical and the antihistorical themes come together in their thinking?

Foucault and the End of Man

After publishing his innovative *Madness and Civilization* in 1961, Foucault made clear his wider ambitions in *The Order of Things* (1966) and *The Archaeology of Knowledge* (1969).[8] In specifying his starting point, he offered some

7. See, for example, Donald MacKenzie, *Inventing Accuracy: A Historical Sociology of Nuclear Missile Guidance* (Cambridge: MIT Press, 1990). Though it preceded the peak of Foucault's influence among historians, Allan Megill's quasi-neopositivist, slightly tongue-in-cheek "The Reception of Foucault by Historians," *Journal of the History of Ideas* 48, no. 1 (January–March 1987): 117–141, remains a helpful introduction to the subject.

8. Foucault reflected frequently on his own intellectual evolution, noting especially the import of the Days of May uprising of 1968 and pinpointing the changes in his conception of power. See, for example, Michel Foucault, *Power/Knowledge: Selected Interviews and Other Writings, 1972–1977*, ed. and trans. Colin Gordon (New York: Pantheon, 1980), 115–116. This is not the place to consider Foucault's life and death, both the subject of recent controversy in light of his homosexuality and AIDS. See Alan Ryan, "Foucault's Life and Hard Times," *New York Review of Books*, 8 April 1993, 12–17, for an introduction to the recent literature. The most influential recent biography, Didier Eribon's *Michel Foucault*, trans. Betsy Wang (Cambridge: Harvard University Press, 1991), finds homosexuality central to Foucault's intellectual itinerary. See also Jerrold Seigel, "Avoiding the Subject: A Foucaultian Itinerary," *Journal of the History of Ideas* 51, no. 2 (April–June 1990): 273–299, for a sensitive reconsideration of Foucault's intellectual itinerary, especially his ongoing concern with subjectivity and freedom, in light of his homosexuality.

particularly forceful characterizations of the reduction to history. At the outset of *The Order of Things*, he adapted Jorge Luis Borges's "Chinese" classification to show the merely historical constructedness of what we take to be natural ways of dividing things up.[9] And he insisted that what we are, our very subjectivity, is fundamentally historical. The notion that "man," the human subject, afforded a stable object for human self-understanding was itself a historical product. Far from being a discovery, the coming to light of something hitherto concealed, "man" was an invention, even a mere "effect of a change in the fundamental arrangements of knowledge."[10]

Foucault's periodization was slightly idiosyncratic. Rather than emphasize the Cartesian break, he argued that this focus on "man" became possible with the crystallization of the modern *episteme* toward the end of the eighteenth century. It was only then, with the disappearance of "discourse" and the shift of language toward objectivity, that it became possible to envision apprehending human being objectively and scientifically. Thus "man was constituted at a time when language was doomed to disappear." In our own time, however, that whole episteme seemed to be ending; it seemed possible that "man is in the process of perishing as the being of language continues to shine ever brighter upon our horizon." Indeed, man might be simply "erased, like a face drawn in sand at the edge of the sea."[11]

With these apocalyptic notions, Foucault popularized the idea that something fundamental to our self-understanding was dissolving in our own time. In one sense, the "man" that was ending was the more or less Marxian version, with an essence that might be realized through some sort of "emancipation." History no longer admitted of such grandiose and teleological metanarratives. But though he focused in *The Order of Things* on the relatively recent modern episteme, Foucault implied that what was ending was something deeper and older—essentially the metaphysics that led us to posit essences and to take stability as privileged in the first place.

For us, what most obviously ends is the notion that human being is defined by some stable essence that we are capable of apprehending. Although he was hardly the first to make this argument, Foucault has been a major source of the postmodern notion that "man," which once seemed the transcendent and enduring subject, dissolves into impersonal systems that are historically specific. As Ian Hacking has put it, "It is a Foucaultian thesis that every way in which I can think of myself as a person and an agent is something that has been constituted within a web of historical events. Here is one more step in the destruction of Kant: the noumenal self is nothing."[12]

9. Michel Foucault, *The Order of Things: An Archaeology of the Human Sciences*, trans. Alan Sheridan Smith (New York: Random House, Vintage, 1973; orig. French ed. 1966), xv.

10. Ibid., 387.

11. Ibid., 385–387.

12. Ian Hacking, "The Archaeology of Foucault," in *Foucault: A Critical Reader*, ed. David Couzens Hoy (Oxford: Basil Blackwell, 1986), 36.

So the reverse side of the end of man is the eruption of history.[13] In *The Order of Things*, Foucault described how during the nineteenth century "man as such is exposed to the event," or radically historicized. Among the responses were various attempts—from Karl Marx to Oswald Spengler to social science—to interpret the whole of history, but history overflowed all such efforts: "Since the human being has become historical, through and through, none of the contents analyzed by the human sciences can remain stable in itself or escape the movement of History." Those contents can only be directed at "synchronological patternings within a historicity that constitutes and traverses them." Moreover,

> the forms successively taken by the human sciences, the choice of objects they make, and the methods that apply to them, are all provided by History, ceaselessly borne along by it, and modified at its pleasure. The more History attempts to transcend its own rootedness in historicity, and the greater the effort it makes to attain, beyond the historical relativity of its origin and its choices, the sphere of universality, the more clearly it bears the marks of its historical birth . . . ; inversely, the more it accepts its relativity, and the more deeply it sinks into the movement it shares with what it is recounting, then the more it tends to the slenderness of the narrative, and all the positive content it obtained for itself through the human sciences is dissipated.

History, then, "surrounds the sciences of man with a frontier that limits them and destroys, from the outset, their claim to validity within the element of universality."[14]

At best, the reach of science is limited, as for Saussure, to the synchronic dimension that abstracts from the disruptive flow of time. But that synchronic dimension was bound to seem ever more artificial as the experience of the historicity of things, including finitude and incompleteness, became more intrusive. Thus Foucault suggested that we can only approach ourselves historically.[15] And we need to do so, for our fundamental problem is how we came to understand ourselves as we have. Thus Foucault invited a radically new form of

---

13. The periodization Foucault developed, in seeking to specify this complicated historical relationship, has bred some uncertainty. In *White Mythologies: Writing History and the West* (London: Routledge, 1990), 20, Robert Young suggests—plausibly—that man dissolved at the end of the eighteenth century as the classical age of reason gave way to the historicizing modes of the nineteenth century. The transition Foucault had in mind was ultimately more complex, however, and thus his suggestion that it is only in our time that man disappears. Indeed, confidence in the scope for a suprahistorical science of man seems to have reached its peak around 1960. So whereas the nineteenth-century eruption of history was central in one sense, its way of historicizing proved a kind of holding action, as I emphasized in chapters 2 and 3. And thus my emphasis on the more radical break that came with the crisis of the first historicism around the beginning of the twentieth century. "Man," of course, had been the latest incarnation of what I have called metaphysics, and in the wake of that break we have come ever more lucidly to grapple with postmetaphysical cultural possibilities. Foucault's own efforts were moves in that ongoing exploration.

14. Foucault, *The Order of Things*, 370–371.

15. Michel Foucault, "What Is Enlightenment?" trans. Catherine Porter, in *The Foucault Reader*, ed. Paul Rabinow (New York: Pantheon, 1984), 45–46.

historical questioning that does not take a certain human essence or transcendent subjectivity for granted. As he put it in a 1977 interview,

> One has to dispense with the constituent subject, to get rid of the subject itself, that's to say, to arrive at an analysis which can account for the constitution of the subject within a historical framework. And this is what I would call genealogy, that is, a form of history which can account for the constitution of knowledges, discourses, domains of objects, etc., without having to make reference to a subject which is either transcendental in relation to the field of events or runs in its empty sameness throughout the course of history.[16]

At the same time, Foucault made explicit the reflexivity essential to any acceptance of the reduction to history. Our assumptions, categories, and objectives are themselves historical resultants, yet they tend to remain unthought, to be hidden or held back. So as we question the past, we need to be attentive to the historical constructedness of our own ways of asking and knowing, bringing them to critical awareness, putting ourselves at risk.[17]

Foucault, then, explicitly embraced Nietzschean genealogy as he proposed a more radical role for historical inquiry. In his noted essay "Nietzsche, Genealogy, History," first published in 1971, he probed as no one had before the concerns that led Nietzsche to his novel genealogical approach. Nietzsche, Foucault tells us, had reacted against the too-easy historical consciousness of the nineteenth century, which had led historians to assume "that words had kept their meaning, that desires still pointed in a single direction, that ideas retained their logic." Still drawing on the residues of metaphysics, the mainstream historical approach had not been radical enough in grasping the historicity of things. Nietzsche, in contrast, had come to feel that everything we believe immutable in what we are—even the most basic instincts and sentiments—has a history, has come to be as it is through a process of development. Even the physiology of our bodies is historical, because it depends on what we do with our bodies, on nutrition, work, and rest, and these, too, are historically specific.[18]

Whereas conventional, metaphysically grounded historical thinking sought "origins," Nietzsche's sense that history is radically ungrounded led him to eschew any such approach. As Foucault puts it, the long-standing emphasis on origins "is an attempt to capture the exact essence of things, their purest possibilities, and their carefully protected identities, because this search assumes the existence of immobile forms that precede the external world of accident and

---

16. Foucault, *Power/Knowledge*, 117.

17. Michel Foucault, "The Subject and Power," afterword to Hubert L. Dreyfus and Paul Rabinow, *Michel Foucault: Beyond Structuralism and Hermeneutics*, 2d ed. (Chicago: University of Chicago Press, 1983), 209. See also Paul Bové, "The Foucault Phenomenon: The Problematics of Style," foreword to Gilles Deleuze, *Foucault* (Minneapolis: University of Minnesota Press, 1988), xiii-xix, for an excellent sense of what such disciplinary reflexivity would entail.

18. "Nietzsche, Genealogy, History" is included in Michel Foucault, *Language, Counter-Memory, Practice: Selected Essays and Interviews*, ed. Donald F. Bouchard, trans. Donald F. Bouchard and Sherry Simon (Ithaca: Cornell University Press, 1977). See p. 139 for the passage quoted.

succession." The origin, in short, was assumed to be "the site of truth," prior to the fall into the capricious change of history, so the quest for origins is the refuge of metaphysics against history.

> However, if the genealogist refuses to extend his faith in metaphysics, if he listens to history, he finds that there is "something altogether different" behind things: not a timeless and essential secret, but the secret that they have no essence or that their essence was fabricated in a piecemeal fashion from alien forms. . . . What is found at the historical beginning of things is not the inviolable identity of their origin; it is the dissension of other things. It is disparity.[19]

What we find in the past, then, are not pristine "origins" but mere "beginnings," a haphazard intersection that ends up as some present configuration only as the result of the contingent historical concatenation that follows, not because the present resultant was somehow implicit from the outset. And the difference has fundamental implications for the status of the present, for "historical beginnings are lowly: . . . derisive and ironic, capable of undoing every infatuation." We come to sense that what seems true to us today started as some particular error and only became hardened into truth "in the long baking process of history."[20]

Thus, as noted in chapter 4, the postmetaphysical form of historical understanding new with Nietzsche was fundamentally debunking, unmasking. And this, of course, is unnerving to us, just as it was to Nietzsche. As Foucault puts it, "we want historians to confirm our belief that the present rests upon profound intentions and immutable necessities. But the true historical sense confirms our existence among countless lost events, without a landmark or a point of reference."[21]

All that is left to us, then, is the genealogy that probes "the details and accidents that have attended every beginning." Whereas conventional history had tended to find "continuity," the step-by-step unfolding of a present implicit in the past, genealogy focuses on the errors, the accidents, the contingencies through which whatever there is, has come to be. In this sense its focus is not continuity but *dis*continuity, which is to be true to the singularity of the single event, "the singular randomness of events." And genealogy seeks this singularity "in the most unpromising places, in what we tend to feel is without history," even by attending to what did not become actual.[22]

The metaphysical belief in eternal truth had led mainstream historians to

19. Ibid., 142–143. See also p. 181.
20. Ibid., 143–144. See also pp. 146, 154, for the overall argument, and pp. 145, 148, on Nietzsche's use of *Entstehung* (emergence) and *Herkunft* (descent), as opposed to *Ursprung*.
21. Ibid., 155.
22. Ibid., 139–140, 144, 146, 154–155; see also pp. 175–176. In addition, see Michel Foucault, *The Archaeology of Knowledge*, trans. A. M. Sheridan Smith (New York: Harper and Row, Colophon, 1976; orig. French ed. 1969), 3–17, 166–177, for Foucault's way of contrasting conventional history, taken as developmentalist in assumption and implication, with the sense of discontinuity that had informed *The Order of Things*.

seek to be objective by plugging into the realm of what is completed and fixed. The genealogical approach, in contrast, rests on the reflexivity that follows from the eclipse of metaphysics. Historians are not sovereign over the events of the past but part of the history they study; their categories are themselves historical resultants. Historical knowledge is finite, provisional, interested.[23]

When brought to this point, Foucault's line of argument includes much that, it might be argued, had been discussed for decades everywhere but France. But Foucault, thanks partly to his confrontation with Nietzsche, interjected these ideas into humanistic discussion with renewed bite, based on a deeper sense of their implications. Only now, Foucault felt, were we ready to grasp Nietzsche's novel experience of the historicity of things and the import of the genealogical approach he had offered in response.

For Foucault, as for Nietzsche, history might claim our attention as never before, although it would have to be approached without a good deal of conventional baggage. So we must be wary of the widespread tendency to characterize Foucault, because of his assault on historical "continuity," as an antihistorical thinker. In a 1977 interview, Foucault claimed to be flabbergasted at the way his emphasis on discontinuity had been misconstrued. As in his earlier essay on Nietzsche, he identified "continuity" with a progressive developmentalism implying a reassuring anthropocentrism. These metaphysical residues, he felt, were still at work in much historical writing. In his effort to counter them, he was specifying an alternative approach to history, not turning from history altogether.[24] With no metaphysical frame affording an evolutionary shape, all that remains is the naked history itself, with its quirks and contingencies and *relative* discontinuities. As Foucault framed the crucial distinction in 1979, "The time of men does not have the form of an evolution, but precisely that of a history."[25]

It was tempting to view Foucault as a radically antihistorical thinker partly because in *The Order of Things*, especially, he seemed to be concerned with mapping successive cultural strata that were simply discontinuous; there seemed no scope for explaining change over time, how each stratum emerged from the preceding. But he later insisted that he had intended, in a subsequent work, to try to account for the change at work in *The Order of Things*. The point was not simply to shift from delineating an explanatory structure to describing a singular configuration or event but to realize "that there are actually a whole order of levels of different types of events differing in amplitude, chronological breadth, and capacity to produce events." And, crucially, these ruptures or discontinuities do not defy understanding: "History has no 'mean-

23. Foucault, *Language, Counter-Memory, Practice*, 153, 156–157, 158.
24. Foucault, *Power/Knowledge*, 111–112. See also Foucault's account of his own development in the introduction to *The Archaeology of Knowledge*, 3–17, esp. pp. 5, 8, 12, 14.
25. Michel Foucault, "Is It Useless to Revolt?" *Philosophy and Social Criticism* 8, no. 1 (Spring 1981): 8.

ing,' though this is not to say that it is absurd or incoherent. On the contrary, it is intelligible and should be susceptible of analysis down to the smallest detail."[26]

Understanding, in other words, may require shifting from one layer to another to do justice to the quirks and contingencies in the coming to be of anything in history. To play up discontinuity is not to turn away from historical inquiry but to show, as Croce and Gadamer did not, how such inquiry might be radical, genuinely disruptive. Up to this point, then, Foucault's emphasis on discontinuity is precisely congruent with a radical but reconstructive understanding of deconstruction.

In a series of historical works, Foucault probed such discontinuities as he sought to illuminate present modes of understanding and the societal practices bound up with them. In general terms, his overall aim was "to create a history of the different modes by which, in our culture, human beings are made subjects."[27] This entailed showing, above all, how we have come to divide our experience as we have, thereby warranting the particular sciences, from linguistics to economics to biology, through which we have developed our particular ways of studying and conceiving ourselves. He also probed what he called "the dividing practices" by examining the historical process through which we have come to confer normality on some and to marginalize others through various categories, procedures, and institutions—madness and illness, criminality and punishment, hospitals and prisons. Finally, he asked how we came to turn ourselves into sexual subjects, to conceive ourselves as sexual beings—as opposed to other ways we might have come to conceive ourselves.

Although he helped popularize the notion that even sexuality has been constructed historically, with certain forms taken as normal and others marginalized as "deviant," Foucault's own history of sexuality was more broadly encompassing, focusing on our particular way of relating to our bodies by conceiving and organizing pleasure. In probing as deeply as he did, Foucault envisioned not merely freeing up repressed forms of sexuality but opening the way to "desexualization," a new general economy of pleasure not based on sexual norms.[28]

Foucault's approach to all these modes of human self-definition was loosely congruent with the more rigorous form of deconstruction that Derrida developed. To understand how "sanity" or "normality" or "rationality" got constituted historically, we must attend to the marginalized or excluded term in the binary opposition at issue. Each of those categories took on its historically specific meaning as we defined certain individuals as insane, or irrational, or ill, or delinquent, thereby marginalizing them.

26. Foucault, *Power/Knowledge*, 113–114.
27. Foucault, "The Subject and Power," 208.
28. Foucault, *Power/Knowledge*, 190–191.

By unearthing the contingencies in fundamental societal practices, Foucault's histories compelled a reassessment of certain of those practices. Indeed, no one has better shown how deconstructive historical inquiry can serve criticism and change. Yet, as critics have noted, there was at the same time something curiously bloodless about Foucault's histories. Purposes other than societal reconstruction seemed to have been at work in them, purposes that I seek to identify below.

Foucault came to recognize that what had attracted his historical attention were particular constellations of power, bound up with particular claims to knowledge. So during the 1970s, the two-sided coin of power/knowledge came more clearly into focus as the object of study. And at first this seemed to deepen the reconstructive potential of the form of historical inquiry he advocated.

Foucault admitted that he himself had first viewed power in the conventionally negative way, as a juridical prohibition that might then be resisted by appeal to rights. But when working on *Discipline and Punish* during 1971–1972, he was struck by the positive function of power in constituting whatever there is—some particular configuration of knowledge or pleasure, for example. Power is everywhere, as the glue that, in a situation of nothing but history, enables things to come together as some particular present world. Yet the traditional legal and institutional categories, reflecting the tendency to see power as negative, could not account for its positive dimension in a world reduced to history: "for power relations we had no tools of study."[29]

In probing the constructive role of this diffuse power, Foucault fastened on the interrelationship between power and a particular claim to knowledge and casting of truth. "Each society has its régime of truth, its 'general politics' of truth: that is, the types of discourse which it accepts and makes function as true; the mechanisms and instances which enable one to distinguish true and false statements, the means by which each is sanctioned; the techniques and procedures accorded value in the acquisition of truth; the status of those who are charged with saying what counts as true." Specific effects of power are attached to the true, so " 'truth' is linked in a circular relation with systems of power which produce and sustain it, and to effects of power which it induces and which extend it."[30]

At first glance, Foucault might seem simply to be recasting the familiar notion that what passes for truth is merely ideological or superstructural, but he explicitly eschewed the "ideology" category. In light of the reduction to history, he found it essential to posit a nonreductionist concept of power, not bound up with some class subject or some ambiguous notion of ideology, implying that there are degrees of blindering or distortion to be measured

29. Ibid., 119, 183–184; Foucault, "The Subject and Power," 209.
30. Foucault, *Power/Knowledge*, 131–133.

against a criterion of objective truth. Because there is nothing else, no "really" true standard, the aim cannot be to unmask some ideological claim to truth. All we can do instead is to see "historically how effects of truth are produced within discourses which in themselves are neither true nor false."[31]

What is most generally at work in any present configuration is a particular regime of power/knowledge that is open to historical questioning. The resulting understanding may nurture attempts to resist some aspect of our present world. To probe the present configuration of power by examining the expansion of the state and the web of relationships among government, business, and societal institutions such as the family might enable us, first, to pinpoint objects of struggle, then to adapt the methods of struggle to the present realities of power. The forms of struggle must change just as power does.[32]

By thus destabilizing things, does Foucault invite, or at least have room for, a global unearthing of the whole regime of power/knowledge that holds sway at present? In some of his moods, he seemed to envision a post-Marxist radicalism, with no metanarrative of telos and liberation, no claim to strong totality, yet still pointing the way to a global uprooting of our historically specific system of power/knowledge. Thus, in part, his appeal at a time when the radical tradition centering on Marxism was in crisis.[33]

With our deeper sense of the historicity of things, we come to see that the target of present struggles is not simply an institution or practice "but rather a technique, a form of power," bound up with the way knowledge has come to circulate and function. We seek not simply to free the individual from a totalizing state "but to liberate us both from the state and from the kind of individualization which is linked to the state. We have to promote new forms of subjectivity through the refusal of this kind of individuality which has been imposed on us for several centuries."[34]

Although the resulting transformation would be global in one sense, it would open the way to various "local" forms of criticism and resistance. The metanarrative of liberation has fallen away, so there is no role for the universal intellectuals who once seemed to enjoy privileged access to the truth of things.[35] Rather, Foucault accented the scope for the specific intellectual with a definite

31. Ibid., 118. See also Barry Smart, "The Politics of Truth and the Problem of Hegemony," in *Foucault*, ed. Hoy, 157–173, esp. pp. 170–171, for an excellent discussion of Foucault's divergence even from Gramsci, who, with his accent on "hegemony," seems the Marxist thinker closest to Foucault.

32. Foucault, "The Subject and Power," 212–216, 224; Foucault, *Power/Knowledge*, 187–188.

33. Two influential assessments of the scope for using Foucault to recast the radical tradition are Barry Smart, *Foucault, Marxism, and Critique* (London: Routledge and Kegan Paul, 1983); and Mark Poster, *Foucault, Marxism and History: Mode of Production versus Mode of Information* (Oxford: Basil Blackwell, 1984).

34. Foucault, "The Subject and Power," 216. See also Foucault, *Power/Knowledge*, 122–123, 133.

35. Foucault, *Power/Knowledge*, 80–81, 130–132. See also Smart, "Politics of Truth," 167, 169.

area of expertise. Even in his studies of particular domains of control, Foucault did not pretend to indicate alternatives but only to open the way for those more directly involved to speak up and resist. Such local criticism might take advantage of subjugated forms of knowledge. In any case, a genuine alternative could only be local, because what most needed to be undone was the pretense of universal knowledge.

But though Foucault's form of radical historical inquiry seems at first to serve action and the endless remaking of the world, some of his accents suggest a premium on ongoing resistance itself, apart from any reconstructive aim. Indeed, those accents tend to compromise the reconstructive potential of his mode of deconstruction.

Moreover, Foucault's whole enterprise rested on his own historical account, which was apparently intended to help clarify our present self-understanding and thus our present possibilities. Yet surely a historical account is but another human construction, another deployment of power/knowledge. In what sense, then, does history remain a distinguishable and reliable mode of self-understanding, and what is the status of Foucault's own historical account? Not only is any particular historical account a historical product but so is our sense that history is the way to approach things. So perhaps Foucault's approach was too conventional. Derrida thought so; thus his attempt at a more radical reduction.

Derrida and the Dissolution of Metaphysics

Speaking in 1968, Derrida suggested that "if the word 'history' did not in and of itself convey the motif of a final repression of difference, one could say that only differences can be 'historical' from the outset and in each of their aspects."[36] To move beyond structuralism was to admit a fundamental historicity, but Derrida found "history" too loaded to characterize a poststructuralist world. Thus, in dissolving stable essences and meanings into a play of differences, he did not explicitly invoke history as Foucault did. Moreover, changes in the character of Derrida's work by the mid-seventies seemed to carry him ever further from any concern with history. But even the more playful accents of his maturity responded to the change in the overall cultural framework that has been at issue for us in this study. Those accents presuppose earlier, apparently more rigorous categories that Derrida elaborated in an effort to make provisional sense of the postmetaphysical situation before decid-

36. Jacques Derrida, "Différance," in *Margins of Philosophy*, trans. Alan Bass (Chicago: University of Chicago Press, 1982; orig. French ed. 1972), 11. This piece is also included in Jacques Derrida, *Speech and Phenomena and Other Essays on Husserl's Theory of Signs*, trans. David B. Allison (Evanston: Northwestern University Press, 1973); see p. 141 for a slightly different translation of the passage quoted.

ing how to respond. And though they differed from Foucault's, those categories, too, sought to make deeper sense of the reduction to history.

Derrida became associated in the English-speaking world with literary theory, but he was trained as a philosopher and established his reputation through a sustained, rigorous assault on the Western metaphysical tradition. He studied with Jean Hyppolite and read Hegel, Husserl, and Heidegger intensively during the early 1950s. By the end of that decade, however, his encounter with the thinking of Georges Bataille, Maurice Blanchot, and Roland Barthes had begun to interest him in a subject long off-limits for serious philosophy—the implications for philosophy of its own textuality and thus, more generally, the relationship between philosophy and literature.

By the early 1960s, Derrida was confronting Husserl and Lévi-Strauss, exploring the limits of each in light of his new interest in textuality. Especially influential was his critique of structuralism in "Structure, Sign, and Play," first presented at a conference at Johns Hopkins University in 1966 and a major vehicle for his influence in the United States. Then in a series of works centering on *Of Grammatology* (1967), Derrida offered a historical deconstruction of the philosophical tradition, from its ancient Greek roots through Rousseau and Hegel and on to Husserl, Saussure, and Lévi-Strauss, showing how the tradition not only claimed more than it could deliver but sought to hide what it could not encompass—and to hide the attempt to hide as well. Like Nietzsche, Croce, and Heidegger, Derrida sought to put the whole thing into question, but his confrontation with Lévi-Strauss and structuralism enabled him to approach the tradition from a French angle—and thus to make a distinctive contribution.

Derrida's historical account rested on his seemingly extravagant insistence that the Western tradition has privileged speech and "suppressed" writing, which is in fact prior in some sense. This notion has appeared arbitrary, perverse, or merely silly to numerous critics, and Derrida had to amend and stretch it considerably. Yet even in its earlier formulations, it made a fundamental point about the metaphysical tradition and its limits.

Derrida was not claiming that writing literally preceded speech in the evolution of language. At issue, rather, were two ways of understanding language and the human relationship with it, each of which carried a particular set of assumptions. Privilege to speech was bound up with all that made the Western tradition fundamentally metaphysical. That tradition assumed there is a certain way things are and that language mirrors or represents the way things are. When we speak, language seems direct, unmediated, pure, transparent, self-present. It seems to put us in immediate touch with things. Writing, in contrast, is more obviously compelled to take its own "languageness" seriously, so it has seemed derivative, at one remove from speech. Indeed, as we have afforded priority to speech, we have had to devalue and even suppress writing, because writing is always already slipping and destabilizing the restricted economy of language and representation. Writing continually undermines our image of stable truth, immediate presence, pure origins—and thus metaphysics itself.[37]

To make it clear that what he had in mind in opposing writing to speech was not simply marks on a page, or even some "textuality" that could be clearly separated from some real world "outside," Derrida used the term "arche-writing" for the problematic side of language, for all that eludes our assumption of an easy correspondence with a stable reality, for all that subverts our assumption that through language we can reduce the world to rational sense. Part of the point was to show that our philosophical tradition had inevitably been wound around contingency and circumstance, despite its tendency to believe itself pure, suprahistorical. Indeed, that tradition had always hidden, and hidden from, its own historicity.[38]

But thanks to the deconstructive history that Derrida offered in his works of the late 1960s, we can at last begin to see through our tradition and out the other side. Derrida's history focused on all that got marginalized or covered over as our tradition developed. Although he remained especially concerned with the recent outcome of the tradition in Husserl, Saussure, and Lévi-Strauss, he devoted particular attention to Rousseau and his cult of origins and to Hegel and his teleological conception of history.

With its assumption that truth, purity, self-presence, and stable identity were to be found in a "state of nature," the cult of origins was at one with the bias for speech and the attendant suppression of writing. Rousseau was an especially tempting target because his longing for original purity and transparency was bound up with a self-conscious preoccupation with the problematic nature of writing.

Although he wanted to attribute inequality and other negative characteristics to a "fall" into civilization, Rousseau could not conceive the original state of nature without codes and conventions that entailed difference, even hierarchy and repression. He discovered, but tried to deny, that no matter how far back we push, we find instability, slippage; there was always already a "supplement," something that could not be contained within a consistent logic. There was not, for example, some healthy original sexuality, with deviance resulting from the fall into civilization. Rousseau sensed, but hid the fact, that the desires underlying sexuality are inherently contradictory; admitting of no complete satisfaction, they are a source of endless instability.[39]

Just as Vico insisted on "metaphor," Derrida insisted on "writing" to show

37. See especially Jacques Derrida, *Of Grammatology*, trans. Gayatri Chakravorty Spivak (Baltimore: Johns Hopkins University Press, 1976), 229. See also Norris, *Derrida*, 69, 71, 83–84.

38. Derrida, *Of Grammatology*, 70–71; Norris, *Derrida*, 87, 93, 122, 188–189, 193.

39. Thus Derrida's conclusion to *Of Grammatology*, "The Supplement of (at) the Origin," 313–316; see also p. 229. In addition, see Jacques Derrida, *Limited Inc.*, trans. Samuel Weber (Evanston: Northwestern University Press, 1988), 93, where he holds that the notion of pure, unproblematic origins rests on privileging one term in an undecidable, unstable dualism. See also Norris, *Derrida*, 34, 50–51, 86, 91, 105–106, 118, 121, on Derrida's treatment of Rousseau and the cult of origins.

that appeal to origins affords no stable, suprahistorical truth of things. As soon as human beings can be said to be human at all, they are caught up in a language that is already in motion, referring, differentiating, deferring. Language confers meaning, but at any point, meaning refers backward, since it functions only in relationship with preexisting terms, and defers forward, since it is never stable and finished.[40]

Denial of an end entailing completion and closure is thus the other side of the denial of pure, privileged origins.[41] For the most part, belief in the purity of origins had been bound up with the ahistorical chord of the Western metaphysical tradition. There is a certain way things are, evident at the origins, so history either obscures what things really are or can be dismissed as superficial squiggling. But Hegel, especially, twisted the cult of origins around so that the truth, implicit at the beginning, was to be found only at the other end, as the outcome of a historical process. History became at once meaningful and teleological. But Hegel, Derrida insisted, had been no more successful than Rousseau. Derrida featured in Hegel the strains and contradictions that resulted from his metaphysical effort, including his subordination of "writing" to "speech."[42]

As the problems with enterprises like those of Rousseau and Hegel became clear, Husserl, Saussure, and Lévi-Strauss sought more self-consciously to establish some basis for certainty, science, stable meaning. But again Derrida fastened on what they left out, on what eluded their attempts to integrate and control. These were last-ditch efforts, and as such each made especially clear the impossibility of the whole enterprise of Western metaphysics, with its suppression of writing. Derrida's determination to confront the legacies of Husserl and structuralism in tandem enabled him to make his powerful contribution to the assault on metaphysics—and to reach his distinctive understanding of what remains, of what can be said, once metaphysics has dissolved.[43]

Structuralism had featured the sense in which signs have meaning only through their place in a synchronic system of contrasts and differences. But Derrida fastened on what was being bracketed as it did so, the endless disruption of the structured system, the instability occasioned by the excess of meaning, which is forever eluding the form, the structure, the logic. In chapter 3 it was noted that Croce, writing at the same time as Saussure, featured the endless novelty of language, the individuality of every usage, as opposed to the synchronic system in terms of which particular uses of language can be meaningful

40. See, for example, Derrida, *Of Grammatology*, 158–159, for suggestions that recall Vico's move.

41. Richard Rorty notes that Derrida's "great theme is the impossibility of closure"; see *Essays on Heidegger*, 92. See also Norris, *Derrida*, 89.

42. Norris, *Derrida*, 75; Derrida, *Margins of Philosophy*, 69–87.

43. See especially Derrida, *Writing and Difference*, 154–168. See also Norris, *Derrida*, 225–227, on the import of confronting Husserl and structuralism in tandem.

at any one time. Derrida's reversal paralleled Croce's, but his need to confront the structuralist enterprise led him to deepen the point considerably. Even on its own terms, Derrida showed, the synchronic system is never self-contained, complete, and stable. Meaning is not synchronically present in language at all, and Derrida found it necessary to propose new terms to characterize what happens instead. Because, as Christopher Norris has put it, meaning "is always subject to a kind of semantic slippage (or deferral)," Derrida coined the word *différance* "to suggest how meaning is at once 'differential' and 'deferred,' the product of a restless play within language that cannot be fixed or pinned down for the purposes of conceptual definition."[44]

For Derrida, then, language is not the synchronic system but the diachronic chain of disruptions and deferrals. Meaning is an endless web, each part of which depends on and refers to others, so that we never get a full, final grasp of what is being referred to. Meaning is always deferred; there is always further *différance*. When we seek the level of settled meaning or certain interpretation, we find no stopping place but only "traces" of earlier traces, as sequences, linkages, referring us back, back, endlessly back.[45]

But we cannot think simply in terms of a single chain of meaning or truth. As David Hoy has emphasized, Derrida was not denying the possibility of truth but admitting the plurality of truths, even as he fastened on Nietzschean play.[46] In this sense, Derrida avoided the Nietzschean overreaction from a metaphysical confidence in truth to a claim that there are only lies or fictions. What the postmetaphysical situation involves is an undecidable infinity of possible truths and readings, a luxuriant overflow, an ongoing dissemination of meaning. The term "dissemination" makes it clear that there is no dialectic that reabsorbs in some higher synthesis what gets marginalized when we assert this or that.[47]

In deconstructing the philosophical tradition during the 1960s, Derrida was at once developing an interpretive strategy and seeking to characterize what is left, or what is happening, if metaphysics falls away altogether. His way of working back through the tradition owed much to Heidegger, but he felt that Heidegger had gotten trapped in the metaphysical tradition he was seeking to sidestep. Thus Heidegger's alleged nostalgia for some original, now-forgotten

44. Norris, *Derrida*, 15. For Derrida's fullest elaboration of this key category, see "Différance" (1968), in *Margins of Philosophy*, 1–27 (also in *Speech and Phenomena*, 129–160).

45. Christopher Butler, *Interpretation, Deconstruction and Ideology: An Introduction to Some Current Issues in Literary Theory* (Oxford: Oxford University Press, 1984), 62.

46. David Couzens Hoy, "Jacques Derrida," in *The Return of Grand Theory in the Human Sciences*, ed. Quentin Skinner (Cambridge: Cambridge University Press, 1985), 57. Hoy here follows especially Jacques Derrida, *Spurs: Nietzsche's Styles*, trans. Barbara Harlow (Chicago: University of Chicago Press, 1979), 103.

47. Derrida made the point in an especially arresting way in discussing Mallarmé's image of fold upon fold. See "The Double Session," in *Dissemination*, trans. Barbara Johnson (Chicago: University of Chicago Press, 1981; orig. French ed. 1972), esp. pp. 252–273.

experience of being, for a time when language was in touch with the ultimate truths of experience. Although Derrida did not do justice to Heidegger's later thinking, his determination to avoid the taint of metaphysics that he found even in Heidegger enabled him to deepen our characterization of the postmetaphysical situation.[48] Indeed, Derrida derived some of his key categories by thinking through Heidegger's emphasis on the epochal character of being and treatment of the ontological difference between being and beings.

> *Différance,* in a certain and very strange way, [is] "older" than the ontological difference or than the truth of Being. When it has this age it can be called the play of the trace. The play of a trace which no longer belongs to the horizon of Being, but whose play transports and encloses the meaning of Being: the play of the trace, or the *différance,* which has no meaning and is not. Which does not belong. There is no maintaining, and no depth to, this bottomless chessboard on which Being is put in play.[49]

There was much dispute, however, about the status of such categories, which Derrida worked out to his satisfaction by the mid-seventies. Some, like Rorty, charged that Derrida was simply offering another metaphysics, establishing transcendental conditions of possibility. In response, Derrida insisted "that the trace is neither a ground, nor a foundation, nor an origin."[50] And indeed différance, trace, and dissemination were not metaphysical categories but simply ways of characterizing a world that cannot be fixed, that opens to the play of interpretations. So Derrida had no need to repudiate them as he moved on to the more playful responses that Rorty preferred. Those playful responses presupposed the world that his earlier categories characterized.

Leftist critics, especially, have worried that Derrida was proposing a reduction to textuality that would preclude access to a real, "outside" world and thus the possibility of concrete change. Marian Hobson has shown convincingly that this line of criticism fundamentally misconstrues Derrida's point. Accusing critics like Edward Said of a "stunning misunderstanding" of Derridean terms like "différance" and "trace," she contends that "far from collapsing what Said deems to be outside the text back onto it and into it, these concepts are exploring what could be called the historical nature of thought without using any kind

---

48. In *Of Grammatology*, 50–51, Derrida stressed the need to follow Husserl and Heidegger through to the very end; at that point, scope for play opens. For Derrida's treatment of Heidegger, see especially *Margins of Philosophy*, 21–27, which makes it clear that Derrida, in hammering out his own radical categories, was responding to the perceived inadequacies of Heidegger. See also pp. 64–67, 123–136; as well as Jacques Derrida, *Positions*, trans. Alan Bass (Chicago: University of Chicago Press, 1981; orig. French ed. 1972), 9–11, 52. In addition, see Norris, *Derrida*, 160–161.

49. Derrida, *Margins of Philosophy*, 22.

50. Derrida, *Positions*, 52. Rorty, *Essays on Heidegger*, 102, finds Derrida's response here "puzzling." See also Rorty's assessment of Derrida on pp. 112–113, 117.

of position of even momentary transcendence."[51] And Hobson goes on to show that what Derrida was seeking to characterize was essentially the postmetaphysical history at issue in this study. Although seeking a way of thinking about radical contingency, with no origin, direction, or goal that would afford a measure to history, Derrida was not denying the coherence necessary for a kind of historical trajectory. On the contrary, says Hobson, "Derrida's *trace* is itself a trajectory. The back and forth makes a set of plies—strands in a yarn or rope, which provide the strength through tension. We are left not with a scatter of points but with a trajectory."[52]

The approach to texts that Derrida developed as he worked back through the philosophical tradition came to be known as "deconstruction" in the precise, delimited sense of the term. His encounter with structuralism and the workings of structured systems enabled him to develop an actively deconstructive approach without the implication, prominent in Heidegger's second stage, that we might achieve some definitive uprooting or recovery.

Although Derrida was not offering just another position within Western metaphysics, neither did he believe that the tradition was simply foolish, a trivial mistake that now simply dissolves. It remains inescapable for us—a destiny or fatality—as much for Derrida as for Heidegger. So we must continue to address our particular history, reading the philosophers, but now in a deconstructive way.[53]

Whether it was featuring the purity of beginnings, the completeness of ends, or the logical consistency of a structured system, the metaphysical tradition had always had to deny or marginalize something—something that kept sticking out nevertheless. So Derrida featured the strains and contradictions, the attempt to marginalize, the effort to hide the fact that the intelligibility of a philosophical claim always presupposes a larger space that is not made intelligible.[54] In this way he uncovered the undecidability, instability, deferral, and dissemination that have always been fundamental to the philosophical tradition.

In its more general form, Derrida's deconstructive strategy could be applied to any text, showing that the text cannot fully situate, control, or exhaust the matter at hand and disrupting the text's effort to impose limitations on its own meaning or implication.[55] The loose ends stick out, despite the effort of the text to exclude or hide them. And with the end of metaphysics, there can be no "transcendental signified," so the deconstructive reader can show that appeals

51. Marian Hobson, "History Traces," in *Post-Structuralism and the Question of History*, ed. Attridge et al., 101–115. The quoted passage is on p. 102.
52. Ibid., 113; see also p. 109.
53. Derrida, *Writing and Difference*, 288.
54. Throughout his *Derrida*, Norris characterizes effectively what Derridean deconstruction may unearth, including even the prelogical possibility of logic. See p. 183 for this example, as well as pp. 61, 77, 79–80, 82–83, 86.
55. Derrida, *Positions*, 23–24. See also Butler, *Interpretation*, 61, 80.

to reality in the text are simply efforts to claim an unwarranted authority over subsequent interpretation. As "method" such deconstruction could become formulaic and mechanical, but Derrida was showing, as no one had before, how to probe the diachronic workings of language. Here, perhaps, was where to look and how to proceed if we seek a more radical kind of historical questioning in a postmetaphysical world.

In seeking to undermine the pretenses of philosophy, Derrida sought to work into the distinctions on which its whole self-understanding has rested, showing that they do not hold up. This did not entail simply inverting the binary oppositions at work and assigning priority to the hitherto suppressed term. Not even writing is to be assigned privilege through such a reversal, as if the point was finally to grasp, once and for all, that everything is motion, flow, happening, or event. The point is to destabilize dualistic opposition itself, for it is through systems of such oppositions that we believe we fix the world.[56] By showing how the terms intersect, presupposing and affecting each other in undecidable ways, we demonstrate not only that philosophy cannot deliver what it claims but ultimately that our world itself cannot be stable, centered, self-identical in the way that the metaphysical tradition led us to expect.

In the same way, Derrida was not simply reversing some reality-textuality dichotomy to offer a textualist recasting of idealist metaphysics, suggesting that only textuality is real. Rather than saying "everything is language," or some such, he proposed to shake us from the metaphysical prejudice that we capture and fix the world in language. Thus his concern was with what he called the "other of language," but that "other" was not to be conceived simply as an independent reality that language does, or does not, mirror or represent.[57] Language, textuality, representation, reality—we may go on adding terms that serve in various dichotomies, but those terms are all linked in an undecidable, tension-ridden way. So, again, rather than simply reversing the hierarchy, deconstruction burrows its way "beneath" our usual dualistic distinctions, even including reality and textuality, reality and representation. There is no clear line between them.

Thus, in trying to characterize the sense in which philosophy is literary, Derrida insisted that even the notion of metaphor was misleading because it implies

56. Norris, *Derrida*, 23–24, 56, 133. See also Brook Thomas, *The New Historicism and Other Old-Fashioned Topics* (Princeton: Princeton University Press, 1991), 123, for an especially effective way of making the point. Derrida was not opting simply for Nietzschean play as opposed to some binary alternative; rather, he was seeking to put even that opposition in play. Play has meaning only in tandem with the alternative, so there is no end, no moment of deliverance.

57. See Derrida's comments in his illuminating interview with Richard Kearney, *Dialogues with Contemporary Continental Thinkers: The Phenomenological Heritage*, trans. Richard Kearney (Manchester: Manchester University Press, 1984), 123–124. See also Norris, *Derrida*, 121, 142–144, 213. On p. 213, Norris argues convincingly that Derrida's often-cited dictum, "There is no 'outside' to the text," makes the same point, that there can be "no ultimate appeal to 'lived' experience," no stopping point.

an independent reality to which the metaphorical text refers—indirectly, figu-
ratively. When we work back from the philosophical text seeking a reassuring
connection to some preexisting real world, we find no stopping point, no solid
ground.[58] The founding concepts of metaphysics are instances not of metaphor
but of *catachresis*—"a violent production of meaning, an abuse which refers to
no anterior or proper norm."[59] If we insist on the literal-metaphor distinction, it,
too, can be destabilized as undecidable.

Derrida's first response, then, was to subject the texts through which we
organize our world to such disruptive deconstructive readings. But a number of
questions intrude themselves about the purposes of this strategy, and even the
most sympathetic students of Derrida do not answer them in the same way.
Once we get Derrida's point, do we need to keep the deconstructive pressure
on, or have we liberated ourselves to go on to something else? Beginning with
Glas in the midseventies, Derrida himself began trying out radically new kinds
of writing, seeking more actively to force open the tradition. *Glas* was an
encounter with Hegel that Derrida characterized as "neither philosophy nor
poetry" but "a reciprocal contamination of the one by the other, from which
neither can emerge intact." Indeed, Derrida noted explicitly that in *Glas* and
other such works he was trying to introduce new forms of catachresis.[60] In one
sense, he was simply extending the deconstructionist enterprise in these later
works, going back to the tradition, finding ever more imaginative ways to disrupt it, open it, play with it. But was Derrida thereby offering us a richer understanding of our history, or did the element of play take precedence, affording
self-creation, edification, or entertainment? Whatever Derrida's purposes in his
later works, can the deconstructive strategy serve ongoing reconstruction, endlessly yielding some provisional reality, or is the notion of reconstruction itself
suspect? Is dissemination and even catachresis compatible, on some level, with
Gadamerian gathering, or coming back together?

In his *Radical Hermeneutics*, Caputo emphasized the negative value of Derridean deconstruction in endlessly puncturing authoritarian pretense. Others
sought to show how deconstruction could serve reconstruction, building up
something to replace what dissolves. In his often-cited *Marxism and Deconstruction*, Michael Ryan sought to show that Derrida might serve to open and
expand Marxism.[61] Perhaps most relentless in drawing out the critical yet

58. Derrida, *Of Grammatology*, 15; Butler, *Interpretation*, 20; Norris, *Derrida*, 82, 170.
59. Derrida in Kearney, *Dialogues*, 122–123. See also Derrida's "White Mythology" (1971), in
Margins of Philosophy, 207–271.
60. Derrida in Kearney, *Dialogues*, 122–123. See also Jacques Derrida, *Glas*, trans. John P.
Leavey, Jr., and Richard Rand (Lincoln: University of Nebraska Press, 1986; orig. French ed.
1974), and the accompanying *Glassary* by John P. Leavey, Jr.
61. John D. Caputo, *Radical Hermeneutics: Repetition, Deconstruction, and the Hermeneutic
Project* (Bloomington: Indiana University Press, 1987); Michael Ryan, *Marxism and Deconstruction: A Critical Articulation* (Baltimore: Johns Hopkins University Press, 1982). Ryan worried,
however, that Derridean deconstruction, taken alone, points to nihilistic passivity. See esp.
pp. 37–40.

reconstructive potential in Derrida was Christopher Norris, who sought ultimately to combine Derrida with Habermas.

Part of Norris's effort was to rescue Derrida from the popular understanding of deconstruction that he associated especially with American literary intellectuals. What Derrida offered was neither a technique for textual interpretation nor a license for a more inventive, playful mode of reading. Rather, his way of attending critically to our language, starting with the language of philosophy, afforded the key to "real changes in the present institutional structures of power, knowledge and politics." And Norris insisted repeatedly that this enterprise entailed rigorous analysis; there was nothing playful about it.[62]

Norris's suggestion is surely plausible. By drawing our attention to the way what has come to be said plays off, even precludes, what is not said, Derrida significantly deepened our sense of what might be questioned. This critical approach to language might help us grasp the contingency of sociocultural practices and to discern what changing them would entail. But of course the conventional radical tradition, too, might be subject to deconstruction. Based on categories like domination and emancipation, it, too, had been constructed historically around absences, margins, preclusions. So deconstruction could not be assumed to buttress some existing radical position. Indeed, by indicating what had been unquestioned in our own thinking, it invited a form of reflexive self-criticism. And this reflexivity entailed putting everything at risk.[63]

We have seen that Foucault, by pointing to the constructedness of relations of power/knowledge, showed how we can contest existing practices in a radical but reconstructive mode. In a sense, Derrida cut deeper by showing how any such constructedness works in language. However, Foucault was more obviously looking beyond the philosophical tradition. So whereas Derrida showed how to probe language in our quest for answers, Foucault showed that all cultural practices may be questioned on the same basis, in terms of some defining, historically specific discourse. It would seem, then, that Foucault and Derrida, taken together, might afford the radical but reconstructive component missing in the combination of historicism and hermeneutics discussed in the last chapter. In both Foucault and Derrida, however, the premium on disruption was so relentless and exclusive that the scope for reconstruction remained uncertain at best.

---

62. Norris, *Derrida*, 26. See also p. 109, where Norris insists that Derrida's approach "requires a rigour and a scrupulous adherence to the letter of the text which could scarcely be further removed from [the] popular idea of what 'deconstruction' is all about," and pp. 21, 24, 27, 112–113, for variations on the same theme. Marian Hobson similarly criticizes the overemphasis on undifferentiated "free play" among some of those embracing Derridean deconstruction; see "History Traces," 103–104.

63. Though more a critic of Derrida than a supporter, Christopher Butler is especially good on the uses of the critical approach to language that can be developed from Derridean deconstruction. See *Interpretation*, 20–22, 64.

The Premium on Disruption

At some points Foucault's way of emphasizing the "other" or underside of power, "that which responds to every advance of power by a movement of disengagement," seems to suggest the scope for change, for it "forms the motivation for every new development of networks of power."[64] New forms of power emerge through the intransigence of freedom vis-à-vis the power relations that have crystallized so far. But rather than emphasize the scope for reconstructive action, Foucault insisted on leveling things out; whatever happens, the outcome will simply be another instance of power, which conflates with subjugation, domination: "Domination is in fact a general structure of power whose ramifications and consequences can sometimes be found descending to the most incalcitrant fibers of society." The construction or coming to be of the world necessarily entails "a multiform production of relations of domination."[65] Wherever we look in history, then, we find only some particular power configuration that is subject to condemnation. Thus Rorty charged that "Foucault's work is pervaded by a crippling ambiguity between 'power' as a pejorative term and as a neutral, descriptive term."[66]

Foucault's refusal to allow distinctions among crystallizations of power drew the criticism of both liberals and radicals. As liberals charged, he could not admit that the development of the liberal state over the past three centuries might have increased choice and decreased suffering.[67] And Foucault's suggestions that *all* dominant forms of power are suspect encompassed even the dominant opposition. Marxism, too, had come to dominance through exclusion, subjugation, spurious claims to privilege. Thus radical critics from Fredric Jameson to Jean Baudrillard charged that Foucault offered only a futile neo-anarchism, a useless protest.[68]

Foucault's way of reducing everything to the same level precluded the measure of positive identification with something in particular that would afford a foothold for criticism to serve positive reconstruction. Seeking to pinpoint what was missing in both Foucault and Jean-François Lyotard, Rorty referred to "the extraordinary *dryness* of Foucault's work[,] . . . a dryness produced by a lack of identification with any social context, any communication. . . . It is as if thinkers like Foucault and Lyotard were so afraid of being caught up in one

64. Foucault, *Power/Knowledge*, 138.
65. Foucault, "The Subject and Power," 226; Foucault, *Power/Knowledge*, 142. See also Foucault, *Power/Knowledge*, 188; and Mark Philp, "Michel Foucault," in *Return of Grand Theory*, ed. Skinner, 75–76, for indications of Foucault's way of conflating power with domination.
66. Rorty, *Essays on Heidegger*, 195.
67. See especially the influential critiques by Michael Walzer, "The Politics of Michel Foucault," and Charles Taylor, "Foucault on Freedom and Truth," both in *Foucault*, ed. Hoy, 51–102. See also Rorty, *Essays on Heidegger*, 194–195.
68. See Bové, "The Foucault Phenomenon," xxix, for a good summary of these charges and references to several examples.

more metanarrative about the fortunes of 'the subject' that they cannot bring themselves to say 'we' long enough to identify with the culture of the generation to which they belong."[69]

In the final analysis, Foucault seemed to allow only a grim, endless, ritualistic kind of resistance, a struggle against power itself, with its tendency to organize a world, to crystallize things into something in particular.[70] Rather than portray his own effort as an exercise of power intended to respond to the challenges of his own time and contribute to the next moment of truth and reality, he found it necessary to subvert the whole ideal of truth and reality in our culture, as merely one aspect of this historically specific power configuration. Because even the notion of "objective reality" confirmed the extant order, he sometimes suggested that lying and rhetoric were necessary instruments in the ongoing struggle.[71] And he insisted on the fictional nature of historical works— including, of course, his own—even while conceding that some fictions may function as "true."

> I am well aware that I have never written anything but fictions. I do not mean to say, however, that truth is therefore absent. It seems to me that the possibility exists for fiction to function in truth, for a fictional discourse to induce effects of truth, and for bringing it about that a true discourse engenders or "manufactures" something that does not as yet exist, that is, "fictions" it. One "fictions" history on the basis of a political reality that makes it true, one "fictions" a politics not yet in existence on the basis of a historical truth.[72]

Up to a point, this passage usefully characterizes the element of creativity in historical truth and the broadly political role that historical accounts play in shaping the next moment. But because he had other axes to grind, Foucault gave the insight a particular spin, folding historical truth within politically inspired fiction. During his lifetime, at least, his dismissive characterizations of "objective reality" and historical truth led practicing historians to view his historical works with suspicion. Specialists in early modern Europe like Lawrence Stone and H. C. Erik Midelfort pinpointed what they found to be unacceptable license in Foucault's handling of the historical evidence.[73] But while they

69. Richard Rorty, "Habermas and Lyotard on Postmodernity," in *Habermas and Modernity*, ed. Richard J. Bernstein (Cambridge: MIT Press, 1986), 172.

70. Foucault, "The Subject and Power," 211–212, 221–223, 225.

71. Allan Megill, *Prophets of Extremity: Nietzsche, Heidegger, Foucault, Derrida* (Berkeley, Los Angeles, and London: University of California Press, 1985), 243–244, 252–254.

72. Foucault, *Power/Knowledge*, 193. See also pp. 118, 131–132.

73. H. C. Erik Midelfort, "Madness and Civilization in Early Modern Europe: A Reappraisal of Michel Foucault," in *After the Reformation: Essays in Honor of J. H. Hexter*, ed. Barbara C. Malament (Philadelphia: University of Pennsylvania Press, 1980), 247–265; and Lawrence Stone, "Madness," *New York Review of Books*, 16 December 1982, 29–30. See also *New York Review of Books*, 31 March 1983, 42–44, for an exchange between Foucault and Stone occasioned by Stone's essay.

continued to put off many mainstream historians, Foucault's characterizations increasingly seemed to others to justify an overtly political element in the construction of historical accounts—or fictions.

But Foucault was not settling for this relatively familiar instrumentalist understanding of historical interpretations as effective fictions. He argued that the categories around which our mental life has come to be organized, and even what we take to be our intelligence itself, are historically specific and necessarily imply a precluded other that might be liberated: "by creating a space for the operation of truth and falsity, by situating the free supplement of error, categories silently reject stupidity. In a commanding voice, they instruct us in the ways of knowledge and solemnly alert us to the possibilities of error, while in a whisper they guarantee our intelligence and form the a priori of excluded stupidity." Much like Derrida, however, Foucault envisioned not simply a reversal that would make "stupidity" privileged instead of intelligence; nor was his simply a romantic emphasis on the superiority of feeling, sentiment, imagination, or some other "Other" of conceptual intellect. Rather, he wanted to keep the tension before us, to operate in the crease, thus endlessly resisting the imperious demands of intelligence. If anything, we might afford privilege to paradox: "The philosopher must be sufficiently perverse to play the game of truth and error badly."[74]

Derrida's premium on perversity paralleled Foucault's. As Caputo has emphasized, Derrida's dialectic was always negative, his praxis always disruptive.[75] Even if it did not call simply for straightforward reversal, Derridean deconstruction explicitly afforded privilege to what has been marginalized, to uncanonical texts, to the blind spots or the margins of texts. And although Norris was surely right to deny that Derrida simply offered interpretive license, neither could Derrida consistently be made the reconstructive radical that Norris was seeking. Derrida's approach was ultimately too playful. Thus Rorty accented Derrida's refusal to take philosophy seriously and lauded the comic element in Derrida's mature work, which included a systematic evasiveness as Derrida played with the status of his own texts.[76]

Rorty was prominent among those distinguishing the playful "later" Derrida from the earnestly philosophical Derrida of the works prior to *Glas* in 1974. But the more playful approach followed from the sense of the cultural situation that Derrida had already developed. As early as 1966, in "Structure, Sign, and Play," he explicitly welcomed the opening to a more playfully active interpretation that seemed to follow once we grasp that the language in which we are enmeshed is neither solidly referential nor solidly structural but end-

74. Foucault, *Language, Counter-Memory, Practice*, 188, 190.
75. Caputo, *Radical Hermeneutics*, 189–196, esp. pp. 189–190.
76. Rorty, *Essays on Heidegger*, 113; see also pp. 117–118.

lessly open, lacking a stable center or stable points of reference.[77] As we interpret texts, there is no privileged authority that can either limit us or judge us, holding us responsible. We are free to read in an innocently active way, disseminating new meanings—even new truths—but without seeking even provisionally to close the circle by bringing understanding of the text back to the coherence of a unified—even "true"—account. Such reading even involves finding ways not to pretend to do so, to subvert any claims to do so.

The playful, endlessly disruptive thrust of Derridean deconstruction has prompted critics like John Ellis to emphasize that Derrida's thinking is antithetical to any constructive approach. It is incongruent, for example, with Marxism, or with the feminist attempt to unmarginalize women's voices.[78] Such approaches seek to overcome a historically specific situation, putting something deemed superior in its place, but Derrida's accent on the instability of things was so extreme that it undercut the foothold necessary both for criticism and for constructive action. More generally, Ellis showed that Derrida's premium was on subversion itself, as opposed to replacing a subverted idea with a better one.

So the Foucault and Derrida currents converged in their mistrust of authority and their premium on disruption. In the final analysis, the sort of reconstruction Ellis had in mind was not the point for either thinker, and the question is why they wanted to do something else instead. But even critics like Ellis who effectively pinpointed the elements of extremity found it difficult to account for the priorities of deconstruction. Still thinking in terms of the "intellectual progress" through which better ideas supersede older ones, Ellis could not see the rationale for Derrida's way of keeping ideas in eternal purgatory. He was simply puzzled by Derrida's premium on endlessly putting the whole thing into question, on backing off from the finitude of particularizing language, on subverting the whole central/marginal dichotomy and thus the possibility of discerning/judging degrees of importance.[79]

To explain such apparent extravagance, some, at least some of the time, repaired to reductionist categories, referring to the authoritarianism of the French university system, or to the uncertainties of radicalism after 1968, or to the resentments these particular individuals felt as intellectuals and outsiders.[80] But others sensed that the extremity in deconstruction stemmed from deeper impulses, perhaps reflecting new preoccupations coming to the fore with the eclipse of metaphysics.

77. Derrida, *Writing and Difference*, 292–293. Though helpful, Butler's account in *Interpretation*, 86, seems better to characterize the embrace of Derridean deconstruction by literary intellectuals than the basis for Derrida's own more playful response by the mid-1970s.

78. Ellis, *Against Deconstruction*, esp. p. 96.

79. Ibid., 41–42, 53–54, 69–71, 73, 75, 78, 81–82, 87, 93–94, 140–141, 151.

80. Ibid., 83–84; Butler, *Interpretation*, 88. See also Perry Anderson, *In the Tracks of Historical Materialism* (London: Verso, 1983), 38–42.

In a brief but brilliant article, Rorty maintained that Foucault's enterprise mixed two purposes that were better kept separate. Foucault wanted to help people, but as an intellectual he was also seeking personal autonomy and self-creation. In his quest to help people he bent over backward to respect *their* autonomy, so he declined to take over their vocabularies or to relate them to the wider historical process. The extreme, anarchical tendency in Foucault was "the result of a misguided attempt to envisage a society as free of its historical past as the Romantic intellectual hopes to be free of her private past."[81] Rorty was suggesting, then, that a loosely Nietzschean concern with self-creation, necessarily standing opposed to reconstructive, history-making action, undermined Foucault's desire to help people, to make a difference in the wider world around him. At issue was a tension between ways of relating to the world as historical, but though Rorty's discussion was especially suggestive, it left only a few indications of what those might entail.

Norris, as part of his effort to save Derridean deconstruction for radical reconstructive purposes, distinguished Derrida from "Foucault, Deleuze or the adepts of post-structuralist apocalyptic discourse," whom he associated with a leap into some unknown, beyond reason and critical thought.[82] Norris was suggesting, then, that some quasi-religious concern had made Foucault too extreme to serve reconstruction.

Rorty was still more explicit in finding something "religious" at work in the vogue of Derridean deconstruction, although he considered Paul de Man far more responsible than Derrida for the mixture of elegy and polemic that set the tone for the movement in the United States. Reading literature in a de Manian mode became a kind of religious ritual for a postmetaphysical age. In contrast with scientific, philosophical, and everyday uses of language, literature always attends to its own relationship with reality; literary language always manifests the impossibility of the full presence, the oneness with things, that we desire. So by endlessly encountering the literariness of language, deconstruction offered what Rorty called "a way of mourning a *Deus absconditus*, of participating in a divine absence[,] . . . an ascetic practice that confronts one ever and again with 'the presence of a nothingness.' "[83]

81. Rorty, *Essays on Heidegger*, 195–196.
82. Norris, *Derrida*, 224–225. See also 216–217, 222, for Norris's effort to separate Derrida from Foucault.
83. See Rorty, *Essays on Heidegger*, 113–118, for this reading of de Man and his influence; the quoted passage is on p. 114. On p. 116n, Rorty refers in a similar vein to "the worship of a Dark God, the celebration of perpetual absence." See also pp. 129–139, esp. p. 131, for Rorty's analysis "De Man and the American Cultural Left." In developing this point about deconstruction, Rorty draws partly on one of de Man's closest and most influential colleagues, J. Hillis Miller, in *The Ethics of Reading* (New York: Columbia University Press, 1987), pp. 41–59, esp. pp. 53–54, 57–58. Miller makes it clear that the "reading" at issue is a mode of human interaction with the world, not a delimited encounter with literary texts. See also Miller's much earlier *The Disappearance of God: Five Nineteenth-Century Writers* (Cambridge: Harvard University Press, 1963),

When he considered Derrida himself, Rorty accented Derrida's playful side. In Rorty's account, in fact, Derrida sought to make the whole philosophical tradition look enigmatic by treating it as a joke.[84] Yet that response, too, seems to manifest preoccupations new to a world of nothing but history.

In any case, a premium on enigma, systematic evasion, or ritualistic participation in divine absence is utterly incongruent with an emphasis on endless reconstruction. The problem is how to account for these impulses and how to place the overall extremity of deconstruction in perspective.

Plausible Extremity

One possibility, which convinces up to a point, is to say that the claim to a spurious authority is ongoing and so must endlessly be disrupted. Whatever comes to be always seeks to mask its own historicity and constructedness; our concepts always tend to harden, hiding their instability. Because we can expect no definitive deliverance from metaphysical temptations, deconstruction is endlessly necessary, at least as one cultural moment among others, to loosen, to disrupt, and thereby to subvert the "logocentric" conception of things that takes the world as graspable in language.[85]

Derrida noted that philosophers were trying to erect suprahistorical theories even in response to insights akin to his own about difference and instability. Thus his noted encounter with Searle, who developed an influential theory of speech acts largely from J. L. Austin's form of ordinary language philosophy. Like Wittgenstein in his later works, Austin offered insights into the radical pluralism, the unsystematic nature of language, that were congruent with the wider retreat from metaphysics. Although he remained too much the conventional philosopher for Derrida's taste, Austin was more interested in following problematic cases as they broke down prior speech act classifications than in incorporating them into some overarching theory. Searle, in contrast, sought to develop from Austin's insights a rigorous theory of speech acts, laying out classifications, as if philosophy could specify in advance how language must work to make sense. Thus Derrida sought to deconstruct speech act theory by pinpointing what Searle had played down or marginalized in systematizing

---

for his sense of the overarching religious issue. On pp. 9–12, he portrays historicism as the desolate outcome of the disappearance of God by the end of the nineteenth century. Rorty may be too quick to dismiss attempts like those of de Man and Miller to work through the ruins of the old to new forms of religiosity. But he argues convincingly that Derrida cannot serve de Man's project, because Derrida did not assume that our way of conceiving the dualism of language and reality is at last the right one, or that we have finally discovered what language and reading have been all along.

84. Rorty, *Essays on Heidegger*, 117–118.
85. This is Norris's implication throughout *Derrida*; see esp. pp. 16, 60, 84, 184.

Austin's insight.[86] Whether Derrida's assault was successful remains in dispute, but Searle's response to Austin made it clear that even as we abandon foundationalism, we may seek to fix, to classify, to specify in advance, as opposed to getting on with our business, using language, putting it to work.

It might be argued, then, that deconstruction provides the cultural lubricant that is endlessly necessary to bring human being together with the process of endless deferral. To be sure, the world is in slippage in any case, but the constant lubrication frees up human creativity, so that we mesh in a history-making mode with this slipping world of interlacing contingencies. In fact, however, Foucault and Derrida each seem to have had deeper reasons for placing priority on ongoing resistance, disruption, and destabilization.

The impetus toward extremity in deconstruction derived from the universe of new preoccupations, stemming from the reduction to history, that we found emerging first in Nietzsche and Heidegger. The premium on endless loosening, distancing, and disrupting responded not simply to an ongoing metaphysical tendency but to a new sense of confinement, even suffocation, in a *post*metaphysical world. At first, the extremity in Foucault seems to differ from the extremity in Derrida, both in origin and in cultural implication. Foucault seems more earnest and at least quasi-political, Derrida more playful. Foucault criticized precisely the apparently apolitical implications of Derrida's more playful approach.[87] For each, however, there was something suffocating, yet also insubstantial and inadequate, about a world newly experienced as merely historical. Seeking to respond, each moved back and forth between Nietzsche and Heidegger, interlacing themes from each, thereby thickening the web of postmetaphysical extremity.

Part of what compromised the reconstructive potential of deconstruction was an element of quasi-Heideggerian alienation. It is evident well before Foucault and Derrida in the late reflections of the cultural critic Walter Benjamin, who is worth considering briefly as a link between Heidegger and this wider cultural tendency. Loosely within the orbit of T. W. Adorno and the Frankfurt school, Benjamin was one of the most imaginative of the generally Marxist cultural critics of the twentieth century. Especially in his "Theses on the Philosophy of History," however, a Heideggerian element came together with his radicalism, resulting in a blurring that compromised both.[88]

---

86. Derrida, *Limited Inc.* In *Essays on Heidegger*, 86n, 103n, Richard Rorty endorses Searle's criticism of Derrida for attributing to Austin traditional motives and attitudes that he in fact avoided. But though Derrida may not have done justice to Austin, he effectively criticized metaphysical assumptions common to both Austin and Searle. In *Derrida*, Norris accents Derrida's feeling that he was considerably closer to Austin than to Searle; see pp. 179–186, 189–190.

87. See Hoy, "Jacques Derrida," 58–60, for a good summary.

88. Walter Benjamin, *Illuminations*, ed. Hannah Arendt, trans. Harry Zohn (New York: Schocken, 1969), 253–264, esp. p. 255. The "Theses" date from 1940. On p. 46 of her introduction to *Illuminations*, Hannah Arendt notes that Benjamin, without realizing it, was closer to one side of

Benjamin resented the domination by the historical victors, including the selective remembering and enforced forgetting that seemed to be involved in any actualization in history. What is ultimately troubling in this syndrome is not some isolable power configuration, or even the strong notion of progress that justifies the victors, but the mechanisms through which any and every moment comes to be through history. In the nature of things *any* reality will be particular, resting on the power of the victors and the particular remembering and forgetting that are bound up with their victory. The appropriate mode of response to such a world was ultimately more religious than political. Indeed, a way of reappropriating the whole of history was central to Benjamin's image of redemption. "A chronicler who recites events without distinguishing between major and minor ones acts in accordance with the following truth: nothing that has ever happened should be regarded as lost for history. To be sure, only a redeemed mankind receives the fullness of its past—which is to say, only for a redeemed mankind has its past become citable in all its moments."[89] Short of such redemption, Benjamin implied that we may respond through a kind of ritualistic disruption that recalls Heidegger's mature strategy. We refuse to distinguish major and minor events, thereby keeping the whole of what has happened alive "for its own sake," in defiance of the endless resulting in some actual present through some particular winning and marginalizing.

In the last analysis, however, Benjamin remained suspended between radical politics and religious alienation. His condemnation was so global that it undermined the foothold necessary for his historical deconstruction to result in reconstruction, yet the element of hope against hope for radical change impeded the disengagement necessary for an alternative, more or less Heideggerian religiosity.

Despite the power of his historical questioning, Foucault ended up in a similar ambiguity. Like Benjamin, he wanted to be radical, but extremity got the upper hand in his thinking, so even historical inquiry served him not so much to prepare subsequent action but to disrupt in a ritualistic way. Power is wherever anything has resulted; the winning that has resulted in that power has always entailed exclusion; that power pretends to an unwarranted authority and is tantamount to domination. What Foucault offered, in response, was a neo-existentialist, self-justifying, and, yes, "humanistic" gesture of resistance to power itself, to the mechanisms through which any world at all comes to be. As he put it in 1979, "My ethic is . . . 'anti-strategic': to be respectful when something singular arises, to be intransigent when power offends against the universal. A simple choice, but a difficult work. It is always necessary to watch out

---

Heidegger than to the subtle Marxism of his friends. Julian Roberts similarly suggests that the later Benjamin had more in common with Heidegger than he was willing to admit. See his *Walter Benjamin* (Atlantic Highlands, N.J.: Humanities Press, 1983), 91.

89. Benjamin, *Illuminations*, 254.

for something, a little beneath history, that breaks with it, that agitates it; it is necessary to look, a little behind politics, for that which ought to limit it, unconditionally."[90]

Still, to achieve purity, integrity, in response to the mechanisms of world-resulting as history, it is not enough to pull back and disengage altogether. Precisely because the reduction to history was a crucial datum for Foucault, he envisioned that we keep resisting and disrupting power *in its historical specificity*; we cannot resist it in general, or simply turn our gaze heavenward. Because the target of resistance is necessarily different at any moment, we need different strategies. In our own time, for example, commodification is central to the diffusion of power, so we have to learn to resist that. And we still need historical understanding—in order to understand how to resist such particular crystallizations of power.

Paul Bové, disputing Gilles Deleuze's claim to find a "utopian" element in Foucault, insisted that there is instead only endless subversion—subversion even of any such utopian aspiration. Bové suggested, consistently enough, that in Foucault's world perhaps only "failure" can be counted as success, the only genuine mode of opposition.[91] This is true even for the opposition intellectual, of course, for even the dominant modes of opposition came to dominance through the same particularizing mechanisms. Any such premium on failure-as-resistance reflects the ultimate in alienation from the mechanisms of world-making as history, which, by definition, entails succeeding, winning, excluding.

Foucault's response may be seen as loosely religious in the sense that it stemmed from this sort of alienation, which was ultimately deeper even than Heidegger's. Heidegger was alienated from the particular world resulting from our particular history, but Foucault resented "history" itself, the way the world happens, the mechanisms bound up with the coming to be of anything at all. Although the element of religious disengagement Heidegger afforded was spare and limited, his orientation was more hopeful than Foucault's because to resist closing up in the actual and to attune oneself to the giving itself was, first, to experience positively the fact that there is anything at all and, second, to hold open for a different dispensation, a different actuality. For Foucault, in contrast, resistance becomes an end in itself—again, an existentialist gesture of authenticity.

Moreover, for all his debt to Nietzschean genealogy, Foucault's radicalism was ultimately anything but Nietzschean, because the mode of affirmation Nietzsche envisioned was to dissipate precisely the postmetaphysical resentment we find in Foucault. For Nietzsche, power was simply the neutral glue of world-resulting and not "domination," understood as inherently illegitimate.

90. Foucault, "Is It Useless to Revolt?" 9.
91. Bové, "The Foucault Phenomenon," xxix-xxxvi; see esp. p. xxxvi. See also Thomas, *The New Historicism*, 47, on the antireconstructive thrust of Foucault.

To be sure, power for Nietzsche might well entail domination, but it can be exercised with a good conscience in light of Nietzsche's affirmative embrace of the particularity of the world. For Nietzsche, critical discrimination among power configurations remained possible, and a particular configuration may be subject to condemnation as life-debasing. It will not be so, however, simply because it is an instance of power and entails the exclusion or concealment that *any* instance of power entails.

Although it was more playful, Derrida's response stemmed from the same family of preoccupations as Foucault's. An acute sense of confinement to our particular history was central to his thinking from the outset. Referring to the developing radical critique of the bases of the tradition, a critique to which Nietzsche, Freud, and Heidegger seemed to have been central, Derrida noted,

> But all these destructive discourses and all their analogues are trapped in a kind of circle. This circle is unique. It describes the form of the relation between the history of metaphysics and the destruction of the history of metaphysics. There is no sense in doing without the concepts of metaphysics in order to shake metaphysics. We have no language—no syntax and no lexicon—which is foreign to this history; we can pronounce not a single destructive proposition which has not already had to slip into the form, the logic, and the implicit postulations of precisely what it seeks to contest.[92]

So our particular history continues to happen no matter what we say, no matter how radically we deconstruct it. We may "seek to contest," but we are "trapped," in the sense that whatever we say or do grows from, belongs to, and returns to the idiosyncratic history that surrounds us.

Still, we may resist, even establish a fleeting measure of personal autonomy, though only through an ongoing encounter with endlessly suffocating history. We noted that Derrida, like Heidegger, found it essential to continue working through the texts of our tradition, but he concluded that unprecedented approaches were necessary if he was to avoid simply assuming a place behind Heidegger in the Western lineage.[93]

We have noted that a kind of playfulness was central to Derrida's response virtually from the start. At first, Derridean play seemed a form of the innocent, posthistoricist self-affirmation that Nietzsche had posited. In 1966, in fact, Derrida explicitly linked his approach to Nietzsche's notion of "the innocence of becoming." As an antidote to the sense of loss and even guilt that threatened to befall us in this newly decentered world, Nietzsche had envisioned the "joyous affirmation of the play of the world and of the innocence of becoming, the affirmation of a world of signs without fault, without truth, and without origin

92. Derrida, *Writing and Difference*, 280–281.
93. Derrida, *Margins of Philosophy*, 134–136. See also Rorty, *Essays on Heidegger*, 118n, for a good characterization of Derrida's move.

which is offered to an active interpretation."[94] Rather than trying to get something right or claiming some definitive overcoming of our predecessors, we have fun uncovering the inevitable destabilizing elements in the efforts of others to do so. Or we play reflexively with our own tendency to cover over and marginalize all that does not fit. The game was innocent because the players claimed to be doing nothing more than keeping the thing in play—and having some sophisticated fun in the process.

To understand interpretation as play undercuts any pretense, of the sort that crept into the wider current of deconstructive criticism, that the interpreter enjoys a privileged epistemological status vis-à-vis the author, a status enabling the interpreter to reveal the blindness of the author. It is crucial that for Derrida everything is leveled out. We keep in mind that we are playing, so we avoid the temptation to claim objectivity or some privileged meaning. For the obvious questions about the status of his own texts, Derrida was more than ready. Indeed, he welcomed the occasion they afforded him to play to the next level "down." Although in one sense his accounts of Hegel, Nietzsche, and other historical figures presuppose the sort of objective truth to the texts that he wanted to destroy, he assured us that his own texts have no decidable meaning.[95]

Despite the fun, however, there was something grimly relentless about Derrida's approach.[96] His sense of suffocation made him increasingly preoccupied with the bizarre, contingent character of the process whereby whatever anyone writes is taken up by those who follow—and enters history. Because they were doomed to write, philosophers from Plato on laid themselves open to all manner of unauthorized interpretations. In "Otobiographies" (1979), Derrida pondered both Nietzsche's preoccupation with the future fate of his own writing and the actual fate of his writing—so far. Nietzsche's masks, pseudonyms, and dissimulation had not prevented the Nazis from bending him to their own purposes. Like Nietzsche, we all die before our name; what becomes of what we write always eludes our intention or control.[97] So Derrida himself became more self-conscious about his own place in the endless chain of partial interpretations as he became "Derrida," as his own work was disseminated in, for example, American literary deconstruction. Even more than Nietzsche, he did his

94. Derrida, *Writing and Difference*, 292.
95. For example, on pp. 135–137 of *Spurs*, his analysis of Nietzsche's treatment of women, Derrida reassures us that *Spurs* itself has no decidable meaning. See also Butler, *Interpretation*, 62–63, 77–79.
96. As Frederick Crews has put it, Derrida had no way out of the web of inherited ideas "he has doomed himself to deconstruct ad infinitum and thus to retain in a limbo of combined attention and nonassertion. His contentment with that annotative role marks him as an intellectual nihilist, though a learned and exuberant one." Frederick Crews, "In the Big House of Theory," *New York Review of Books*, 29 May 1986, 40–41.
97. Derrida, "Otobiographies," in *The Ear of the Other: Otobiography, Transference, Translation*, ed. Christie V. McDonald, trans. Peggy Kamuf (New York: Schocken, 1985), 1–38. See esp. pp. 9, 28–29, 31–32, 36, 38.

best to obstruct expository treatment of his own texts.[98] Thus the ever more imaginative modes of disruption that characterized his work. With *Glas* in 1974, he began using several voices and producing several texts at once.

Derrida's preoccupations recall those that led Foucault to shift his ground in order not to be fixed, trapped, suffocated. Responding to charges that he was seeking simply to sidestep or one-up his critics, Foucault suggested that a deeper preoccupation was at work.

> Do you think that I would keep so persistently to my task, if I were not preparing—with a rather shaky hand—a labyrinth into which I can venture . . . in which I can lose myself and appear at last to eyes that I will never have to meet again. I am no doubt not the only one who writes in order to have no face. Do not ask who I am and do not ask me to remain the same: leave it to our bureaucrats and our police to see that our papers are in order. At least spare us their morality when we write.[99]

Although Foucault was most obviously concerned to elude the present regime of power, he was responding to the snares of the world as historical itself, with its tendency to make something arbitrary and unforeseeable, delimited and particular, of what we do, say, are.

But it was Derrida who most consistently pursued this theme. He understood that subsequent treatment of his own thinking would inevitably delimit and impoverish it by treating it in some particular, contingent way, precisely as we are doing now. To put it in Heideggerian terms, much is held back or conceals itself as "Derrida" passes into the cold but malleable marble of the tradition. In 1966, Derrida had welcomed the Nietzschean innocence that seemed to become possible in a postmetaphysical world, but it quickly came to seem that though we are no longer responsible in the old sense, we cannot simply flow innocently either. We are left with particularizing as history, which occasions resentment; we must actively confront our history—not to build on it but to spite it.

Although his responses constitute a single consistent strategy, Derrida leaves us in tantalizing uncertainty. Is it that we find ways of perpetually undercutting ourselves to avoid stating a position that time and history will undercut? Is it that we one-up even history itself, by doing what it will do—erase, though leaving traces—before it gets the chance? Or is it that we simply give in to the inevitability of history, which will do with us as it will, and passively but poisonously set ourselves up for further deconstruction?[100]

However it is characterized, Derrida's playful response proved distinctly

---

98. Norris, *Derrida*, 64, 187, 194–195, 199–200.

99. Foucault, *The Archaeology of Knowledge*, 17.

100. In an exchange in the *New York Review of Books*, 2 February 1984, 48, John Searle notes this tendency in Derridean deconstruction—and finds something essentially phony about it. My point is that a plausible postmetaphysical preoccupation is at work in this way of relating to the ongoing particularizing, so the tendency need not be characterized so dismissively.

non-Nietzschean, despite his endorsement of the innocence of becoming in 1966. For Nietzsche claimed, at least, to have dissolved the basis for precisely the sense of historical suffocation that preoccupied Derrida. Nietzschean innocence of becoming entails innocence even in the face of an endlessly capricious history. The key to such innocence was not the allegedly "fictional" basis of all human construction but the experience of eternal recurrence, the endlessness of this same particular world. Insofar as I grasp and affirm this endlessly particularizing world as all there is, I am freed from the anxious preoccupation that what I do will be swallowed up by a history imposing its own meaning on what I have done. In affirming the whole as particular, the Nietzschean affirms not only the past and present but also the "future"—what history will make of what I do, the fact that particularizing will encompass this as well. There is nothing I can do about it—but I feel no need to do anything about it. Because it rests on affirmation of an interconnected whole, Nietzschean play is not to one-up history.

Although Derrida sometimes conflated "history" with Hegel and then found in Hegel the source of the problem, it is crucial that even weak, postmetaphysical history, with no specifically Hegelian admixture, was sufficient to occasion his preoccupations. Indeed, it is precisely the absence of any controlling telos that makes my belonging to history so appalling; not only does history make what it will of whatever I do but it does so capriciously, contingently.

From one perspective, both Foucault and Derrida seem less consistent than Nietzsche and Heidegger, less able to embrace a postmetaphysical and posthistoricist orientation. Thus the resentment and shrillness in their responses. It is axiomatic that, as extremes, their strategies do not serve history-making reconstruction, but neither do they afford affirmative self-creation or religious disengagement. From this perspective, Foucault offers a resentful ritual of perversity, Derrida, a futile play of shadows.

But it is possible to view the responses of each thinker more sympathetically. Even if we grasp the preoccupations that occasioned the earlier responses of Nietzsche and Heidegger, we may not find those responses convincing. And because neither Foucault nor Derrida was content simply to recapitulate the extreme moves of the two earlier thinkers, each was able to broaden our sense of what we may experience, and how we may respond, in a merely historical world. Our modes of relationship with that world may include ritualistic disruption and play, each of which reflects both religious alienation and concern for personal autonomy. On occasion we may seek to disengage from the actual, attuning ourselves to what was not said, to what was hidden or held back, even if we do not believe, with Heidegger, that in doing so we attend to the sending or particularizing itself. Severed from Heideggerian religiosity, this approach to our history becomes ritualistic disruption. Though it affords no disengagement, let alone deliverance, it still may constitute a privileged moment in our experience. Or we may, on occasion, find ourselves unconvinced by Nietzsche even as, backing away from Crocean faith in history, we find our own autonomy to be of ultimate interest in a postmetaphysical world. In such moods, we may find the play of futility precisely the right way of relating to the history happening around us.

Overreaction and Preclusion

Up to a point, then, the extremity in deconstruction may be taken as plausible, even insofar as it stands in tension with the reconstructive potential. There is room for both in a postmetaphysical culture; the tension is at least appropriate—and possibly fruitful. But another dimension, involving dualistic conflation and overreaction, led deconstruction to prejudicial characterizations that tended to preclude any scope for a reconstructive orientation.

Certain well-known features of the French intellectual tradition, culminating in structuralism, helped nurture this tendency toward overreaction. The Cartesian and positivist traditions remained especially strong in France well into the twentieth century, and, as a consequence, French intellectuals were much less concerned than their German and Italian counterparts with the problems surrounding historicism. In historiography the French developed the *Annales* paradigm, which was brilliantly innovative in certain ways but limited in others—especially because of its still-positivistic orientation.[101] Hegel came late to France; Alexandre Kojève's lectures of 1933–1939 were especially central.[102] But Hegel was taken very seriously at that point, so in France the shadow of Hegelianism lay over any understanding of the world as historical, any association of knowledge with history, any attempt to conceive alternatives to the positivism of the *Annales* school. In Germany and Italy, Hegel had been a more familiar feature of the landscape, so German and Italian intellectuals proved better able to conceive the world as historical in a post-Hegelian way.

The ongoing concern with science and certainty in France led to structuralism, but by the 1960s thinkers like Foucault and Derrida were beginning to find the structuralist enterprise unsustainable on its own terms. In seeking an alternative orientation, poststructuralists looked partly to Nietzsche and Heidegger, but their way of conceiving the new cultural challenge reflected French preoccupations. They viewed time and historicity as especially disruptive,

101. See Massimo Mastrogregori, *Il genio dello storico: Le considerazioni sulla storia di Marc Bloch e Lucien Febvre e la tradizione metodologica francese* (Naples: Edizioni Scientifiche Italiane, 1987), for a balanced assessment of the French historiographical tradition from an Italian perspective. Because historicist traditions were so strong in Germany and Italy, historians in those countries were slow to embrace the Annales approach.

102. Michael S. Roth, *Knowing and History: Appropriations of Hegel in Twentieth-Century France* (Ithaca: Cornell University Press, 1988), is invaluable on these dimensions of the French intellectual landscape.

undermining the possibility of knowledge; and they understood "history" in a quasi-Hegelian way, entailing a certain baggage. Conceiving the alternatives in extreme terms, they proved especially prone to assume that, though we now find ourselves without it, we need the sort of grounding that the old metaphysics claimed to provide.

Moreover, French thinkers from Lévi-Strauss to Foucault were especially prone to afford privilege to some "other" of the dominant historical process— to nature as opposed to culture, even to the uncivilized as opposed to the would-be civilizers.[103] Thus it has been hard to sort out the elements that have made the French response at once so distinctive and so influential. In some of its guises, French thinking seems an innovative response reflecting a deepening sense of the unity of the world, in all its historical specificity. In others, it seems a mere overreaction against largely discredited metaphysical and Eurocentered pretenses.

In a widely read critique of Derridean deconstruction, the American philosopher John Searle pinpointed a major source of this overreaction. Thanks especially to Wittgenstein and Heidegger, wrote Searle, the search for foundations central to the philosophical tradition has come to seem simply misguided. Yet Derrida's response to the absence of foundations ended up mirroring the Cartesianism he claimed to reject.

> Derrida correctly sees that there aren't any such foundations, but he then makes the mistake that marks him as a classical metaphysician. The real mistake of the classical metaphysician was . . . the belief that unless there are foundations something is lost or threatened or undermined or put in question.
>
> It is this belief that Derrida shares with the tradition he seeks to deconstruct. Derrida sees that the Husserlian project of a transcendental grounding for science, language, and common sense is a failure. But what he fails to see is that this doesn't threaten science, language, or common sense in the least. As Wittgenstein says, it leaves everything exactly as it is.[104]

103. See Hayden White, *Tropics of Discourse: Essays in Cultural Criticism* (Baltimore: Johns Hopkins University Press, 1978), 268–270, for an especially cogent characterization of this tendency.

104. John R. Searle, "The Word Turned Upside Down," *New York Review of Books*, 27 October 1983, 77–78. This essay, nominally a review of Jonathan Culler's *On Deconstruction*, proved a major document in the developing controversy over deconstruction. See the follow-up exchange, including a critique of Searle's review by Louis H. Mackey and a reply by Searle, in *New York Review of Books*, 2 February 1984, 47–48. While endorsing parts of Searle's critique, Richard Rorty charged that Searle was himself too caught up in conventional notions of philosophy to grasp Derrida's overall point. Derrida was not doing amateurish philosophy of language, as Searle assumed, but asking metaphilosophical questions about the value of such philosophy. See Rorty, *Essays on Heidegger*, 93n–94n. Although I agree that Searle missed much of what Derrida was up to, Searle's charge that Derrida labored under the shadow of the metaphysics he rejected seems to me on target. Derrida himself found Searle's piece to be "an article of unbridled resentment." See his afterword to *Limited Inc.*, 125.

But while the eclipse of metaphysics leaves everything the same in one sense, in another it surely does not, and thus our need to reassess our cultural proportions. The deconstructionist current has made a greater contribution to that effort than Searle's characterization suggests. Provocative though they are, Derrida's categories—dissemination, slippage, undecidability, différance, erasure, trace—deepen our understanding of what "there is" in a postmetaphysical world. It remains true, however, that deconstruction sowed confusion about postmetaphysical possibilities because, just as Searle suggested, the shadow of metaphysics made it too rigidly dualistic and extreme in characterizing the alternatives.

One critic after another noted the French tendency to overplay metaphysical authority, to fight the straw ghosts of Hegel and Husserl, to beat horses that seemed quite dead to others within the postmetaphysical space. Rorty argued that over the last two hundred years the discourse of high culture has been chattier, more fluid and playful than Derrida recognized. Except occasionally and rhetorically, nobody claims that there is universal agreement on conditions of intelligibility or rationality.[105] Others charged that American literary intellectuals fastened on Derridean deconstruction only because they assumed that old-fashioned positivism was lurking everywhere else, as if no one else had caught on that language does not simply mirror reality.[106]

Inflating the metaphysical danger, the deconstructionists tended to assume that theirs was the only alternative and thus to preclude competing ways of characterizing postmetaphysical possibilities. Indeed, they tended to go from one extreme to the other. Searle noted Derrida's eagerness to conclude "that without foundations we are left with nothing but the free play of signifiers." And Gerald Graff charged that an "understandable but misconceived reaction against positivistic certainty" had led Geoffrey Hartman and other deconstructionist critics to invoke the ghost of authoritarian rationalism "in such a way as to make irrationalism look like the only alternative. The fact that there is no '*last* judgment' in criticism is used to make judgment as such sound suspect."[107]

Most important, for our purposes, the deconstructionists' extreme characterizations sowed confusion about the place of history in a postmetaphysical

105. Rorty, *Essays on Heidegger*, 99–101.
106. See, for example, Ellis, *Against Deconstruction*, 37–38; and Searle, "The Word Turned Upside Down," 78–79. Brook Thomas notes another aspect of the deconstructionist tendency to fight straw persons when he observes that ideas of progressive, linear time were long since undermined; we did not need Paul de Man to make the point, effective though his characterizations proved. See Thomas, *The New Historicism*, 106–107.
107. Searle, "The Word Turned Upside Down," 79; Gerald Graff, *Literature against Itself: Literary Ideas in Modern Society* (Chicago: University of Chicago Press, 1979), 145. Graff was an early, persistent, and particularly astute critic; see, for example, his "Deconstruction as Dogma," *Georgia Review* 34 (1980): 404–421. See also Ellis, *Against Deconstruction*, 49, 66, 122–123. 137–140, on the tendency of deconstructionists to go from one extreme to the other.

world. It has been widely assumed, in fact, that French deconstruction definitively refuted the "humanist historicism" that apparently attaches to virtually
any notion of history.[108] But their tendency to overreaction led the French to
load all sorts of unnecessary, prejudicial baggage onto "history" and thereby
to preclude the recasting of reality, continuity, and truth necessary for a postmetaphysical understanding of the world as historical.

Although Foucault, in *The Order of Things*, offered a suggestive analysis
of the nineteenth-century inflation of history, his way of characterizing historicism and hermeneutics did not do justice to their scope for development in a
postmetaphysical way. He argued plausibly that historicism was an effort to
posit a measure of coherence in a world reduced to partial perspectives and
individual bits and pieces. Hermeneutics served that wider effort by providing
a method for understanding across time and difference. But Foucault found historicism so concerned to establish partial totalities and relative justifications
that it precluded attention to finitude as such and ultimately to what the possibility of relative coherence required. So Foucault distinguished historicism
from what he called "the analytic of finitude," which

> never ceases to use, as a weapon against historicism, the part of itself that his-
> toricism has neglected: its aim is to reveal, at the foundation of all the positivities
> and before them, the finitude that makes them possible; where historicism sought
> for the possibility and justification of concrete relations between limited totalities
> . . . the analytic of finitude tries to question this relation of the human being to the
> being which, by designating finitude, renders the positivities possible in their
> concrete mode of being.[109]

Foucault thus found something superficial in the historicist emphasis on
knitting together a world; thus the premium he placed on the analytic of finitude as one aspect of his larger deconstructive strategy of playing up what is
hidden or excluded as anything comes to be. But in radicalizing historicism
and hermeneutics, Croce and Gadamer went beyond Dilthey to incorporate precisely the deeper understanding Foucault had in mind. It proved possible to
conceive partial totalities as finite, to reconceive understanding and justification
for a finite world, and thereby to cease worrying about relativism. In a sense,
Croce and Gadamer showed how we might carry the analytic of finitude with
us as we proceed, in a fully reflexive mode, with the endless reconstruction of
the world.

As I have emphasized, there are plausible reasons for eschewing this recon-

---

108. See, for example, Michael Roth's characterizations in a review essay in *History and Theory* 27, no. 1 (1988): 70–80. On p. 73, following Gilles Deleuze, he notes that Foucault's is "a
project that rejects the assumptions of humanist historicism." See also Megill, *Prophets of Extremity*, 271–274, 295–298.

109. Foucault, *The Order of Things*, 367–373. The quoted passage is on p. 373.

structive but still postmetaphysical response, and, if stretched a bit, Foucault's premium on the analytic of finitude can point the way to one form of the posthistoricist extremity that has emerged as an alternative. But his way of framing the opposition suggests that the analytic of finitude is privileged because it grasps the deeper suppositions of historicism in a way that historicism itself cannot. In this sense, Foucault was not doing justice to the scope for an alternative to Dilthey's brand of historicism.

Although Foucault brilliantly drew out the implications of Nietzschean genealogy, his accents even in "Nietzsche, Genealogy, History" ended up quite different from Nietzsche's own. Foucault featured three uses of historical writing that assaulted what he took to be the still-metaphysical underpinnings of mainstream history: "parodic, directed against reality," "dissociative, directed against identity," "sacrificial, directed against truth."[110] In accenting each, he afforded privilege to disruption in an effort to keep the elements suspended, to prevent reconstructive reassembling.

Most basically, Foucault wanted to puncture the *identity* we derive from history as we connect ourselves to the past in a certain way: "the purpose of history, guided by genealogy, is not to discover the roots of our identity but to commit itself to its dissipation." We may do so by calling attention to the masks and disguises, or to the alternate identities that are constantly proliferating, reappearing, but that somehow get marginalized. Or we may show how what seems a stable identity dissolves into intersecting but competing systems that cannot be combined in a stable synthesis. Thus, as Foucault put it, genealogy "seeks to make visible all of those discontinuities that cross us." And rather than claim to criticize past injustices on the basis of some present truth, we disrupt the present claim to knowledge—and with it the injustice essential even to that claim. We do not exempt even ourselves but reflexively disrupt our own claims.[111]

Foucault was true to Nietzsche in pointing out that because things emerge "in between," in a "nonplace," with no purpose or intention behind them, no one is responsible for them. But when he went on to contend that in refusing "the certainty of absolutes," genealogy "disperses, . . . liberating divergence and marginal elements," Foucault not only departed from Nietzsche but fell into the dualistic characterization typical of deconstruction: such endless dispersal is the only alternative to the pretense of metaphysical certainty.[112]

This rigid dualism led Foucault to find something spurious and authoritarian in any effort to let things come together by finding continuities and similarities, by inventing concepts and, beneath them, the categories that shape the world.

---

110. Foucault, *Language, Counter-Memory, Practice*, 160–164.
111. Ibid., 162, 164.
112. Ibid., 150, 152–153.

No matter how lucid and unpretentious the enterprise might be, no matter how weak and provisional the results are taken to be, *any* such shaping entails suppressing "the anarchy of differences." So Foucault's priority was on disruption to liberate singularity and difference: "On the one side, [cognitive categories] can be understood as the a priori forms of knowledge, but, on the other, they appear as an archaic morality, the ancient decalogue that the identical imposed upon difference. Difference can only be liberated through the invention of an acategorical thought."[113]

Let us recognize, again, that there may be plausible reasons for this extreme response, affording privilege to disruption and difference. Even our cognitive software is particular, finite, and comes to be only as something else is held back. But the element of dualistic overreaction led Foucault to assume that categories or concepts are inherently suprahistorical, fixed, stable, yet even Croce's way of conceiving concepts as ragged, ad hoc, provisional, merely practical, eludes Foucault's characterizations. By means of an implicit conflation with metaphysics, Foucault precluded weak, postmetaphysical ways of conceiving categories and concepts—including those like reality, identity, continuity, and truth that are bound up with the world as historical.

In the same way, Foucault contrasted his own disruptive approach with dialectics, which "does not liberate differences" but "guarantees, on the contrary, that they can always be recaptured"—as if endless disruption was the only alternative to a teleological dialectic. And he opposed masks and theater to "reality," which he associated with Platonism and metaphysics.[114] He was suggesting not only that masks and theater were the only alternative to metaphysics but also that what is left, with the eclipse of metaphysics, has the lightness of masks and theater. And thus he afforded privilege to all that prompts us to experience ourselves and our world as a series of masks, with no weight, with nothing for keeps.

Despite periodic disclaimers, Foucault's characterizations tended to conflate "continuity" with progress and Hegelian telos and thus to preclude the weaker conception of continuity that others had already posited. Not only did that weaker conception eschew progress and telos but it had plenty of room for rupture and relative discontinuity as well. It neither assumed nor required the metaphysical justification that Foucault associated with any emphasis on reality, identity, or continuity. As we approach the present historically, we may indeed feature the discontinuities as we loosen and deconstruct our world, showing how it came to be. But we produce a *different* provisional continuity as we go on to reconstruct, partly by answering our historical questions as we do. This is

113. Ibid, 181–187; the quotation is on p. 186.
114. Ibid., 171, 192, 196, and, for the passage quoted, p. 184.

true even insofar as the new power-knowledge construction is content to remain local and specific.[115] To establish some provisional continuity simply serves the moment of "gathering," or coming back together, that balances the ongoing disruption. Such an understanding of continuity does not require positing the unity of being in the old metaphysical way, yet it was against that conventionally metaphysical view that Foucault measured his own position.[116] He had room only for the old metaphysics and his own one-sided emphasis on disruption.

This tendency toward dualistic overreaction led Derrida, too, to impose prejudicial baggage on "history," especially through conflation with Hegelianism. He noted, for example, that "history and knowledge . . . have always been determined . . . as detours *for the purpose of* the reappropriation of presence."[117] Even more radically than Foucault, Derrida sought to disrupt the historical approach in general by deconstructing the linearity it required. Not only was linearity arbitrary and exclusionary but it was inherently "Hegelian" in its implication of privileged origins and ends.

Also like Foucault, Derrida understood his categories to be antithetical to hermeneutics, which he viewed as an attempt to reestablish coherence by deciding among possible interpretations and settling on some definitive meaning. This attempt inevitably fails; we cannot decide how to distinguish proper from improper, or possible from impossible, readings. So hermeneutics can only cover over the endless dissemination to which the world has been reduced. In pretending to determine meaning where no determinate meaning exists, hermeneutics was still operating within the framework of metaphysics.[118] Derrida was assuming that any alternative to endless disruptive decentering involves a metaphysical claim to definitive meaning.

In his playful encounter with the Western tradition in *The Post Card*, Derrida posited two postal systems. One is policed, legalistic, and efficient, while the other, as Norris has put it, "opens up a fabulous realm of messages and meanings that circulate beyond any assurance of authorized control."[119] So again there are two alternatives, characterized in terms of one extreme or the other. And of course Derrida's accent was on freeing up all that the dominant tradition had repressed or marginalized. Again and again, he, like Foucault,

---

115. Compare Mark Philp, "Michel Foucault," 76–78. Although his account is excellent overall, Philp's way of accenting the "local" blurs the constructive potential of Foucault's thinking.

116. See, for example, Foucault, *Language, Counter-Memory, Practice*, 186–187.

117. Derrida, *Of Grammatology*, 10. (Emphasis in original.) See also pp. 85–87.

118. Hoy, "Jacques Derrida," 54, 56–57, 63–64, is especially good on Derrida's reading of hermeneutics. On pp. 63–64, Hoy notes the overreaction that results from Derrida's assumption that hermeneutics insists on a final reading.

119. Norris, *Derrida*, 116, 188, 192–193; Jacques Derrida, *The Post Card: From Socrates to Freud and Beyond*, trans. Alan Bass (Chicago: University of Chicago Press, 1987).

afforded an a priori privilege to the other, to difference, partly because he allowed no other alternative to the old authoritarian metaphysics.[120]

Their preoccupation with showing that "the disruptive movement of time" undermines system, completeness, and thus any hope of definitive knowledge kept Foucault and Derrida from considering what happens as that disruptive movement proceeds.[121] That it continually disrupts is not in doubt, but because there is still a web of influence, there is not blank flux but thick and messy continuity. In fact, Foucault and Derrida grasped precisely this particularizing continuity, but their responses tended prejudicially to preclude any affirmative, constructive way of relating to the world that endlessly results from dissemination, slippage, and the play of power.

Although he implied that his own reaction against metaphysics precluded history, Derrida could not help positing a measure of continuity and coherence sufficient for a postmetaphysical form of history to survive even his own extreme reduction. "Defer," for example, is a category that entails not only temporality but also continuity. In insisting that "no element can function as a sign without referring to another element which itself is not simply present," Derrida was not positing merely a synchronic structure. He tells us that "this interweaving, this textile, is the *text* produced only in the transformation of another text," and the notion of "transformation" entails the essential measure of temporality and continuity.[122] To say that nothing simply "is," without presuppositions and effects, without itself being a presupposition and effect of other things, is already to have posited the prior and the subsequent and the connectedness necessary for continuity and history.[123] That history is even linear; the "line" is ragged and thick but still finite and particular.

As a major intellectual presence, moreover, Derrida at once responded to the traces of earlier ideas and left traces of his own for us to respond to, as we are doing now, incompletely, provisionally, undecidably—but still particularly, in this way and not that. The particularizing continues as a particular understanding of Derrida and his cultural place emerges—incompletely, provisionally, undecidably. Despite all Derrida's efforts to preempt anything we can say about him, he becomes part of a continuous history as some provisional understanding of him emerges; the tradition grows to encompass him. As noted

120. The same quick conflations, limiting us to one extreme or the other, were evident in the uses that others made of Derrida. John Caputo, for example, featured the value of Derridean disruption, but he had room for only one alternative, which entailed totalizing metaphysics, police, the shedding of blood. If these are the only alternatives, then any accent on positive construction will be conflated with metaphysics. Thus, for example, Caputo assumes that construction entails giving a definition of justice. See Caputo, *Radical Hermeneutics*, 195–196.

121. The phrase is from Mark C. Taylor's introduction to *Deconstruction in Context: Literature and Philosophy*, ed. Mark C. Taylor (Chicago: University of Chicago Press, 1986), 16.

122. Derrida, *Positions*, 26. As noted above, Marian Hobson has put it nicely in discussing Derrida's notion of the trace: "we are left not with a scatter of points but with a trajectory." See Hobson, "History Traces," 113.

123. See also Ryan, *Marxism and Deconstruction*, 50, on this implication in Derrida.

above, his premium on disruption responded to his preoccupation with precisely that. Conversely, we deal with him now in full knowledge that we cannot fix him definitively, getting him "right." But that is not what we are trying to do, or what the ongoing construction-resulting of some particular world requires.

In stressing undecidability, Derrida showed that as we go about interpreting the world, we cannot specify in advance what is to count and what is possible. But "deciding" does occur—as a continuing process, event, or happening. Although we have no basis for choosing a definitive interpretation, we go on offering particular, partial interpretations, some of which prove influential, helping to shape the culture's understanding of whatever "text" is in question. Through the competitive interaction of interpretations, some consensus develops, some authority is established, some meaning is conferred, and our particular history endlessly results.[124] The event of interpretive understanding continues, taking its direction from the interpretations that in fact are offered and prove influential.

Even on Derrida's own terms, then, it is undeniable that, unstable and provisional though it is, a particular world endlessly results even as the dissemination and slipping continue. The question is what we make of that world, how we experience it and relate to it. In this sense, the issue that Derrida raises is "ethical," just as Norris has emphasized.[125] But it is necessary to do justice to the alternatives that open from Derrida's conception before any genuinely ethical decision is possible. Derrida's insight into the mechanisms of the world does not require his own cultural strategy in response.

How we relate to the endlessly slipping world and to this provisional moment depends on our assessment of the mechanisms through which things come to be. Does the world seem so light and capricious that we are struck mostly by the futility of what we do? Or does a purely historical world seem so heavy that we can hope for some measure of autonomy only through a single-minded emphasis on resistance and disruption? And what about the competitive interaction through which some prove powerful, through which the winners win? We can invariably find power, authority, and exclusion. Are they to be understood as instances of coercion and domination? There is no right answer to these questions. As we have taken pains to emphasize, extreme responses are possible. But deconstruction, in its prejudicial mode, has precluded even consideration of the moderate answers.

In overreacting, deconstruction sometimes overemphasized the heaviness

---

124. Without accenting the happening of history, John Ellis contributes effectively to this side of the reconstructive alternative; see *Against Deconstruction*, 128–129.

125. Norris, *Derrida*, 225. Norris argues that Derrida points us beyond the epistemological concerns that have long dominated our intellectual life. Once we realize that we cannot synthesize structuralism and phenomenology into a new epistemology, we confront a choice of direction that is essentially ethical.

of the world, sometimes the lightness. On the one hand, it assumed that a claim to metaphysical authority attached to the resulting of anything at all. Indeed, the deconstructionists tended to conceive power and authority in such a way that even persuasion is domination.[126] To be convinced is to be determined or hood-winked, because we take whatever has convinced us to be justified in a final and exhaustive way. In postmetaphysical terms, however, the particular consensus and authority that has won so far is provisional and tension-ridden and makes no claim to strong authority.

On the other hand, deconstruction sometimes portrayed the actual world as light and inadequate, precisely because it lacks the grounding and stability that we have come to associate with "reality." Derrida tells us that rather than the stuff that metaphysicians used to talk about, that simply was what it was, "there are only, everywhere, differences and traces of traces," because meaning is never settled and dissemination continues. There is no outside to the text, nothing outside the text.[127] Fine, except that Derrida's way of saying "only traces" and "nothing outside" betrays the shadow of metaphysics, the standard of something else. Thus there seemed something inadequate about a world with a texture of this sort; the lack of a procedure for deciding seems somehow debilitating. But why the implication of inadequacy? Who said something was missing?

We have seen that even a world reduced to the play of traces has some measure of solidity and coherence. And our experience of that world may be sufficiently affirmative that we seek to mesh with its endless incompleteness and slippage in a history-making mode. Thus we may accent the scope for ongoing reconstruction, for endlessly renewing the common world, as opposed to either the stifling authority or the futile lightness of that world.

Once we have pinpointed both the plausible extremity and the prejudicial overreaction, we can see how aspects of deconstruction can mesh with historicism and hermeneutics to serve such reconstructive purposes. Deconstruction and hermeneutics have sometimes been viewed as cultural allies, but primarily by those accenting the antimetaphysical or postmodern elements they share. It has been harder to understand how they might complement each other once the common antimetaphysical elements are taken for granted, and the task is to discern the contours of a postmetaphysical culture. Indeed, with Gadamer trumpeting the authority of tradition, and Foucault and Derrida endless disruption, hermeneutics and deconstruction have seemed antithetical.[128]

---

126. See, for example, Michael Roth's characterization in his review essay in *History and Theory* 27, no. 1 (1988): 73.

127. Derrida, *Positions*, 26; Derrida, *Of Grammatology*, 158.

128. Derrida and Gadamer interacted directly at the Goethe Institute in Paris in 1981. Although the outcome was disappointing, their encounter elicited some illuminating comment. See *Dialogue and Deconstruction: The Gadamer-Derrida Encounter*, ed. Diane P. Michelfelder and Richard E. Palmer (Albany: State University of New York Press, 1989).

   Although Gadamerian hermeneutics emphasized the moment of reconstruction and gathering, it did not pretend to the decidability, to the complete and determinate reading, that Derrida associated with hermeneutics in general. In the hermeneutic and historicist mode of experience, we know that there are only traces bearing traces, undecidable texts piled on earlier undecidable texts; we know that meaning is unstable, that we go on disseminating new meanings. But these titillating ways of characterizing the postmetaphysical situation are neither as damaging nor as liberating as they seem.

9

Pragmatism, Historicism, Aestheticism

Rorty's Neopragmatism

As the assault on metaphysics and modernity gathered force in the 1970s and 1980s, a new strand emerged with Richard Rorty's departure from Anglo-American analytical philosophy. Although the American pragmatist tradition was fundamental to him, Rorty refurbished that tradition and developed a particular understanding of the postmetaphysical possibilities, partly in confrontation with Nietzsche, Heidegger, Foucault, and Derrida. And though he owed no debt to Croce, his intellectual framework had some striking similarities with Croce's, and for a while, at least, he found a significant kinship with Gadamerian hermeneutics. Rorty was navigating precisely the space at issue for us, and his distinctive way of sorting out its possibilities made him the most influential American contributor to the wider humanistic discussion by the late 1980s.

Rorty's contribution proved so valuable because he was able to bridge the gap between Anglo-American and Continental approaches; he moved comfortably, for example, from Quine and Davidson to Heidegger and Derrida. Partly because of his unique range, Rorty became as trenchant a critic of the metaphysical and modern as we have had, deepening the characterization of the overall cultural displacement. And in Rorty's thinking, one measure of that displacement was precisely a reduction to history. He characterized as "historicism" the harvest of Dewey, Heidegger, and Wittgenstein. Moreover, taking for granted the contingency and historicity of things, he himself proposed an orientation to the postmetaphysical world that was explicitly historicist.[1]

1. Richard Rorty, *Philosophy and the Mirror of Nature* (Princeton: Princeton University Press, 1979), 9–10.

That orientation was explicitly moderate as well, so it paralleled Croce's and Gadamer's up to a point. For Rorty, too, removing the metaphysical props does not warrant the giddy or debilitating cultural consequences that some were drawing.[2] He, too, sought to show that we need not become preoccupied with skepticism and relativism as we recognize that, lacking any suprahistorical vantage point, we are doomed to become outdated. But coming later than Croce and Gadamer and from a different tradition, he was able to add considerably to what they had offered.

Rorty sought especially to reconnect with the American pragmatism of John Dewey, who had distanced himself from Croce in a celebrated dispute over aesthetics during the late 1940s and early 1950s. Croce recognized a general kinship with Dewey, however, and the cultural reorientation he proposed included many of the themes that Rorty found valuable in Dewey's legacy. Most basically, Croce, too, had deflated philosophy in favor of engagement with the ordinary world.[3] Indeed, Rorty's line of argument was arguably more congruent with Croce's way of doing so than with Dewey's.

Starting from a radical empiricism, pragmatism in Dewey's hands came to warrant a still-deeper cultural privilege for science. The question was how science comes up with what it does and how we can adapt scientific procedures to other forms of activity. As Rorty himself put it, Dewey held that things would be better "if only we could adopt the attitude and the habits of the natural scientist."[4] Indeed, a scientific approach to value choice and conflict resolution could lead us to the millennium. At the same time, the American pragmatists paid little attention to the problems surrounding history and historical knowledge.[5] During

2. Ibid., 281–288, 294–295, 309–310, 316–317.

3. For a good summary of the dispute between Dewey and Croce over aesthetics, see George H. Douglas, "A Reconsideration of the Dewey-Croce Exchange," *Journal of Aesthetics and Art Criticism* 28, no. 4 (Summer 1970): 497-504. While stressing his kinship with Dewey, Rorty recognized an important ambivalence in Dewey's career: Dewey wanted to be a conventional system builder even as he offered a new therapeutic conception of philosophy. See especially Richard Rorty, *Consequences of Pragmatism (Essays: 1972–1980)* (Minneapolis: University of Minnesota Press, 1982), 35, 73, 82–83, 85. We have seen that Croce, too, seemed to place a premium on philosophical system early in his career, but he made it ever clearer that what had initially seemed systematic categories were merely ad hoc clarifications. Though Rorty admitted the complexity of Dewey's legacy, some students of Dewey have plausibly accused Rorty of overemphasizing those aspects of Dewey's thought that anticipate his own. See especially Robert B. Westbrook, *John Dewey and American Democracy* (Ithaca: Cornell University Press, 1991), 539–542.

4. Richard Rorty, *Essays on Heidegger and Others* (Cambridge: Cambridge University Press, 1991), 129. See also p. 137.

5. Cushing Strout, *The Pragmatic Revolt in American History: Carl Becker and Charles Beard* (New Haven: Yale University Press, 1958), 14. See also Brook Thomas, *The New Historicism and Other Old-Fashioned Topics* (Princeton: Princeton University Press, 1991), 97. In his relatively late *Logic: The Theory of Inquiry* (New York: Henry Holt, 1938), 220–244, esp. pp. 234–239, Dewey considered aspects of historical knowledge, but his argument echoed Croce's of a quarter-century before—as Croce noted with some exasperation. And even as he addressed questions about historical knowing, Dewey did not develop an overarching historicist framework like Croce's—or like Rorty's of a half-century later.

the 1920s and 1930s, as Deweyan pragmatists were seeking to take over social science departments in the United States, Croce was attacking social science and proposing, from his historicist perspective, cultural priorities that were closer than many of Dewey's to those Rorty would later emphasize.

Like Croce and Gadamer, Rorty took it for granted that we can no longer take our cultural cue from the natural sciences—that we must look to the other, "humanistic" culture instead. Moreover, Rorty seemed to echo Croce and Vico in focusing on the winding of history around creative language. And his way of conceiving language was central to the moderation of his position. Still, Rorty's pragmatism led him to focus not on truth but on the consequences, or "cash value," of saying this as opposed to that; we use language in different ways simply to get what we want under different circumstances. As we have seen, both Croce and Gadamer explicitly opposed any such pragmatist dissolution of truth. So despite the areas of convergence, a crucial difference between Rorty's neopragmatism and historicist hermeneutics is apparent from the outset.

During the 1980s, Rorty's effort to establish a postmetaphysical middle ground attracted many who, while valuing the deconstructionist assault on metaphysics, found the cultural prescriptions of deconstruction excessive or extravagant. Christopher Butler, for example, embraced Rorty's pragmatist categories as he sought to show how to sidestep the apparent dualism of reality and deforming language that he felt had led Derrida to excess. For Butler, the distinction between literal and figurative uses of language is a pragmatic one; theoretical adjudication is neither possible nor necessary. Rorty similarly criticized Derrida for failing to assume a relaxed, pragmatic, naturalistic view of language.[6]

We noted that Derrida seemed to take the philosophical tradition too seriously and thus his overreaction as it apparently dissolved. From Rorty's down-to-earth, American perspective, that tradition had not been all that important in the first place. Intellectuals have had their particular hang-ups, and some even managed to get worked up about the problems of metaphysics. But those problems were of no general import. In seeking a postmetaphysical alternative to Heidegger, Rorty even dared confess that he himself "forgets about Being and thinks that beings are all there are."[7] But he denied that in doing so he had fallen into Heidegger's darkening and night.

Still, for all its moderate valences, Rorty's neopragmatism diverged from the reconstructive neohistoricism it sometimes seemed to entail. Although not denying history as one kind of writing, Rorty gravitated toward the wider aes-

6. Christopher Butler, *Interpretation, Deconstruction and Ideology: An Introduction to Some Current Issues in Literary Theory* (Oxford: Oxford University Press, 1984), 23–25; Rorty, *Essays on Heidegger*, 3.

7. Richard Rorty, *Contingency, Irony, and Solidarity* (Cambridge: Cambridge University Press, 1989), 113n.

theticism, which seemed to have no room for history as an autonomous cultural strand.[8] His departure from historicism proves symptomatic and illuminating.

From Foundations to History

Rorty's *Philosophy and the Mirror of Nature*, published in 1979, was fundamental to the overall assault on foundational philosophy. Although there his immediate target was epistemology, his subsequent writings made it clear that he was criticizing metaphysics and any notion of stable essences.[9] And Rorty showed that an array of innovative recent philosophers had all been pulling in the same antimetaphysical direction. Thus, for example, Wittgenstein, Quine, Dewey, Davidson, and Derrida had all come to the antiessentialist, radically holistic conclusion that things have no intrinsic properties "in themselves," only relational properties. Saussure's notion that language is a play of differences was for Rorty the same as Wittgenstein's notion "that the meaning of a word is its use in the language." Thus we grasp the futility of our long-standing quest for the conditions of possibility of "language," or for some big metavocabulary specifying the least common denominator of all the possible uses of language.[10]

More generally, we give up the "ancient hope" that Rorty found lurking in the whole philosophical tradition: "the hope for a language which can receive no gloss, requires no interpretation, cannot be distanced, cannot be sneered at by later generations. It is the hope for a vocabulary which is intrinsically and self-evidently final, not merely the most comprehensive and fruitful vocabulary we have come up with so far. Such a vocabulary would have to be adequate to 'place' all of history and all of contemporary culture."[11] To give up that hope for completeness and closure is to recognize that the world is ever provisional and that we are caught up in endless history.

At first, the end of foundational philosophy might seem to portend some

8. In ibid., 119n, Rorty considers the notion of aestheticism that Allan Megill developed in his *Prophets of Extremity* to account for the common thread in the thinking of Nietzsche, Heidegger, Foucault, and Derrida. Here, and throughout this book, Rorty seeks to distinguish the private quest for aestheticist edification from the neoliberal politics he advocates, but I will argue that even in Rorty's universe public and private are not so easily separated.

9. See, for example, Rorty, *Contingency*, 74–75, 96. Though less explicit, Rorty's antimetaphysical posture had been clear in *Philosophy and the Mirror of Nature*; see, for example, 269, 272–273. See also Richard Rorty, "Habermas and Lyotard on Post-Modernity," in *Habermas and Modernity*, ed. Richard J. Bernstein (Cambridge: MIT Press, 1985), 170, 173.

10. Rorty, *Essays on Heidegger*, 127, 130. This is not to suggest that Rorty was equally comfortable with all the more innovative Anglo-American philosophers of his time. In *Philosophy and the Mirror of Nature*, 259–262, he found greater kinship with Davidson and Nelson Goodman than with Quine, Hilary Putnam, Wilfrid Sellars, and Saul Kripke. The former were more "radical" and potentially historicist.

11. Rorty, *Essays on Heidegger*, 89.

sort of crisis or abyss. But Rorty reacted against the extreme, apocalyptic tendencies of Continental thinkers from Nietzsche and Heidegger to Derrida, all of whom assumed that something deeply significant was ending. The end of essentialism and logocentrism, even the death of God, was not a world-historical pivot, requiring some radically new self-understanding.[12]

For Rorty, it was not philosophy but the history of concrete social engineering that made North Atlantic civilization what it is—with all its glories and dangers. The canonical sequence of philosophers from Descartes to Nietzsche was a mere distraction. Our philosophical tradition remains back there, of course, but it need not traumatize us; we can simply circumvent it, recognizing it for what it was—and is.[13]

Conversely, even when such foundations dissolve, we have what we need, so no apocalyptic response is necessary. Rather than assume that the insights of Derrida, for example, demand an altogether different cultural orientation, we can simply proceed without taking the inevitable binary oppositions very seriously—as most of the culture has been doing for a long time. We are increasingly conscious, said Rorty, of resting on nothing more solid than a fountain of puns and metaphors. Because we are constantly reading several texts at once, we do not need, for example, the new kind of writing that Derrida offered in *Glas*. Although it required real brilliance for Derrida actually to do it on paper, *Glas* was not the novel catachresis that Derrida intended but a realistic rendering of what goes on in our heads. As we go about our business, we can find room for Derrida, too, of course, but we should take him simply as the great comic writer he is.[14]

Rorty recognized, however, that Nietzsche, Heidegger, and Derrida had been instrumental in the assault on metaphysics. And despite their apocalyptic tendencies, they had managed some of the generally pragmatist insights that Rorty valued. Although giving it a very different political spin, Nietzsche had done most to convince European intellectuals of the doctrines purveyed to Americans first by James and Dewey, then by "the later, linguistified pragmatists" Quine, Hilary Putnam, and Davidson, who, Rorty maintained, could as easily be grafted onto Nietzsche as onto Dewey. Although their accents sometimes differed, "pragmatists" from Nietzsche and Heidegger to Derrida, Putnam, and Nelson Goodman have taught us to focus on human uses and to accept the relativity of our descriptions, rather than worry about correct representation and suprahistorical essences.[15]

Although Rorty sometimes portrayed the new, more pluralistic culture he envisioned as "postphilosophical," it was clear that it had room for philosophy as one kind of discourse or conversation. In *Philosophy and the Mirror of*

12. Ibid., 132; his targets here are Heidegger, Derrida, and de Man.
13. Rorty, "Habermas and Lyotard," 172–173.
14. Rorty, *Essays on Heidegger*, 100–105.
15. Ibid., 2–6, 126.

Nature, he suggested that Dewey, Heidegger, and Wittgenstein pointed the way for philosophy to become appropriately therapeutic, as opposed to foundational or systematic.[16] At the same time, however, Rorty implied that philosophy had always performed something like this therapeutic function, even as it claimed to offer something more grandiose. Much like Croce, he denied that the important philosophers have all been doing the same thing, as if there was a set of enduring philosophical problems to be addressed. Rather than give new answers to the same enduring enigmas, the notable philosophers have endlessly formulated new questions.[17] Even what have seemed the "deep" philosophical questions are historically specific and provisional.

As therapy, philosophy's aim is simply to continue the conversation. Croce argued in a similar way that philosophy's role was to provide ad hoc clarification—to enable the growth of the world to continue. For both Rorty and Croce, the point of repairing to the philosophical level is not to claim the last word and stop the discussion, or even to stop and rest. The point, rather, is to clear up a cluster of historically specific confusions to enable us to move back down, to get back to work, so that the discussion—and the growth—may continue. Rorty followed Wittgenstein in arguing that philosophical clarification can work— can be "true" or adequate for the particular historical moment or language game.[18] And he valued Gadamerian hermeneutics because it was not simply another attempt to fill the old epistemological space, to specify a method for attaining truth; rather, it was an attempt to show what happens and how we proceed once the epistemological effort at commensuration, or finding decision procedures, is abandoned.[19]

Even as he offered his reassuring, easygoing pragmatism, Rorty translated the eclipse of metaphysics into precisely the reduction to history at issue for us. The dissolution of metaphysical foundations leaves us with contingency, with historicity, with things in their individuality.[20] Much like Croce and Gadamer, Rorty accented the novelty that endlessly results from the creative ways that human beings use language. Thus, for example, "our repertoire of sentences grows as history goes along, and . . . this growth is largely a matter of the literalization of novel metaphors." We are forever responding to new and perplexing cases "by reweaving our web of linguistic usage." More generally, "the realm of possibility expands whenever somebody thinks up a new

16. Rorty, *Philosophy and the Mirror of Nature*, 5, 393–394.

17. Ibid., 63, 263–264; Rorty, *Essays on Heidegger*, 123n; Rorty, *Consequences*, xxxi.

18. Rorty, *Philosophy and the Mirror of Nature*, 393–394; Rorty, *Consequences*, 104.

19. Rorty, *Philosophy and the Mirror of Nature*, chap. 7, "From Epistemology to Hermeneutics," esp. pp. 315–322. See also pp. 357–358. For a penetrating critique of Rorty's use of Gadamer, see Georgia Warnke, "Hermeneutics and the Social Sciences: A Gadamerian Critique of Rorty," *Inquiry* 28, no. 3 (September 1985): 339–357. See also Georgia Warnke, *Gadamer: Hermeneutics, Tradition and Reason* (Stanford: Stanford University Press, 1987), chap. 5.

20. See, for example, Rorty, *Consequences*, 158; Rorty, *Contingency*, 74; and Rorty, *Essays on Heidegger*, 108.

vocabulary, and thereby discloses (or invents—the difference is beside any relevant point) a new set of possible worlds."[21]

In some of his formulations, Rorty was concerned to show especially the
historicity of the philosophical tradition. At any one time, philosophy centers
on one topic rather than another, not because of some dialectical necessity, but
because of the mundane accidents of who happened to encounter what idea
when, or because of the contingent intervention of a brilliant new question or
idea.[22] But contingent interaction with innovations elsewhere in the culture—
the French Revolution, for example, or the new science, or the advent of the
modern novel—also shaped philosophy, so in the final analysis it is not just
philosophy that is merely historical but the whole of our world, encompassing
everything from selfhood to language.[23]

On every level, "what we are today" is nothing but the contingent resultant
of earlier contingent interaction, when the very measure of what we now "are"
was not yet "there." That measure is "always already" in the process of being
hammered out—as, of course, it is at this moment as well. In one striking
instance of this argument, Rorty invoked both Foucault and Kuhn as he considered the significance of Galileo's triumph over Robert Bellarmine for what
subsequently counted as rationality. Even the sort of evidence that would count
for this or that was the contingent outcome of the competition of interpretations at that point in the past.

> The "grid" which emerged in the latter seventeenth and eighteenth centuries was
> not there to be appealed to in the early seventeenth century, at the time that
> Galileo was on trial. No conceivable epistemology, no study of the nature of
> human knowledge, could have "discovered" it before it was hammered out. The
> notion of what it was to be "scientific" was in the process of being formed. . . .
> We are the heirs of three hundred years of rhetoric about the importance of dis-
> tinguishing sharply between science and religion, science and politics, science
> and art, science and philosophy, and so on. This rhetoric . . . has made us what we
> are today.[24]

Along the same lines, Rorty insisted that the quest for a theory of meaning
change, in response, especially, to Paul Feyerabend's radically open-ended conception of scientific innovation, was doomed. Indeed, the division of labor
between the historian and the philosopher no longer made sense, because what
comes to seem the rationality of change always depends on new discoveries.
Thus, for Rorty, the philosopher has nothing to add to what the historian shows.[25]

21. Rorty, *Essays on Heidegger*, 3, 109, 127; see also p. 103.
22. Rorty, *Philosophy and the Mirror of Nature*, 264; see also pp. 389–392, as well as Rorty,
Consequences, 62; and Rorty, *Essays on Heidegger*, 88n–89n, 98.
23. See especially Rorty, *Contingency*, chap. 1; see also pp. 50–51.
24. Rorty, *Philosophy and the Mirror of Nature*, 327–331. The quotation is from pp. 330–331.
25. Ibid., 272.

So Rorty's conception of what there is, what is happening, as the roles of both philosophy and science contract, seemed first to suggest a deeper premium on historical inquiry. Indeed, for Rorty, even more than for Croce or Gadamer, philosophy plays its therapeutic role by becoming a radical kind of historical inquiry. He insisted explicitly that we can only refer to history for self-understanding, and he himself resorted frequently to historical interpretation—some of the most effective we have had.

Rorty's immediate target was the philosophical tradition. To get rid of the vexing but unnecessary mind-body problem, for example, we must relive its history.[26] But of course it is ultimately the whole of our history, not simply an isolable history of philosophy, that opens for such questioning. Rorty noted that we find ourselves asking why we have philosophy in our culture in the first place—and this is a broader historical question.[27]

Our cultural situation invites big, encompassing histories that, Rorty suggested, stem from contemporary concerns and can significantly affect contemporary practice. Considering, for example, the enduring desire for some suprahistorical grasp of the conditions of free discussion, he observed that he would like "to replace both religious and philosophical accounts of a suprahistorical ground or an end-of-history convergence with a historical narrative about the rise of liberal institutions and customs." That history would have immense practical import—as the only way to get our bearings in a postmetaphysical world: "Such a narrative would clarify the conditions in which the idea of truth as correspondence to reality might gradually be replaced by the idea of truth as what comes to be believed in the course of free and open encounters."[28]

Rorty's sense of what historical inquiry might accomplish enabled him to bring out the reconstructive potential in Foucault's approach, though he also offered some illuminating criticism of Foucault's tensions and ambiguities. Envisioning a fully postmetaphysical culture, in which we no longer believe we need "a theory of communicative competence as backup," Rorty suggested that we would simply turn our attention "to some concrete examples of what was presently distorting our communication." Approaching them historically opens the way to the sort of salutary

> "shock" we get when, reading Foucault, we realize that the jargon we liberal intellectuals developed has played into the hands of the bureaucrats. Detailed historical narratives of the sort Foucault offers us would take the place of philosophical metanarratives. Such narratives would not unmask something created by power called "ideology" in the name of something not created by power called

26. Ibid., 33–34, 123–126, 136. See also pp. 10, 389–392; as well as Rorty, *Consequences*, 186.
27. Rorty, *Philosophy and the Mirror of Nature*, 229. See also Rorty, *Consequences*, 60–71.
28. Rorty, *Contingency*, 68.

"validity" or "emancipation." They would just explain who was currently getting and using power for what purposes, and then (unlike Foucault) suggest how
some other people might get it and use it for other purposes.[29]

So whereas Foucault left uncertainty about the practical import of historical
questioning, Rorty explicitly connected history as thought with history-making
action. Indeed, his way of conceiving the mechanisms whereby the world
grows as we respond and question, act and interact, is almost precisely Croce's
of over fifty years before. In interacting, we all hope our modicum of novelty,
our creative response in language, will be carried into the future, becoming part
of the stock of what are taken to be literal truths.[30] But for Rorty, again as for
Croce, pluralism and humility follow from historicism; we understand ourselves as collaborators in the process through which the world is endlessly
remade.

These accents led Rorty, like Croce, to insist that the overall intellectual
reorientation was neoliberal in its political implications. Rorty opposed his historicist neoliberalism to the effort of those like Habermas "to ground moral
obligation, and thus social institutions, on something universally human."[31]
Exactly like Croce during the 1920s, Rorty held that we cannot specify in
advance what counts as undistorted, or ideological, or true, or good; all we can
do is set up free, pluralistic, democratic institutions and trust in the ever-
provisional outcome of the resulting interaction.[32] In interacting, we seek to
persuade, but we also seek an ever-renewed yet always provisional consensus
within a tolerant, broadly liberal framework.

Whatever Rorty's own characterizations, critics like Jonathan Culler and
Christopher Norris found his thinking politically conservative in implication,
especially when compared with the radicalism of deconstruction. Rorty claimed
in response to be striking a balance.[33] He found a place for Foucault's radical
historical questioning, yet he embedded Foucault's approach within a quasi-
Gadamerian framework. Thus his concern for "reinforcing our sense of identification with our community," though always in a postmetaphysical mode,

29. Rorty, "Habermas and Lyotard," 173.
30. Rorty, *Contingency*, 42; see also p. 61. For a few of Croce's many statements along these
lines, see *Cultura e vita morale: Intermezzi polemici* (Bari: Laterza, 1955), 206–209 (1916),
210–211 (1917); and *Filosofia e storiografia: Saggi* (Bari: Laterza, 1969), 64–65 (1945).
31. Rorty, *Essays on Heidegger*, 197. Although Rorty here refers to Habermas as "my fellow
liberal," the crucial difference is explicit; Rorty was determined to do without the suprahistorical
element that Habermas still seemed to find necessary.
32. Ibid., 132–133; Rorty, *Contingency*, 84, 176–177. Up to a point, Rorty's pluralism was
congruent with Foucault's emphasis on local knowledge and the wider postmodern reaction against
"metanarrative," or the pretense of global solution.
33. In *Essays on Heidegger*, 119–120, 120n, 132–136, Rorty opposed his tolerant, democratic
pluralism to the American cultural Left, with its tendency, derived partly from Foucault and de
Man, to view contemporary democratic states as "disciplinary" and reformist politics as complicit
with the discourses of power.

without "a theory of communicative competence as backup."[34] Conversely, this Gadamerian dimension was not prejudicially conservative because it was balanced with Foucault's invitation to ongoing critical questioning. The community Rorty envisioned was liberal as opposed to conservative precisely in inviting this endless self-examination through deconstructive historical inquiry.

In general, then, Rorty's cultural prescriptions seemed to point to the synthesis of deconstructive questioning and Gadamerian gathering, or community, that seems necessary for postmetaphysical moderation. But rather than focus on the scope for a new culture of history, he reached out to the literary culture and prescribed a variety of aestheticism. Even as he found kinship with Gadamer, Rorty's accents diverged from Gadamer's own, for Rorty was concerned with edification while Gadamerian hermeneutics, though departing from epistemology, was still concerned with the happening of truth. In the same way, Rorty posited a relationship between individual experience and the world as historical that compromised the accents on history-making that were prominent in much of his writing. From within his aestheticized neopragmatist framework, history seemed unlikely to play the cultural role Rorty himself sometimes seemed to suggest for it.

From Philosophy to Textualism

Rorty's assessment of contemporary cultural possibilities rested on his historical account of the process whereby the claims of both philosophy and science began to diminish. In "Nineteenth-Century Idealism and Twentieth-Century Textualism" (1980), he offered an arresting historical sketch of the cultural falling out that resulted from the breakdown of modern philosophy.[35] Though brilliant in many respects, the essay moves quickly over the crucial changes, and it is illuminating to pinpoint its accents and omissions.

Much, plausibly, turns on Hegel's departure from the Kantian notion that the task of philosophy was to provide a stable cultural framework by accounting for the success of science. By subordinating any such framework to the overall historical process, Hegel not only occasioned a break into historicism but opened the way to a recasting of the intellectual hierarchy. With the scientific study of nature forced down a notch or two, a new kind of literary culture, from Samuel Taylor Coleridge and Ralph Waldo Emerson on up to those like the American literary intellectual Harold Bloom in our own time, began to assume the role of cultural arbiter that philosophy had previously played.[36]

34. Rorty, "Habermas and Lyotard," 173.
35. Reprinted in Rorty, *Consequences*, 139–159. See esp. pp. 146–153 for the points at issue for us.
36. Ibid., 149. More specifically, this meant, with romanticism, the hope "that what the philosophers had been seeking, the inmost secrets of the spirit, were to be discovered by the new literary genres which were emerging" (p. 150).

Thus, initially, the claims of romanticism, but with Nietzsche and William James late in the nineteenth century, romanticism gave way to pragmatism; we understand the new vocabularies we devise not as bringing secrets to light but simply as tools for getting what we want. At about the same time, the new modernist literature depicted life without hope of metaphysical comfort. Then a more general culture of textualism emerged in the twentieth century, attempting to think through the pragmatist break, the "thorough-going abandonment of the notion of *discovering the truth* which is common to theology and science."[37]

Rorty contended that one variant of that textualism did not fully make the break. Even in our own time there are "weak textualists" who believe that with everything reduced to linguistic structures or some such, we can at last get it right, by means of the correct method, whether structuralist or poststructuralist. Rorty identified instead with the "strong textualist," who embraces the twin legacies of pragmatism and literary modernism and who seeks autonomy and novelty, rather than truthfulness to experience or the discovery of preexisting significance.[38] With his premium on strong textualism, Rorty was following Bloom, whose concern with "the anxiety of influence" proved central to Rorty's way of conceiving the cultural challenge and whose corresponding emphasis on "strong misreadings" influenced Rorty's sense of current priorities.[39]

Rorty's way of dividing things up recalls the long-standing bifurcation into "the two cultures" made famous by C. P. Snow but also to be found in important subsequent assessments of cultural proportions.[40] The alternative to the scientific culture, more or less buttressed by philosophy, more or less dominant for the past couple hundred years, is a literary culture that offers certain kinds of things instead. In embracing that literary culture, Rorty placed a relatively conventional emphasis on the value of poetry, the novel, the literary mode in general, but it was his way of embracing Bloom's categories that gave particular bite to his cultural prescriptions.

In one sense, Rorty's way of associating the decline of science with the fallout from Hegel was idiosyncratic. The breakdown of the Hegelian synthesis is widely viewed as the charter for the great age of science that followed, with

37. Ibid., 150–151; emphasis in original.
38. Ibid., 151–153.
39. In addition to ibid., 151–154, 157–158; see Rorty, *Contingency*, 24, 24n–25n, 29–30, 40–41, 41n–42n, 53, 61, for his debt to Bloom and his way of embracing these two categories. For Bloom's elaboration of those categories, see *The Anxiety of Influence: A Theory of Poetry* (New York: Oxford University Press, 1973) and *A Map of Misreading* (New York: Oxford University Press, 1975).
40. C. P. Snow, *The Two Cultures: And a Second Look* (New York: New American Library, Mentor, 1964). Rorty invokes Snow approvingly in introducing *Consequences*; see pp. xli and xlvii, n. 50. See also W. T. Jones, *The Sciences and the Humanities: Conflict and Reconciliation* (Berkeley, Los Angeles, and London: University of California Press, 1967). Although he probes more deeply, Jones ends up, like Snow, positing a cultural dichotomy between science and literature that leaves history suspended ambiguously.

each branch of inquiry detaching itself from what had been the philosophical center to become, or seek to become, an autonomous science. But Rorty's underlying point is convincing. Although the cultural apogee of science came in the late nineteenth century, Hegel was central to historicizing ways of conceiving the philosophical foundations, and ultimately scientific inquiry itself, which ultimately helped to undermine the hegemony of science. The question is what was left, or what alternatives emerged, as both systematic philosophy and science were historicized.

Rorty jumped quickly from nineteenth-century Hegelianism to twentieth-century textualism rather than pull back to encompass the whole broadly humanistic culture that emerged in tension with science and foundational philosophy during the nineteenth century. The several strands of that culture included those Rorty featured, culminating in pragmatism and modernism, but also a historicist strand that had also come through Hegel, that was not limited to Dilthey, and that had in Gadamer one major contemporary exemplar. In conflating historicism with Hegel, and in featuring romanticism as what emerges as the space of science proves circumscribed, Rorty neglected that historicist strand, its relationship with the pragmatist and modernist strands, and its prospects for development.[41] Thus he tended toward a limiting bifurcation as he characterized the cultural possibilities that have resulted from our recent intellectual history.

To be sure, Rorty embraced Gadamer as an ally in *Philosophy and the Mirror of Nature*, but problematically and, ultimately, unconvincingly. Because Gadamer was reacting against epistemology, Rorty assumed that he, too, was interested in edification and a kind of aestheticism, that he, too, was showing that in a postphilosophical world we simply try to get what we want. The alternative to the metaphysical pretense of a final vocabulary was a quest for autonomy on the private level. But this was to gloss over Gadamer's concern with truth and the endless gathering, or coming back together, of the public world, the continuing tradition to which we belong. Rorty's use of Gadamer reflected his tendency to characterize postmetaphysical alternatives in a narrowly dualistic way.

Irony, Redescription, Autonomy

Rorty, then, was quick to find common cause with the literary culture, but what, more specifically, did he find most important for us, now that we seem at last to be coming to terms with the break from idealism to textualism? His initial suggestion was that we follow the lead of edifying thinkers like Dewey, Heidegger, and Wittgenstein, who seek not to mirror reality but simply to keep the conversation going—in the face of our ongoing attempt to close it through

41. Rorty, *Consequences*, 76, 82, 85.

appeal to objective truth. Although they know their work is historically specific and thus loses its point when their historical period has ended, such edifying thinkers are a source of new descriptions, of ongoing novelty.[42] For
example, the greatness of Dewey's work

> lies in the sheer provocativeness of its suggestions about how to slough off our
> intellectual past, and about how to treat that past as material for playful experi-
> mentation rather than as imposing tasks and responsibilities upon us. Dewey's
> work helps us put aside that spirit of *seriousness* which artists traditionally lack
> and philosophers are traditionally supposed to maintain. For the spirit of serious-
> ness can only exist in an intellectual world in which human life is an attempt to
> attain an end beyond life, an escape from freedom into the atemporal. The con-
> ception of such a world is still built into our education and our common speech,
> not to mention the attitudes of philosophers toward their work.[43]

Whatever the scope for edification, this characterization indicates Rorty's
tendency to limit us to two alternatives, one traditional, bound up with the conventional function of philosophy, and the other generally artistic. In the traditional philosophical mode, our past imposes "tasks and responsibilities upon
us," and we find ourselves seeking escape into the atemporal; in the artistic
mode, we treat our intellectual past "as material for playful experimentation."

In Rorty's later works, the edifying philosopher took more general form as
the ironist, his major postmodern protagonist. The ironist seeks autonomy.

> He is trying to get out from under inherited contingencies and make his own con-
> tingencies, get out from under an old final vocabulary and fashion one which will
> be all his own. The generic trait of ironists is that they do not hope to have their
> doubts about their final vocabularies settled by something larger than themselves.
> This means that their criterion for resolving doubts, their criterion of private per-
> fection, is autonomy rather than affiliation to a power other than themselves. All
> any ironist can measure success against is the past—not by living up to it, but by
> redescribing it in his terms, thereby becoming able to say, "Thus I willed it." . . .
> He wants to be able to sum up his life in his own terms.[44]

In emphasizing ever-provisional self-making, Rorty was explicitly seeking to
turn from the "modern" premium on self-expression, with its still-metaphysical
assumption of a given essence.[45] But the Nietzschean notion of "thus I willed
it" prompts another line of questioning. Does the autonomy resulting from successful redescription have some wider public purpose, or is it simply an end in
itself?

In some of his moods, Rorty seemed to want to box out not just the philo-

---

42. Rorty, *Philosophy and the Mirror of Nature*, 368–369, 377–378.
43. Rorty, *Consequences*, 87–88; emphasis in original.
44. Rorty, *Contingency*, 97.
45. Ibid., chap. 2; see esp. pp. 42–43.

sophical tradition but the concerns of intellectuals more generally, as idiosyncratic and of marginal importance.[46] The intellectual, from this perspective, is a
special type, preoccupied with self-creation and novelty, needing to use words
that are not part of anybody else's language game. Intellectuals are not serving
a *social* purpose when they fulfill this idiosyncratic personal need—and thus
they are prone to feelings of alienation and guilt.

Generally, however, Rorty had in mind a wider cultural function, responding to reality-as-history, even as he accented novelty, originality, and self-
description. Intellectuals may be more original than others, but the question of
creativity and change is at issue for the culture as a whole.[47] In one sense, the
intellectual ironist serves as a cultural spearhead or pioneer; in another, all
actors are "intellectuals" to the extent that their responses rest on some understanding of a given situation. Ultimately, the imperative of irony applies to all
of us. But how does that imperative, and how does the function of the ironist,
relate to the neohistoricist conception Rorty seemed on his way to positing?
Distinguishable questions about both thought and action are at issue.

Among other things, the ironist is looking for a redescription of the philosophical tradition that will cause it to lose its hold over him. In both his prescriptions and his practice, Rorty sometimes suggested that a historical account,
revealing the contingency of the tradition, is precisely what is needed to
achieve the desired autonomy. But is such a historical account simply a creative, ironic redescription, or is it in some sense true and, on that basis, distinguishable from other kinds of redescription?

Moreover, Rorty apparently sought, in publishing his own historical
accounts, to influence the subsequent culture—as indeed he has. He recognized, let us recall, that we hope that our modicum of novelty, or metaphor,
will carry into the future, becoming part of the future's stock of what are taken
to be literal truths. Moreover, he noted explicitly that some influence others in
the process of social interaction; new metaphors connect with earlier ones,
influencing the future. Thus there is "a web which stretches backward and forward through past and future time."[48] The world is an ongoing conversation,
as opposed to a series of unconnected assertions or descriptions. And a particular history results from the provisional triumph of some particular set of

46. See, for example, Rorty, "Habermas and Lyotard," 174–175; and Rorty, *Essays on Heidegger*, 136–137.

47. Nancy Fraser has astutely analyzed the tensions between the "pragmatic" and "romantic,"
or "public" and "private," themes in Rorty's thinking. See especially her "Solidarity or Singularity?
Richard Rorty between Romanticism and Technocracy," in *Consequences of Theory*, ed. Jonathan
Arac and Barbara Johnson (Baltimore: Johns Hopkins University Press, 1991), 39–62. On
pp. 44–46, Fraser nicely characterizes the tack Rorty takes when claiming that strong poets serve a
wider sociopolitical function, but she finds him unpersuasive. See also Nancy Fraser, "From Irony
to Prophecy to Politics: A Response to Richard Rorty," *Michigan Quarterly Review* 30, no. 2
(Spring 1991): 259–266.

48. Rorty, *Contingency*, 41–42. See also pp. 29, 61.

contingent metaphors. So creative redescription could be conceived as history-making, reshaping the culture as an aspect of the ongoing particularizing and growth. How, then, do irony and redescription relate to the connectedness, the web of influence, that Rorty could not avoid positing?

Rorty went out of his way to link irony and redescription to discontinuity, as opposed to the reconnection of history-making action. What I seek, in coming up with new metaphors, is a redescription that will prove useful for my own purposes of self-creation, not for reconstructing the public world. Indeed, creativity is bound up with wriggling free of history. Suggesting that contingency precludes continuity, Rorty implied that creation requires discontinuity and even conflated "the continuity-seeking historian" with the discredited philosopher.[49]

Rorty's tendency to jump from philosophy to literature, bypassing or precluding history, is especially clear in the striking passage below, in which he first implies that a form of postmetaphysical history is what we most need but then finds literature to be the only alternative to metaphysically grounded theory. From a consideration of Proust, contrasted favorably with Nietzsche in this context, Rorty concluded

> that novels are a safer medium than theory for expressing one's recognition of the relativity and contingency of authority figures. For novels are usually about people—things which are . . . quite evidently time-bound, embedded in a web of contingencies. . . . By contrast, books which are about ideas, even when written by historicists like Hegel and Nietzsche, look like descriptions of eternal relations between eternal objects, rather than genealogical accounts of the filiation of final vocabularies, showing how these vocabularies were engendered by haphazard matings, by who happened to bump into whom.[50]

Rorty's implication is that such genealogy is what we most need in this contingent world, and it is *not* afforded by the novel, insofar as novels deal with people as opposed to ideas. There is a particular cultural place for something "between" more or less metaphysical theory, on the one hand, and literature, on the other. The genealogies we need look at first glance like histories. Yet Rorty leaves us with a cultural premium on "novels," implying that anything not focused on contingencies of people will seem like something *more* than the desired genealogy, will be taken as claiming metaphysical sanction or suprahistorical status. Although not focusing explicitly on history in this passage, Rorty implied that history necessarily claims too much, *looks like* something more. And thus he assigned to literature a role that initially seemed to fall to history in a postmetaphysical culture.

49. Ibid., 28, 107. See also p. 25 n. 2, for Rorty's way of understanding continuity: "Metaphysicians look for continuities—overarching conditions of possibility—which provide the space within which discontinuity occurs."
50. Ibid., 107–108.

As one especially effective thrust in his assault on the philosophical tradition, Rorty showed that we are misled by the assumption of a prelinguistic consciousness, or intuition of the way things are, that we should be able to get at in language, with philosophy showing us how. In fact, however, "what is described as such a consciousness is simply a disposition to use the language of our ancestors, to worship the corpses of their metaphors."[51] Our philosophical tradition, in other words, leads us to take the contingent metaphors of our language to be more than they are. This tendency seems to be built in: "each generation's irony is likely to become the next generation's metaphysics. Metaphysics is, so to speak, irony gone public and flat—liquefaction congealed, providing a new ground on which to inscribe new figures."[52]

For Rorty, the ironist, or forger of "new ways of speaking," responds to precisely this tendency to congeal. We might assume that the ongoing process of freeing up our creativity would include recognizing that the constituents of our present language *are* dead metaphors, that our world is wound around contingent dead metaphors—the sort of thing deconstruction might help us do. But, in this instance as well, Rorty turned away from any premium on historical inquiry and played up the role for literature. Although literature cannot have the political import that some leftists envision, "literary study helps one realize that today's literal and objective truth is just the corpse of yesterday's metaphor."[53] No doubt it can, in a loose, general sort of way, but historical inquiry encompassing the insights of Derridean deconstruction might do so with considerably more bite.

Whether accenting edification or irony, redescription or strong misreading, Rorty continually bypassed history and plugged into the wider aestheticism. His accents in doing so stemmed from his way of framing the relationship between individual experience and the historical world. Anxiety about autonomy in the postmetaphysical situation, in which we find ourselves trapped within an ever-congealing history, gave a particular spin to his assessment of the possibilities.

Suffocation, Weightlessness, and the Prophets of Extremity

I noted that when seeking to deflate the apocalyptic tendencies of deconstruction, Rorty insisted that we increasingly understand ourselves as resting on a fountain of puns and metaphors. But I also noted that there seems to be an ongoing tendency, in Rorty's universe, for once-molten metaphors to "objectify" or congeal and for human beings, in their metaphysical necrophilia, to

51. Ibid., 21.
52. Rorty, *Essays on Heidegger*, 128n.
53. Ibid., 134.

worship the corpses. So we need to keep showing up and undermining that still-metaphysical tendency. But do the particular metaphors that have in fact resulted—become ours, us—*have* to be the objects of such misplaced worship? What if we were to experience them as nothing more than what they are, as nothing but history? We would no longer worship them, certainly, but we have seen that new preoccupations intrude as metaphysics fades, as we escape even its shadow.

Fundamental to Rorty's response was the suffocating experience, explored first by Nietzsche, of being always already caught up in a particular history— determined by a past not chosen and confined to a present that is nothing but the haphazard resultant of the whole of that past. With the reduction to history, the anxiety of influence that Bloom explored with respect to poetry becomes general, because *everything* is wound around metaphor coming to us from a past that threatens our autonomy.[54]

Thus Rorty, still following Bloom, advocated the actively "strong misreadings" that yield new metaphors; the alternative, merely to "read," is to be confined to the particular line of the actual, with the present seemingly encompassing the embryo of any future. More specifically, to seek "truth" as opposed to a disruptive irony is to remain subservient to metaphors now congealed. Our tendency to worship corpses is the other side of the tendency of particularizing history to ensnare us, limiting what we can say, do, even be, in ways we have not chosen. So the premium is on irony, even quirkiness, as opposed to truth or reconnection.

Although Rorty, as noted, posited a web of influence, we experience the inevitability of connection not as an opportunity to help shape the future but as a limitation to be eluded as much as possible. Thus the act of strong misreading is not experienced as history-making but as liberating from the confining world of nothing but history. And the effort of wriggling free is endless because the future as well as the past occasions the experience of suffocation; the anxiety of influence works in both directions.

Again Rorty invoked Bloom, who "reminds us that just as even the strongest poet is parasitic on her precursors, just as even she can give birth only to a small part of herself, so she is dependent on the kindness of all those strangers out there in the future."[55] Even insofar as each of us manages to redescribe the whole past into "thus I willed it," we will continually be redescribed in contingent ways we have not chosen by those who come after us. It is happening to Rorty precisely now, as it will be happening to me "now." In a sense, in fact, history is precisely that ongoing process of redescribing. Recognition of that fact leads not only to anxiety over what will become of what I do but also to resentment of history itself, for arbitrarily making of what I do, even what I

54. Rorty, *Contingency*, 40–41.
55. Ibid., 41.

am, something I cannot choose or foresee. Although Rorty did not engage in Derridean preemptive moves to one-up history and undercut the subsequent redescription, he, too, placed a premium on endlessly wriggling free of the particularizing coils.

But such anxiety toward the future may give way to its opposite, to a giddy sense of weightlessness or lightness. Not only is it impossible to foresee how things will connect but, in light of the radical contingency of things, there seems no good reason why they end up connecting as they do. Since what will happen to what I do is almost literally up in the air, it does not matter what I do, so I come to feel that reality as mere history lacks sufficient weight to hold together, to come back together. The anxiety of suffocating submergence within the particular history gives way to a feeling of lightness warranting a premium on edification or irony without any concern for shaping the future.

So though Rorty's neopragmatism seemed at first a way of boxing out poststructuralist excess, his response paralleled certain aspects of the poststructuralist reaction and left him, too, in the broadly aestheticist camp as he accented edification, quirkiness, and play at the expense of disciplined criticism to serve history-making change. His way of conceiving the cultural possibilities was broadly pluralistic in one sense, but it proved dualistic in a deeper sense as he afforded privilege to the generally literary alternative to foundation-seeking philosophy. The scope for a postmetaphysical culture of history, operating "between" the old philosophy and the new literary culture, got lost.

In both deconstruction and neopragmatism, the aestheticist tendency stemmed from both the "modern" preoccupation with metaphysical authority and the twin "postmodern" preoccupations with claustrophobia and weightlessness. But because Rorty was less subject to philosophical traumas and more comfortably within the postmodern space, his thinking manifested more clearly the postmodern preoccupations.

In his effort to sort out cultural possibilities, Rorty confronted Nietzsche, Heidegger, Foucault, and Derrida directly. His analyses were unusually helpful because they sought to pinpoint the tensions that resulted from the disparate components in the thinking of each. More specifically, Rorty featured the extreme impulses in each, probing their sources and questioning their relationship with his own cultural strategy.[56] In the final analysis, however, his characterizations fed his tendency to present an aestheticized pragmatism as the only alternative to still-metaphysical positions.

Although he initially dismissed Heidegger as simply another Platonist with a newer jargon, Rorty's later work did greater justice to the postmetaphysical dimension in Heidegger's confrontation with the tradition. More specifically,

56. I focus especially on Heidegger and Derrida in what follows. For Rorty's assessment of Foucault, see especially his 1988 essay, "Moral Identity and Private Autonomy: The Case of Foucault," in *Essays on Heidegger*, 193–198. See also *Contingency*, 61–69, where he considers Foucault in tandem with Habermas.

he played up Heidegger's preoccupation with the world as historical. In a particularly telling passage, Rorty found Heidegger, like Hegel and Nietzsche, to have been caught up in a "quest for the historical sublime."

> Whereas Plato and Kant had prudently taken this sublimity outside of time altogether, Nietzsche and Heidegger cannot use this dodge. They have to stay in time, but to view themselves as separated from all the rest of time by a decisive event.
>
> This quest for the historical sublime—for proximity to some event such as the closing of the gap between subject and object or the advent of the superman or the end of metaphysics—leads Hegel, Nietzsche, and Heidegger to fancy themselves in the role of the "last philosopher." The attempt to be in this position is the attempt to write something which will make it impossible for one to be redescribed except in one's own terms—make it impossible to become an element in anybody else's beautiful pattern, one more little thing.[57]

Rorty recognized, then, that for both Nietzsche and Heidegger, the priority was no longer a suprahistorical metaphysics but a certain relationship with our particular history. But each was concerned to keep from becoming merely a piece of the history like everything else. There seemed something suffocating about confinement to the particular contingent history, knowing that what I do will become part of it in a way I cannot determine. Autonomy thus required not simply redescribing the past but also bringing some part of the history itself to an end, so that I will not be subject to the capriciousness of the merely historical future.

In one sense, Rorty concluded, Heidegger achieved "the sublimity he attempted," eluding the snares of the tradition and creating himself.[58] By reformulating philosophical language, he made the elemental words of our tradition poetic, so that the sounds, not the uses, are what matter; the words are no longer tools, means to ends, or counters in a game others can play. They become opaque, so we are not drawn to recontextualize them, thereby redescribing Heidegger himself. Heidegger, then, forced us to see him as a thinker of a different kind, *not* as just another metaphysician, just another footnote to Plato.

For Rorty, Heidegger's quasi-ironic disengagement could serve subsequent efforts on the part of those who have been formed by our philosophical tradition, who have worried about the esoteric problems of metaphysics, and who now stand in ironic relation to those problems: "Despite himself, what Heidegger did to the history of philosophy was not to deconstruct it but to further encapsulate and isolate it, thus enabling us to *circumvent* it." Those few, including Rorty himself, found encounter with Heidegger essential as they made their

---

57. Rorty, *Contingency*, 105–106.
58. Ibid., 118–119. Rorty offers this assessment, however, in contrasting Heidegger with Proust, who, Rorty holds, succeeded in a way that Heidegger did not. See pp. 108–120 for the overall contrast.

own comparable efforts at redescription. But Heidegger had not solved some general problem of the age, as he thought he was doing. Indeed, Rorty insisted, Heidegger's enterprise was "entirely useless to people who do not share his associations."[59]

On one level, the conception of cultural possibilities implicit in Rorty's assessment of Heidegger was radically pluralistic. Some, like Heidegger and Rorty themselves, had to engage philosophy, but that particular sphere and that particular confrontation were not privileged. Other kinds of people develop their own edifying relationship to what, thanks to history, they have become. Rorty also featured the uses of novels, as we have seen, but the list might be expanded to include, for example, the carnivalesque, or cross-dressing, or certain forms of popular music.

In a deeper sense, however, Rorty had room for only two alternatives—the old monolithic, philosophically grounded culture, and the ironic, edifying redescription that he valued. Heidegger was suspended in the middle. He was sufficiently ironic that he could not be redescribed, but he still assumed there was a privileged list of books and words to be confronted; he still thought the most important thing for us was to spruce up Greek terms. What kept Heidegger bound to the philosophical tradition was his refusal or inability to embrace the more relaxed aestheticism that Rorty found the only genuinely postmetaphysical response. Heidegger, said Rorty, "wanted to find a way of being neither metaphysical nor aestheticist," but for Rorty, there was no such space.[60]

Rorty found Derrida, too, guilty of overvaluing the philosophical tradition, especially in his earlier phase, before the mid-1970s. At that point Derrida was still operating as a traditional philosopher, seeking "to go transcendental" and deduce the noncausal conditions of possibility—in this case, for the *im*possibility of closure. Though Derrida claimed to show how to avoid the traps of philosophy, his terms like "trace" and "différance" were attempts to devise a new metavocabulary claiming superior status, even closure. But for Rorty, it was simply inconsistent to contend that the possibilities for recontextualization are boundless, that there can be no closure, while also offering transcendental arguments, based on a claim to grasp the condition of possibility of all possible contexts. The categories Derrida derived through his form of transcendental deduction were unnecessary, dispensable.[61]

But Rorty recognized that after the mid-1970s Derrida had become more consistently preoccupied with sidestepping the limiting philosophical tradition. Derrida had been especially concerned to avoid the mistake of Heidegger, who

59. Rorty, *Essays on Heidegger*, 105 (emphasis in original); Rorty, *Contingency*, 118–119. See also Rorty, *Philosophy and the Mirror of Nature*, 12.

60. Rorty, *Contingency*, 112. See also Rorty, *Essays on Heidegger*, 104.

61. Rorty, *Essays on Heidegger*, 2, 93–94, 110n, 112–113, 118, 124n, 121–128. Rorty argues especially against Rodolphe Gasché's *The Tain of the Mirror*, which accents, and values, the philosophical rigor of Derrida's work.

had sought mightily to be a postphilosophical thinker, yet who, Derrida felt, had ended up mired within the tradition nevertheless. Derrida sought to be more radical by trying out brutal, disruptive ways of changing terrain, or by interlacing the horns of the dilemma by embracing several languages or texts at once.[62]

Up to a point, Rorty valued that enterprise: "What Derrida has done, despite himself, is to show us how to take Heidegger with Nietzschean gaiety, how to see his handling of the metaphysical tradition as a brilliantly original narrative rather than as an epochal transformation."[63] But when Derrida turned from philosophy, his writings seemed to lack focus and point. It appeared that in Derrida's hands, at least, writing utterly emptied of philosophical content would lack subject, context—would be so open as to be merely babble.[64] So Derrida kept returning to philosophy to tell the story over and over, showing how philosophy invariably eludes itself. But even this, for Rorty, remained too close to what philosophers had always done, giving transcendental arguments, establishing general propositions—in this case about the impossibility of a completed vocabulary.

By the latter 1980s, Derrida seemed to have abandoned definitively any attempt to establish categories, so Rorty proposed that Derrida's earlier, apparently more traditional phase had simply been a false start that need not compromise the value of later works like *The Post Card*. No longer was Derrida concerned to say how things *are* on some level by finding the correct words; no longer was he just another philosopher, concerned to give rigorous arguments for a position that would settle things on some level. Now Derrida was "content to have fun rather than feel haunted." And Rorty heartily approved: "I think he was on the right track when he suggested that the only strategy of evasion that is going to work will be to write in a way that makes the discourse of philosophy look enigmatic rather than ubiquitous. At his best, Derrida realizes that one good way to make something look enigmatic is to treat it as a joke."[65] Thus Rorty's praise for the later Derrida as "a great comic writer" whose way of treating the tradition was "splendidly original." For Rorty, then, Derrida had become one of those valuable edifying thinkers who serve the culture by loosening, opening things up, in the face of the ongoing tendency to congeal.[66]

Rorty's characterizations of Heidegger and Derrida remain invaluable, but his way of opposing aestheticism to metaphysics limited what he was prepared to draw from them. From his perspective, the two thinkers were postmeta-

---

62. Rorty, *Essays on Heidegger*, 95–98. Here Rorty relies especially on the key passage in Derrida's *Margins of Philosophy*, trans. Alan Bass (Chicago: University of Chicago Press, 1982), 135.
63. Rorty, *Essays on Heidegger*, 105.
64. Ibid., 93–94.
65. Ibid., 117–118.
66. Ibid., 113, 113n, 128, 128n.

physical only insofar as they treated the ensnaring tradition as a joke and embraced an edifying irony, with a premium on creativity, novelty, and quirkiness. The central postmetaphysical impulse is a quest for autonomy in opposition to a tradition that grows to encompass whatever we say or do.

Rorty's accents, stemming from his dualistic framework, kept him from doing justice to certain of the postmetaphysical extremes. Although he found an element of religious ritual in the recent vogue of deconstruction, Rorty was not attuned to the possibility that new forms of religiosity might open up, in opposition to the workaday world he generally featured. Thus he did not do justice to Heidegger, who came to recognize precisely what Rorty charged against him, that "we need to create our own elementary words, not spruce up Greek ones."[67] That, however, was not so easy. We may *think* we are on our own, but we will not be, until we experience the sense in which we are nothing but this particular destining—and then find a way of distancing from the whole of it. Only by thus preparing ourselves might we serve the creating/receiving/disclosing of those new elementary words. Heidegger envisioned an alternative to Rorty's easygoing pragmatism *and* to the sort of personal edification Rorty assumed he must have been seeking.

Even as he pinpointed the quasi-religious element in Paul de Man's version of deconstruction, Rorty did not do justice to the point of telling our story over and over, in a ritualistic way. And his lack of sympathy for any such aim affected his treatment of Derrida as well. Even in Derrida's hands, telling it over and over is new and different, not simply a variation on transcendental argument.[68] It is an extreme response to history, not just another philosophy, precisely because Derrida was fully self-conscious and reflexive. Moreover, even if such ritualistic retelling is done in a semicomic mode, it may stem from preoccupations and aspirations quite different from the personal concern for autonomy.

Reconnection and Truth

Rorty's treatment of the extremists fed his tendency to sidestep the reconstructive alternative to both metaphysics and postmetaphysical extremity that he initially seemed to invite. In approaching Derrida's earlier, more conventional works, he was quick to assume that Derrida was doing old-fashioned philosophy rather than the historically informed "theory" that may be necessary even as we leave the old philosophy behind.[69] Derrida's categories may be understood as attempts at ad hoc clarification, specifying, for now, some of the conditions of our postmetaphysical situation so that we might respond to

67. Ibid., 104.
68. Note the telling ambiguity in ibid., 93–94.
69. Ibid., 101–102.

historically specific problems. In positing différance as "older," for example, Derrida was seeking a way to say what seemed essential at his moment of rupture—that slippage is built in, is "always already," so that we cease appealing to a ground or origin.[70] Any such enterprise yields nothing more than "new metaphors," in Rorty's terms, and even those that prove most persuasive need not pretend to transcend history. From within his dualistic framework, Rorty could not do justice to the sense in which Derrida could "argue," even offer some new categories, without claiming the last word.

Rorty charged that in their different ways both Heidegger and Derrida suggested they had finally gotten language right, as it actually is. Rather than "take a relaxed, naturalistic, Darwinian view of language," each tended to let " 'Language' become the latest substitute for 'God' or 'Mind'—something mysterious, incapable of being described in the same terms in which we describe tables, trees, and atoms."[71] Although for Heidegger, to be sure, new insight into language might open the way to the quasi-religious "mystery" Rorty was determined to do without, it may not be enough, in light of contemporary confusions, simply to relax and put language to work. Even insofar as we aim to return to the workaday world as soon as we can, we may need to ask big questions about how we have come to conceive language as we have; we may need to say something new and *relatively* theoretical about how it relates to us and the world. But we need not claim that now, at last, we have said everything that will ever need to be said. We simply seek to do better at saying what language has been so far.

We noted that Rorty, in accenting autonomy and redescription, was taking over some of Nietzsche's imperatives, partly as mediated by Bloom. With his accent on "thus I willed it," Nietzsche appeared to warrant a concentration on the private or personal level, apart from the public world of history. But, as emphasized in chapter 4, he experienced the freakish present world not simply as a blurry backdrop, or as raw material for his own edifying self-creation. Though only the contingent outcome of a chain of accidents, it was the fatality, and Nietzsche sought an affirmative relationship with it to overcome both resentment and fear of judgment, including historical judgment. So the mode of life that Nietzsche posited cannot be understood as private as opposed to public; it entailed a certain relationship with the whole, newly experienced as nothing but the particular history.

If we eschew the Nietzschean extreme, we must devise an alternative understanding of the relationship between individual and postmetaphysical totality. With his neoliberal accents, Rorty was no Nietzschean extremist, but he tended to settle for a private-public bifurcation, partly because of the loosely Nietz-

---

70. Derrida, *Margins of Philosophy*, 22. Derrida's denial that he was offering another set of philosophical categories left Rorty puzzled. See Jacques Derrida, *Positions*, trans. Alan Bass (Chicago: University of Chicago Press, 1981), 52; and Rorty, *Essays on Heidegger*, 102.

71. Rorty, *Essays on Heidegger*, 3–4. See also p. 5.

schean emphasis on self-creation at work in the culture. His emphasis on the private produced prejudicial characterizations, mixed uneasily with his liberal and historicist accents, and led him simply to neglect certain possibilities.[72]

So quick was Rorty to place a premium on personal redescription that he did not fully consider the scope for a mode of belonging to the historical totality that does not preclude creativity but invites it. In their different ways, Croce and Gadamer each specified an affirmative relationship that entails such ongoing criticism and reconstruction. We identify with the actual world sufficiently to care for it, to feel responsibility for it, and to respond to it, seeking not autonomy but reconnection with the world even as we help to change it.

In associating Dewey with playful experimentation as opposed to seriousness, Rorty reacted plausibly against philosophical pretense, but he also neglected the scope for a kind of weak seriousness as the middle term. Croce, in contrast, suggested that precisely because there can be no "escape from freedom into the atemporal," as Rorty put it, our ongoing making of history is of ultimate seriousness and that we are ultimately responsible—though only to history, that apparently capricious judge.[73]

Although Rorty denied to literature the grandiose political role that the American literary Left seemed to envision, he suggested that certain forms of writing—from novels to newspaper stories to Foucault's histories—can make a difference. There was scope for effective criticism and constructive change, underpinned by some measure of positive identification with the actual.[74] Even redescription that starts on the personal level might have public or broadly political effects, reconnecting with the actual and helping to shape the future. But Rorty's emphasis on individual self-creation stood in tension with that mode of identification—and with the way of experiencing ourselves as public actors that follows from it. The edification Rorty valued tended toward quirky brilliance, originality for its own sake. Indeed, his conflation of "seriousness" with metaphysics tended to undermine any emphasis on reconnection and the enduring, history-making weight of what we do.

An effort to reconnect, to influence, to participate in the process and shape the future leads to a premium on knowing the world as history. Conversely, the more we play down the history-making weight of what we do, the less we need worry about the autonomy of historical inquiry, the sense in which historical inquiry can yield truth in a way that literary modes do not.

We noted that Rorty called for historical narrative as the way to clarify the

72. See, for example, ibid., 127, where Rorty discusses the different purposes that language, as a set of tools, may perform. Like Alexander Nehamas, on whose interpretation of Nietzsche he draws, Rorty did not do justice to Nietzsche's confrontation with the totality that results from the reduction to history. See *Contingency*, 27n, for Rorty's acknowledgment of his debt to Nehamas.

73. Rorty offered the quoted phrase in discussing, approvingly, Dewey's retreat from seriousness. See Rorty, *Consequences*, 87–88. See also above, p. 238.

74. See Rorty, *Essays on Heidegger*, 119–120, 120n, 134–136; and Rorty, "Habermas and Lyotard," 173, for indications of the scope for that positive identification.

conditions in which a new conception "of truth as what comes to be believed in the course of free and open encounters" could emerge to replace our long-standing "idea of truth as correspondence to reality."[75] This would be to redescribe our past to make certain consequences possible. But no matter how brilliant and original the narrative, it could have the consequences Rorty envisioned only if it was specifically historical, seeking truth. The point of such a redescription is to reconnect, and brilliance and originality are not sufficient. The truth to be sought would not claim to be definitive, and it would be congruent with precisely the notion of truth to which Rorty refers here and elsewhere.

There is obviously more to be said about how specifically historical truth happens, about what distinguishes it from its contraries, and about the difference its autonomy makes to the culture. Croce and Gadamer offered some indications. With Rorty's inflation of the literary sphere, however, a historical account becomes just another form of irony, metaphor, or strong misreading. Again and again, Rorty's aestheticist accents blurred the sense in which historical truth still stands opposed to literary fiction *even* in a postmetaphysical world where no one claims some finished and complete account. Despite Gadamer's concern to recast truth, Rorty invoked Gadamer in insisting that from the "educational" point of view that replaces epistemology, "the way things are said is more important than the possession of truths."[76] Because he was so eager to embrace an aestheticized pragmatism as the alternative to the conventional belief in definitive "truths," Rorty took no account of Gadamer's effort to offer a postmetaphysical understanding of truth.

In the same way, Rorty's strong misreader "is in it for what he can get out of it, not for the satisfaction of getting something right."[77] Fair enough, but this formulation invites overreaction unless we recognize, with Croce, that what such misreaders need and seek, even if they have no illusions about "getting something right," is a true account, precisely insofar as such knowing is to serve action. The fact that it will simply be a finite and provisional true account, not complete or definitive, does not dissolve it into literature or generic redescription. Insofar as that difference is blurred, any assessment of cultural proportions will preclude prejudicially the scope for an autonomous historical strand, and the postmetaphysical culture will be unnecessarily irrationalist and capricious.

Rorty admitted that we all hope our metaphors will connect. At the same time, he noted the possibility that the quest for originality can lead to pointless babble. In criticizing Foucault, he seemed to place a premium on the community, belonging, and endless reconnection that Foucault seemed determined to

---

75. Rorty, *Contingency*, 68. See above, p. 233.
76. Rorty, *Philosophy and the Mirror of Nature*, 359.
77. Rorty, *Consequences*, 152.

disrupt.[78] To avoid babble, what Derrida or anyone else needs is precisely to reconnect. Because he was a philosopher, Derrida needed to reconnect with the philosophical tradition—as he did, even as he radically deconstructed it. But there is scope for such deconstruction-reconnection in all reaches of the culture. Try it with the bases of our sociopolitical thinking, or with the discourse of business and ethics or of gender and sexual harassment. But Rorty's concern with autonomy and edifying personal redescription kept him from developing this point, even led him to turn in the opposite direction and emphasize autonomy and shaking loose as opposed to any such reconnection.

As I have emphasized, plausible new preoccupations result as we contemplate being recontextualized in an endlessly slipping world of contingent particularizing. Thus, in part, the tendencies toward extremity I have noted. Insofar as Rorty responded to such preoccupations, his assessment of our cultural possibilities became one-sided. Yet that response coexisted with his historicist and reconstructive impulses. Although he sought to sidestep the issue by bifurcating private and public, or the idiosyncratic concerns of intellectuals and the concerns of everyone else, he was simply ambivalent in responding to the reduction to history. I have accented the plausibility of an array of responses, including various extremes, even while seeking to specify the terms of a moderate alternative. The components will jostle, and Rorty's ambivalence is itself plausible. But what is most therapeutic at this point is to sort out the components—in a way that reconnects.

78. As discussed in the preceding chapter. See Rorty, "Habermas and Lyotard," 172.

10

Past, Process, and Contest in Contemporary Historiography

Historiographical Openness

In their different ways, hermeneutics, deconstruction, and neopragmatism all seemed to suggest a more central role for empirical historiography. To be sure, historiography still embodied legacies of positivism and nineteenth-century historicism that would have to be jettisoned, but the assault on metaphysics seemed to yield the elements for the necessary recasting. However, other impulses, evident in thinkers from Nietzsche and Heidegger to Derrida and Rorty, seemed to undercut the historical discipline altogether.

In chapter 1, I noted that by the late 1980s practicing historians were becoming attuned to the wider discussion in the humanities. Some suggested that historians, freed at last from the misguided imperative of representation, could do more kinds of things and thereby expand their cultural function. But this confidence betrayed presentist and aestheticist accents that provoked more traditional historians to insist more tenaciously on the old self-understanding. The result was confusion and a debilitating polarization in historiography.

With the eclipse of metaphysics, there seemed deeper reasons for each of the competing foci long at work in historiography—the past moment, apprehended on its own terms, and the process connecting the past moment with the present. Insofar as present conditions have resulted from nothing but history, historical understanding seems all we have to go on. So we feel a deeper urgency to focus on processes leading from the past to our present, not to grasp the goal or shape of history as a whole, but simply to understand where our present has come from. In this mode, we feature in the past moment what fits into and furthers some such process.

Such inquiry may serve action in response to our present situation. As with gender, the now-familiar example, to show that what had seemed natural was contingent and historical is to loosen the present configuration and open the way to new construction—in this case, a new way of making social sense of sexual difference. So historical inquiry that probes contingent constructedness may be *re*constructive—not in the sense of reconstructing the past as it actually happened, but serving the ongoing reconstruction of the world.

The example of gender shows that we need not take what formerly seemed the *dominant* processes, especially political-constitutional development, to be most worthy of our attention. The whole historical terrain seems subject to arrangement in one such process or another, connecting the past to us. The arrangement of those processes in some hierarchy of importance is itself historically specific—and at this moment is up to us. In the reflexive mode that follows from the inflation of history, we understand that we are ourselves historical actors as we choose, on the basis of present needs, to ask about this as opposed to that.

Alongside the renewed emphasis on presentist involvement and process, we find a renewed emphasis on the past moment for its own sake, quite apart from, even *as opposed to*, its place in the process resulting in our present. Indeed, it may be partly because we have new reasons for accenting presentism and process that we feel, at the same time, a deeper need to disembed our predecessors from the processes connecting their experience with our own. To apprehend their experience for its own sake might entail at once suppressing the distance and restoring the real difference between the present and the past moment. In any case, we apparently need to reconceive *both* terms of the past/process dichotomy and the relationship between them in light of the eclipse of metaphysics.

It was noted in chapter 1 that Simon Schama's semifictionalized history, *Dead Certainties*, published in 1991, seemed symptomatic of the perplexities that wider theoretical innovations had occasioned for historiography. Most obviously troubling was Schama's apparently willful blending of fact and fiction, but the relationships among past, present, and process were still more fundamentally at issue.

Dead Certainties followed hard upon Schama's *Citizens: A Chronicle of the French Revolution* (1989), which eschewed temporal distance in order to convey events from the perspective of the participants. Schama seemed to suggest that *even* in the maelstrom of "the French Revolution," which had long seemed the founding event of our era, what was most real and worthy of our attention was a world of experience that we can grasp only if we do *not* worry about where it was all leading, which we know in a way that those involved did not. That world is defined, in fact, by its tension with the process that has led to us.

In *Dead Certainties*, Schama took a more radical step, teasing into the creases between involvement and detachment, fact and fiction, past and process, and exploring their interconnections. In his critical review, Gordon Wood understood that in this work, too, Schama assumed "that participants have a privileged access to knowledge of the events they are involved in," whereas, Wood pointed out, most historians assume the opposite. Precisely insofar as they are removed from events, historians are better able to put disparate, confused, often contradictory accounts by participants into a plausible whole.[1]

But in invoking "objectivity" to characterize what he took to be the alternative to Schama's willful foreshortening, Wood sidestepped important aspects of Schama's challenge. The point is not simply that the accounts of the participants themselves are fragmentary and thus inadequate, as if the participants simply were not as good at doing the same thing historians do. The question concerns the alternative foci of historical inquiry—and the purposes at work in each. In what sense is history about the process leading to the present, and in what sense is it about the past, apart from any such process? Insofar as it is about both, what purpose does each mode of inquiry serve, and what is the relationship between them?

Schama's provocative book usefully dramatized the central issues facing historiography by the early 1990s, when an unprecedented sense of possibility, risk, and danger marked the historical discipline. The historiographical focus continued to expand as never before, yet historians were subject to gnawing doubts as the bases of their earlier self-understanding eroded. Schama had managed to play with the ambiguities in an especially entertaining way, but the challenge was more deeply to clarify the central dichotomies—involvement and detachment, fact and fiction, past and process—and the relationships among them.

Processes to the Present

During the 1980s, historians and theorists coming from very different directions explicitly embraced presentism as the key to a more open and resonant historiography. They included students of historical narrative like Hayden White and Hans Kellner, innovative "new historians" like Joan Wallach Scott, and proponents of "the new historicism" like Brook Thomas. Despite significant differences in accent, each played up the active role of the historian in connecting the present with the past for broadly political purposes.

As noted in chapter 1, Hayden White's *Metahistory* (1973) launched a narrativist current that examined the construction of historical accounts in language and thereby forced renewed attention to the historian's active role. In

---

1. Gordon S. Wood, "Novel History," *New York Review of Books*, 27 June 1991, 14; Simon Schama, *Dead Certainties (Unwarranted Speculations)* (New York: Random House, Vintage, 1992), 319–326.

that work White delineated the cycle of rhetorical strategies that afforded historiography a certain resonance during the nineteenth century but that led to a curiously sterile outcome by the beginning of the twentieth, when historiography settled into the "ironic" mode that henceforth characterized professional historiography. The irony lay in the disjunction between present and past that enabled the historian to assume a stance of superiority. The historian understands what was happening in a way that past participants themselves did not; indeed, the historian can see the inevitable disparity between their self-understanding and what we, from our privileged perspective, know to have been happening *really*. Thus irony was bound up with the assumption that realistic representation of the past is possible—and is the defining mode of historiography as an autonomous discipline.[2]

This outcome proved ironic in a double sense, because the assumption of present superiority and the imperative of realistic representation left historiography confined to the temple of art, cut off from the broadly political world of present action.[3] White sought to contest that outcome by showing that historical accounts are actively constructed in language through particular rhetorical strategies, which stem from political assumptions and have political implications. By undercutting the long-standing assumption that history affords a realistic rendering of a past that is sharply distinguishable from the present, he hoped to point historians toward a more overtly active and reconstructive present role.

White and his narrativist allies added an important dimension to what deconstruction in the loose sense had offered historiography. Any present understanding is simply one contingent narrative construction. And what we deconstruct is never unvarnished reality, the historical "thing-in-itself," but some particular account, constructed in language. To be more precise, what we might find it liberating to deconstruct is some *dominant* account, central to our present self-understanding and intertwined with our present practice. So deconstructive historical inquiry focuses on the constructedness not of some present actuality but of our historical understanding itself.

Still, even with much clarification in the two decades after *Metahistory*, White's work proved a problematic bridge between the wider discussion and

2. Hayden V. White, *Metahistory: The Historical Imagination in Nineteenth-Century Europe* (Baltimore: Johns Hopkins University Press, 1973); see esp. pp. 36–38, for White's understanding of "irony" in this context. For a nice summary of the point, see Lloyd S. Kramer, "Literature, Criticism, and Historical Imagination: The Literary Challenge of Hayden White and Dominick LaCapra," in *The New Cultural History*, ed. Lynn Hunt (Berkeley, Los Angeles, and London: University of California Press, 1989), 104.

3. In *Metahistory*, chap. 10, White portrayed Croce as the embodiment of that ironic culmination. I have disputed White's use of Croce elsewhere, but the issue is secondary here. White does not do justice to Croce, but neither does his larger argument rest on his use of Croce. And his overall point that realist assumptions and imperatives led historiography to settle into a relatively "safe," circumspect cultural role is convincing and important.

practicing historians. In an essay published in 1989, White took particular care
to head off the many misrepresentations that had come to surround his argument. He emphasized, most fundamentally, that his understanding of historical
discourse, with its accent on the constructedness of history in language, "does
not imply that past events, persons, institutions, and processes never really
existed," or that we cannot have genuine knowledge about the past. He was
not suggesting that everything is language or discourse, or that we cannot refer
to and represent extradiscursive entities. Nor was he denying that events occur
in chronological sequence. Rather than collapsing the distinction between fact
and fiction, he was simply trying to reconceive the relationship between them.[4]

White recognized that there is an archive of information and a naked chronology; historical inquiry presupposes them. Indeed, the scope for "scientific"
research, for access to information about the past, could simply be taken for
granted. What required attention was the process through which the historian
transforms information and chronology into a specifically the historical, and
inherently interpretive, kind of knowledge. Although the transformation at issue
can entail very different degrees of complexity, it always involves the production of a historical text in language. More precisely, it is always through the narrative mode of representation that we grasp referents as distinctively historical.
In that sense historical discourse constructs its own subject matter.[5]

So the key, for White, was to understand the function of narrativity in historical writing. From the same historical subject matter, it is always possible to
construct a variety of narratives—and thereby to confer different meanings.
Whatever the meanings they confer, historians construct plots using the same
rhetorical strategies, or modes of linguistic figuration, that imaginative writers
use. And those strategies are more tropological than logical in nature.[6]

When he argued that the rules of discourse formation are not fixed, so that
particular instances cannot be predicted in advance, White seemed on his way
to a radical historicism. But instead he accented the scope for classifying strategies of emplotment in terms of the four tropes delineated in neoclassical rhetorical theory—metaphor, synecdoche, metonymy, and irony. By understanding
how historical writing is wound around these tropes, we better understand how
historical discourse works like fictional narrative.[7]

Because White played up this convergence, many failed to recognize that
within the wider humanistic discussion he was seeking a middle ground.
Though the current developing from structuralism had been crucial in drawing

4. Hayden V. White, " 'Figuring the nature of the times deceased': Literary Theory and Historical Writing," in *The Future of Literary Theory*, ed. Ralph Cohen (New York: Routledge, 1989),
19–43. See pp. 20, 34–35, for the points here. On pp. 31–36, White summarizes, and responds to,
the standard objections to his argument.

5. Ibid., 20–22.

6. Ibid., pp. 25–26. See also Hayden V. White, *Tropics of Discourse: Essays in Cultural Criticism* (Baltimore: Johns Hopkins University Press, 1978), 98.

7. White, " 'Figuring the nature of the times deceased,' " 28–29.

our attention to the narrativity of historical writing, White pulled back from the extremes into which the resulting insights had led many of the French post-structuralists. Thus he did not join those who sought to undermine the narrative form as itself ideological and repressive, and he insisted again and again that histories differ from fictions in a culturally significant way.[8] Although a narrative history does not provide a scientific account of events, it still affords the scope for truth as opposed to ideology.

At the same time, White sought to avoid the other extreme, the quasi-structuralist determinism that his way of relying on the rhetorical tropes seemed to suggest. "Far from implying linguistic determinism," his conception "seeks to provide the knowledge necessary for a free choice among different strategies of figuration." The particular culture affords a finite range of possibilities—culturally specific conventions governing the construction of *any* narrative—but within that culturally specific range, choice of plot structure is relatively free.[9] As White put it in 1986, "narrative accounts of real historical events . . . admit of as many equally plausible versions in their representations as there are plot structures available in a given culture for endowing stories, whether fictional or real, with meanings."[10]

But this aspect of White's thinking betrayed a tension that Kellner, one of his ablest allies, astutely analyzed. Because the desired openness entailed the danger of excess, White continued to accent some version of the initial structural tropology that had informed *Metahistory*. The possibilities for narrative construction, and thus for historical understanding or meaning, were radically open in one sense, but they were limited and structured by a "bedrock of order," the prior, implicitly stable modes of emplotment available in the particular culture.[11]

Moreover, White's argument grew slippery when he accented the possible truth value of historical texts, and his way of drawing the distinction between historical and literary narratives proved elusive at best. Thus, for example, his insistence that historical narrative tests "the capacity of the culture's fictions to endow real events with the kinds of meaning that literature displays to consciousness through its fashioning of patterns of 'imaginary' events."[12] Rather than specify the source and nature of the truth value of history, White turned in

---

8. Hayden V. White, *The Content of the Form: Narrative Discourse and Historical Representation* (Baltimore: Johns Hopkins University Press, 1987), 26–57 (article originally published 1984); see esp. pp. 34–40, 44–45. Even during the 1970s, as deconstruction gathered force, White questioned the tendency to take its insights to the extreme of "the absurdist moment." See White, *Tropics*, 261–282; but see also Dominick LaCapra's critique in his *Rethinking Intellectual History: Texts, Contexts, Language* (Ithaca: Cornell University Press, 1983), 72–83.

9. White, " 'Figuring the nature of the times deceased,' " 34; see also p. 27.

10. Hayden V. White, "Historical Pluralism," *Critical Inquiry* 12, no. 3 (Spring 1986): 489.

11. Hans Kellner, "A Bedrock of Order: Hayden White's Linguistic Humanism," *History and Theory* 19, no. 4 (Beiheft 19: *"Metahistory": Six Critiques*, 1980): 1–29.

12. White, *Content of the Form*, 45. See his use of factual and "factological" in " 'Figuring the nature of the times deceased,' " 35, for a comparable example.

the other direction to insist that literature, too, teaches us about reality. After noting that the criteria of realism vary from one culture to another, he asked, "Anyway, does anyone seriously believe that myth and literary fiction do *not* refer to the real world, tell truths about it, and provide useful knowledge of it?"[13] Again and again, what he found most worthy of emphasis was the fact that historical and literary texts rely on the same strategies for providing the structure, coherence, and meaning necessary to produce what we accept as an image of "reality."[14] Historical narratives were realistic and produced the *effects* of truth.

To be sure, White insisted that it was still proper to assess historical discourse in terms of the truth value of its factual statements, taken individually. Otherwise, history could not justify its claim to represent and explain "specifically real events." This suggested that historians operate within certain constraints; they cannot make up documents, for example. But it is one thing to apprehend some set of events; it is something altogether different to emplot them, to make up a coherent narrative out of them. And for White, truth is no longer at issue once we move from the archive and the chronicle into the narrative telling. So even though the mode of narrative emplotment affects the very content of the historical account, there is no scope for assessing modes of emplotment and narration in terms of the truth/fiction dichotomy. The scope for assessing the truth value of historical accounts is confined to the lower, prenarrative level. And, again, White's own priority was to show not how truth becomes possible but "how historical discourse produces its characteristic knowledge-effects."[15]

In the last analysis, *all* stories for White are fictions and can be true only in a metaphorical sense. Thus his insistence that "stories are not true or false, but rather more or less intelligible, coherent, consistent, persuasive, and so on. And this is true of historical, no less than fictional stories."[16] Conversely, arguments about the meaning of events are as much about the plot structure as the events themselves, so neither can they be true or false. Rather, they constitute second-order fictions.

So even though White, in eschewing the extremes, still posited something distinctive about historical writing, he could seem to be giving away much of the store. Yet the essentials of his argument about emplotment and narrative were unassailable. The question was whether, in light of a postmetaphysical emphasis on construction as opposed to correspondence, White's account of

13. White, " 'Figuring the nature of the times deceased,' " 39. See also White, *Content of the Form*, 44.

14. White, *Tropics*, 121–122; White, "Historical Pluralism," 492.

15. White, *Content of the Form*, 45–46; White, " 'Figuring the nature of the times deceased,' " 26, 39.

16. White, "Historical Pluralism," 492. See also White, " 'Figuring the nature of the times deceased,' " 27.

what happens when historians emplot in narrative did justice to the scope for recasting the distinction between fiction and truth. As White took care to note, Paul Ricoeur's *Time and Narrative* defended the adequacy of narrative by positing "nothing less than a metaphysics of narrativity," showing that the past is actually structured like narrative.[17] But several earlier thinkers—most notably Croce, Heidegger, and Gadamer—had attempted a more radical recasting of the relationship between human inquiry and the happening of the particular world in history. In their different ways, each concluded that it is only when we reach the level of—in White's terms—narrative emplotment that truth begins to happen.

White almost recalled Croce in asking if "the question of narrative in any discussion of historical theory is always finally about the function of imagination in the production of a specifically historical truth."[18] In this passage and elsewhere he seemed to suggest as much, but his argument generally severed imagination from the sphere of what can be true or false. It was not clear how, for White, the production of truth relates to imagination, creativity, and the practical concerns that inform the choice of any particular strategy of emplotment.

Like White, Kellner insisted that he emphasized narrativity and emplotment not to undermine historiography but to deepen its cultural impact. Practicing historians, in contrast to their literary colleagues, were quick to avoid confrontation with language, to view rhetoric as merely ornamental, and to take narrative representation as unproblematic. In jettisoning the confining legacy of nineteenth-century realism, they would be free to construct more creative, and resonant, historical accounts.[19] And understanding why they never get the story straight would make historians more cognizant of the cultural stakes when they choose their particular mode of narration and construction from among those available in the culture. The result, as Kellner saw it, would be a more open and fruitfully pluralistic historical culture.[20]

Kellner deconstructed historians from Jules Michelet to Fernand Braudel in an effort to promote this crooked self-understanding, but, like White, he also placed some premium on quasi-structuralist classification. We find order and experience some sense of mastery in showing how any historical narrative follows an identifiable rhetorical program, beneath authorial intention. Kellner's celebrated reading of Braudel's *The Mediterranean* as a Menippean satire is

17. White, *Content of the Form*, 49–54. The quoted phrase appears on p. 49. David Carr similarly argues that narrative is appropriate to the structure of historical reality in *Time, Narrative, and History* (Bloomington: Indiana University Press, 1986).

18. White, *Content of the Form*, 57.

19. Hans Kellner, *Language and Historical Representation: Getting the Story Crooked* (Madison: University of Wisconsin Press, 1989), x–xi, 7, 24–25, 122–123.

20. See ibid., 291–292, 315–316, 319, 323, on the role of will. Kellner explicitly follows White in much of this discussion.

the most notable example.[21] As applied on an ad hoc basis to historical texts, such historiographical criticism tended toward the "weak textualism" that Rorty found one, somewhat ambiguous response to the eclipse of foundationalist philosophy. Like the methodological form of deconstruction that became prominent in American literary criticism, such criticism was at once sophisticated and playful. But it pulled back from the quest for a fully postmetaphysical alternative.

Kellner was one of a number of historians and theorists who, in the wake of White, accented rhetoric and narrative emplotment and deflated the loosely positivist ideal of getting the story straight. Most, like White and Kellner, claimed to foster reflexivity and creativity among historians.[22] And many did so partly by uncovering the rhetorical strategies that structured historical writing in the past; nineteenth-century French historians drew particular attention.[23] At the same time, some of these narrativists pulled back from what seemed an unnecessary extravagance in White to seek a more moderate recasting of historiography. But their accents differed considerably.

Linda Orr stressed the irony that results when, with "the revenge of literature," the long-suppressed fear of language comes to the historiographical surface. Taking it for granted that historians seek some Rankean "as it actually happened," she assumed that the inevitable linguistic slippage means failure; we never grasp it, never get it right, never arrive—but precisely thus the history continues.[24] However, her characterizations betray the shadow of a stable object and finished truth that we have encountered especially among those influenced by the French tradition. As her reference to the continuing history suggests, what she characterizes may not be failure but adequacy in an ever-provisional world.

Lionel Gossman implied that a more radical reconsideration was necessary when, after examining the relationship between fiction and history in

21. Kellner's "Disorderly Conduct: Braudel's Mediterranean Satire" was first published in 1979, then revised for inclusion in *Language and Historical Representation,* 153–187. On p. 184, Kellner found Braudel's book to be "a continuous satire on the means available to historical comprehension" and as such, comparable to modernist literature. See also p. 176. In addition, see the essays on Guizot, Michelet, and Goethe and Spengler in the same volume. Kellner argues on pp. 323 and 333 that such deconstructive readings promote a more open historical culture.

22. For example, Robert Berkhofer found positive implications in the historiographical reflexivity that followed from the new literary theory. By breaking down the distinction between construction and representation, that theory forced historians at last to cease denying the personal element in their offerings and thus opened the way to a richer historical culture. See Robert F. Berkhofer, Jr., "The Challenge of Poetics to (Normal) Historical Practice," *Poetics Today* 9, no. 2 (1988), esp. pp. 444–446, 449–450.

23. Among the notable examples are Lionel Gossman, *Between History and Literature* (Cambridge: Harvard University Press, 1990); and Stephen Bann, *The Clothing of Clio: A Study of the Representation of History in Nineteenth-Century Britain and France* (Cambridge: Cambridge University Press, 1984).

24. Linda Orr, "The Revenge of Literature: A History of History," *New Literary History* 18, no. 1 (Autumn 1986): 1–3, 10, 13, 18.

nineteenth-century France, he called for a new pragmatics of historical truth, transcending the opposition between naive realism and absolute relativism.[25] In a similar way, F. R. Ankersmit suggested that White, though his contribution had been essential, had left much undone. Thanks to White, the philosophy of history had at last plugged into the wider linguistic turn in the culture, but the strong influence of literary theory in White's work kept essential questions about the distinctiveness of historical writing in the background. For Ankersmit, the question was how, in light of White, we are to conceive histor- ical rationality and where we are to find it. Textualism did not exhaust the issue because something that could still be called historical reality continued to have priority over the text, constraining the historian.[26]

So whereas the narrativists raised essential questions about language and the element of creativity in historical writing, they did not agree on the answers. And though much of their argument offered a healthy challenge to historio- graphical assumptions seriously in need of reexamination, some of their accents seemed extravagant and provoked confusion or overreaction. While stressing that White's argument was, from the start, considerably more subtle than many of his critics grasped, Peter Novick noted that White had proven a perfect focal point for the restiveness of those reluctant to abandon the "noble dream" of selfless, objective history and finished truth.[27]

Even as he insisted provocatively on "getting the story crooked," Kellner sought to reassure his readers that

> to challenge the ideology of truth is not to champion lies, falsify documents, or suppress information; it is to assert the constructed nature of the human world, to follow Vico in asserting that any meaning that can be gotten from the world is a meaning for some human purpose, and gotten with human tools. Historians do not "find" the truths of past events; they create events from a seamless flow, and invent meanings that produce patterns within that flow.[28]

Although some of his argument had become common currency by the late 1980s, Kellner's emphases were bound to provoke doubts unless attention was paid to the other side of the coin. Why *not* lie and falsify documents, especially if all our purposes are ultimately "political" anyway? Kellner wanted us to rec- ognize that any historical representation is an allegorical creation for a human purpose, but why do *some* of our purposes dictate that we do something other

---

25. Gossman, *Between History and Literature*; see esp. the concluding essay, "The Rationality of History," 285–324. See also R. B. Kershner, "Dances with Historians," *Georgia Review* 45, no. 3 (Fall 1991): 589, for a strong endorsement of Gossman's effort.

26. F. R. Ankersmit, *History and Tropology: The Rise and Fall of Metaphor* (Berkeley, Los Angeles, and London: University of California Press, 1994), 6–18.

27. Peter Novick, *That Noble Dream: The "Objectivity Question" and the American Histori- cal Profession* (Cambridge: Cambridge University Press, 1988), 596–603, esp. p. 599.

28. Kellner, *Language and Historical Representation*, 24.

than falsify documents to serve some worthy moral or political purpose? Why might a need to learn inform our inquiries into the past, and what happens when it does so? Kellner's accent on crookedness betrayed the image of straightness, taken as an impossible ideal. What scope is there for a postmetaphysical conception of truth that eludes that dichotomy altogether?

Fundamental though it was, the narrativist contribution remained incomplete, so it proved a shaky bridge between the wider cultural discussion and practicing historians. The question was how the narrativists' insights could be embedded in a constructive postmetaphysical framework that made new sense of the defining imperatives of historiography.

White and Kellner had been trained as historians, but to other historians they could seem marginal figures who, having been sucked into the abyss of "theory," found themselves more comfortable in the company of literary intellectuals and Continental philosophers than "working historians."[29] Scott, in contrast, was already a distinguished practicing historian when, during the 1980s, she began invoking Foucault and Derrida and arguing for a politically conscious presentism in historiography. In addressing historiographical issues, she articulated the aims of historians working in relatively new fields like women's or ethnic history, who tended to embrace political presentism and perspectivism without apology.[30] Like the narrativists, she claimed to invite a more open and resonant historiography.

By embracing wider humanistic theory, Scott was able to explain with particular force the sense in which history is contemporary, interested, competitive, and "political" in the broadest sense. Even the process through which some subjects come to be studied at the expense of others is politically contested. And Scott argued convincingly that the long-standing assumption of a single master narrative had tended to exclude certain categories of historical subjects—and even certain modes of historical inquiry. Thus she called for a "democratic history [that] would accept the facts that there will always be a plurality of stories, that telling them involves contests about power and knowledge, and that the historian's mastery is necessarily partial."[31]

More specifically, Scott linked her own line of historical inquiry to a particular present political concern—feminism—and to the deconstructive strand of French poststructuralism.

---

29. Gordon Wood spoke for many practicing historians when, in his review essay on Schama's *Dead Certainties*, he referred to "Hayden White, who carps at the margins of the discipline and preaches skepticism and subversion to the halfway converted but writes no history." See Wood, "Novel History," 12.

30. See Novick, *That Noble Dream*, 593–602, esp. p. 598, on the tendency of many "new historians" casually to abandon the objectivity ideal.

31. Joan Wallach Scott, "History in Crisis? The Others' Side of the Story," *American Historical Review* 94, no. 3 (June 1989): 691. See also pp. 681, 692, as well as Joan Wallach Scott, *Gender and the Politics of History* (New York: Columbia University Press, 1988), 3–5.

A more radical feminist politics . . . seems to me to require a more radical epistemology. Precisely because it addresses questions of epistemology, relativizes
the status of all knowledge, links knowledge and power, and theorizes these in
terms of the operations of difference, I think post-structuralism (or at least some
of the approaches generally associated with Michel Foucault and Jacques Derrida) can offer feminism a powerful analytic perspective.[32]

Indeed, Scott's forceful case for the relevance of deconstruction in her introduction to *Gender and the Politics of History* made the book something of a
watershed in the self-understanding of practicing historians. To grasp how
much has come to be constructed historically is but a first step. We then recognize that what, most fundamentally, get constructed are meanings. And
deconstruction helps us understand *how* meanings get constructed—and thus
how historiography as deconstruction might proceed.[33]
    Scott looked to deconstruction as she developed her influential argument
for the import of gender as a historical subject and category of analysis. Rather
than reflecting or implementing "fixed and natural differences between men
and women," Scott maintained, "gender is the knowledge that establishes
meanings for bodily differences. These meanings vary across cultures, social
groups, and time since nothing about the body, including women's reproduc-
tive organs, determines univocally how social divisions will be shaped." What
was necessary, then, was not simply another step in the expansion of social
history: "The story is no longer about the things that have happened to women
and men and how they have reacted to them; instead it is about how the subjective and collective meanings of women and men as categories of identity
have been constructed."[34]
    Deconstruction affords an understanding of the broadly political process—
involving differentiation and opposition, negation and exclusion—through
which such meanings emerge and change. The view that becomes dominant
always entails a positive term defined through its difference from, or opposition
to, a term taken as antithetical. Although we come to understand our world
through unitary concepts or fixed oppositions, they are always unstable, provisional, because the repressed negative is never fully integrated or mastered but
continues in tension with the positive. So the process remains open, despite the
tendency of the dominant view to try to close debate by hiding its own historical contingency and constructedness. The binary opposition at issue in gendering has informed not only our way of sorting out the roles of women and men

32. Scott, *Gender*, 4. See also p. 3, on her own "avowedly political" motive, and pp. 7–8, on
the historian's active role in the production of knowledge.
    33. In addition to *Gender*, 1–11, Scott's remarkable introduction to the volume, see Joan W.
Scott, "Writing History," in *Behind the Lines: Gender and the Two World Wars*, ed. Margaret Ran-
dolph Higonnet et al. (New Haven: Yale University Press, 1987), 21–30, esp. pp. 26, 29–30.
    34. Scott, *Gender*, 2, 6. See also the unsigned introduction to *Behind the Lines*, ed. Higonnet et
al., esp. pp. 3–4, for a cogent argument for gender as a historical subject.

but also far wider reaches of our cultural practice, as we have come, for example, to understand public and private, or political and social, as we have.[35]

Thus, for Scott, historical inquiry informed by deconstruction can be especially effective politically, opening the way to change. By analyzing "in context the way any binary opposition operates, reversing and displacing its hierarchical construction, rather than accepting it as real or self-evident," deconstruction enables us to see beyond the array of societal practices that depend on our way of casting the male-female difference.[36] At the same time, deconstruction entailed the reflexivity and risk necessary for openness. Thus the mode of practice that Scott envisioned developing from deconstruction: "politics that are not only critical of existing social hierarchies but able to point out the premises of their operations; politics that are self-consciously critical of their own justifications and exclusions, and so refuse an absolutizing or totalizing stance."[37]

Although her way of drawing out the historiographical potential of deconstruction was superb, and though much of her point about politics was unassailable, Scott's emphases seemed to traditionalists to invite excess by reducing history to a mere *instrument* of political struggles, reflecting a priori political positions. Was a politically inspired historical inquiry into gender to be open to an array of possible answers, so that the inquirers might genuinely learn from their inquiries—and perhaps adjust their present political positions as a result? Or do such inquirers simply find ammunition for their effort to alter present ways of gendering? Do we need a *true* history of gender, or, as thinkers from Foucault to Kellner seemed to suggest, do appeals to truth and reality simply serve the authoritarian hegemony of the winners, the powerful? The questions are obvious; the answers are not.

Moreover, Scott offered several imperatives at once, and it was not clear how they cohered around the political presentism at issue here. Her emphasis on "the pluralization of the subject of history" sometimes seemed to suggest that we settle for parallel group stories, that any emphasis on the unity of a master narrative was authoritarian and elitist. Yet in playing up the broadly political contest at work in historiography, she was implicitly recognizing that even as the subject of history expands and splinters, there is still a kind of unity, totality, or master narrative; it is simply the endlessly provisional outcome of our debates over what to include. In addition, some of Scott's accents suggested an a priori privilege to "Otherness" that defies *both* process to the present *and* open contest. Scott, then, left an array of questions as she offered her stimulating contribution; I return to those questions below.

35. Scott, *Gender*, 4–7.
36. Ibid., 40–41. See also pp. 10–11.
37. Even as she made her own political and reconstructive aims explicit, Scott recognized that diverse tendencies were at work in deconstruction, which thus did not need to be taken whole: "It may be that some deconstructive critics pursue an endless exposure of contradiction and are thereby unable to endorse or comfortably advocate a political program of their own. But there are also evident examples of a politics empowered by this approach." See ibid., 9. See also pp. 7, 11; and Scott, "History in Crisis?" 691, on provisionality and reflexivity.

Like Scott and the narrativists, Thomas embraced an explicit presentism as he sought to draw out reconstructive possibilities from the new historicism that emerged in literary studies in the United States during the 1980s. The movement's most prominent representative was Stephen Greenblatt, who referred to "the new historicism" almost in passing to characterize a new determination to contextualize literary artifacts after the various loosely structuralist ways of treating them formalistically, as self-contained systems of relations. The point, however, was not simply to return to the old way of explaining works of literature in terms of some prior, stable sociocultural bedrock but to interject them into a field of reciprocal relations with other historically specific cultural practices.[38]

New historicists like Greenblatt were not presentists, but Thomas thought it possible to adapt their insights for presentist purposes. He took it for granted that in our postmetaphysical era there can be no transcendence or utopian telos to show us the way beyond our historically specific present. But we are not merely stuck, precisely because our present is a hinge between past and future, "a moment of historical *translation*, not one of mere transition within an inevitable historical process."[39] By means of exchange with texts from the past, we gain perspective on our own points of view and a sense of possibility that provokes us to grope for alternatives to the present.

What Thomas found in the new historicism was a way of restoring the difference, the strangeness, the uncanniness of the past moment, as disembodied from some apparently inevitable chain leading to us. The new historicists sought access not simply to the past moment for its own sake but to the *excluded* past moment; they afforded privilege to what did not become actual, to what stood in tension with what had come to seem the dominant processes. But, for Thomas, their insights made possible a deeper, more challenging way of understanding precisely the processes leading to us—as radically contingent and open-ended. Reconnection with what had been excluded or marginalized would enable historical inquiry to serve present action with greater bite. Because the point was to loosen the present configuration, this way of focusing on process to the present would entail anything but some Whiggish justification of the present outcome.

At the same time, Thomas credited the new historicism for working to overcome the separation between literary and historical studies. Although this promised to revitalize both, he envisioned especially a new culture of history taking advantage of literature as a form of historical evidence. Literary evidence could be particularly revealing, especially once deconstruction had

38. The new historicism was associated especially with the journal *Representations*, launched in 1982. See Stephen J. Greenblatt, *Learning to Curse: Essays in Early Modern Culture* (New York: Routledge, 1990), 146, 162–163, on how "the new historicism" came to be used. Greenblatt admitted that the term was misleading and advocated "cultural poetics" instead.

39. Brook Thomas, *The New Historicism and Other Old-Fashioned Topics* (Princeton: Princeton University Press, 1991), 211; emphasis in original.

taught us to question it in a more unsettling way. As the new historicism showed that texts are not self-contained but bound up with societal practices, we understand that the strains in the text may illuminate societal tensions, contradictions, and suspended possibilities. Thomas noted Greenblatt's interest in theater, which seemed to have special value as historical evidence because of its broad license to present potentially subversive themes that might otherwise have remained hidden. But literature in general embodies what was held back and offers scope for dialogue with our own provisionally lost possibilities. As historical evidence, then, literature no longer needed to be understood in the familiar way, as a mere reflection of society, but could release transformative potential and serve present action.[40]

Thomas's way of confronting the history-literature-action relationship was moderate and measured. Indeed, he addressed explicitly the reasons for nervousness about the narrativist way of bringing history together with literature and about Scott's more freewheeling political emphasis. In the accents of some of White's followers, he found "the risk of resubordinating history to literature," which would compromise the reconstructive uses he had in mind. So as he proposed a new way of bringing history and literature together, Thomas also found it essential to reaffirm the distinction between them, based on their different cultural functions.[41]

Thomas's effort to avoid the excesses he found at work in the wider discussion led him to accents that recall Croce and Gadamer. Exactly like Croce, he sought to strike a balance by emphasizing that though our sense of the present as history does not mean we can shape the future at will, historical understanding maximizes our chances to act effectively: "the *probability* of overcoming particular historical forces that unnecessarily limit us is increased if we are aware of them." Moreover, Thomas linked the presentist desire for effectiveness to a certain mode of inquiry: "So long as our situation in the world has been partially determined by the past, the most empowering studies will be the ones that come as close as possible to telling us how it really was or perhaps more importantly why it was the way it was." Thus, "it is in our interest to maintain disinterested inquiries into the past."[42] Croce and Gadamer made the same crucial point about openness to learning, though each framed it more radically, without relying on the long-standing imperative of disinterestedness.

Thomas took care to emphasize that a radical sense of the historicity of the

40. Ibid., 153, 166, 171. Thomas's argument for the particular value of literature as historical evidence recalls a major theme in the work of Dominick LaCapra over the years. See, for example, his chapter on Mikhail Bakhtin in *Rethinking Intellectual History*, chap. 9, esp. pp. 313–314.

41. Ibid., 155–156, 206.

42. Ibid., 18 (emphasis in original), 76, 77. From a Crocean perspective, of course, the notion of "telling us how it really was" comes carelessly close to assuming the historical "thing-in-itself" that Thomas presumably wanted to avoid.

present need not confirm any particular radical or leftist agenda. We may question everything, but we cannot know in advance what we will find. The very conditions of our political judgments are open to such questioning—and are at risk.[43]

Thomas's way of framing the case for presentism was particularly valuable partly because it was itself historically informed. Although he was interested especially in American pragmatism, he at least considered the impasses of the first historicism in Europe. Thus he could find the potential he did in the new historicism, and thus he was able to place deconstruction in useful historical perspective. Deconstruction was not, as so many assumed, simply an ahistorical formalism or an assault on historical-mindedness; it was rather a response to a historicized world—a world still wrestling with the problems of the first historicism.[44] And thus Thomas was able to draw out the uses of deconstruction for presentist, reconstructive historical inquiry.

Still, tendencies now familiar to us compromised the force of Thomas's case for presentism. Despite his care to avoid aestheticist blurring, he left uncertainty about the respective cultural contributions of literature and history as his focus shifted from literature as historical evidence to the role of literature at any present moment. Some of his accents suggested a privileged present role for literature vis-à-vis the historical approach that he otherwise seemed to emphasize. And he sometimes blurred the distinction, which elsewhere he understood his argument to require, between literature, with its capacity for inventiveness and play, and history, with its sober concern for truth, understood as preparing the way for effective action. Those trained in literature are especially equipped to use literature as historical evidence in the way Thomas envisioned. But they do so as historians, seeking a true account. They are attentive to play and what it can teach us, but they themselves are not playing, because they understand that what they need is truth, or history, as opposed to fiction, or literature.

Moreover, Thomas was subject to the widespread tendency to view any accent on process or continuity in strong, still-metaphysical terms. Thus he could not do justice to the array of ways of conceiving the past-process relationship. Admirable though it was, his effort to assess contemporary priorities in light of the outcome of the first historicism proved a source of limitation. He associated that earlier historicism with strong justification and the image of "progressive emergence," but though this Whiggish tendency lurked in the nineteenth-century embrace of history, it was not the dominant thrust in Ranke, let alone Dilthey.[45] Croce and Gadamer explicitly eschewed any such tendency

43. Ibid., 18. See also p. 162.
44. Ibid., 16, 31–32, 35.
45. See, for example, ibid., 95. On p. 33, Thomas cites the point, by now associated especially with Walter Benjamin, that history is always written by the victors.

as each reacted against nineteenth-century historicism to probe more deeply the terms of a merely historical world.

Thomas considered Gadamer, but he did not do justice to Gadamer's way of dealing with the tensions in the first historicism, and thus he misrepresented Gadamerian fusion of horizons. Although what Gadamer envisioned was surely a renewal of tradition, it was not a form of "mimesis," seeking to re-present a lost presence, to reproduce the thing-in-itself. Indeed, Gadamer specified precisely what Thomas found most important about our way of conceiving the world as historical; rather than re-presenting some "lost originary moment," we are endlessly bringing something new into being.[46]

Although much of Thomas's argument for the reconstructive uses of historical questioning was superb, his dualistic reading of the alternatives ultimately precluded the scope for the moderate postmetaphysical orientation he seemed to envision. He did not grasp the scope for a weak, postmetaphysical kind of continuity or for a weak, provisional "totalization" that does not preclude openness and contingency. Thus he conflated continuity with strong telos and process with inevitability. The resulting accents—the premium on "disrupting the chain of temporal continuity," for example—gave Thomas's argument an element of extravagance that blurred the cultural possibilities and compromised his reconstructive aims.[47]

Finally, in assessing the impulses at work in the new historicism, Thomas did not quite grasp the scope for the alternative to presentism that we have begun to encounter in other thinkers—as an extreme, nonreconstructive response to the uncanny new experience of nothing but history. To be sure, Thomas was well aware that new historicists like Greenblatt, as they fastened on the excluded past moment, were not interested in the presentist effort to create a new future.[48] But what were they doing instead? What other reason was there for affording privilege to that excluded moment?

The Uncanny Past

To place the offerings of the presentists in perspective, we must probe the impulse that led some in the opposite direction, to a renewed emphasis on the past "for its own sake," apart from its connection with us through some process. That impulse responded partly to the strong, Whiggish conceptions of process that still lurked in the culture, but it also responded—more interestingly—even to the weak, postmetaphysical emphasis on process to a present utterly lacking in metaphysical justification.

In a world of nothing but history, we seem to have reason to eschew any

46. See especially ibid., 209–210, for Thomas's treatment of Gadamer.
47. Ibid., 72, 179, 208–209, 211. On p. 203, Thomas views any notion of temporal continuity as conservative. Even the fact of change confirms a status quo that takes change as normal, inevitable.
48. Ibid., 5–6, 37.

emphasis on what fits into some dominant process and to focus instead on what did *not* become actual, what did *not* fit into what are agreed to be the dominant processes leading to us. As we come to feel that our present is but the resultant of such contingent processes, we find something precious about what lies "outside history" and place a premium on gaining access to it.[49] So we emphasize what was left along the way, the "other" that any focus on dominant process tended to ignore or exclude.

As noted above, Thomas argued convincingly that attention to that excluded other may be preliminary, serving the wider aim of presentist reconstruction by deepening what we can learn from historical inquiry. The other stands in tension with the dominant process, threatening to disrupt it. But focus on the excluded other may serve purposes that stand opposed to any such concern with presentist reconstruction. In such a nonreconstructive mode, we do not make the past moment more familiar by connecting it with us across historical distance; we do not make those in the past part of our narrative. We do not even seek dialogue with them, for the aim of dialogue is still to overcome difference for our present purposes. Rather, we leave the past moment disembedded, outside, and revel in its difference. We afford privilege to what did not become actual, to the other in all its strangeness. This is to reverse the direction of presentists like White, Kellner, Scott, and even Thomas.

Several ways of handling historical material in this mode have opened up. We may simply display the uncanniness that surrounds the past moment or excluded other when disembedded, left to itself. Or we may take disembedded past artifacts as materials for aesthetic construction, for a good story, so that, yet again, history converges with literature. The combination is evident in the "microhistories" that historians like Carlo Ginzburg, Emmanuel Le Roy Ladurie, and Natalie Davis began offering in the early 1970s and that came to enjoy a considerable vogue by the 1980s, when they seemed characteristically postmodern. Microhistory overlapped in significant ways with Greenblatt's new historicism. But in a looser form the same impulses could be discerned in much innovative historiography.

Microhistory developed from within the *Annales* paradigm, but whereas much of the *Annales* accented quantification and the "longue durée," the microhistorians fastened on the individual case, the concrete, the local, the immediate sequence of life as lived, apart from long-term trends or abstractions, apart from any privilege to what could be quantified.[50] This was to focus on ordinary

49. It is striking, for example, that Eavan Boland grouped her poems on the experience of women under the rubric "outside history." Only as history inflates could the world as historical become the foil in this way. See her *Outside History: Selected Poems, 1980–1990* (New York: W. W. Norton, 1990).

50. For a good introduction, see Edward Muir, "Introduction: Observing Trifles," in *Microhistory and the Lost Peoples of Europe*, ed. Edward Muir and Guido Ruggiero (Baltimore: Johns Hopkins University Press, 1991), vii–xxviii. This is a collection of articles from the Italian journal *Quaderni storici*, which was a fruitful and influential locus of the new microhistory.

people as shapers of their own lives quite apart from, even in tension with, what had seemed the mainstream development.

Often, in fact, microhistory entailed a close narrative account of apparently isolated, anecdotal, trivial, or bizarre events. Ginzburg's *The Cheese and the Worms*, one of the best-known examples of the genre, fastened on a sixteenth-century Italian miller to reconstruct a pantheistic peasant cosmology woven around an earthy material culture. That cosmology turned out to have survived in uncanny difference within official Christian culture—yet it was precluded, and virtually forgotten, by subsequent historians.[51]

In focusing on what had seemed marginal, the microhistories dramatically brought home difference. Conversely, it was a premium on difference that led the microhistorians to seek out what seemed most opaque and uncanny, most opposed to the dominant processes that had led to us. Some stressed explicitly that in seeking to *dis*connect the past moment from any process to the present, they were seeking a mode of historical inquiry that does *not* serve some present concern, which would entail getting caught in contemporary political squabbles. Focusing on Ginzburg's effort within the ideologically charged Italian academic world, Edward Muir made the point nicely: "To [Ginzburg] the proper goal of the historian is not to explore the historical implications of a contemporary theory or problem, but to write about things that are totally forgotten and completely irrelevant to the present, to produce a history that is 'really dead.' "[52]

But to what end? Raking through the debris of the past sometimes turned up material for a good story, as with Davis's *The Return of Martin Guerre*, which became the basis for a popular film. Such stories worked like fictions, though the element of distance and uncanniness gave them a particular resonance. But even the best expressions of the microhistorical imperative did not make clear why it had become so important to focus on those hitherto lost to history, why there was something privileged about defying presentism and process.

Justifications for microhistory often betrayed the now-familiar tendency to argue against various straw persons. In one of the best discussions of the genre, Muir recognized that questions about selectivity and concerns about triviality intrude as the historical scale goes "micro." But he went on to observe that the ablest microhistorians "have been struggling to eliminate the distortions produced by the giantification of the historical scale, which has crushed all individuals to insignificance under the weight of vast impersonal structures and forces."[53]

51. Carlo Ginzburg, *The Cheese and the Worms: The Cosmos of a Sixteenth-Century Miller*, trans. John Tedeschi and Anne Tedeschi (New York: Penguin, 1982). See also Carlo Ginzburg, *Clues, Myths, and the Historical Method*, trans. John Tedeschi and Anne Tedeschi (Baltimore: Johns Hopkins University Press, 1989).
52. Muir, "Introduction," xii.
53. Ibid., xx–xxi.

Although Whiggish tendencies remain part of the mix, we surely need not conceive the historiographical alternatives in such terms as these. As we have noted, historians have sought to get at things in their concreteness and individuality at least since the nineteenth-century reaction against Hegel. To be sure, some strands of the *Annales* school, when asking certain kinds of questions, played up impersonal structures, but surely no one advocates crushing "all individuals to insignificance under the weight of vast impersonal structures and forces." Who is the target of such charges? Where is such giantification to be found?

This tendency to attack straw persons made it difficult to grasp the postmetaphysical point of the microhistorical impulse. The question concerns the cultural uses of the genre once the earlier ways of playing down individuality, from Hegelianism to cliometric quantification, are no longer at issue. What is the point of disembedding individual lives and episodes and leaving them opaque—in defiance *even* of weak process to the present, embedded in weak totality? Conversely, what did the success of the microhistorical approach say about the scope for an orientation admitting a weak totality and focusing on weak processes to the present?

The turn to a new historicism in literary studies entailed a comparable emphasis on the disembedded past moment.[54] In one sense, the new historicism was a predictable reaction against formalism, including not only structuralism but also poststructuralist deconstruction, insofar as it, too, tended to become simply another critical method. As noted briefly above, new historicists argued that the work of art is a historically specific artifact, not a self-contained system of oppositions and relations. But because the legacy of deconstruction remained, it was not possible simply to return to an older contextualism, explaining the literary artifact in terms of some prior, deeper, stable context. The relationship between artifact and context was one of dynamic interplay that eludes our attempt to fix either of them. In accenting the historicity of literary artifacts, moreover, the new historicists were not embracing conventional historiographical approaches but opposing them. However, they sometimes blurred still-metaphysical and postmetaphysical targets as they did so, and thus it was hard to specify their place within the universe of new responses to the merely historical world.

Greenblatt reacted explicitly against what he termed the "relentlessly celebratory character" of much historical narrative.[55] Such a celebratory mode had been especially prominent in the literary and art historical disciplines, which long had concentrated on the canonical sequence of great masterpieces. But

---

54. It was symptomatic that both currents embraced the insights of Bakhtin, who enjoyed a particular vogue during the 1980s. A prominent American advocate of the microhistorical approach, Guido Ruggiero, starts with Bakhtin in his recent *Binding Passions: Tales of Magic, Marriage, and Power at the End of the Renaissance* (New York: Oxford University Press), 1993.
55. Greenblatt, *Learning to Curse*, 168–170.

new historicist priorities suggested that *any* historical narrative of dominant
processes is inherently justifying and celebratory. In their opposition to celebration, the new historicists were, up to a point, usefully resisting a still-
metaphysical tendency. But much like the microhistorians, they tended to tilt
with shadows because they did not do justice to the scope for endless Gadamerian dialogue, for knowledge that is taken to be no more than provisional. Still,
again as with microhistory, something more novel and interesting was at work
in the eruption of the new historicism, even if its practitioners sometimes
blurred the point. What happens when there is no longer some metaphysically
grounded metanarrative to link us securely to our predecessors, whom we can
no longer understand as not-yet-Christian, for example, or as "less developed"?
The new historicists sought to explore the sense in which the difference
becomes uncanny.

More generally, the new historicists sensed that the categories that had
enabled us to posit coherent past moments begin to shatter as the culture
places ever more weight on the historical. Reviewing the evolution of his
own work, Greenblatt confessed that he had grown "increasingly uneasy with
the monolithic unities" that his work on the Renaissance had posited. He had
partaken of the conventional approach to the historical world, which had
taken for granted a measure of unity, stability, and integration. But it now
seemed that the effort to posit such unities "repeatedly fails for one reason:
there is no escape from contingency." So in embracing the new historicism,
Greenblatt was seeking to overcome the temptation "to conceal cracks, conflict, and disarray" by organizing his work around some power network, hidden structure, or master discourse.[56] This required pulling back from *any*
totalizing or integrating vision, even of the relatively local sort at issue when
we think not in terms of some coherent process but simply of some coherent
past moment.

So, for Greenblatt, the objective could not be simply a reversal, condemning what had been celebrated—not even a reversal in the name of the
oppressed. Nor was it enough simply to let this deeper sense of the contingency of the past moment serve the more radical and fruitful presentism that
Thomas envisioned. Rather, the new historicists sought to disembed the artifact from any process to the present *and* from any present unifying category.
Thus we might experience the naked contingency of things, real difference
across time, the uncanniness of the artifact—and of the whole past moment
with which it is problematically bound up. In this mode the past elicits not the
veneration we once felt for the succession of masterpieces, but "wonder." "By

56. Stephen Greenblatt, *Shakespearean Negotiations: The Circulation of Social Energy in
Renaissance England* (Berkeley, Los Angeles, and London: University of California Press, 1988),
2–3.

wonder," said Greenblatt, "I mean the power of the object displayed to stop the viewer in his tracks, to convey an arresting sense of uniqueness, to evoke an exalted attention."[57]

Objects displayed in a museum sometimes evoke this sensibility, and pioneering twentieth-century visual artists from Giorgio de Chirico to Joseph Cornell have explored the possibilities surrounding it. The museum, however, houses a special class of objects, and even they, most of the time, can be fitted as stepping-stones in a path leading from the past to us, or at least can be related to each other in a way that some present category enables us to grasp. But with the inflation of history, our relationship to the universe of such objects becomes more problematic because we understand such ways of integrating to be themselves contingent and historical. So those artifacts are not so easily confined, controlled, rendered familiar, fitted into our experience. Yet the past comes to seem a collection of such objects—artifacts that can evoke feelings of uncanniness and wonder.[58]

Early in the century, Croce had sought an orientation radical enough to dissolve the basis for any such approach to the world as historical. With his way of collapsing the past into the present, there is no tension—and no scope for uncanniness. Because there is no independent past, it is obvious that there is nothing but our present questions and categories to give history coherence, to make the world "history" at all. The artifacts from the past are now present, available to us. But in some of our moods, Croce does not quite convince. Even as we go on making a certain sense of our historically specific world, our sense of the arbitrariness and contingency of the process leaves us glimpsing the shadow of an uncanny remainder. The new historicists fastened on that remainder and sought to bring it to the center of our experience.

Much like the microhistorians, the new historicists often focused on the anecdote, the single disconnected episode, naked in its contingency. The only way to get at what was real, they suggested, was by simply presenting such an episode through narrative, without trying to explain it in terms of some larger structure or process.[59] And as Joel Fineman has argued, there is no basis for confining the anecdote to some particular level, where it might be assumed to stand in tension with some higher-level process. Indeed, the anecdote may inflate to totality.[60] To suggest that the whole thing, all "there is," is one big anecdote is a way of characterizing the weak, finite, particular totality of a world of nothing but history. Generally, however, the new historicists fastened on something apparently trivial or everyday, sometimes isolating it, sometimes

57. Greenblatt, *Learning to Curse*, 170.
58. Ibid., 10, 14, 169–170, 180–181.
59. Ibid., 5; Joel Fineman, "The History of the Anecdote," in *The New Historicism*, ed. H. Aram Veeser (New York: Routledge, 1989), 56.
60. Fineman, "History of the Anecdote," 61.

juxtaposing it with other such bits and pieces, sometimes piling up detail, but always in an effort to produce a certain resonance, a new experience of the uncanniness of the stuff of the historical world.

Greenblatt was fascinated especially with the collectible artifacts—fossils, exotic animals—that were assembled in the early modern "cabinet of curiosities." Like the collectors of centuries past, he seemed to find satisfaction in skillful aesthetic arrangement, and he hoped to convey a comparable experience to his readers. But critics found something arbitrary in his approach. Anne Barton suggested that Greenblatt's collection "is itself a cabinet of this kind, an assemblage of disparate and fragmented things, arbitrarily juxtaposed, their asserted cultural interconnections all too often depending on Greenblatt's skill at arrangement."[61] R. B. Kershner asked what is to keep the new historicist enterprise "from lapsing into a quirky kind of impressionism"?[62]

Especially in this premium on arresting assemblage, the new historicism participated in the wider aestheticist tendency to fold history within fiction or literature. But whatever the arbitrariness of his constructions and whatever the pleasure he may have derived from his own creativity, Greenblatt explicitly sought to avoid the aestheticist blurring that threatened as metaphysically grounded philosophy falls away. The poststructuralist way of destabilizing the relevant distinctions remained essential, but it did not exhaust the issue, so we keep coming back to the tensions between fiction and fact, literature and history. There is still a real world distinguishable from fictional ones, and historical texts have different uses than fictional texts.[63]

For Greenblatt, it clearly mattered that the entertaining anecdotes and resonant curiosities of the new historicism were not invented whole cloth. And despite its interest in fictional artifacts and its suspicion of conventional historiographical modes of ordering, the new historicism was a response—a post-metaphysical response—to the world as historical. For the new historicists, as for all our major figures, it mattered fundamentally that the coming to be of the world has been some particular way, so that there are these artifacts and not some others that we might imagine—or forge. The uncanniness of those artifacts lies in their combination of naked actuality and bizarre contingency. Part of what stops us in our tracks is the sudden awareness that our world, all of it, consists of nothing but such stuff as this. So even the newly privileged experience of the marvelous required truth and thus a distinctively historical text.

Still, Greenblatt's way of framing the alternatives meant that only the form of historical writing that evoked wonder by disembedding the past could be taken as postmetaphysical and culturally valuable. Any reconstructive uses of historical understanding smacked of the conventional historiographical modes of ordering that needed to be disrupted. Greenblatt noted, for example, that

61. Anne Barton, "Perils of Historicism," *New York Review of Books*, 28 March 1991, 56.
62. Kershner, "Dances with Historians," 585.
63. Greenblatt, *Learning to Curse*, 13–15.

"while philosophy would seek to supplant wonder with secure knowledge, it is the function of the new historicism continually to renew that marvelous at the heart of the resonant."[64] "Philosophy" entailed the still-metaphysical quest for closure that Greenblatt and others found lurking in conventional historiography. And the antidote is the relentless effort of the new historicism to keep things in their uncanny individuality.

But though relentless in one sense, that enterprise could be relaxed and pleasurable. Much like Ginzburg on microhistory, Greenblatt stressed that the new historicist approach lacked particular political implications. Precisely as we pull back from any effort to illuminate the present for reconstructive, broadly political purposes, we experience a new admiration and wonder in relationship to the past. For Greenblatt, this experience was a particular achievement of our time, and it afforded "one of the most intense pleasures" our culture has to offer.[65] In terms of our overall cultural economy, this sort of experience might afford a welcome counterpoint to the ongoing contest that followed from the alternative emphasis on process to the present. Thus Kershner liked the "tentative, playful, and sometimes ironic quality" of the new historicism, especially in comparison with the stridency that results when, in a presentist mode, we approach the past with some present concern in mind.[66]

From the new historicist perspective, then, evoking the uncanniness of difference, the wonder of arbitrariness and contingency, became the fundamental raison d'être of historical writing. It is crucial for our purposes to understand why this emphasis on the disembedded past crept into the culture when it did and how that impulse relates to the renewed emphasis on presentism and process.

Thomas had difficulty understanding why the new historicists eschewed presentist, reconstructive purposes like his own. He could only assume that Greenblatt and his colleagues were still tied to the mimetic model; thus they were seeking fixed original meaning, even continuity. In the final analysis, he charged, the new historicists had ended up sanitizing the paradoxes of literature by fitting them back into the reigning historical constructions, thereby undercutting their capacity to challenge received opinion.[67]

But this characterization missed much of what was innovative in the new historicism and did not do justice to the scope for a nonconstructive orientation to the world as history. More specifically, Thomas did not grasp the point of keeping the past moment from reconnecting, *even* in the subversive way he himself had in mind. To restore strangeness to the past moment or artifact is not simply, as Thomas put it, "to re-present an original presence."[68] Greenblatt's

64. Ibid., 181.
65. Ibid., 180.
66. Kershner, "Dances with Historians," 586.
67. Thomas, *New Historicism*, 214–215. See also pp. 184–185, 199–200, 208–210; compare Greenblatt, *Shakespearean Negotiations*, 18–19.
68. Thomas, *New Historicism*, 209.

aim, after all, was hardly the security we might gain from rendering the past as it actually happened, or the past moment as it actually was. Rather, we experience the strangeness of the disembedded past moment, not to serve the presentist aim of changing the provisional outcome, but as a quasi-religious end in itself. This was to expand the spectrum of experience that opens as we adjust to a world of nothing but history. That experience is akin to, but ultimately distinguishable from, the ritualistic resistance and disruption we found especially in the extreme side of deconstruction. With the new historicism, the element of resentment falls away.

The emphasis on past as opposed to process lurked more generally in historiography by the last decades of the century; it was not limited to the specific genre of microhistory, nor did it require the exotic new historicism. Much of what came to be called simply the new history, as social history expanded, reacted against the long-standing emphasis on *some* dominant elite strand to focus on formerly neglected groups or dimensions of human experience.

Initially, historians turned from the dominant political or intellectual strand to focus on excluded others like women, out of the sense that women, too, were agents—whether in the larger public sphere or in their own "local" sphere. This was simply to say that power to affect the world was diffused more widely than it had seemed when we relied on a master narrative with a particular, delimited set of foci. Insofar as that was the argument, the focus was still on world-making—even if world-making involved strands that ran parallel, intertwining only problematically. But in some instances the claim to the actual agency of such excluded others weakened, so the focus and rationale of the inquiry changed. From this perspective, history was not about world-making at all.

Sometimes, the aim seemed simply to rescue from condescension those who did not affect the outcome, whose significance lies instead in the dignity, the coherence, of their having lived the lives they did, apart from dominant processes. But some took another step and, at least implicitly, afforded privilege to those who were left outside or marginalized by the dominant processes, processes *agreed to be* dominant. To focus on their stories was not simply to propose that we study a different process to the present but to disrupt focus on *any* process. There seemed something inherently illegitimate about the process of particularizing itself, because particularizing necessarily entails winning, leaving a great deal to fall by the wayside. Characterizing the "other" of the dominant processes, those approaching the past in this way almost universally eschewed neutral terminology such as "left outside," "did not result," or even "precluded" as they spoke of the "suppressed" and afforded privilege to the "suppressed other."[69] They took as most important what was *not* most impor-

69. Even Ankersmit, who has approached this set of issues with balance and discernment, sometimes uses such phrasing; see, for example, *History and Tropology*, 173–174.

tant in the older sense of having had a disproportionate influence on some dominant process to the present. Rather than focusing on the coming to be of the actual, this was to resist winning itself by giving privilege to what is excluded as a result of the winning.

In some of its expressions, this approach manifested an overt hostility to the political-constitutional and "high" intellectual-cultural processes that had long seemed especially worthy of attention. Historians found satisfaction in showing that ordinary people—most people—lived their lives little touched by such processes as the Renaissance, the American Revolution, or the Italian Risorgimento. Or they afforded privilege to the experience of those most directly the victims of dominant processes, such as the aboriginal populations in areas taken over by Europeans.

The focus of this approach might even expand beyond long-excluded groups to encompass long-neglected aspects of the experience of all of us. The coming to be of the particular world entails particular ways of understanding, experiencing, conferring meaning. And whichever strand we choose to emphasize, this particularizing process can be understood as preclusion or suppression, so that a mode of experience that was nipped in the bud could be conceived as an excluded other.

To afford historiographical privilege to any such other undercuts a focus on world-making, even as expanded to encompass a much larger class of historical agents or dominant processes. So that impulse among practicing historians stood opposed not only to the old exclusionary master narrative but even to the middle ground of weak process and reconstruction. And it participated in the wider tendency toward ritualistic subversion, or reversal, that we found in the extreme side of both Foucault and Derrida, and that reflected a quasi-religious resentment of the particularizing mechanisms through which any world comes to be in history.

Some contended that the narrative form itself is ideologically charged and entails preclusion, so that the alternative to an emphasis on process must entail subverting, or at least eschewing, the narrative form.[70] Even as he resisted moves in this direction, White pointed out that whereas we have good constructive reasons for emplotting the stuff of history in various kinds of narrative accounts, it is also possible to take an antinarrativist approach, showing how any narrative seeks to cover over its own constructedness—and undermines itself in the process.[71] So White suggested that whereas we *may* want to devise historical stories, thereby constructing some particular meaning, the

70. See White, *Content of the Form*, 34–40, for a good account of this notion, especially as it informed the effort of Roland Barthes and found its way into French poststructuralism. In *Historical Culture: On the Recoding of an Academic Discipline* (Berkeley, Los Angeles, and London: University of California Press, 1986), Sande Cohen seeks to point the way to a recoding of historiography to free it from the allegedly prejudicial—and reactionary—effects of narrative.
71. White, "Historical Pluralism," 490–491.

constructive impulse that leads us to do so is not privileged. We might instead approach the stuff of history in a more ritualistically deconstructive spirit, constantly undercutting the pretense of coherence itself.

Indeed, our deeper understanding, thanks to White, of what is entailed in narration/construction may well stimulate this countervailing will to antinarrative deconstruction. The postmetaphysical space has room for this impulse as part of the array of new ways of addressing the past apart from process, just as it has room for the variety of the presentist accents discussed in the preceding section. Sometimes, however, these ways of affording privilege to the past moment rested on the conflations and overreactions we have encountered again and again.

In specifying the uses of microhistory, Ankersmit was quick to assume that the alternative boils down to a quest for the key to the workings of history or for some essence or unifying principle tying everything together. He implied that insofar as we seek to understand ourselves as historical resultants by focusing on some process connecting past and present, we repair either to a speculative, quasi-Hegelian metanarrative or to a justifying, celebratory master narrative. By fastening on the scraps, the margins, as opposed to those aspects of the past that led most directly to us, the microhistories afforded a welcome antidote, a kind of defamiliarization that resisted our tendency toward a too-easy essentialism. To concentrate on what was most different, on what most resisted processes that proved dominant, keeps us from assuming that anything we might find back there can be integrated into our present identity, taken as privileged or "given."[72]

We have good reasons for focusing on the past margins and scraps that stand opposed to all that most readily connects with us. But we cannot understand those reasons if we impute essentialism or Hegelianism to the postmetaphysical way of experiencing ourselves as historical products or resultants. To connect, in a continuous narrative, our present understanding of death, for example, with a very different earlier understanding, and to concentrate on those aspects of the past that fit into that narrative, is not necessarily to make the present privileged and inevitable, or even to make the historical account reassuring. Rather, that historical account may defamiliarize and destabilize the present by showing up as merely historical what was assumed to be given, natural, essential.

Yet we *still* have reason to emphasize instead the past moment for its own sake—even the margins and scraps of that past moment. We have reason to turn the sense of belonging to a particular history inside out by attending to the preclusion, or by experiencing the uncanniness of the past moment left disconnected, not subjected to the construction that follows from our present need to act. Even insofar as, with Gadamer, we grasp the scope for a dialogical approach that values difference and even surprise, we have reason to depart

72. Ankersmit, *History and Tropology*, 174–177.

from Gadamer's way of seeking dialogue and reconnection. These new ways of concentrating on the past for its own sake yield an experience of the historical world that stands in fruitful tension with our renewed emphasis on process to the present.

But though there is room for both sets of impulses, confusion about past-process interaction produced uncertainty about historiographical priorities and fed polarization among historians. And whereas historiography seemed to become more open and inclusive in one sense, some noted a renewed tendency to claim predominance and to exclude. Criticizing Ginzburg's *The Cheese and the Worms*, Dominick LaCapra pinpointed the interlocking tensions that lurked in some of the popular microhistories and in much of the new history. As noted previously, Ginzburg revealed a popular peasant culture that had been hidden in our mainstream cultural history, but LaCapra found contradictions both in Ginzburg's conception of agency and in the relationship between that popular culture and the elite culture that had seemed dominant. Ginzburg seemed to view the popular culture as at once autonomous and caught up in a reciprocal relationship with "high" texts. Moreover, LaCapra charged that Ginzburg's approach entailed preclusions of its own; his "empathy with the oppressed" yielded a limited perception of those taken to be their oppressors.[73]

Paradoxically, the tendency to afford privilege to some excluded other entailed the danger of a new form of vulgar presentism. Reviewing several books on "1492," the moment of Columbian encounter, J. H. Elliott lamented "the absurdities and evasions that arise from efforts to view the past through the lens of such contemporary preoccupations as environmentalism and multicul-turalism. . . . This litany of deformations of the past [suggests] . . . the attitudes of an essentially ahistorical civilization, unwilling or unable to recognize the complexity of the processes that have gone to the shaping of the present." Elliott found a sad irony in the tendency of historians to denounce insensitivity to the otherness of the others while refusing to recognize that the earlier Euro-peans, especially the missionaries, were different from us precisely in seeking not differences but resemblances, a common humanity: "Ironically, it is the otherness of these early European observers and ethnographers which now tends to be overlooked, as their efforts at understanding are . . . found lamen-tably wanting by the standards of our own more enlightened age."[74]

Such ahistorical tendencies fed implicit claims to privilege among some "antiprocess" historians. As noted in chapter 1, LaCapra found "a bizarre and

73. Dominick LaCapra, "*The Cheese and the Worms*: The Cosmos of a Twentieth-Century Historian," in Dominick LaCapra, *History and Criticism* (Ithaca: Cornell University Press, 1985), 45–69; see esp. pp. 60, 62. See also Roger Chartier, "Texts, Printing, Readings," in *The New Cultural History*, ed. Hunt, 169–170, 173–174, for another indication of exasperation with the tendency to dichotomize "high" and "popular" culture, coupled with some helpful suggestions about how we can transcend the dichotomy.

74. J. H. Elliott, "The Rediscovery of America," *New York Review of Books*, 24 June 1993, 37–38.

vicious paradox" in the stance of many of those disrupting claims to privilege in the past: "a vicarious relation to the oppressed of the past serves as a pretext for contemporary pretensions to dominance" within contemporary historiography.[75] So even as calls for openness and pluralism grew more insistent, historians found it ever harder to agree on the criteria as the relationship between past and process became more problematic.

Scott versus Himmelfarb

The whole array of new impulses, some inviting a politically charged presentism, some defying traditional historical narrative, provoked more traditional historians. None responded more forcefully than Gertrude Himmelfarb, a distinguished historian of nineteenth-century England.[76] Although no single individual or direction manifested all the tendencies Himmelfarb deplored, the opposition between Himmelfarb and Joan Wallach Scott proved especially illuminating. By the late 1980s, Himmelfarb and Scott had emerged as prominent advocates of the opposing "old" and "new" historiographical positions, and each explicitly denounced the other as representing what most threatened the discipline. Each produced a widely discussed book on historiography, and their papers highlighted a notable opening session at the annual meeting of the American Historical Association in 1988.[77]

Although Himmelfarb and Scott were surely representative, neither side in the debate between old and new historians was monolithic, and certain of the emphases of each of these two exemplars have been controversial even among historians who have no use for the other. Scott was criticized by women's historians both for taking the generally poststructuralist orientation too much to heart and for downplaying the experience of women as she emphasized gender.[78] And not all those bothered by Scott's overtly political stance were as traditionalist as Himmelfarb in insisting that the political-constitutional sphere must remain privileged as the organizing core for historiography. But the disagreement between these two prominent historians, and the ways they talked past each other, proved highly symptomatic.

Although immediate political differences had their place in the dispute between Scott and Himmelfarb, it would be facile to account for that dispute in

75. LaCapra, *History and Criticism*, 69.

76. Gertrude Himmelfarb, "Telling It as You Like It: Post-modernist History and the Flight from Fact," *TLS: The Times Literary Supplement*, 16 October 1992, 12–15.

77. Gertrude Himmelfarb, *The New History and the Old* (Cambridge: Harvard University Press, 1987); Scott, *Gender*. See also Scott's review of Himmelfarb's book in *American Historical Review* 94, no. 3 (June 1989): 699–700. The two papers were published in *American Historical Review* in June 1989 and are discussed below.

78. For a lucid discussion of Scott's role among historians of women and gender, see the review essay by William H. Sewell, Jr., on Scott's *Gender* in *History and Theory* 29, no. 1 (1990): 71–82. See esp. p. 79 on the criticisms that Louise Tilly and Claudia Koonz raised against Scott.

politically reductionist terms. Their disagreement proves more instructive because it cut to the level of the framework for that undoubted political difference. At issue was how the politically charged historiographical terrain might be contested most fruitfully.

As Himmelfarb saw it, Scott had fallen into presentist bias by adopting a feminist stance that those in the past, the subjects of her history, did not share.[79] As Scott saw it, Himmelfarb would confine the subject of history to the dominant strand of mainstream political development, thereby precluding the stories of the others, stories that might, among other things, subvert the mainstream story and the particular reality it buttresses.

Himmelfarb's conception of history rested on two established pillars: There is a determinate, stable past, and the historian's aim is to understand it as contemporaries did. In her view, the new history was problematic because, picking up on dubious intellectual innovations from outside historiography, it moved away from the former imperative and thus, apparently, from the latter as well: "There is no fixed reality in the past, we are told; the whole of the past is indeterminate." And the consequence: "It is only by making the past indeterminate, making it a *tabula rasa*, that historians can impose upon the past their own determinacy."[80] If the object of inquiry is not understood as some stable reality—the past as it actually happened, or actually was experienced—historians feel liberated from the imperative to reconstruct the past as well as possible; they seem to have license to impose anything they like, even to see how creative and inventive they can be.

Whereas for the old history, Himmelfarb went on, contemporaries invented a world that the historian then seeks to reconstruct, for the new, it is the historians who invent, thereby distorting the experience of those they should be seeking to understand.

> What is being deprivileged and deconstructed is not only history as traditional historians have understood it but the past as contemporaries knew it. Contemporaries may have thought that their history was shaped by kings and statesmen, politics and diplomacy, constitutions and laws. New historians know better. . . . The new history . . . is in danger of fostering a new kind of condescension, a condescension toward those contemporaries who left few records of their "consciousness" and are at the mercy of the historian who can "invent," "imagine," "create," or "construct" a consciousness that is suspiciously in accord with the historian's own consciousness.[81]

79. Gertrude Himmelfarb, "Some Reflections on the New History," *American Historical Review* 94, no. 3 (June 1989): 668. Himmelfarb includes Scott's *Gender*, pp. 3, 6, among the examples of the avowed, conscious bias she finds in the new history.

80. Himmelfarb, "Some Reflections on the New History," 665–668; the quoted passages are on pp. 666 and 668.

81. Ibid., 667–670. See also Himmelfarb, *New History*, 15–24.

Himmelfarb emphasized that she welcomed the expansion of focus associated with the new history; of course we should study the historical experience
of women and blacks, for example. But she worried that the new historians
were placing such emphasis on the disparate subjects of the new history that
unity and any hierarchy of importance came to seem inherently illegitimate.[82]
The result was fragmentation and leveling, bound up with a prejudice against
"greatness," all of which led Himmelfarb to suggest that, despite everything,
political history, especially as focused on the development of constitutions and
institutions, remained central. It is the political realm that affords scope for the
free and rational shaping of our collective world.[83]

Scott, in contrast, claimed to want a more democratic history in a double
sense. Most obviously, this meant widening the focus to include the stories of
the long-excluded others. But it also meant a freer, more open contest over
what was important in history, what should be asked, taught, learned. And Scott
found traditionalists like Himmelfarb unwilling to countenance either form of
democratic expansion. First, they insisted that we continue to focus on elites
rather than encompass those excluded others. The pluralization of the subject of
history, wrote Scott,

> challenges the notion, dear to Himmelfarb and her associates, that "man" can
> be studied through a focus on elites. Instead, attention to women, blacks, and
> other Others demonstrates that history consists of many irreconcilable stories.
> Any master narrative—the single story of the rise of American democracy or
> Western civilization—is shown to be not only incomplete but impossible of
> completion in the terms it has been written. For those master narratives are
> based on the forcible exclusion of Others' stories. They are justifications
> through teleology of the outcomes of political struggles, stories which in their
> telling legitimize the actions of those who have shaped laws, constitutions, and
> governments—"official stories."[84]

At the same time, Scott found the traditionalists prone to insist on a unified
master narrative based on a restrictive conception of what is important. In
doing so, they were refusing contest over historiographical priorities, over
how that master narrative is to be configured. And their reasons were merely
self-serving.

> It is finally the plurality of stories and of the subjects of those stories, as well as
> the lack of any single central narrative that conservatives find intolerable because
> it undermines the legitimation of their quest for dominance. Their defense of their

82. Himmelfarb, *New History*, 5, 9–10, 16, 18, 99.
83. See Himmelfarb's assault on "History with the politics left out," in ibid., 13–32, esp.
pp. 17–21, 31–32. At the very least, she suggested, the determined turning from political subjects
that was a hallmark of the new history reflected a change in our self-understanding that called for
fuller examination.
84. Scott, "History in Crisis?" 689–690.

subject—elites in the past, their own hegemony in the present—is a repudiation of the possibility of contest and conflicting interpretation, a refusal of change, and a rejection of the possibility for what I would call democratic history.[85]

Although reaction against a master narrative that had indeed been prejudicially restrictive was surely justified, these are strong words. Whereas "old" historians like Himmelfarb, in defending "their subject," repudiate "the possibility of contest," we new historians, Scott apparently wanted to say, welcome such contest, as we . . . what? Defend *our* subject, while they defend theirs? Or do we do something different? Why, from Scott's perspective, did making one choice in the contest entail repudiation of the contest itself—a refusal to play by democratic rules—while to make a different choice did not?

Groups, Processes, and Axes of Contest

In arguing for the continued centrality of political and constitutional history, Himmelfarb was advocating a particular organizing frame, but she was also insisting, more generally, that some hierarchy of importance is essential to provide unity and coherence to the culture's historical self-understanding. Some persons, events, and processes are more important than others, and history must feature those who, from *some* perspective, seem to have been disproportionately powerful, affecting the course of things. By implication, historians perform one of their roles in determining which such persons, events, and processes are most worthy of our attention, arranging them in a hierarchy of importance. But questions about that process of decision quickly intrude themselves. How open can it be? What range of possible processes does it encompass? Is the outcome always to be conceived as provisional, subject to further contest, or might it be privileged, carrying more than a merely historical sanction?

Insofar as Scott and other new historians emphasized excluded groups, irreconcilable stories, and the scope for disrupting the master narrative, they seemed to suggest that *any* such emphasis on unity, dominant process, or hierarchy of importance was to afford privilege to the elite and thereby to exclude others. A plurality of parallel stories seemed the only alternative to a master narrative that both privileges the strand leading to the current outcome and justifies that outcome, buttressing the hegemony of the winners. In the passages quoted above, Scott seemed first to envision only these two dichotomous alternatives. And she seemed to suggest that if embracing parallel stories entailed splintering the once-unified historical narrative and leveling the once-hierarchical way of assigning importance, that was an acceptable price.

85. Ibid., 691.

Because older approaches did tend to confine the past to a single dominant strand, there was good reason for the bravado with which new historians like Scott and Lawrence W. Levine pointed to different histories and accented the conflicts or irreconcilabilities among them.[86] Still, Scott's argument, too, suggested that there is always a kind of master narrative, *some* overall historical self-understanding in the culture, though we come to see it as provisional, tension-ridden, open to contest. In one of the passages above, she contended that our way of organizing history around a particular elite strand had precluded stories that might *undermine* that dominant way of telling and the overall cultural self-understanding it yields. And she charged that her opponents were refusing the contest that she thought desirable. So in her account the various possible histories are at least potentially in interaction and competition.

Thus Scott's irrefutable argument that history in both the making and the telling is inherently political. The process of interaction, competition, and conflict through which the particular world results is political; the decision to tell this and not that, the process whereby the wider culture comes to learn this and not that, is part of that overarching political process.[87] Historians are historical actors—significant ones—as they compete to shape the culture's self-understanding.

In her influential argument on behalf of gender as a historical subject, Scott was claiming not only that our present way of giving meaning to sexual difference has been constructed historically but also that we need to recast our hierarchy of importance. We long took the political sphere to be especially important; those successful in that sphere, that particular "elite," had a special claim to our attention. But for now, at least, we have more to learn from a history of gendering than we do from the political or constitutional histories that traditionalists like Himmelfarb continued to favor. Although focus on gender may reveal that gendering has affected even our political categories and thus lead us to some fresh questions about our political tradition, we turn from politics to gender not because the politicians we formerly studied were men, marginalizing women, or because, through their power, they marginalized others. Rather, to focus on gender is to take as more important a different aspect of our common historical experience. As part of her effort to help alter our hierarchy of importance, Scott probed historically the process whereby gender was restricted to a particular place in the hierarchy—or kept from becoming a historical subject altogether.[88] Thanks partly to that historical account, I, for one, am persuaded that gender merits a higher place, even at the expense of politics, in the hierarchy of our historical self-understanding.

86. Lawrence W. Levine, "The Unpredictable Past: Reflections on Recent American Historiography," *American Historical Review* 94, no. 3 (June 1989): 671–679.
87. Scott, "Introduction," in *Gender*, esp. pp. 2–3, 5–8.
88. In this connection, see *Gender*, 83–84, part of Scott's critique of E. P. Thompson's classic *The Making of the English Working Class* (New York: Vintage, 1963).

The larger point, however, is that in accenting contest and in arguing for gender, Scott implicitly agreed that there is a hierarchy of importance and thus something like a master narrative, a common world, a common history. Moreover, in accenting political contest, she implicitly recognized that some prove more powerful than others, exerting a disproportionate influence over the direction of things, as the world comes to be some particular way. Whether what is at issue is an institution or a way of affording meaning to experience, each historical strand encompasses winning, or becoming actual, and exclusion. And the process of winning has a special claim to our attention. Recounting the triumph of whatever has triumphed at present may serve to justify the outcome, as Scott suggested, but celebratory accounts may be contested as well. And as Scott's treatment of gender makes clear, to elevate a particular winning strand in the hierarchy is not necessarily to justify or celebrate but may instead serve deconstruction and change.

In implicitly accepting this larger framework, Scott found herself going beyond her emphasis on irreconcilable stories to a deeper understanding of democratic expansion and pluralism in historiography. Two steps were involved. First, that expansion encompasses not simply formerly excluded groups but a wider array of processes, a wider array of the winning strands that have resulted in our present. Thus gendering and much else compete with conventional political development for our attention. Second, a democratic expansion makes that competition itself freer, broader, more open. There is room for more perspectives, more voices, in the process whereby a particular hierarchy of importance is hammered out. In calling for greater pluralism, Scott seemed to suggest, as the traditionalists did not, that the master narrative is forever tension-ridden and provisional—and thus *invites* ongoing contest.

In one sense, this broadly political contest has always gone on, but it has not been as open, pluralistic, and democratic as it might have been. The old master narrative was "strong," presenting its particular understanding of the hierarchy—Western, male, political, and so forth—as necessary and inevitable. But as we come to experience our world as nothing but history, we recognize that the master narrative is itself merely historical and thus open to contest. It encompasses whatever historians put into it; historians endlessly compete to get this or that included and to get the hierarchy of importance arranged in this way as opposed to that. As we grasp the cultural import of that competition, our historical self-understanding becomes more tension-ridden than ever before.

Still, both sides of the coin must be remembered. Thick and messy though it is, some particular cultural self-understanding endlessly results from that competition. The point is not to deny unity and totality but to insist on weakness and provisionality. At the same time, it is crucial that though Scott was more concerned than Himmelfarb to accent openness and contest, she did not envision putting everything in, treating everything as equally important. The point was not that the traditionalists insisted on hierarchy and exclusion, whereas Scott did not. Scott simply wanted an expanded and more open contest in the double sense I have described. *Any* such choice in this contest will leave something out, and the leaving out, or particularizing, can always be characterized as marginalizing, precluding, or suppressing.

Scott's argument, then, suggested a number of points essential for a moderate, open-ended, yet reconstructive understanding of the place of historiography in a postmetaphysical culture. But though her contribution was invaluable, certain tensions blunted her argument and blurred some of its essential points. In her dispute with the traditionalists, Scott's plausible reaction against the old master narrative tended toward overreaction, precluding even the weak, postmetaphysical understanding of unity and hierarchy that can be derived from the main lines of her argument. So she tended to restrict with one hand even as she invited openness with the other.

Scott's way of using the loaded term "elite" blurred the difference between expansion to encompass excluded groups and expansion to encompass more of the dominant processes that produced our present. Insofar as history in both the making and the telling is political and contested, it is about winning and losing—and the winners, by definition, have had a disproportionate impact on the outcome, the configuration of the present. Whatever their initial status, those winners constitute a sort of elite, but they are not necessarily an elite in the usual sense, a group that is recognizable and advantaged even as it enters the contest, mixing it up with other groups.

Political and cultural leaders command our attention not simply as "the elite," one social group among others, but as dominant agents, as those who turned out to wield disproportionate power in shaping what was, like it or not, the particular totality of our common world. We focus not so much on *them*, as if their experience as winners was somehow more significant, as on the process itself—the process through which some set of agents proves more powerful and through which our particular world results. A conventional political or intellectual history need not be any more *about* elites, as an advantaged grouping, than is a history focusing on how we have come to understand gender as we have.

Moreover, once we understand that the outcome of this contest is weak and provisional, to argue for the importance of some particular strand of the overall process is not in itself to seek to justify the outcome—neither the present resultant of that strand nor the overall hierarchical arrangement in which, at present, it has its particular place. In a postmetaphysical mode, we are not tempted to celebrate that master process as the providential march to the present—or to a future that we can discern through reason. We view the privilege that attaches to any present outcome as weakly historical, not strongly metaphysical. But to understand and possibly change some aspect of the present, we must focus on those historical processes that we suspect have been most important in giving our present its particular shape.

Obviously Scott, in focusing on gender, was seeking not to justify our present way of gendering but very nearly the opposite: To show how it emerged historically might enable us to change that provisional outcome. So we afford historiographical privilege to the coming to be of one strand of the actual, even though this particular process of winning entailed the marginalization of women.

Yet Scott tended to preclude any such "moderate," weakly postmetaphysical understanding when she suggested that to focus on a dominant process is *necessarily* to celebrate its outcome, that historical recounting leads us to associate the winners with some suprahistorical justification. She assumed, moreover, that those who focus on the dominant processes are affording privilege to elites and "forcibly excluding" the rest. And they could wish to do so only because, belonging among the elite winners themselves, they seek to cement their own hegemony. Because of this spurious justification, "their defense of their subject" comes to seem "a repudiation of the possibility of contest."

Thus Scott imputed a claim to strong justification to more traditional historians like Himmelfarb who found the relatively conventional political-constitutional sphere still to be most important. Some of those historians *may* seek, or lapse into, such strong justification, but unless we are prepared to distinguish strong justification from weak, merely historical justification, we will not be able to judge any particular instance.

Even as Scott invited political contest as opposed to parallel stories, her initial solicitude for excluded groups continued to inform her thinking. An element of posthistoricist extremity, with its accent on the disembedded past, fed her tendency to afford privilege to those marginalized by dominant processes. Thus the vehemence of her reference to "the forcible exclusion of Others' stories."[89] In this mode, Scott was not saying simply that what had seemed the dominant processes are less important. Nor was it that, disliking their outcomes, she wanted to deconstruct them. This would leave them most important, most worthy of our attention. Because such reconstructive purposes also informed her thinking, Scott did not embrace the more global extremes of Derridean disruption or Heideggerian disengagement. But her way of affording privilege to the excluded other carried her beyond the argument, which she shared with Thomas, that attention to the excluded element can deepen our understanding of any process to the present.

Scott's solicitude for others reflected the resentment of a world of nothing but history that we have encountered in several forms. That world endlessly results in a present that is what it is only because some have been marginalized or left out along the way. In light of this preoccupation, focus on the excluded other, or whatever has been held back, takes on the quasi-religious function we have discussed. The other has a special claim to our attention. Otherness disrupts dominance and so is privileged—is even, quite literally, next

89. Scott, "History in Crisis?" 689–690.

to godliness. In a world of nothing but history, the others are the meek, and there is only the history for them to inherit. But inherit it they do, thanks to the historian.

As I have emphasized, this new way of focusing on past in opposition to process is a plausible response to a world of nothing but history. But because Scott did not sort out the disparate concerns that nourished her thinking, this element of extremity reinforced her tendency to conflate telling with justifying and compromised her understanding of "democratic expansion." Her solicitude for a certain class of others led her to claim, implicitly, an unwarranted privilege in her contest with the traditionalists over the hierarchy of importance.

Whereas focusing on gender as a long-excluded process genuinely expanded the master narrative, Scott's way of affording privilege to the stories of women as a forcibly excluded other made it seem that to elevate political history over gender history was not simply to judge one process more important than another but to preclude the stories of women as a group. And this could only serve the interests of those whose stories had *not* been precluded—namely, "the elite." By blurring the two axes, Scott was able to make a choice for a different process look spurious, self-serving. Thus, again, her charge that the traditionalists' "defense of their subject—elites in the past, their own hegemony in the present—is a repudiation of the possibility of contest and conflicting interpretation."[90] Such purposes *may* be at work when more traditional historians make their more conventional choices, but to refuse to reduce history to a collection of group stories, and even to marginalize the stories of certain groups, is not in itself to deny the contest or to refuse to expand the focus.

At the same time, Scott's solicitude for excluded groups compromised the reconstructive potential she had in mind in arguing for gender as a historical subject. Insofar as that solicitude intrudes into gender history, it leads the historian to focus on women's experience for its own sake and diminishes the presentist bite. Although our way of gendering left men politically and economically dominant, it diminished the range of possible experiences for both men and women. A history of gender stemming from reconstructive purposes would probe what was precluded, but rather than focus on groups, it would probe experience and meaning, examining the marginalization of possibilities for men as well as for women—precisely as historians have recently begun to do. Scott, however, got caught up in the ambiguity at the intersection between gender and women's history. Thus she did not fully develop the argument for the reconstructive potential of gender as a historical subject, yet neither did she satisfy historians like Claudia Koonz who were more concerned with the parallel history of women as a group.

---

90. Ibid., 691. See also pp. 685–686, 689–690, for Scott's tendency to restrict the axis of debate by assuming that groups are necessarily at issue.

Although Scott sometimes disparaged the "elite" winners, her often-reconstructive aims entailed a positive evaluation of some aspects of the process that had resulted in the present—and even of some of those elites who had most powerfully shaped that present. She implicitly valued, for example, the steps in our "high" intellectual history that made Foucault and Derrida possible and that brought them to her attention. That was precisely what we presently take to be the master narrative of our intellectual history in the West, a history that is more obviously "elitist" than most of the strands we presently take to be dominant.

To Scott, at least, it did not seem necessary to study and convey that history, although in principle she might have, as she sought to show other historians how the "more radical epistemology" of Foucault and Derrida could deepen the impact of feminist historiography and, more generally, serve the greater pluralism she sought. But she surely had to applaud the success of intellectual historians like LaCapra whose works extended the master narrative to encompass these figures. Though that narrative was about elites in one obvious sense, that was not why it mattered to Scott. It mattered because it deepened her understanding of the possibilities for present action.

Despite the frustration she professed at the outset of *Gender and the Politics of History*, Scott made herself heard. So powerful was her voice, in fact, that she herself assumed a place in that elite, not as a woman, participating in a parallel history of women, but as an intellectual leader, affecting the priorities of the culture. She assumed a place in that continuous history of the elite that, in some of her moods, she affected to despise. And in my judgment, obviously, she merits that place; that is why I have read and discussed her, as opposed to some random, typical, ordinary, or marginal historian writing at the same time. But, just as obviously, the master narrative in which Scott had become central was only provisional. Her influence might diminish; others marginalized by her triumph might be resurrected.

Polarization and Revitalization

As translated into historiography, the themes of the wider humanistic discussion tended to produce confusion, restriction, and a debilitating polarization, as opposed to the revitalization that had seemed possible. The Himmelfarb-Scott encounter dramatized that tendency with particular force. Scott pinpointed much that was essential for historiographical renewal, but her prejudice against elites and even greatness betrayed excesses that Himmelfarb was quick to fasten on. Partly because of those excesses, Himmelfarb managed to sidestep some of what was most challenging—and ultimately essential—in Scott's contribution. In turn, Scott and her followers fell into prejudicial characterizations, including a facile political reductionism, partly because they had to respond to those like Himmelfarb who were quick to repair to unsustainable traditional categories.

Against Scott's presentism, Himmelfarb insisted that historians should reconstruct past experience as contemporaries lived it. But this was to blur the problematic relationship between their experience and our history. Thanks partly to presentists like Scott, Kellner, and Thomas, we better understand that insofar as we seek to deconstruct some present configuration, our purpose is not to write "their" history but our own. We do not willfully falsify past experience, but neither do we simply reconstruct it, because we can know, as our predecessors did not, what was resulting from the processes in which their lives were enmeshed.

In light of the expanded role history was called on to play, Himmelfarb's concern—the past as contemporaries knew it—was indeed being deprivileged, and needed to be. Still, Himmelfarb's complaint that new historians like Scott were forcing their concerns onto the experience of those in the past could not be dismissed as conservative prejudice. But it was not possible to head off the excesses in Scott's thinking by repairing to the old self-understanding as Himmelfarb did.

A more thoroughgoing postmetaphysical recasting of historiography was necessary to overcome the polarization. That recasting required a reconsideration of hierarchy, unity, and totality; of past and process; of commitment and risk; and of the terms of the endless contest to which Scott drew our attention. It required showing why focus on *our* history and even denial of a stable past do not authorize historians to treat those who came before as mere proxies for present struggles. It was essential to show why, on the contrary, we need to learn—and why truth may result when we seek to learn. On that basis, we might recognize that an invitation to political conflict need not warrant a political-reductionist understanding of the process of interaction. Most basically, that reconsideration had to make sense of the variety of impulses that inform the human encounter with history in a postmetaphysical world, probing the interplay of presentist reconstruction and the plausible extremes.

11

Responding to the World as Historical

Postmetaphysical Moderation

From Nietzsche to Scott, major thinkers who eschewed metaphysics found it essential to ask new questions about the relationship between human being and history. The discussion that developed encompassed aestheticist tendencies, plausibly extreme responses, and prejudicial conflations, but also an ongoing effort to articulate a moderate orientation based on a particular embrace of the world as historical. Despite different concerns and accents, thinkers from Croce and Gadamer to such contemporaries as Richard Bernstein, David Kolb, F. R. Ankersmit, and Brook Thomas envisioned something like the same cultural alignment. Navigating between the extremes of "authoritarianism" and "play," they sought to foster openness, risk, dialogue—the ongoing conversation of humanity. And they accented the sense in which, as a result of that process, the world is endlessly remade.

That alignment included, at least by implication, a renewed understanding of the cultural role of empirical historiography. To be sure, the notion of postmodern or postmetaphysical moderation seemed almost oxymoronic to mainstream historians like Perez Zagorin and Gordon Wood. But Ankersmit, for example, sought to assemble various postmodern tendencies in a way that boxed out willful extravagance and provided a more convincing understanding of what historians offer the culture.[1]

"Moderate" in this context did not stand in any simple, dualistic opposition

---

1. F. R. Ankersmit, *History and Tropology: The Rise and Fall of Metaphor* (Berkeley, Los Angeles, and London: University of California Press, 1994); see especially the introduction and chaps. 6 and 7.

to "radicalism." Among the questions at issue was what radicalism might mean in a postmetaphysical world, in which any scope for a metanarrative of "emancipation" had apparently fallen away. A moderate orientation might specify, among other things, how a radical mode of historical questioning might affect what the world becomes, rather than serving self-cultivation, ritualistic disruption, or disengagement. But it would have to make the case without the still-metaphysical claim to privilege that some found necessary to keep radicalism alive in light of such extreme tendencies.

The possibilities remained unclear partly because intellectuals like Perry Anderson, Terry Eagleton, and Frank Lentricchia, with roots in the older, generally Marxist radical tradition, often seemed the most determined—and the best equipped—to rescue "history" from the excesses of poststructuralist deconstruction. Yet the deconstructionists seemed to uncover hidden metaphysical assumptions in conventional notions of history, including those that such radicals at least implicitly embraced. The prominence of this axis of debate contributed to the limiting bifurcation we have encountered in this study again and again. History apparently dissolves—unless it has Hegelian-Marxian buttressing. The question, then, is the scope for an understanding of history that does not posit metaphysical forms of totalization and closure, that does not claim to fix things for good, that entails a reflexive sense of historicity.[2]

That understanding would be part of the weak but constructive culture of history that proves essential to postmetaphysical moderation. We have found elements for such a cultural component emerging during the course of this study, but the complexities of the ongoing adjustment to the postmetaphysical situation, including the postmetaphysical encounter with history, have kept the bits and pieces from coming together in a convincing way. Thus the effort to outline that moderate orientation must understand its place in the whole field of forces at work in the settling out of a postmetaphysical culture. This requires, first, pinpointing the prejudicial conflations, stemming partly from the shadow of the old metaphysical dualism, that have impeded assessment of the cultural alternatives. But even when that shadow dissipates and we find ourselves fully within the postmetaphysical space, we find room for an array of plausible responses to the world as historical, not all of them moderate. So it is also necessary to differentiate the weak but constructive strand from the plausible extremes we have encountered.

A dualistic conception of the relationship between human being and reality persisted especially in the French thinking that narrativists like White and Kellner were quick to embrace. Standing opposed to reality "in itself" is human language, which orders or represents reality yet, because of its figured nature,

2. Geoff Bennington and Robert Young outline nicely the opposition between poststructuralist and generally Marxian positions, but they tend to settle for this unnecessarily limited dichotomy in their "Introduction: Posing the Question," in *Post-Structuralism and the Question of History*, ed. Derek Attridge et al. (Cambridge: Cambridge University Press, 1987), 1–11.

always falsifies reality in the process. Because we are trapped in language, reality and truth are ultimately beyond our grasp.

From this perspective, the eclipse of metaphysics left us without the older congruence between us, with our way of knowing and need for meaning, and the world, or reality, or whatever else there is. That congruence, of course, had been the positive, reassuring side of the tradition in eclipse; the human mind apparently had access to stable being, so that truth, even meaning, were somehow grounded, really "there," apart from the contingent, finite side of human being and the human world. Bridging the gap between mind and world had always been a problem, but that gap became ever more troubling as the historicity of both the human inquirer and the reality to be known became more intrusive. Suprahistorical mind seemed to reduce to "language," which, more obviously than mind, was "embedded," cultural, merely historical.

Thus cultural modernism entailed irony, stemming from the representation problematic. For structuralism, to be sure, it seemed possible to take advantage of the sign/signified dichotomy to devise a science of signs and through language, writ large to encompass a multiplicity of cultural usages read as rule-governed systems of signs, even to gain access to mind—the mind that underlies and generates culture. But finally, with the break into poststructuralism, "history" submerged even that possibility, and claims that once seemed reassuring came to seem authoritarian pretense instead.

In one sense, then, we are well rid of the old metaphysical claims. In parading as what they could not have been, they now seem but glosses for particular ideological positions, affording a spurious privilege. But insofar as the shadow or image of congruence remained, the eclipse of metaphysics seemed to leave us with meaninglessness, nothingness, mere flux. Instead of the metaphysically grounded world, what "there is" is merely what has resulted from the aggregation of *non*grounded responses. Still looking over our shoulders, we experience this slipping, tension-ridden world as pale and inadequate. At best, it opens to new forms of play or self-creation. Those who claim still to find meaning and truth of any sort seem, if not simply nostalgic conservatives, authoritarians foreclosing a desirable openness for reasons of their own. For some, we have seen, such ideological purposes lurk not only in the claim to reality and truth but also in any imputation of coherence and continuity—or even in the narrative form itself.

From this perspective, then, the tendency was to perceive the postmetaphysical situation in terms of two opposing sets of possibilities. On the one hand were the witting and unwitting forms of authoritarian pretense; on the other were responses that were sufficiently playful to eschew any claim to reality, meaning, or truth.

The situation proved more complicated, however, because some of the extremes that became part of the mix responded not simply to the authoritarian preoccupation but to modes of experience that became possible when even the shadow of the old metaphysics had dissipated. As noted, a world reducing to nothing but a particular history may seem suffocating, so that notions of unity, continuity, tradition, and truth seem limiting. Although its source was distinguishable, the response to this experience intertwined with the tendency to associate such notions with metaphysical pretense. "Authoritarianism" became the shorthand for what needed to be resisted.

We also noted that in proposing antidotes to this authoritarianism, thinkers from Nietzsche to Rorty to Kellner tended toward an aestheticism that, among other things, blurred the distinction between history and fiction. So whereas history, with the eclipse of metaphysics, was coaxed from under the shadow of science, it found itself immediately sucked within the orbit of the ascendent literary culture. But playing down the autonomy of history in this way made it hard to grasp the scope for a moderate postmetaphysical alternative.

Although "authoritarian" appeals to reality and truth still needed to be resisted, the move from metaphysics to aestheticism entailed an unnecessary overreaction, precluding the middle ground, based on a more constructive experience of the actual that did not have to be conflated with the discredited metaphysics. One thinker after another imputed strong, still-metaphysical pretensions to alternatives that could be understood instead as weak—even, for example, to the Gadamerian emphasis on the continuity of tradition. So to indicate the scope for such a middle ground, it was necessary to show that though the postmetaphysical actual is contingent, unstable, and provisional, it has a certain objectivity, consistency, and weight. And it was then necessary to make sense of the difference between the extreme and the moderate ways of experiencing and responding to that world in a fully postmetaphysical mode.

We have noted that a number of those seeking their way out of metaphysics sought to sidestep the dualism that leads us to assume we are somehow trapped in language, cut off from objective reality. In different ways, these thinkers groped toward a new understanding of language as what brings human being together with reality, truth, and meaning. Language becomes the medium through which a particular world comes to be; reality becomes the endlessly provisional human world that happens historically, in and through language.

Especially in recasting language, this effort to eschew dualism reconnected with Vico, whose way of bracketing the natural and the divine made it possible to conceive the human world as utterly on its own. "Natural" is no longer the touchstone, because "reality" is nothing but this human world, which continually comes to be as language responds to what language has done. With Vico's ingenious way of conceiving human origins, human beings are "always already" caught up in linguistic constructions; no matter how far back we go, we never find anything else.

To say, with Vico, that knowing is bound up with doing means that we cannot aspire to the godlike certainty of settled knowledge because we are constantly making over the world. We can know the world we have made, but our knowledge is inevitably partial and provisional. In accenting imagination, moreover, Vico suggested that our way of knowing is creative—or rhetorical. But rhetoric is not inimical to truth; it is simply the measure of our creativity and one aspect of the particularity of truth. Our particular creative way of knowing the world that has resulted so far helps make that world the particular way it next comes to be. So though it is partial, provisional, and rhetorical, the knowledge we can achieve is sufficient, serving our ongoing remaking. Indeed, precisely because they are embedded in the concrete historical world, our rhetorical truths are practical, serving action, in a way that Cartesian, "certain" truths are not.

Among the more recent thinkers moving in the same direction, Heidegger proved central because he addressed explicitly, in light of the eclipse of metaphysics, what human being "is" in relationship to the coming to be of some particular world.[3] Human being is the clearing for coming to be in language. And because it is the nature of being "to be" epochally, merely historically, the becoming actual of anything at all is also a holding back. So as the happening of the particular continues, there is always an other, and always scope for subsequent deconstruction of the actual, and always more history.

Gadamer, eschewing the Heideggerian extreme, sought to characterize the potentially positive, constructive side of Heidegger's insight. More explicitly than anyone else, he insisted that language does not cut us off from reality but is the medium through which some particular world comes to be—over time, as history. The world that comes to be in language is not somehow inadequate but is reality given as particular, the particular reality to which we belong.[4]

Derrida, Foucault, and even Rorty, however, did find something inadequate about that contingent, ever-provisional world. They could not coherently deny that such a world keeps resulting even as metaphysical foundations dissolve, but their extreme responses colored their characterizations of the postmetaphysical situation.

Derrida, for example, fastened on the fact that severing our world from reference to an external reality leaves us with a plethora of truths. But though the world at every moment admits an infinity of possible truths, infinity does not encompass every possibility. Even as Derrida conceived the postmetaphysical

3. Among recent thinkers, the late Ernesto Grassi most fruitfully explored the relationship between the rhetorical tradition, as recast by Vico, and the postmetaphysical efforts of Heidegger and others. For example, see his *Heidegger and the Question of Renaissance Humanism: Four Studies* (Binghamton: State University of New York, Center for Medieval and Early Renaissance Studies, 1983); and *Vico and Humanism: Essays on Vico, Heidegger, and Rhetoric* (New York: Peter Lang, 1990).

4. Coming from a very different intellectual tradition, Stanley Fish similarly argues that institutions and rhetoric simply are the real, not some sort of screen or overlay. See especially his *Doing What Comes Naturally: Change, Rhetoric, and the Practice of Theory in Literary and Legal Studies* (Durham: Duke University Press, 1989). See also Brook Thomas, *The New Historicism and Other Old-Fashioned Topics* (Princeton: Princeton University Press, 1991), 213–214.

situation, finitude remained basic to it. So no matter how freely I play, or how playfully undecidable my interpretation, my response is to play in some particular way, saying this and not that. Even from the mechanisms Derrida posits, a particular world endlessly results, a world with a certain consistency. The question is how we respond to it.

If instead we follow Rorty and view what once seemed stable foundations as a fountain of contingent puns and metaphors, we similarly find that our world is endlessly becoming some particular way because, in the contingencies of history, some metaphors congealed as truths while others washed away. And it matters—it is fundamental—that we belong to the world these particular metaphors have constituted and not some other. Although our particular world allows infinite possibilities for redescription, it does not allow *every* possibility; precisely because it is particular and finite, some redescriptions would be mere babble.

White and Kellner worried that because narrative can present things in a way that seems natural, historical accounts in our culture have seemed to do more than they can. But insofar as we more radically sidestep the old dualistic framework, there is no longer any possibility of telling it straight or establishing settled meanings. We experience any such narrative as merely particular and provisional, as tension-ridden and unstable. We take it for granted that any narrative results from encounter not with unvarnished "reality" but with other narratives, with discourse, with earlier ways human beings made sense of what had resulted from what their predecessors had done. This is not to do violence to some way things *really* are, because there is no such way—not even for the participants, the first to make sense of them. Things come to be as they do in particularizing language. And through our often-contested uses of language, the particularizing continues.

However it is to be characterized, there will be a particular provisional resultant, and an attendant concealing or holding back, as part of the ongoing particularizing of the world. That particular is thick, sufficiently thick to encompass whatever anyone says, the whole web of disseminations and relationships resulting from what is said. But the totality of what is said, and what results, remains particular. In shorthand terms, the element of infinity operates within finitude and results in finitude. There is no limit to the ways we, looking into the past, may sort things out, dividing and combining and relating, but not everything has happened, and thus even the totality is a particular. Still, the thickness of the particularity means that it is not to be confined to a single dominant strand—the dominant strand of the moment—but is always more even than the totality of our ways of understanding it. This is simply one more measure of the holding back that was essential to both Heidegger and Gadamer.

So an actual world remains even with the eclipse of metaphysics, but it is simply the unstable, provisional resultant of our particular history. To recognize the actuality of the present moment is not to afford metaphysical privilege to the process that produced the present; nor is it to justify the present outcome. Our freakish, tension-ridden present *is* what has resulted from history so far; those aspects of the past that led to our present are privileged only in this weak sense. Things are connected but only in the comparably weak sense that whatever happens, becomes actual, responds to and grows on, what has resulted so far. There is weak continuity within a weak totality, but there is no overarching framework or telos, and there is plenty of room for contingency and relative discontinuity or rupture.

Once we adjust to such a world, the need to counter still-metaphysical pretense fades. And beginning with Nietzsche, Croce, and Heidegger, the question was how we might relate to the world of nothing but history that seemed to be left with the waning of metaphysics. To posit a postmetaphysical actuality does not establish a solution but simply opens a new universe of possibilities.

Among those possibilities were the diverse extremes we have noted, from Nietzschean edification to Heideggerian disengagement to ritualistic disruption to privileging the disembedded other. Each of these extremes entails a relationship with the world as historical, yet what they have in common— what defines them as extreme—is their way of eschewing any positive identification with the actual, any scope for experiencing action as reconstructive, or history-making. To respond in the contrasting, moderate way to the experience of nothing but history entails precisely this measure of positive identification, even with the weak, provisional present outcome. We experience ourselves as belonging to and caring about the historically specific world that envelops us.

Care, Learning, and Truth

One of Croce's themes makes this sense of caring responsibility for the world especially clear. In accenting our sense of kinship with all who preceded us, not just the dominant elites, he seemed to share the renewed solicitude for past lives as opposed to process and even to give voice to its quasi-religious basis.[5] But, for Croce, that sense of kinship stems not from a common alienation or from some identification with the other. Rather, it serves simply as a stimulus to us to continue, to transform through our own action the world our predecessors bequeathed to us. This kind of kinship is central to the positive identification with the actual that leads to history-making action informed by responsibility. In this mode, our concern for the world leads us to build upon it rather than disengage from it, disrupt it, or play with it.

We have noted periodic waves of concern that the eclipse of metaphysics dissolves any critical tension, leaving us to acquiesce in the historical outcome,

5. Benedetto Croce, *Ultimi saggi* (Bari: Laterza, 1963), 263–264 (1930). See above, chap. 5, p. 103.

or to accept the authority of tradition.[6] Thus the ongoing concern to specify something suprahistorical—if not actual values, then at least criteria or decision procedures. But for Gadamer and Croce and even for Nietzsche and Heidegger, the reduction to history did not dissolve the possibility of critical response, or even what can be called the moral impulse, but simply the possibility of specifying suprahistorical "principles" or "values."

The situations to which human beings must respond are radically concrete, but evaluating does go on, because human being entails care for the happening of the world, and some of the time, at least, individuals respond to the world on that basis. On one level, that is all that can be said—or needs to be said—because the capacity for such response is a defining attribute of human being. Rather than referring to some transcendent dimension, the ethical is simply our name for one of the things we do, or that happens when we do one of the things we do. The possibility of critical response to the ever-provisional actual is immanent, built into human being. At the same time, the scope for endless moral response suggests that tension between human being and the actual is built into the human condition.

In emphasizing care, Heidegger pointed toward this constructive sense of belonging and responsibility, but it fell to Gadamer to draw out the positive side of Heidegger's notion. Gadamer accented the sense of belonging to some particular tradition that leads us to work within it in a positive, constructive spirit, expanding it through dialogue, participating in its coming back together, or gathering. By implication, moreover, we necessarily affirm some part of the actual world even as we seek to replace some other part of it. No matter how deep the rupture we find necessary, we start with what has already come to be and, even as we change it, build upon it.[7]

Care and the resulting moral response are not "rational" in the sense of telling us what to do in advance, but neither are they irrational, affording the license for some sort of free play. Genuinely to care is to discipline moral response by asking historical questions in an effort to understand the particular situation to which we must respond. What is rational, in postmetaphysical terms, is historical inquiry that seeks to learn, thereby preparing the way for criticism and action.

Moreover, the fact that, at every present moment, we are confronted with something in particular means we need a true account of the historical emergence of what now enmeshes us; edification or propaganda will not do. In Rorty's terms, the tool we need is a special kind of redescription—which we characterize as *true* to distinguish it from an array of contraries, from fiction to

6. Habermas's worries about Gadamer's emphasis on the universality of hermeneutics recalls Guido de Ruggiero's charge during the 1940s that Croce would leave us to acquiesce in the historical outcome, whatever it was. Guido de Ruggiero, *Il ritorno alla ragione* (Bari: Laterza, 1946), 13–19, 27–29, 35–36.

7. Charles Taylor develops a similar argument in "Foucault on Meaning and Truth," in *Foucault: A Critical Reader*, ed. David Couzens Hoy (Oxford: Basil Blackwell, 1986), esp. p. 98.

play. Redescriptions aiming at edification need not be true, and insofar as they are not, they will not be useful in the same way. And the human capacity for inquiry that is open to learning makes such truth possible.

Whereas many of the narrativists played down truth in accenting what historical narratives have in common with fictional narratives, Croce, Heidegger, and Gadamer insisted precisely on truth as they confronted human being as historical. Because they more fully eschewed the shadow of metaphysics than did those within the French orbit, they were less preoccupied with undercutting authoritarian conceptions, and they could simply cease worrying about "representing reality." Once the dualism of language and reality falls away, truth cannot entail representing even an unstable, provisional reality, let alone an original moment of full presence. So these thinkers were able to turn in another direction and consider the scope for a weak, postmetaphysical conception of truth, bound up with what human being is and does and stemming ultimately from care, or ethical capacity. The capacity for the happening of truth is simply an ongoing human attribute, and truth is what results when human beings approach the actual in a certain mode, seeking to learn.

Heidegger made the point most explicitly: truth comes to language through the clearing that is human being. Conversely, it is only in or through us, with our capacity for language, that truth comes to be—comes to language. This abstract notion becomes clearer when translated into the mode of caring, constructive engagement with the world as historical that is implicit in Croce's conception and explicit in Gadamer's.

As noted in chapter 7, Croce and Gadamer each responded to the generally pragmatist challenge by showing that interest and involvement do not undermine truth but make it possible. Because our inquiries have practical stakes, we do not make up just any story about how our world came to be but the particular kind of story we call "true." Our need to learn leads us to eschew the edifying or aesthetic or even moralistic concerns that would lead us to get it wrong. To be sure, as Gadamer recognized in accenting "prejudice," historical inquirers already have some idea of what they expect to find, but insofar as they are doing history, they are open to a range of answers—because they need and seek to learn. Rather than having *completely* decided on some particular political agenda, they are still deciding what to do next and seeking illumination.

At the same time, both Croce and Gadamer distinguished the forms of presentist bias that undermine historical understanding from those that make it possible. Their ways of framing the distinction help us flesh out recent efforts like those of Thomas Haskell to point beyond Peter Novick's neorelativist resignation by showing that "objectivity is not neutrality."[8] Because, in Croce's terms, we are not only truth-seeking and cognitive but also aesthetic, moral,

8. Thomas L. Haskell, "Objectivity Is Not Neutrality: Rhetoric vs. Practice in Peter Novick's *That Noble Dream," History and Theory* 29, no. 2 (1990): 129–157.

and utilitarian, we may prefer an edifying account when we write history, or we may overplay whatever evokes a sense of uncanniness. Although truth is useful, the utilitarian quest for immediate advantage—to secure a promotion by pleasing the reviewers, for example, or simply to avoid effort and risk by sticking to convention—may compromise the happening of truth. And although openness to truth is itself ethical, any attempt to make the historical account serve a particular moral purpose will get in the way of truth. Insofar as such utilitarian and moral concerns creep in, the inquiry is not history, not the sort of thing that can yield truth.

In fact, aims that do not invite learning are always at work, so no one account is pure, unadulterated truth—even in the weak, finite, provisional sense. But even though, as the narrativists showed, ethical and rhetorical components structure any historical narrative, in principle the scope for truth enables us to differentiate historical accounts according to cognitive as opposed to moral or aesthetic criteria.

Although the capacity for truth, for both Croce and Gadamer, is simply an attribute of human being, it is crucial that human being is differentiated into finite, historically specific individuals who ask only particular questions on the basis of particular experiences, concerns, and needs. So our truths do not pretend to be exhaustive, pure, final, or even free of contradiction. What each of us comes up with will be at best only *a* true redescription—partial, provisional, to some degree idiosyncratic and contingent. Such weakness means, moreover, that there is no limit to the number of true accounts that we might find it illuminating to construct at any present moment. The responses of individuals like us determine which in fact get constructed.

What comes to language through any of these individual inquiries is only one linear narrative strand. To say that any such strand may be true is not to claim that the past is *really* linear in the way our historical narratives are. Only if we remain tied to notions of correspondence and representation do we assume we must find such linearity in the way things really are, or in the structure of human experience. Once that ideal has dissipated, any historical account claims to be no more than one constructed linear strand, but that is enough. In Gadamerian terms, what comes to language through dialogue, as the world continues its particularizing growth, is a linear narrative.

As noted in chapter 9, Rorty suggested that a genealogical account of our contingent present is precisely what we need, but his concern that such a genealogical history would *look like* a description of eternal relations led him to pull back from any premium on a distinctively historical approach. However, a history that claims no more than weak truth no longer even looks like a description of eternal relations. Yet though it will be both "metaphorical" and personal, such a genealogical account is not simply generic redescription or literature but a particular kind of redescription—"history," a true redescription.

The Process of Interaction

Still, the notion of weak, postmetaphysical truth opens up an array of questions. By definition, weak truth must get by without epistemology or any theoretical basis for adjudicating truth claims. So even though, in principle, the scope for truth affords cognitive criteria of differentiation, how, in practice, can we distinguish the true from the false, or from whatever else it is that might turn up in redescriptions of the past? And if every offering of truth is partial and provisional, what is the relationship among the various finite, particular truths that in fact come to language? Unless such questions admit plausible answers, the truth at work in historical accounts may seem too weak to play a constructive cultural role.

Instead of decision procedures enabling us to judge the process from above, we have only the ongoing interaction that endlessly results in some provisional, tension-ridden cultural self-understanding. Much rests on the quality of that process and the competition and conflict it entails.

Our particular truths do not remain idiosyncratic and personal because care entails a desire to affect what the world becomes. So individuals keep interjecting new accounts, seeking to influence. As part of that process, truth is winnowed out; some of what would lead us to get it wrong is washed away as a particular way of getting some of it right is established. In this sense the happening of truth is an ongoing, supraindividual process to which we all may contribute as we enter into our particular dialogues and write our particular histories. Because the finite totality of true accounts at any one time is tension-ridden, the conflict continues.

As epistemology has faded, those seeking a moderate alternative to irrationalism have devoted much attention to the procedures whereby particular disciplinary communities make the crucial distinctions, determining what counts, for example, as a respectable work of history. Americans from Thomas Kuhn to Stanley Fish have been especially prominent in this aspect of the overall humanistic discussion.[9] But the fact of such communities and their rule-bound practices does not in itself provide an answer; rather, it invites a particular set of historical questions, because disciplinary communities operate within the weak but constructive framework.

Any set of disciplinary rules will prove relatively solid and effective at some times, problematic and in need of reconstruction at others, depending on changing historical circumstances. There will even be crises, occasioning revolutions—or *relative* discontinuities. It is precisely such a situation of questioning and revision that historiography has experienced in recent years. And because any system of rules is itself historically specific, when such a system begins to

9. See especially Stanley Fish, *Is There a Text in This Class? The Authority of Interpretive Communities* (Cambridge: Harvard University Press, 1980).

lose its force, we can only repair to historical deconstruction to understand where it came from and how it became bound up with our present practices— so that we can begin reconstructing the rules.

However solid they are at any one moment, the paradigms and rules prove to be merely provisional, historically specific crystallizations, more or less effective for dealing with what they have been called on to deal with so far. From a longer-term perspective, they are ragged, weak, never to be fixed but themselves historical, changing partly as the community finds it necessary to understand new, historically specific situations. The disciplinary communities themselves prove comparably ragged; thus, for example, the boundary setting off those who are to be recognized as "real" historians shifts as the rules change. By conceiving such communities as themselves caught up in the ongoing process, we invite openness and risk and avoid the temptation to treat any such community as static and privileged.

But if the insight into the import of disciplinary communities simply takes us back to the process of interaction, the obvious questions about the quality of that process become even more urgent. Even if the process *can* yield the happening of truth, it does not necessarily do so. It might be fair and efficient, or distorted and limiting. Effectiveness and truth seem to require "communicative competence" and a willingness and an ability to listen, to be open to persuasion. If distortions are built into the process, then the outcome is not truth but an instance of illegitimate domination. And if we can only act within the world that has resulted from a distorted process, we seem doomed simply to reproduce the distortion. Under such circumstances, a human situation reduced to history seems a kind of confinement, calling forth extremity, or a renewed appeal to something suprahistorical, or some combination of both.

The essential point about the process of interaction revolves around the relationship between the critical-deconstructive and conservative-hermeneutic elements at work in the culture. Attention to the concerns of Jürgen Habermas, Christopher Norris, and John Caputo will enable us to identify that point and show its import for a weak but constructive culture of history.

Bothered by "the hermeneutic claim to universality," Habermas sought to hold to the possibility of rational or enlightened critique by preserving criteria of distinction between distorted and undistorted forms of communication.[10] Writing in 1979, Richard Rorty found something all too metaphysical about Habermas's enterprise: "we need to know more about what counts as 'undis-

---

10. In considering the process of interaction and the quality of the communication it entails, Habermas criticized first Gadamerian hermeneutics, then both Foucault and Derrida. As noted in chap. 7, he summed up his case against Gadamer with particular clarity in Jürgen Habermas, "The Hermeneutic Claim to Universality," trans. Josef Bleicher, in Josef Bleicher, *Contemporary Hermeneutics: Method, Philosophy and Critique* (London: Routledge and Kegan Paul, 1980), 181–211. See also Jürgen Habermas, *The Philosophical Discourse of Modernity: Twelve Lectures*, trans. Frederick G. Lawrence (Cambridge: MIT Press, 1987), chaps. 7, 9, and 10, on Foucault and Derrida.

torted.' Here Habermas goes transcendental and offers principles."[11] As his thinking developed, Habermas backed ever further from the sort of substantive claim that would require such a transcendental turn, but even in 1988 Rorty noted that "Habermas would like to ground moral obligation, and thus social institutions, on something universally human."[12] What troubled Habermas was the claim that *on every level* there is nothing but hermeneutic interaction, nothing but history.

Rather than seek to lay down rules, principles, or criteria of rationality, Habermas sought to establish a regulative principle empty and abstract enough to transcend historical specificity and claim universality. As noted in chapter 7, he held that in interacting at all, we presuppose "a theory of communicative competence" and recognize a regulative principle of undistorted communication. Insofar as we find distortions in present forms of communication, we act to remove them, so our goal is an "ideal speech situation" of undistorted communication.[13]

Habermas, then, was not content simply to criticize what he took to be present distortions, seeking to persuade others. If we rely on nothing but the interaction itself, we seem doomed to acquiescence in a tradition embodying myriad contingent distortions. Thus Habermas's insistence on a quasi-teleological regulative principle to do some, at least, of what we used to believe a universal criterion of rationality could do for us. What unites us, making communication possible, is not simply the tradition but the regulative principle itself, "the formal anticipation of an idealized dialogue."[14]

Although Habermas was critical of Derrida, Norris, one of Derrida's most prominent advocates, offered an explicitly Habermasian reading of Derrida, seeking to show that Derridean deconstruction affords an essential complement to the enlightened or rational critique that Habermas sought to warrant—and that Norris, too, found essential. Norris's immediate aim was to secure the critical bite of Derridean deconstruction against what he took to be the wayward appropriation of Derrida among American literary deconstructionists, who found in Derrida a warrant for loose, undisciplined play. Peeling away the literary excess revealed the rigorously critical, Habermasian Derrida that Norris found essential to counter an array of more worthy cultural adversaries, from Gadamerian hermeneutics to the permissive postmodern neopragmatism of

---

11. Richard Rorty, *Consequences of Pragmatism (Essays: 1972–1980)* (Minneapolis: University of Minnesota Press, 1982), 173. See also Richard Rorty, *Philosophy and the Mirror of Nature* (Princeton: Princeton University Press, 1979), 380–383, 385, for this line of criticism against Habermas.

12. Richard Rorty, *Essays on Heidegger and Others* (Cambridge: Cambridge University Press, 1991), 197. In the same vein, Rorty implies that there is little to be said in advance about what counts as undistorted or ideological; thus we can only rely on democratic procedures. See Richard Rorty, *Contingency, Irony, and Solidarity* (Cambridge: Cambridge University Press, 1989), 82–84.

13. Habermas, "The Hermeneutic Claim to Universality," 202–203.

14. Ibid., 206–207.

Rorty and Jean-François Lyotard.[15] The thinking of each seemed prejudicially conservative in implication.

According to Norris, Habermas established the "basis for a critical theory independent of prevailing consensual norms," while Gadamer seemed to leave reason powerless to criticize the context of prereflective meanings in which all understanding is embedded.[16] But Norris's concern emerged especially in opposition to Rorty, whose way of separating the wheat from the chaff in Derrida was essentially the opposite of Norris's own. Norris worried that the thrust of Rorty's neopragmatism, including his way of reading Derrida, was "to give up any hope of informed rational critique."[17] And for Norris, this denial of "enlightened critique" was "implicitly conservative," because "for Rorty, as for Lyotard, the only justification that truth claims can have is their persuasive efficacy, their power to convince in the context of existing belief systems." More generally, Norris found in Rorty and Lyotard "a form of unprincipled pragmatism which renounces the very possibility of reasoned critique. And in doing so they are effectively depriving thought of any power to engage with social and political realities on other than passively conformist terms."[18] Simply to collapse the distinction between ideology and criticism, as the neopragmatists seemed to advocate, was to give up all hope of rational understanding, limiting us to acquiescence in the myths and ideologies of commonplace wisdom—precisely what Lyotard seemed to welcome. Thus, for Norris, the great value of deconstruction, which afforded a critique of "explanatory systems *without* giving way to a 'post-modern' outlook of passive liberal consensus."[19]

Norris might simply have settled for "critique"—and actually criticized something, seeking to persuade us to change the world. But much like Habermas, he pulled back to insist on the scope for *rational* or *enlightened* critique, out of fear that plain old critique is not enough, would become but another element in the blandly liberal babble. If some particular critique could be enlightened, it would enjoy a special claim to our attention. Conversely, Gadamer and Rorty did deny what Norris, like Habermas, found it essential to preserve—any scope for "reason" that is not merely consensual and historical.

15. Christopher Norris, *Derrida* (Cambridge: Harvard University Press, 1987), 161, 168–169. For Norris's overall cultural aim, see his *The Contest of Faculties: Philosophy and Theory after Deconstruction* (London: Methuen, 1985), 27. Norris continued to refine his argument in the subsequent essays now collected in *What's Wrong with Postmodernism: Critical Theory and the Ends of Philosophy* (Baltimore: Johns Hopkins University Press, 1990). He recognized, of course, that Habermas himself, far from seeking alliance with Derrida, was a formidable critic; thus he sought to defend Derrida against Habermas in the most important of these essays, pp. 49–76. See also pp. 134–163, for Norris's critique of John M. Ellis's *Against Deconstruction*, and pp. 194–207, for Norris's continuing effort to place Derrida in the tradition of Kantian critique.

16. Norris, *The Contest of Faculties*, 25.

17. Norris, *Derrida*, 156–157; the quoted passage is on p. 157. Norris confessed that much of his thinking had developed in creative disagreement with Rorty; see Norris, *The Contest of Faculties*, vii, and pp. 139–166 for "Philosophy as a Kind of Narrative: Rorty on Post-Modern Liberal Culture," one of the key documents in Norris's important interchange with Rorty during the 1980s.

18. Norris, *Derrida*, 153, 155, 169.

19. Norris, *The Contest of Faculties*, 36; see also p. 15.

I have noted certain limits in both Gadamer and Rorty, and it is surely plausible to seek in deconstruction at least a critical complement, if not a full-blown alternative. Although "play" was more prominent in Derrida than Norris admitted, the critical potential of Derridean deconstruction remains fundamental. But does that side of Derrida require a Habermasian gloss or admixture? And is the relationship between Derridean deconstruction and Gadamerian hermeneutics, or even Rorty's neopragmatism, necessarily as antagonistic as Norris assumed?

Before addressing these questions, let us add Caputo, whose stimulating *Radical Hermeneutics* similarly sought to use Derrida for critical purposes. Caputo, however, moved in the opposite direction from Norris and rational critique, for he was concerned with what seemed an ongoing authoritarian tendency to freeze the present outcome and stop the play. And rather than opposing deconstruction to hermeneutics, he sought to bring them together in a postmetaphysical way. In the final analysis, however, Caputo's thinking stemmed from much the same family of concerns as Norris's, for he, too, was worried about the process of interaction and the possibility of domination or distortion. And he was comparably nervous about the implications of leaving everything to history. Moreover, Caputo, like Norris, sought to box out Gadamer as prejudicially conservative.

Although Caputo, in attempting to develop a *radical* hermeneutics, made Heidegger too much like Derrida, he offered superb characterizations of each, and he had enough room for their differences to explicate the tension between them. His aim, plausibly enough, was to use each as a check to the other.[20] Taken together, Derrida and Heidegger undercut claims to privilege and invited ongoing conversation or dialogue—precisely, it would seem, what I have been pointing toward in this chapter.

Yet Caputo's premium was ultimately on disruption at the expense of the moment of agreement, of coming back together, that Gadamer represented. Caputo valued in Derrida's thinking "a deconstruction of hermeneutics as a nostalgia for meaning and unity"—which is what he found in Gadamer. And Derrida, Caputo went on to say, was more Nietzschean than either Heidegger or Gadamer, more suspicious, with "a greater sense of the fragility of our thought constructions and the contingency of our institutions."[21] Following Derrida, Caputo warned against taking ourselves seriously, thereby putting an end to the play, so that disagreement means "drawing blood." Indeed, our major concern must be to resist the authoritarian tendency to draw blood that seems to lurk everywhere in a world endlessly reducing to something in particular; thus Caputo invited us to play "out of bounds."[22]

20. John D. Caputo, *Radical Hermeneutics: Repetition, Deconstruction, and the Hermeneutic Project* (Bloomington: Indiana University Press, 1987), 98; see also pp. 186, 250–251.

21. Ibid., 97. See also pp. 111–112, 210–211; as well as John D. Caputo, "Gadamer's Closet Essentialism: A Derridean Critique," in *Dialogue and Deconstruction: The Gadamer-Derrida Encounter*, ed. Diane P. Michelfelder and Richard E. Palmer (Albany: State University of New York Press, 1989), 258–264.

22. Caputo, *Radical Hermeneutics*, 113, 258.

But Caputo's way of aligning Heidegger, Gadamer, and Derrida betrayed the blurring, the combination of prejudicial conflation and plausible extremity, that we have found in a number of efforts to adjust to a postmetaphysical perspective. As a result, there was something limiting about his way of conceiving the intersection between deconstruction and hermeneutics.

Between Rational Critique and Disruptive Play

In thinkers like Habermas, Norris, and Caputo, concerns about the process of interaction and the nature of its outcome led to a premium on rational critique, on the one hand, and disruptive play, on the other. But there is scope for aligning hermeneutics and deconstruction in a weak but constructive way, so that we no longer feel the need either to grasp for a rational admixture or to play out of bounds. By pinpointing three intersecting problems with Norris's way of infusing a dose of Habermas into Derridean deconstruction, we begin to discern that alternative alignment.

First, Norris claimed to seek, with Habermas and against Gadamer and Rorty, a form of rigorous critique that does *not* repair to metaphysically based "principles."[23] But the questions Rorty asked of Habermas intrude themselves immediately: How do we decide what is "informed," or "rational"? Who decides what counts as distorted or enlightened, and on what grounds? If, in a playfully deconstructionist mood, we were to seek an example of rhetoric disrupting the philosophical text, we would need look no farther than Norris's, which consistently offers characterizations of the alternatives freighted with his particular political orientation. Part of what Derrida showed was that some such freighting is inevitable—even when we claim to specify what counts as rational or enlightened.

Second, insofar as Norris was seeking not to claim privilege for some particular critique but to avoid passive acquiescence, his Habermasian admixture was simply unnecessary. Those like Norris insist on "enlightened critique" because dualistic thinking leads them to misconstrue the effects if we do without it. Their reading of convention, tradition, embeddedness in some particular history leads them to assume that the only alternative to enlightened critique is a pragmatist mishmash, ultimately passive and conservative. But there is a moderate alternative, which specifies simply that the process continues, on all levels, and invites whatever critique anyone cares to offer.

Third, Norris's conflation of deconstruction with enlightened critique is not true to Derrida—*even* to the radical side of Derrida. Although Norris was central in bringing out the critical, reconstructive potential of Derridean deconstruction, his effort to make Derrida congruent with Habermas required

---

23. Norris, *The Contest of Faculties*, 7.

marginalizing much that is essential to Derrida's thinking. Indeed, a deconstructionist number is easily done on Norris's own "margins"—the asides, the parentheses, the "to be sures" that tend to play down everything in Derrida's text that overflows the Habermasian mold. Norris tells us, for example, that "the issues [Derrida] raises belong within the tradition of Kantian enlightened critique, even while pressing that tradition to the limits (and beyond) of its own self-legitimizing claims."[24] Norris makes the "and beyond" seem merely parenthetical, yet in fact it is essential, for it entails a denial and a flip-flop into something quite different from that Kantian tradition.

To be sure, Norris had good reason for dissociating Derridean deconstruction both from the "anarchist," relentlessly negative, sometimes apocalyptic side of Foucault and from the frivolous or methodical literary deconstruction prominent in the United States. But it was not necessary to invoke Habermas or to play down Derrida's departure from enlightened critique to avoid such limiting conflations.

To combine critical theory and deconstruction in opposition to Gadamer's relative conservatism was to miss what Gadamer and deconstruction had in common—and thus the scope for a radicalism no longer relying on metaphysically scented conceptions of reason and enlightenment. The radical side of Derridean deconstruction, insofar as it could serve the reconstruction Norris had in mind, was congruent with Gadamer and, up to a point, with Rorty but not with Habermas—or Norris himself. The key is that, in its critical mode, deconstruction meshed with Gadamerian hermeneutics and *not* enlightened critique.

Much like Habermas, Norris made leaving it to the "power to convince in the context of existing belief systems," which he associated with Rorty and Lyotard, more restrictive than it is.[25] Indeed, those like Norris tend to view such "belief systems" as a fixed grid or box, rather than an unstable, tension-ridden, and thus moving historical constellation. Norris worried, for example, that Rorty mistrusted all those grand theories, including even the tradition of Kantian enlightened critique, "that claim to know more and see further than current beliefs would allow."[26] What a curious worry. "To know more and see further than current beliefs would allow" is surely impossible a priori. But that is merely to confine us to our particular, finite, but still open and moving history, not to some rigid, fixed structure.

The sense of suffocation that may result from the experience of nothing but history was at work in Norris's way of characterizing the alternatives. The present set of beliefs or "principle of reason" allowed any critique Norris could come up with; once he had actually offered some such critique, it would be possible to ascertain if it had been sufficiently persuasive to connect with the

24. Norris, *Derrida*, 169. See also pp. 139–140, 178, 219, for additional examples of this tendency.

25. Ibid., 155.

26. Ibid., 153.

actual and help transform it.[27] From within a weak but constructive culture of history, we see why "power to convince" is enough, why we need not claim some enlightened or rational admixture.

Caputo's fear of the authority of tradition was comparable, though it led him to accent play rather than the scope for enlightened critique. Because he linked Gadamer to a combination of nostalgia and metaphysically buttressed authority, Caputo could not find room for one of the essential dimensions of Gadamerian hermeneutics—the moment of cohesion, consensus, coming back together *within* the kind of postmetaphysical framework Caputo seemed to want. Gadamer showed how to conceive both sides of the coin: Some particular outcome endlessly results from the dialogue, the endless conflict of interpretations, so there is a measure of agreement, and the tradition maintains some measure of authority. Nevertheless, the outcome is not authoritarian and menacing, requiring a premium on disruption, but sufficiently weak to invite our creative and reconstructive engagement with it. To posit play, even play "out of bounds," as the alternative to drawing blood was to preclude precisely the weak but constructive alternative that Caputo first seemed to be seeking.

Just as Habermas insisted, we have a common interest in undistorted communication but what leads us to interact is not the ideal of agreement based on undistorted communication but the desire to learn about this particular world from our need to act within it. We know ourselves to be partial and incomplete, yet in belonging to the totality of the actual, we have something in common with others. Care entails the need and the willingness to learn from them. Although each individual must decide which of those others might offer most, in principle we might learn from everyone else who shares this whole growing particular world with us, everyone both past and present. Thus the rational and moral willingness to learn encompasses a willingness to engage in dialogue, an openness to persuasion.

But because some seem unwilling or unable to learn from us, or incompetent to teach us, so that we cannot learn from them, the dialogue and conflict may be distorted, and thus the process may seem inadequate. We may suspect that those who persist in disagreement are not open to learning and persuasion. And it is true, of course, that any of us may resist, clinging to our own prejudices— from laziness or egotistical interest, from fear, from various forms of contextual interference. So openness and learning must operate not only "horizontally" but also along a vertical axis. Although we cannot establish criteria that would enable us to distinguish the distorted from the undistorted once and for all, our present rules and criteria are subject to contest, so it is possible to appeal from the level of conflict to the more abstract or theoretical level where the particular conflict might be adjudicated. In shifting to that level, the effort to persuade becomes an effort to point out and to account for the element of distortion or

---

27. Compare ibid., 161. Norris's agenda is especially clear and explicit in the discussion here.

blindness that informs the competing position. Indeed, we may find it necessary to step back to suggest why our opponents do not recognize such distortion even when it is pointed out to them. There is room for contest all along this axis.

Habermas proved an especially worthy contestant as he probed for distortions in our present communication and interaction. Rather than simply charge distortion, he backed up to talk about what distortion might mean, starting with his fruitful recasting of Marx and Freud. And thus he, more than anyone, taught us to look for systematic distortion even in the contingent rules that have come to govern our present forms of interaction.

But fearing acquiescence in the authority of a distorting tradition, Habermas offered his critical diagnosis in the guise of an abstract regulative principle, not simply as a higher-level effort to persuade.[28] Although he made that principle as empty as possible, his conception of what counts as enlightened or rational stemmed partly from his particular understanding of present obstacles. His way of postulating an ideal speech situation betrayed his understanding of "distorted"—and thus of "undistorted," "ideal," and "competent" as well. Despite the gloss of neutral abstraction, Habermas, too, was seeking to persuade. Many efforts to adapt Habermas or Derrida, like those of Norris, or Michael Ryan, or even Richard Bernstein, similarly slipped something substantive, resting on some particular conception of human needs and present inadequacies, into what purported to be an empty regulative principle. Whether consciously or not, such efforts sought to preempt the discussion by specifying in advance what counts as such and such. In the test of history so far, those particular critiques have proven especially fruitful, but, inevitably, each was too specific to merit the last word.

We can maintain the distinctions that Habermas and Norris found essential—between ideology and enlightened criticism, for example—without assuming there are suprahistorical criteria that some, at least, might know in advance. Those criteria are continually being hammered out within history, as part of the interaction. Deciding on the rules is part of the game, the particularizing, the test of power. The same is true even for deciding on the rules for determining the rules—take it as many steps as you like.[29] All along the vertical axis, the debate continues as part of the history. There is no way to transcend the process of interaction and specify what counts as rational or competent once and for all. But though the ongoing interaction never yields suprahistorical rules or criteria, its weak, provisional resultants afford the measure of coherence necessary for dialogue and learning—and for a continuing history.

28. See, for example, his treatment of "falsity" and "distortion" in "The Hermeneutic Claim to Universality," 206–207.

29. As Stanley Fish has repeatedly argued, theory is just one more form of practice. See also Thomas, *The New Historicism*, 232 n. 2.

In positing the ideal of undistorted communication as a regulative principle, Habermas suggested that history is wound around an ongoing effort to free up human being from distortion. Despite its quaintly old-fashioned quality, Croce's dictum that history is "the story of liberty" is similar in important respects. Although Habermas was far more helpful than Croce in pinpointing present obstacles to freedom, comparison with Croce's unrelenting historicism indicates the residually metaphysical tendency of Habermas's thinking.

Croce emphasized that obstacles and distortions recur endlessly and thus our endless effort to free up human creativity. There is nothing anomalous about the fact that we *still* need to address distortions; present distortion is simply another historically specific challenge. And there is nothing anomalous about the fact that agreement has not been reached, that we still disagree in our diagnoses and priorities. In contrast, Habermas implied that there ought to be undistortion, even, on some level, agreement. Present distortion is anomalous; to undercut it is to be in touch with the ideal and to merit privilege. Thus the tendency to "go metaphysical" that continued to lurk in Habermas's thinking, even as it became ever more historicist.

We can be persuaded to view aspects of our historically specific framework as distorting without assuming that we should be able to agree, or that we are working toward an ideal situation in which distortion is overcome for good and agreement becomes possible. In a world of nothing but history, distortion is endless, always taking historically specific form as an aspect of particularizing or concealment. And thus disagreement and conflict are built in, endless. But so is the impulse to free up the human capacity for fruitful interaction; and so is the process of persuasion; and so is the coming to provisional agreement. We simply proceed, embracing interaction at all levels within the immanent totality. Meshing with the world as historical in this way, we do not acquiesce in some flawed outcome but participate in the endless overcoming and growth.

Because that process encompasses all conceivable levels, it obviously includes not only Derrida and Habermas and Norris and Caputo but Croce and Gadamer as well. Croce and Gadamer do not specify what counts as distortion-free interaction or how we are to decide on the provisional rules. They, too, are simply part of the interaction, seeking to persuade. Croce made this point explicitly, but his reflexive self-consciousness led not to a paralyzed acquiescence in the actual, nor to play, nor to a renewed quest for something suprahistorical. Rather, he outlined a framework from within which he could offer his own contribution in a constructive, history-making mode.

In seeking to link Derrida with Habermas, Norris did not do justice to the reflexivity that distinguishes deconstruction from rational critique and places it squarely within the terrain that opens with the reduction to history. Knowing itself to be radically immanent, deconstruction invokes no "rational" principles, procedures, or standards. Derridean "undecidability" means precisely that there can be no such enlightened basis for decision, because although things do get decided, *in and as* history, they cannot be decided *in advance.* Deconstruction understands any claim to reason—including Norris's—as suspect precisely as a claim to suprahistorical privilege.

To be sure, a reflexive preoccupation with the status of its own enterprise led deconstruction, in some of its forms, to retreat into the playful self-deconstruction that Norris plausibly feared would undermine the critical force of the Derridean insight. But the key to rescuing the reconstructive potential in Derrida is not to marginalize his relentlessly playful side but rather to account for it historically. A historical account enables us to distinguish the several sides of Derrida's thinking and to keep the elements of both plausible extremity and unnecessary excess from compromising the critical, reconstructive potential. At the same time, it is necessary to grasp the Gadamerian complement that adds the essential measure of weight to deconstruction by showing that endless gathering accompanies endless slippage; the results even of our ongoing deconstructions continually come back together—and even, in one sense, last.

While Norris wanted sharply to distinguish the critical bite in deconstruction from play, Caputo found deconstruction's playful, endlessly disruptive, out-of-bounds tendency essential to the radical role he believed necessary. Caputo's accent was so different because the obstacle he saw, even in hermeneutics, was not bland liberal consensus but authority. He assumed that hermeneutics and historicism somehow play down contingency so that what results from their mechanisms is strong enough to arrest the play. To counter this tendency, Caputo found necessary an exclusive emphasis on the deconstructive side of the equation. But he was missing the scope for a middle term as he conflated the authority that results from Gadamerian mechanisms with still-metaphysical authority.

It is certainly true that persuasion and coming to agreement are essential to the historicist-hermeneutic conception, and they entail power and even authority. But whatever has resulted is contingent, merely provisional, more or less riddled with tensions, and does not claim determinate meaning or final authority. As we have emphasized, the happening of a particular world entails the ongoing competition of interpretations, and this encompasses ongoing judgment about the particular power and authority, even ongoing judgment about the way we go about judging. In this framework of contingency, weakness, and provisionality, deconstruction need not be confined to the task Caputo had in mind, appropriate to a still-metaphysical culture; it can play a more constructive critical role in tandem with the Gadamerian emphasis on the sense in which we continually come to *some* measure of agreement.

To put it simply, because hermeneutics can be weaker than Caputo assumed, deconstruction can play a more constructive role. At the same time, deconstruction, to play that role, need not be so strong as Norris believed necessary, claiming a privileged enlightened status. If there remains a tendency to stop the play, justifying Caputo's fears, it lies in some a priori claim to rationality, not in the provisional authority of a merely historical tradition.

We saw that Caputo, in his uneasiness with a world endlessly becoming particular, invites us to play "out of bounds." Surely anyone may seek to do so, but if you are *really* out of bounds, you will not connect; no one will notice. If you *do* connect—as has Derrida, for example—then even if you started out of bounds, you end up helping to expand the boundaries. You are not really out of bounds at all but rather part of the particular growing tradition. To say you become part of the tradition, however, is not to make you safe or reassuring in the limitingly conservative sense that troubles Caputo. You may play a fruitfully deconstructive, disruptive role within the totality of the particular history—precisely one of the possibilities in Derrida.

The terms of a weak but constructive culture of history enable us to see through the extreme characterizations of the situation that the contingent interaction of the hermeneutic and deconstructive elements often occasioned. To emphasize the moment of consensus, the endless renewal of the authority of tradition, is not to leave us paralyzed within some particular historical outcome. Rather, it simply enables us to continue, without futility, in a postmetaphysical mode. At the same time, deconstructive disruption need not become so all-encompassing that we are left simply to play—or to long for an impossible alterity. While remaining radical and critical, it becomes constructive, serving the endless remaking of the tradition. Tradition makes possible, invites, even demands, its own criticism, deconstruction, reinterpretation. We are constantly affirming as well as deconstructing, looking for what we share, as well as competing. Things slip but continually gather and cohere as particular as the world is endlessly remade.

To bring human being together with history in this way, based on a recasting of truth, continuity, and totality, need not be viewed as nostalgic weakness, stemming from an inability to bear the "real" meaningless of things. Rather, it is to find an even keel after the giddy or despairing overreaction, so that we do justice to the sense in which, even with the eclipse of metaphysics, we are participants in the ongoing happening of a particular world in history.

Openness and Risk in Historiography

Understanding the weak but constructive framework makes it possible to confront more deeply the imperative of historiographical openness and pluralism that we encountered in the preceding chapter. There seems scope for expanding the kinds of questions we ask, the range of answers we are prepared to hear, even the levels of abstraction on which historical inquiry can usefully operate. A greater sense of our own historicity seems to entail, above all, putting more of ourselves and our world at risk. Even the assumptions, categories, and commitments that inform our historical inquiries are merely historical resultants, and they are implicitly at issue whenever we ask historical questions. A willingness to put them at risk would balance the renewed emphasis on present involvement in historiography—which easily leads to excess. Yet how much have we been prepared to put at risk?

Although the narrativists' attention to figured language was invaluable in expanding the sphere of reflexivity and risk, their concern to show the "crooked" constructedness of any historical account tended to neutralize the bite of the reflexivity they opened up. Much like deconstruction in its formalist or weak textualist guise, the narrativists kept finding the same kinds of tensions and oppositions in the historical accounts they analyzed. A certain methodological insight afforded privilege to the present inquirer. At the same time, the narrativists' preoccupation with authority led them to accent the need for every historical text to question its own authority.[30] Such fastidious self-deconstruction could easily become merely playful, and the whole narrativist approach could result in a kind of cynical leveling. If what ultimately matters is the rhetorical constructedness of any historical account, no discrimination is possible, so nothing is genuinely at risk.

Gadamer, especially, pointed historical self-consciousness beyond any such limiting preoccupation with historiographical crookedness. In denying method, he foreclosed any possibility that we might find some privileged way of deconstructing our predecessors. Rather than see through them, we enter into dialogue with them, hoping that they might help us dissolve or overcome some of the tensions in our own constructed world. In suggesting that any truly historical approach thinks its own historicity, Gadamer invited us genuinely to test ourselves, attending to the embeddedness of our questions and categories in the processes we study. Insofar as the historical text understands itself in Gadamerian terms, as part of the ongoing process of interaction, it makes no strong claim to truth and need not be preoccupied with explicitly questioning its own authority.

The new historians, too, invited reflexivity and risk as they expanded the focus to encompass not only excluded groups but forms of experience not formerly thought to be historical. But there was something restrictive about the conception of the historical field that resulted. Even as they invited greater risk in one sense, the new historians tended to pull back from risk in another.

As noted in chapter 10, historiographical conflict yields a particular way of unifying the historical field, a particular cultural self-understanding, a thick, tension-ridden curriculum, canon, or master narrative. With the inflation of history, more strands come to seem historical, and the conflict intensifies. But however great the expansion, any way of arranging the historical field entails downplaying, neglecting, or precluding other ways of looking at those who came before us—their experience and even their connection with us. Even what

---

30. Hans Kellner, *Language and Historical Representation: Getting the Story Crooked* (Madison: University of Wisconsin Press, 1989), 321.

counts as power, elite status, or marginalization depends on our assessment of the relative import of the several spheres at issue. To make gender or ethnicity the focus of concern and grouping is to preclude other possibilities. As with those recent emphases, we arrange the field in a historically specific way in response to present needs. But the process of arranging the field is continuous. There is no end to the ways we might usefully relate to those who came before or to arrange, in a hierarchy of importance, our innumerable connections with them.

The new historians were not only expanding the historiographical focus but fruitfully reshuffling our sense of what was most important in our own history. But they were quick to assume that a suprahistorical moral sanction attached to their particular categories of understanding, their ways of connecting us to our predecessors, and their hierarchies of importance. In emphasizing gender, or popular culture, or social modes of explanation, they implied that we have at last found the right way of understanding what had been marginalized, the right way of ordering the historical universe. But this was to avoid putting at risk their own choices and categories. Genuinely to democratize our historical culture, in contrast, would be to expand the contest, inviting discussion of all aspects of our present connectedness with what went before.

Especially as we accent the broadly political contest at work in historiography, it is tempting to dismiss competing views through the strategies of political reductionism. Political difference becomes an excuse for avoiding engagement and risk. The antidote is to look beneath immediate political differences, to cut as deeply as necessary to find what we share within our common weak totality. Charles S. Maier has noted that "historiography need not simply echo ideological conflicts uncritically"; rather, it can mediate them insofar as historiography is "a shared project of knowledge" that transcends political conditioning through open-minded self-reflection and a "sociable" willingness to listen.[31] To be sure, we may prefer to keep ourselves immune from risk, but our care for the world and our need to learn invite us to seek a basis for discussion, to enable us to profit from difference. The quest for risky dialogue stands opposed to political reductionism.

What we need, then, are riskier histories that more explicitly implicate the categories that inform our own historical questioning. Jane Caplan has astutely invoked deconstruction to show the scope for a riskier history even of fascism; our binary oppositions—starting with rational/irrational—would themselves be at issue in such a history.[32] More generally, as we stress that history is always

31. See Charles S. Maier, *The Unmasterable Past: History, Holocaust, and German National Identity* (Cambridge: Harvard University Press, 1988), 61–64. Maier makes this point in discussing the politically charged debate in Germany during the late 1980s over the scope for "normalizing" the Nazi past.

32. Jane Caplan, "Postmodernism, Poststructuralism, and Deconstruction: Notes for Historians," *Central European History* 22, nos. 3–4 (September–December 1989): 274–278.

written by the victors, we would do well to ponder the fact that the very terms of our present inquiries recapitulate and implicitly endorse *some* contestable winning, some aspect of the provisional present outcome. And of course we, too, are seeking to win, and we are among the victors insofar as our historiographical contributions prove influential—and thereby enter history. This dimension of historical reflexivity need not paralyze us; it simply expands our capacity to learn through historical inquiry and to adjust our present commitments on the basis of what we learn.

At the limit, openness and risk mean that when we question some aspect of what we have become, we are open to answers that prove *not* to undercut the actual. Radical historical questions can yield answers with conservative implications, suggesting, to put it simply, that some actual state of affairs is not so bad after all. To uncover the contingencies and preclusions entailed in the coming to be of the actual does not in itself demonstrate its illegitimacy but simply affords a rational basis for moral response. Insofar as the range of historical answers is restricted a priori, precluding those that seem conservative in implication, the enterprise slides from historical inquiry to edification or propaganda.

Moreover, with the expansion that follows from the inflation of history, there is room for contest over the levels of abstraction on which historical inquiry might operate. The distinctiveness of history has long been based partly on the historians' visceral sense of the drama of the particular case, in its naked individuality. But historical individuality came to connote a certain class of events, on a delimited range of levels, understood in contrast to speculative philosophy of history and to science, which seemed to make higher-order knowledge out of historical events. Thus relatively abstract levels were excluded from historiography through conflation with Hegel or those like Arnold Toynbee who sought laws or regularities. Or those levels were left to the more ethereal, quasi-religious speculation of thinkers like Teilhard de Chardin. To be sure, such efforts to fashion something grandiose from historical material appealed to the wider culture, but they remained suspect, especially because they were always in tension with the historians' emphasis on the particular, in its naked contingency.

With the eclipse of metaphysics, however, the contingencies on what had seemed the merely historical level come to seem ultimate, making the role of the particular all the more dramatic. Insofar as we abstract from those particular events, each higher level, as we become ever more abstract, is shown up to be merely historical as well. Even when we reach the level of what had seemed the suprahistorical frame—metaphysical, teleological, or scientific—we find but a different level of history, itself particular, riddled with contingency. So what is offered to the culture as historical understanding can no longer be confined to the formerly delimited range of frequencies.

Those higher levels can be apprehended only through historical inquiry, which thus has expanded to encompass them. In expanding along that vertical axis, historians encountered those from other disciplines who, with the inflation of history, found themselves compelled to ask historical questions of their own. To be sure, the historical questions of philosophers like Charles Taylor, Alasdair MacIntyre, and Richard Rorty were quite different from those typical of professional historians, but disciplinary lines blurred, and it did not matter whether those who wrote these more abstract histories called themselves historians or not. Although relatively abstract, the "bigger" histories that resulted from their inquiries were not teleological or Hegelian, nor was their aim suprahistorical generalization. They were simply efforts to illuminate the present in the most helpful way possible, by laying out its historical genesis. An expanded and open culture of history will grasp the scope for historical inquiry on such higher levels, but it will also welcome the debate, or contest, that develops along that axis. In any one instance, we will not agree about the level of abstraction that is most likely to afford answers and so is most worthy of our attention.

Questions about levels of abstraction were at work in the disputes over contextualism that marked intellectual history as the scope for historical inquiry expanded. David Harlan and David Hollinger, for example, disagreed not, as it first seemed, over whether intellectual history should be contextualist but over the levels of context that might be appropriate.[33] Hollinger found to be acontextualist the texts by Rorty and Michael Walzer that Harlan admired. They may seem so at first glance, but only because we have grown accustomed to a relatively restricted range of "proper" contexts for understanding ideas. In fact, Rorty and Walzer had filtered out more immediate levels of context in an effort to ask more abstract historical questions—and thus, they hoped, to deepen our understanding of particular aspects of the present. Hollinger proved unnecessarily conservative in this debate partly because, fearing Whiggish deformations, he associated contextualism with the imperative of getting at the past on its own terms. Thus he afforded privilege to a certain level of context, taken as the "original" context.[34] From within a weak but constructive culture of history, it is possible to open and expand in the way Harlan wanted but without inviting the ahistorical anticontextualism that Hollinger feared.

The Extremes and the Middle Ground

Our tendency to think in dualistic, either-or terms has made it difficult to grasp the elements of the moderate postmetaphysical orientation, which proves

---

33. See *American Historical Review* 94, no. 3 (June 1989): 581–626. This includes David Harlan, "Intellectual History and the Return of Literature" (pp. 581–609); David A. Hollinger, "The Return of the Prodigal: The Persistence of Historical Knowing" (pp. 610–621; see esp. pp. 613–615); and Harlan's "Reply to David Hollinger" (pp. 622–626).
34. Hollinger, "Return of the Prodigal," 612–613.

to rest on a weak but constructive culture of history. The reduction to a particular history may seem to freeze the world in a static sameness. Anything that can possibly result from what we do will connect with and reproduce what has come to be so far. Croce and Gadamer can seem conservative partly because each invited us to accept, and work within, such a world of particularity and finitude. An experience of the finitude of the totality of things can induce a sense of limits, even a grim sense of claustrophobia, which perhaps we all feel in some of our moods but which some feel more intensely than others.

Yet whereas finite particularity means sameness in one sense, it does not preclude novelty. The world continuously changes, or becomes other, although the process is bland indeed. Endless human response is the reverse side of the endlessly provisional and tension-ridden quality of what has come to be so far. So the element of continuity does not mean sameness; difference and novelty do not require discontinuity; openness does not require disengagement.

The weak but constructive alternative is weak enough to avoid charges of authoritarianism yet strong enough to avoid aestheticism; it is weak enough to be convincing in light of the wider displacement but strong enough to serve ongoing reconstruction. It establishes a place between play and domination, between endless subversion and enslavement to the tradition. It entails neither innocence nor disengagement but responsibility, weight, and risk. We take ourselves seriously even while recognizing our contingency and finitude—and thus our need for interaction and the impossibility of completeness and the last word.

There is scope for rationality within this framework, but it turns out to mean not "enlightened critique" but historical understanding, stemming from our active involvement with the provisional present world, and it encompasses a deconstructive questioning as radical as we can muster. Indeed, the path opens to a more varied and significant historical questioning even as the pretense of a definitive historical account or master narrative falls away. At the same time, we understand, from within the weak but constructive framework, why a presentist departure from realist representation need not warrant falsified documents or politically prejudiced readings, why others can hope to learn from our historical accounts, partial and provisional though they are.

Our way of realigning the forces at work suggests that as we grow accustomed to the departure from positivism, metaphysics, and modernity, the alternatives before us are more complex, but ultimately more promising, than many have indicated. "Crooked" is not the only alternative to "straight," fiction is not the only alternative to the strong, authoritarian understanding of truth, and Scott's form of politicized presentism is not the only alternative to Himmelfarb's limiting neopositivism. A pinched privilege to excluded groups is not the only alternative to a celebratory master narrative. An appeal to "enlightened critique" is not the only alternative to passive acquiescence, and an invitation to endless subversion is not the only alternative to "drawing blood."

In the weak but constructive mode, we endlessly respond to the actual, or our tradition, in a way that is by turns deconstructive, dialogical, and creative. But at each moment, we may bump up against the limits of the reconstructive impulse and begin to experience the extremes that become possible in a postmetaphysical world. Rather than experience our tradition as an invitation to creative response, we may feel our embeddedness in a particular tradition as limiting, even appalling and grotesque. Rather than seek dialogue, we may afford privilege to the disembedded other. A sense of capriciousness and futility may undermine any premium on historical inquiry to serve history-making action, leaving us to concentrate on self-creation instead. Understanding those extremes enables us to see, in a postmetaphysical world, why we sometimes peer into history in a nonconstructive mode, what happens when we do so, and what role the resulting experience, or form of understanding, has in our lives.

In a postmetaphysical culture the reconstructive strand and the array of extremes can play off each other, working in fruitful tension. Even historical writing can depart from the effort of ongoing reconstruction to foster, or respond to, the extreme experiences of the world as history. And of course there is scope for disagreement and contest even at the intersection of reconstruction and the array of plausible extremes.

The cultural moments issuing from Nietzsche, Croce, and Heidegger are at once competing and complementary. If we experience our postmetaphysical world as nothing but history, we can grasp with Nietzsche the sense in which each of our moments is a timeless culmination, an end in itself, and need not be experienced as simply adding more history to the pile already there. We may, in some of our moments, feel the point of Heidegger's religious disengagement, with its posthistoricist openness to a dimension beyond this particular world and the moments of individual experience that it makes possible. As we have seen, an array of plausible variations have developed on the Nietzschean and Heideggerian extremes. But, conversely, interaction with those extreme responses may reinforce our sense of the scope for a constructive orientation to our merely historical world.

Index

Abbagnano, Nicola, 99
Adorno, Theodor W., 111 n. 1, 208
Aestheticism, 2–3, 12, 46, 48, 49, 89 n. 28,
    165, 167, 177, 252, 267, 269, 274, 294,
    317; in Nietzsche, 58, 79; in Croce, 89,
    91–92; in Rorty, 228–229, 235, 237–238,
    241, 243, 245–246, 250. *See also* Literary
    culture
Anderson, Perry, 292
Ankersmit, F[rank] R., 14 n. 33, 18, 261,
    276 n. 69, 278, 291
Annales School, 215, 269, 271
Apel, Karl-Otto, 167
Arendt, Hannah, 152, 208 n. 88
Austin, J. L., 207–208

Bakhtin, Mikhail, 271 n. 54
Barthes, Roland, 11, 12, 182 n. 6, 193, 277 n.
    70
Barton, Anne, 274
Bataille, Georges, 193
Baudrillard, Jean, 202
Beard, Charles A., 83, 84
Becker, Carl L., 83, 84
Benjamin, Walter, 17, 208–209
Bergson, Henri, 16, 44–46, 52–53, 86, 149
Berkhofer, Robert F., Jr., 260 n. 22
Bernstein, Richard J., 135 n. 68, 151–152,
    170, 291, 309
Blanchot, Maurice, 193
Bloom, Harold, 4–5, 235, 236, 242, 248
Blumenberg, Hans, 23
Boland, Eavan, 269 n. 49

Bové, Paul, 210
Braudel, Fernand, 259–260
Bultmann, Rudolf, 146 n. 108
Butler, Christopher, 228
Butterfield, Herbert, 15, 32

Camus, Albert, 107–108
Capitini, Aldo, 108 n. 72
Caplan, Jane, 14 n. 33, 314
Caputo, John D., 5, 9, 18, 119 n. 19, 120, 145,
    149 n. 117, 153 n. 1, 157, 175, 177, 178,
    200, 204, 222 n. 120, 302, 305–306, 308,
    311–312
Carr, David, 42 n. 5, 259 n. 17
Cartesianism. *See* Descartes, René
Cassirer, Ernst, 24 n. 5, 84
Catachresis, 200, 230
Christianity, 28, 60, 79, 81, 100–102, 113
Coetzee, J. M., 47
Cohen, Sande, 15, 277 n. 70
Collingwood, R. G., 17, 17 n. 39, 83, 110,
    160, 162, 163, 178–179
Comte, Auguste, 34, 38
Cornell, Joseph, 273
Crews, Frederick, 212 n. 96
Croce, Benedetto, 1, 8, 16–17, 81–110, 166,
    215, 218, 220, 249–250, 259, 266,
    267–268, 273, 297–298, 299, 310, 317; in
    common with Nietzsche and Heidegger, 45,
    46, 50–57, 125, 297; and Vico, 87–88, 89,
    91, 93; and Hegel, 84, 86–88, 95; and
    Nietzsche, 89–92, 97–102, 109, 110,
    154–157; and Heidegger, 93, 108, 109,

Croce, Benedetto *(continued)*
110, 115, 117, 118–119, 127 n. 45, 130,
137–138, 143, 146, 157–158, 174; and
Gadamer, 17, 93, 109, 159–160, 164–175,
177–178, 299–300; and Rorty, 107–108,
226–227, 231, 233, 234, 249–250; on
language, 51, 54, 91, 96, 157, 195–196; and
humanism, 55 n. 37, 82, 106, 174; on
philosophy, 84–85, 104, 109–110; on
immortality of the act, 97, 99–100, 102,
167; on faith in history, 85, 100, 102–104,
106–108, 167, 215; as presentist, 83, 91,
94–95, 109, 155, 158, 177; as historian,
96 n. 40, 108–110, 172–174, 178, 189; as
moderate, 81–82, 92, 104, 106–107, 153,
165, 167; as neo-liberal, 102–103, 104–106
Culler, Jonathan, 182 n. 5, 234

Davidson, Donald, 1, 18, 229, 230
Davis, Natalie, 269, 270
De Chirico, Giorgio, 273
Deconstruction, 1, 2–3, 13, 17, 43 n. 8, 63,
180–225, 228, 234, 241, 243, 251, 255,
260, 262–264, 265–266, 267, 271,
276–278, 285, 292, 295, 301–302,
303–307, 310–312, 313, 314, 317; and
Heidegger, 127–128, 178–179, 208; and
hermeneutics, 154, 158, 178–179, 183, 201,
224–225, 302, 305–307, 311–312. *See also*
Derrida, Jacques; and Foucault, Michel
Deleuze, Gilles, 58 n. 1, 72 n. 43, 89, 206,
210, 218 n. 108
de Man, Paul, 182 n. 5, 206, 217 n. 106,
234 n. 33, 247
Derrida, Jacques, 2, 5, 6 n. 16, 8, 11, 17, 44,
175, 179, 180–225, 228, 247–248, 251,
262–263, 289, 295–296, 303–307, 309,
310–312; and Hegel, 193, 194–195, 200,
212, 214, 221; and Nietzsche, 196, 199 n.
56, 208, 211–214; and Husserl, 42, 193,
197 n. 48, 216; and Heidegger, 127 n. 45,
130, 150, 157, 181, 193, 196–198, 208,
211, 214; and Foucault, 180–183, 189,
192–193, 201, 205, 208, 211; Rorty on,
197, 204, 205, 206, 207, 216 n. 104, 217,
228, 229, 230, 243, 245–248, 251; on the
philosophical tradition, 193–201, 204, 207;
and language, 193–196, 198–199, 201,
204–205; and historical inquiry, 198–199,
201; version of deconstruction, 198–200;
on *différance*, 196–197, 217; premium on
disruption, 200, 201, 204–208, 211–215,
221–224, 277, 287
De Ruggiero, Guido, 19, 298 n. 6
Descartes, René; Cartesianism, 7, 23, 24, 34,
41, 42, 44, 55 n. 37, 89, 123, 184, 215,
216–217, 295

Developmentalism, 34, 38, 40, 61, 188
Dewey, John, 1, 226–231, 237–238, 249
Dilthey, Wilhelm, 23, 34–39, 58, 85, 218–219,
237, 267; and Heidegger, 113, 114, 121,
137, 145; and Gadamer, 37, 158–162, 164
Discontinuity, 5, 63, 65, 187–189, 219, 220,
240, 267–268, 297, 301, 317
Disengagement, 113, 115, 128, 143–146, 148,
150, 154, 157, 172, 210, 214, 244, 247,
287, 292, 317, 318
Droysen, Johann Gustav, 33
Dualism (of subject and object, language and
reality, etc.), 18 n. 41, 25, 52–56, 96, 120,
155, 156, 157, 162, 194 n. 39, 199, 206 n.
83, 228, 292–293, 294, 299

Eagleton, Terry, 292
Edification, 18, 96, 101, 150, 164, 200, 235,
237–238, 241, 243, 245–247, 249, 251,
298–299, 315, 318
Eksteins, Modris, 4 n. 8
Eliot, T[homas] S[tearns], 48–49, 50, 149
Elliott, J. H., 279
Ellis, John M., 180 n. 1, 205, 304 n. 15
Ethical (as human capacity or response),
298–300, 308, 314–315
Existentialism, 100, 101, 209, 210; and Croce,
55 n. 37, 99–100; and Heidegger, 118, 143

Feyerabend, Paul, 232
Fichte, Johann Gottlieb, 28
Fineman, Joel, 273
Finitude, 51–53, 55–56, 67, 70, 72 n. 43,
73–76, 78, 117–118, 120, 136, 138,
142–143, 162, 164, 166–167, 185,
218–219, 220, 296, 317
Fish, Stanley, 295 n. 4, 301, 309 n. 29
Foucault, Michel, 2, 5, 6 n. 16, 11, 17, 44, 179,
180–225, 262–263, 264, 289, 295, 307; and
Derrida, 180–183, 189, 192–193, 201, 205,
208, 211; and Nietzsche, 181, 186–188,
208, 210–211, 214, 219; and Heidegger,
210, 214; and historical inquiry, 185–192,
203–204, 210, 219–220; on power,
190–192, 201, 202–204, 209, 210; premium
on resistance or disruption, 192, 201,
202–204, 205–211, 213–215, 219–224, 277;
on historicism, 218–219; Rorty on,
202–203, 206, 232, 233–235, 243, 250–251
Fraser, Nancy, 239 n. 47
Freud, Sigmund; Freudian psychoanalysis, 4,
160, 211, 309
Frye, Northrop, 11
Fussell, Paul, 4

Gadamer, Hans-Georg, 17, 20, 57, 154, 157,
158–179, 218, 224–225, 237, 250, 259,

266, 267–268, 278–279, 294, 295, 296,
298, 299, 303–308, 310, 313, 317; on Vico,
160, 163; on Hegel, 160, 166; and Dilthey,
37, 158–162, 164; on Nietzsche, 158, 160,
166; and Croce, 17, 93, 109, 159–160,
164–175, 177–178, 299–300; and
Heidegger, 124, 128, 132–133, 152,
158–161, 164, 172–175, 178, 295, 298; and
Rorty, 226–227, 231, 233, 234–235, 237,
249–250; on language, 54–55, 167, 175,
295; on dialogue, 158, 162–163, 164–167,
168–169, 171, 172–178, 298, 308, 313; on
historical inquiry, 164, 170–176, 178, 189;
as presentist, 162, 164, 172–175, 178; as
moderate, 158, 165, 167, 170, 175; as
conservative, 175–179
Gasché, Rodolphe, 182 n. 5, 245 n. 61
Gay, Peter, 111 n. 1
Gender (as historiographical category), 183,
253, 263–264, 280, 284–285, 287, 288
Genealogy (as historiographical approach),
61, 69, 79, 186–188, 219, 240, 300
Generations; Generational thinking, 56, 81,
109, 114, 120, 203, 241
Gentile, Giovanni, 173–174
George, Stefan, 126
Gide, André, 46–47, 49–50
Gillespie, Michael Allen, 144
Ginzburg, Carlo, 10, 14, 269, 270, 275, 279
Goodman, Nelson, 229 n. 10, 230
Gossman, Lionel, 260–261
Graff, Gerald, 217
Gramsci, Antonio, 82, 109 n. 74, 191 n. 31
Grassi, Ernesto, 295 n. 3
Greenblatt, Stephen, 10, 265–266, 268, 269,
271–276
Gropius, Walter, 59, 125
Grotius, Hugo, 24

Habermas, Jürgen, 20–21, 201, 302–310; and
Gadamer, 167–171, 298 n. 6; and Rorty,
234, 302–303
Hacking, Ian, 184
Handlin, Oscar, 13
Harlan, David, 316
Hartman, Geoffrey H., 182 n. 5, 217
Haskell, Thomas, 15, 299
Havel, Václav, 6 n. 14, 107
Hawkes, Terence, 26
Hegel, G. W. F.; Hegelianism, 6, 8, 15, 19, 23,
28–32, 38, 51, 55 n. 37, 58 n. 1, 60, 73, 75,
84, 86–88, 95, 123, 139, 145, 150, 160,
166, 193, 194–195, 200, 212, 214,
215–216, 221, 235–237, 244, 315
Heidegger, Martin, 1, 2, 8, 16–17, 110,
111–152, 208, 210, 214, 216, 248, 259,
295, 296, 298, 299, 305, 318; in common
with Nietzsche and Croce, 45, 46, 50–57,
125, 297; beyond Nietzsche and Croce,
115, 137–138, 143, 146; and Hegel, 139,
145, 150; and Dilthey, 113, 114, 121, 137,
145; and Husserl, 42, 51; and Nietzsche,
9 n. 21, 110, 113, 117, 122, 124, 137–138,
154–157; and Croce, 93, 108, 109, 110,
115, 117, 118–119, 127 n. 45, 130,
137–138, 143, 146, 157–158, 174; and
Gadamer, 124, 128, 132–133, 152,
158–161, 164, 172–175, 178, 295, 298; and
Foucault, 210, 214; and Derrida, 127 n. 45,
130, 150, 157, 181, 193, 196–198, 208,
211, 214; and Rorty, 150, 226, 228,
230–231, 237, 243–248; on Greek
philosophy, 129–132; and humanism, 106,
122, 137, 151, 154–155; on nihilism, 110,
116, 122–125, 128–129, 132, 134, 136,
137, 139, 147; and technology, 112,
122–126, 134–139, 156; on historicism,
114, 122, 135 n. 68, 136–139, 142,
146–147; and Nazism, 111–113, 115,
125–126, 134, 148, 152; on historical
questioning, 127–130, 158, 172, 178; and
language, 121, 123, 129, 132, 140, 141,
157, 295, 299; and poetry, 126–127, 136,
146; and "thinking," 128, 143–145,
147–148, 150; and holiness, 116, 122, 146,
148–149. See also Disengagement
Herder, Johann Gottfried von, 32
Hermeneutics, 1, 2–3, 17, 35–37, 121,
159–162, 169, 174–175, 218, 221; and
deconstruction, 154, 158, 178–179, 183,
201, 224–225, 302, 305–307, 311–312. See
also Gadamer, Hans-Georg
Himmelfarb, Gertrude, 13, 14, 280–283, 285,
287, 289–290, 317
Hinman, Lawrence, 170
Historicism, 2, 16, 17 n. 39, 30–34, 37, 41, 52,
59, 85, 114, 159–160, 161, 163, 185 n. 13,
206 n. 83, 215, 218–219, 237, 252,
267–268; and Vico, 23–24, 27–28; and
Hegel, 29–31; and Marxism, 19–20;
Heidegger on, 114, 122, 135 n. 68,
136–139, 142, 146–147. See also Croce,
Benedetto; New historicism
Hobbes, Thomas, 24
Hobson, Marian, 197–198, 201 n. 62
Hölderlin, Friedrich, 113–114, 126
Hollinger, David, 316
Hoy, David Couzens, 18, 29, 196
Humanism, 7, 55 n. 37, 106, 122, 137, 151,
154–155, 209, 218
Hume, David, 41
Husserl, Edmund, 16, 41–42, 44, 51, 114, 117,
123, 181, 194, 195
Hyppolite, Jean, 193

Immortality, 65, 97, 99–100, 102, 167
Irony, 48, 53, 55, 56, 238–247, 250, 255, 260,
    275, 293

James, William, 45–46, 230, 236
Jameson, Fredric, 202
Jaspers, Karl, 114
Jones, W. T., 236 n. 40

Kant, Immanuel; Kantianism, 23, 28, 34–35,
    41, 123, 144, 184, 235, 244, 307
Kellner, Hans, 5 n. 13, 12, 254, 257, 259–262,
    264, 290, 292, 296
Kershner, R. B., 181 n. 4, 261 n. 25, 274, 275
Klossowski, Pierre, 72 n. 43
Kojève, Alexandre, 215
Kolakowski, Leszek, 41
Kolb, David, 17 n. 39, 142–143, 291
Koonz, Claudia, 288
Koselleck, Reinhart, 22
Kripke, Saul, 229 n. 10
Kuhn, Thomas, 8, 159, 232, 301

LaCapra, Dominick, 14, 257 n. 8, 266 n. 40,
    279–280, 289
Language, 24–26, 41–44, 51–55, 57, 132,
    206–208, 292–296, 300; Croce on, 51, 54,
    91, 96, 157, 195–196; Heidegger on, 121,
    123, 129, 132, 140, 141, 157, 295, 299;
    Gadamer on, 54–55, 167, 175, 295;
    Foucault on, 184; Derrida on, 193–196,
    198–199, 201, 204–205; Rorty on, 228,
    229, 231–232, 234, 241, 248, 249 n. 72;
    narrativists on, 11–12, 255–262
Lentricchia, Frank, 292
Le Roy Ladurie, Emmanuel, 10, 269
Levine, Lawrence W., 284
Lévi-Strauss, Claude, 43–44, 182 n. 6, 193,
    194, 195, 216
Literature; Literary culture, 4–5, 11–12, 193,
    206, 260, 265–267, 269–270, 274, 275,
    294; and Rorty, 235–236, 240–241, 243,
    249–250; and narrativists, 257–262. See
    also Modernist literature
Longenbach, James, 49
Löwith, Karl, 19, 106 n. 68
Lukács, Georg, 125
Lyotard, Jean-François, 8 n. 19, 202, 303–304,
    307

Macaulay, Thomas, 32
MacIntyre, Alasdair, 10, 316
Maier, Charles S., 314
Marx, Karl; Marxism, 19–20, 52, 55, 73, 82,
    93, 105, 107, 108, 125–126, 160, 184, 191,
    200, 202, 205, 208, 292, 309
Marx, Werner, 147 n. 111

Megill, Allan, 2, 3 n. 3, 18, 71, 229 n. 8
Meinecke, Friedrich, 37
Metaphor, 24–25, 92, 96, 194, 199–200, 231,
    239–242, 248, 250, 296
Michelet, Jules, 259
Microhistory, 10, 14, 269–273, 275, 276,
    278–279
Midelfort, H. C. Erik, 203
Miller, J. Hillis, 206 n. 83
Modernist literature, 46–50, 232, 236–237,
    260 n. 21
Mooney, Michael, 23, 28 n. 13
Muir, Edward, 270
Musil, Robert, 47–48, 50
Mysticism; Mystery, 45–46, 49, 108, 149, 248

Narrative, 4, 5, 11–12, 181, 254–262, 272,
    273, 277–278, 293, 296
Nehamas, Alexander, 3 n. 3, 67, 70, 71–72,
    249 n. 72
Neo-Kantianism, 19, 35
Neopragmatism, 1, 18, 243, 303–304. See also
    Rorty, Richard
New historicism, 2, 10, 14, 254, 265–268,
    269, 271–276
Niebuhr, Barthold, 30
Nietzsche, Friedrich, 1, 2, 8, 16–17, 58–80,
    81–82, 88, 92, 179, 210–211, 215, 248,
    298, 305, 318; in common with Croce and
    Heidegger, 45, 46, 50–57, 125, 297; and
    Croce, 89–92, 97–102, 109, 110, 154–157;
    and Heidegger, 9 n. 21, 110, 113, 117, 122,
    124, 137–138, 154–157; Gadamer on, 158,
    160, 166; and Foucault, 181, 186–188, 208,
    210–211, 214, 219; Derrida on, 196, 199 n.
    56, 208, 211–214; Rorty on, 206, 230, 236,
    238, 242, 243–244, 246, 248–249; as
    historian, 69, 95, 109, 186–188; as
    posthistoricist, 69–70, 78–79; premium on
    amor fati, 59, 67, 70, 75, 79, 156; notion of
    eternal recurrence, 59, 67 n. 28, 70–77, 79,
    98, 99, 138, 156, 214; on innocence of
    becoming, 59, 70, 76–79, 98, 99, 138. See
    also Will to power
Norris, Christopher, 18, 182 n. 5, 196, 199 n.
    57, 201, 204, 206, 221, 223, 234, 302,
    303–311
Novick, Peter, 13, 15, 261, 299

Oakeshott, Michael, 17
O'Brien, George Dennis, 28, 29
Orr, Linda, 260
Ortega y Gasset, José, 17, 110
Ott, Heinrich, 146 n. 138

Peirce, Charles Sanders, 181 n. 3
Phenomenology, 41, 113 n. 5, 117–119

Phronesis, 23, 27, 151, 167, 175
Plato, 129, 244
Play, 17, 79, 104, 157, 167, 214, 238, 243,
    249, 260, 267, 275, 293, 296, 305–306,
    308, 312, 313; and Nietzsche, 77–78, 98,
    99, 156, 214; and Derrida, 192, 196, 197,
    199 n. 56, 200, 201, 204–205, 207,
    211–212, 221, 305; and deconstruction,
    182 n. 5, 303, 311
Pöggeler, Otto, 113
Positivism, 13, 14, 19, 32–33, 34, 38, 86, 91,
    92, 161, 215, 217, 252, 260
Postmodernism, 8, 62 n. 14, 87, 238, 243,
    303–304; and historiography, 10, 13, 14,
    269, 291
Poststructuralism, 11, 19, 43 n. 8, 44,
    180–182, 192, 193, 195–196, 206, 215–216,
    236, 243, 257, 262–263, 274, 277 n. 70,
    280, 293. See also Deconstruction
Pound, Ezra, 149
Pragmatism, 2–3, 17, 18, 44, 46, 52, 53, 86,
    93, 95, 164, 236–237, 267, 299; and Rorty,
    226–229, 230, 236–237. See also
    Neopragmatism
Presentism (in historiography), 11, 12, 13, 15,
    24, 33, 56–57, 59, 155, 252–269, 272, 275,
    279, 290, 313, 317; and Nietzsche, 68–69,
    95; and Croce, 83, 91, 94–95, 109, 155,
    158, 177; and Gadamer, 162, 164,
    172–175, 178; and Rorty, 233
Proust, Marcel, 240, 244 n. 58
Psychologism, 41, 161
Putnam, Hilary, 229 n. 10, 230

Quine, W. V., 1, 18, 229, 230

Ranke, Leopold von, 15, 31, 32, 33–34, 37,
    38, 56, 94, 260, 267
Rationality, 20, 298, 303–304, 306–309, 311,
    315, 317; in Croce, 85, 87–88, 93, 98–100
Redemption, 28, 66, 70, 74–77, 102, 209
Reflexivity, 56–57, 104, 119, 122, 147–148,
    149, 162, 171, 174, 186, 188, 201, 212,
    218, 219, 247, 253, 260, 268, 310, 312–318
Relativism, 13, 18 n. 41, 20, 33, 35–38, 41,
    42, 52, 57, 114, 185, 227, 230, 261, 299;
    Croce on, 83, 84, 97, 164, 218; Gadamer
    on, 164, 218
Representation, 12–13, 25, 33, 52, 53, 54, 90,
    91–92, 120, 121, 123, 129, 131, 157,
    193–194, 199, 217, 230, 252, 255–262,
    293, 299, 300, 317
Rickert, Heinrich, 16, 40, 85, 114
Rickman, Hans Peter, 37
Ricoeur, Paul, 259
Rilke, Rainer Maria, 126
Rorty, Richard, 1, 3 n. 3, 6, 8, 10, 12, 16, 17,

18, 29, 153 n. 1, 208 n. 86, 226–251, 260,
    295, 296, 298–299, 300, 302–307, 316; and
    Dewey, 226–231, 237–238; and Nietzsche,
    206, 230, 236, 238, 242, 243–244, 246,
    248–249; and Croce, 107–108, 226–227,
    231, 233, 234, 249–250; and Heidegger,
    150, 226, 228, 230–231, 237, 243–248; and
    Gadamer, 226–227, 231, 233, 234–235,
    237, 249–250; on Foucault, 202–203, 206,
    232, 233–235, 243, 250–251; on Derrida,
    195 n. 41, 197, 204, 205, 206, 207, 216 n.
    104, 217, 228, 229, 230, 243, 245–248, 251;
    critique of philosophical tradition, 226, 228,
    229–231, 233, 238, 245–246; on role of
    philosophy, 230–231, 233, 245; and
    pragmatism, 226–229, 230, 236–237; as
    historicist, 226, 232–234, 239; and
    language, 228, 229, 231–232, 234, 241,
    248, 249 n. 72; as liberal, 229 n. 8,
    233–235, 303 n. 12; as moderate, 227–228,
    229–230, 234–235; and literary culture,
    235–236, 240–241, 243, 249–250; and
    deconstruction, 181, 182 n. 5, 206, 241,
    247; and irony, 238–247, 250
Rossi, Pietro, 85, 102 n. 58
Rousseau, Jean-Jacques, 194–195
Ryan, Michael, 8, 200, 309

Said, Edward, 197
Sartre, Jean-Paul, 118
Saussure, Ferdinand de, 16, 41, 42–43, 51,
    185, 194, 195, 229
Schama, Simon, 13, 253–254
Schleiermacher, Friedrich, 35, 161
Schnädelbach, Herbert, 16 n. 37
Schorske, Carl E., 3 n. 4
Scott, Joan Wallach, 11, 12, 13, 15, 266, 317;
    as presentist, 254, 262–265, 288–290; and
    deconstruction, 262–264; and Himmelfarb,
    280–290; and extremity, 287–288
Searle, John R., 181, 207–208, 213 n. 100,
    216–217
Sellars, Wilfrid, 229 n. 10
Skinner, Quentin, 178–179, 180 n. 1
Snow, C[harles] P[ercy], 236
Social science, 32, 36, 42–44, 82, 83, 159,
    185, 227–228
Soll, Ivan, 72
Solomon, Robert C., 8, 28, 29
Spencer, Herbert, 34, 38
Stone, Lawrence, 203
Strauss, David Friedrich, 60
Strauss, Leo, 19
Structuralism, 17, 26, 41, 43–44, 53, 182, 192,
    193, 195, 198, 215, 236, 256–257,
    259–260, 265, 271, 293
Struever, Nancy, 15

Taylor, Charles, 10, 298 n. 7, 316
Teilhard de Chardin, Pierre, 46, 315
Tessitore, Fulvio, 85
Thomas, Brook, 8, 18, 217 n. 106, 266–268,
    275, 287, 291; as presentist, 254, 265–269,
    272, 290
Thompson, E. P., 107
Tocqueville, Alexis de, 33
Totality, 51–52, 125 n. 42, 268, 271, 273,
    285–286, 296, 310, 312, 314; and
    Nietzsche, 70–76, 78; and Croce, 86–87,
    166; and Heidegger, 121, 130; and
    Gadamer, 166; and Foucault, 191
Toulmin, Stephen, 178–179
Toynbee, Arnold, 315
Trakl, Georg, 126
Treitschke, Heinrich von, 32
Trevelyan, George Macaulay, 32
Troeltsch, Ernst, 37

Vattimo, Gianni, 4 n. 6, 9 n. 21, 62 n. 14, 119,
    144, 146 n. 108, 153 n. 1
Verene, Donald Phillip, 27
Vico, Giambattista, 23–28, 29, 35, 38, 51,
    87–88, 89, 91, 93, 127 n. 45, 132, 157, 160,
    163, 194, 228, 261, 294–295
Vienna Circle, 19

Walzer, Michael, 316
Warnke, Georgia, 163, 169, 176 n. 53
Weakness, 9, 27, 52, 69, 75, 107, 157, 166,
    169, 170, 214, 220, 249, 268, 271, 273,
    277, 285–287, 294, 297, 299, 300–302,
    306, 308, 309, 311, 314, 316–318
Weber, Max, 36, 125
Wellek, René, 83, 89 n. 28
Whigs; Whiggish history, 15, 32, 267, 268, 271
White, Hayden, 5, 11–12, 14, 15, 26,
    254–262, 266, 277–278, 292, 296; and
    Croce, 83–84, 94, 255 n. 3
Whitehead, Alfred North, 16, 46
Will to power: as Nietzschean category, 50,
    68, 75, 90–91, 156; Heidegger's critique of,
    124, 137–138, 156–157
Windelband, Wilhelm, 85
Wittgenstein, Ludwig, 1, 8, 54, 167 n. 29,
    181 n. 3, 207, 216, 226, 229, 231, 237
Wohl, Robert, 56, 100
Wood, Gordon S., 13, 254, 262 n. 29, 291

Young, Robert, 185 n. 13

Zagorin, Perez, 291
Zimmerman, Michael E., 114, 119, 135 n. 68,
    137 n. 77
Zunz, Olivier, 11 n. 23

Designer: U.C. Press Staff
Compositor: ComCom, Inc.
Text: 10/12 Times Roman
Display: Helvetica
Printer and Binder: Haddon Craftsmen, Inc.